AL-SHARI'A

(SUNNI & IMAMIYAH CODE)

Deduced from

Fatawa-e-Alamgiri; Fatawa-e-Sirajiyyah; Sharifiyyah; Sirajiyyah; Durrul Mukhtar; Hidaya; Sharhul Vikayah; Jami'ur Ramuz; Sharayaul Islam; Rouzatul Ahkam; Mufatih; Irshad and Tahrirul Ahkam

Vol. II

By

S.C. Sircar

Tagore Professor of Law

KITAB BHAVAN

New Delhi-110002 (India)

Kitab Bhavan
Publishers, Distributors, Exporters & Importers
1784, Kalan Mahal, Darya Ganj
New Delhi - 1100 02 (India)

Phone : (91-11) 23277392 / 93, 23274686, 30906494
website : www.kitabbhavan.com
Email : nasri@vsnl.com
Fax : (91-11) 23263383

Indian Edition 2006

ISBN : 81-7151-374-3 (Set)
ISBN : 81-7151-376-X (Vol.II)

Published in India by :
Nusrat Ali Nasri for Kitab Bhavan
1784, Kalan Mahal, Darya Ganj
New Delhi - 1100 02 [India]

Printed in India at :
Nice Printing Press
Khureji Khas, Delhi-110051

PUBLISHER'S NOTE

Muhammadan Law, technically speaking, means the personal law relating to Muslims as enforced by the British Indian Courts and thereafter on Independence of the sub-continent by the Courts in Pakistan. The Shariat of Islam, in its details, is therefore distinguishable from the so-called Muhammadan Law. This book deals, not with the Muhammadan Law in the above-noted sense, but with the actual law as laid down by the Holy Qur'an and Sunnah, of course, as interpreted by the Imams and Muslim Doctors of acknowledged authority on the bases of *ijma* and *qiyas*, the well-known and established rules of interpretation of Muslim law.

The book starts with a vivid introductory discourse on the origin of Muslim Law followed by a historical account of the great Prophet of Islam (peace be upon him), and traces the growth and development of the law and creation of the various sects through the ages. The principles for the most part have been derived from several Arabic books of paramount authority. Thus, for instance, the principles of the Law of Inheritance have been mainly drawn from the Sirajiyyah and Sharifiyah, the highest authority on the subject, and where they appeared deficient in any respect recourse was had to the Fatawa-i-Alamgiri, Durr-ul-Mukhtar and other works of unquestionable authority. The principles relating to other subjects have been principally deduced from the Hidayah, the Fatawa-i-Alamgiri, Sharhul Viqayah, Jami-ur-Rumuz etc. Care has been taken to insert only such matter as is authentic and the principles, explanations and annotations are versions of passages from the Arabic books as translated by reputed translators. In short, divorced as it is from the case-law and interpretations made by modern writers, this compilation is a thesis on the bare Islamic law as it existed in its original form and as such a very useful guide for Research Scholar of Islamic Law, the Bench and the Bar.

——

PREFACE.

THE principles of Muhammadan law contained in these pages constitute the Lectures delivered by me as "Tagore Professor of Law." Such of them as are inculcated in the first five Lectures, which are according to the *Sunní* School, have been drawn mainly from the *Hidáyah* and *Fatáwá Alamgírí*, and occasionally from the *Sharh-ul-Vikáyah*, *Durr ul-Mukhtár*, and other works of unquestionable authority. Other passages, translated from the above-mentioned authorities, have been appended to almost all those principles with a view to explain and illustrate their meanings in the same manner as has been done in the volume of Lectures published for the last year. The rest of the Lectures is on the Muhammadan law according to the *Imámiyah* School. These constitute the principles contained in page 176 *et seq.*

The above principles have been drawn or extracted mainly from the *Sharáya ul-Islám*, and occasionally from the *Rouzat ul-Ahkám*, *Mafátíh*, *Irshád* and *Tahrír ul-Ahkám*,* books of paramount authority among the *Imámiyahs*. To those principles have been appended other passages from the said authorities to illustrate their meanings. The Annotations are taken from books of great repute, and will serve as authorities or additional authorities (as the case may be) for the principles to

* *Vide* Introductory Discourse, pp. 171—174.

which they refer. Again, all these different matters are so arranged and printed as to be easily distinguishable from one another and not to confuse the reader.* He may easily refer to them, in case he consider any of the principles not sufficient by itself, or require further authorities for the same.

Mindful of the justness of the opinion expressed by the Commissioners appointed under the first Royal Commission issued for considering "the Reform of the Judicial Establishments, Judicial Procedure, and Laws of India,"† and conscious of such being the fact, I have inserted in the present work only such matters as are authentic. The principles, explanations, illustrations and annotations are, with rare exceptions, translations of passages from Arabic books—books which are of very

---

* The principles are, for the above purpose, printed in larger type,—those of great importance being in Pica, and those less so, in Small Pica type, and both are kept clear of the other matters. Then the passages explanatory and illustrative are separately printed in a comparatively smaller type; and under these are placed annotations and foot-notes in different types and under different lines one after the other.

† The first Royal Commission was issued for considering "the Reform of the Judicial Establishments, Judicial Procedure, and Laws of India;" and it did not seem improbable that the subject of the Muhammadan law might, at some period of their labours, come under the notice of the Commissioners. But in the second Report, they gave it as their opinion that—"no portion of the Muhammadan law, or of the Hindú law, ought to be enacted as such, in any form, by a British Legislature," assigning as one of their reasons, that "a Code of Muhammadan Law, or a Digest of any part of that law, would not be entitled to be regarded by Muhammadans as the very law itself, but merely as a exposition of law which might possibly be incorrect."—B. Dig., Introd, . xxiii.

high authority indeed as already noticed, and of which only the *Sharáya ul-Islám* has been translated in part by Mr. Neil Baillie, and printed and published by him under the title—" A Digest of Muhammadan Law, Part Second, containing the doctrines of the Imámiyah Code of Jurisprudence on the most important of the same subjects."

Although the above translation is passed as an authority, and, as such, I ought to have used it wherever the *Sharáya* is cited, yet I have considered it better to adopt in some parts my own version of the same which I had made before Mr. Baillie's translation was published; so I am responsible for those of my versions which differ in any respect from Mr. Baillie's. I have, nevertheless, to offer my grateful thanks to that learned gentleman not only for the valuable aid I have received from his translation, but also for his having rendered the public a great service by translating almost the whole of the forensic part of the *Sharáya ul-Islám*, which (at least in India) is the most prevalent authority of the *Imámiyah* School.

On points difficult and doubtful, I have invariably consulted the *Mujtahid** of Lucknow, who is now with the ex-King of Oudh, and the most learned in the Imámiyah Law in India. This gentleman has very kindly given me every aid that I required of him. I cannot, therefore, conclude these remarks without acknowledging my great obligation to him, for the valuable assistance

* *Vide* Introductory Discourse, p. 166.

that he has herein rendered me. I have endeavoured to collect and incorporate in the present work almost all that was important, and available and practicable within the time allowed me for the purpose.

I have nothing further to add here, having already expressed in the Introductory Discourse all that I had to say with respect to other matters which formed the subject of a Prefatory or an Introductory Lecture. In conclusion I have to observe that as neither time nor labour has been spared in making the present work replete with useful matters, and in rendering it adapted to the study of students,* as well as convenient for reference in the conduct of cases and administration of justice, I hope this work also will meet with the approbation of that august body—the Senate of the University—and be useful to the public in proportion to the pains which I have taken in preparing the same.

* To learn the law inculcated herein, the student is required to study at least the principles printed in Pica type.

SUMMARY OF CONTENTS

OF THE

REMAINING FIVE LECTURES OF THE SUNNÍ CODE.

LECTURE I.

ON GIFTS.

LECTURE II.

ON WASAYAH, OR WILLS.

LECTURE III.

ON EXECUTOR, HIS POWERS, &C.

LECTURE IV.

ON WAKF, OR APPROPRIATION.

LECTURE V.

ON THE WAKF, OR APPROPRIATION, OF MASJIDS, &C.

SUMMARY OF CONTENTS OF THE IMÁMIYAH CODE.

LECTURE VI.

INTRODUCTORY DISCOURSE.

LECTURE VII.

ON INHERITANCE.

LECTURE VIII.

GENERAL AND SPECIAL RULES OF SUCCESSION.

LECTURE IX.

LECTURE X.

LECTURE XI.

ON COMPUTATION OF SHARES.

LECTURE XII.

ON PERMANENT MARRIAGE.

LECTURE XIII.

LECTURE XIV.

LECTURE XV.

ON DIVORCE.

LECTURE XVI.

ON KHULÁ, &C.

LECTURE XVII.

ON THE REVOCATION OF DIVORCE, &C.

LECTURE XVIII.

ON SHUFÁ, OR PRE-EMPTION.

LECTURE XIX.

ON WAKF, OR APPROPRIATION.

POWERS OF THE VOWELS USED IN SPELLING THE ARABIC AND PERSIAN WORDS.

A: as *a* in s*a*lt.

Á: as *a* in f*a*ther.

E: as *e* in th*e*y.

I: as *i* in f*i*t.

Í: as *i* in pol*i*ce.

O: as *o* in g*o*.

U: as *u* in b*u*sh.

Ú: as *u* in r*u*le.

ERRATA.

Page 5, line 22, for *of (a known) part*, read *of part*.

Page 5, line 25, for *of part*, read *of (a known) part*.

Page 109, line 31, for *Testator*, read *Executor*.

Page 163, line 25, for *proprictor*, read *appropriator*.

Page 199, line 27, for 146, & 152, read 146, 152, &c.

LECTURE I.

ON GIFTS.

GIFT (*hibat* or *hibah**), as it is defined in law, is the conferring of a right of property (*tamlík*†) in something specific without an exchange.‡

The person making such transfer is termed "*wáhib*" (donor), the person to whom it is made is "*mouhúb la-hu*" (donee), and the thing given is "*mouhúb*."

DCLXXIII. The pillar (or essential) is the donor's declaration—"I have given."‡ *Principle.*

For that constitutes gift, and it is completed by the act of the owner alone, acceptance being required only for the purpose of establishing the property in the donee.§ However,— *Reason.*

DCLXXIV. Gifts are rendered valid by tender, acceptance, and seizin (*a*).—Hidáyah, vol. iii, p. 291. *Principle.*

(*a*.) Tender and acceptance are necessary, because a gift is a contract, and tender and acceptance are requisite in the forma-

ANNOTATIONS.

dclxxiv. Acceptance and seizin on the part of the donee are necessary, as relinquishment on the part of the donor.—Macn. M. L., chap. v, princ. 2.

---

* "*Hibah*," in its literal sense, signifies the donation of a thing from which the donee may derive a benefit. In the language of the law, it means a transfer of property made immediately and without any exchange.—Hamilton's Hidáyah, vol. iii, p. 290.

† "*Tamlík*" (from *milk*) means owning. Hence *Tamlík-námah* is applicable alike to a deed of sale or of gift.

‡ Fatáwá Alamgírí, vol. iv, p. 520.—B. Dig., p. 507.

§ According to the Hidáyah (vol. iii, p. 673), gift is constituted by declaration and acceptance (*íjáb o kabúl*); and according to the Kifáyah, these are its pillars. The Durr-ul-mukhtár is to the same effect. But they concur with the Ináyah that declaration is sufficient, so far as the donor is concerned.—B. Dig., p 507.

tion of all contracts; and seizin is necessary in order to establish a right of property in the gift, because a right of property, according to *our* doctors, is not established in the thing given merely by means of the contract without a seizin.—Hidáyah, vol. iii, p. 291.

Principle. **DCLXXV. A verbal gift is as effectual as that made under a writing.**

Precedent. A gift orally conveyed is valid, because tender and acceptance are the only essentials to a gift; and complete seizin of the house, none of the donor's property being therein, and its not being used for his benefit, are the only conditions to perfecting the gift. A writing or deed is neither among the essentials nor conditions. Therefore, in a case of gift, if oral tender and acceptance are established, and the condition of complete seizin be also found to exist,—that is to say, that the thing given was in no manner employed for the benefit of the donor, and that it was not undefined,—the gift is valid, although no deed may have been executed.—Macn. Prec., M. L., chap. v, case 22.

Principle. DCLXXVI. The legal effects (of gift) are: 1, that it establishes a right of property in the donee without being obligatory on the donor, so that the gift may be validly resumed or cancelled;* 2, that it cannot be made subject to an option of stipulation; and 3, that it is not cancelled by vitiating conditions (*b*).†

(*b*.) So that if one should give his slave on condition of his being emancipated, the gift would be valid, and the condition void.†

Gift is of two kinds,—*tamlík* (creating ownership), and *iskát* (causing to fall, or to extinguish).†

The words by which gift is effected are of three kinds: *First*, those which have been appropriated to the purpose, as, "I have given this thing to thee," or "I have invested thee with the property of it," or "I have made it to thee," or "this is to thee." *Second*, those in which the meaning of gift is concealed or implied, as, "thy garment is this piece of cloth," or "I have invested thee with this mansion for thy age," which would be a gift. So also if he had said, "this mansion is to thee *umrá*," (for thy age—*umr*), or "*hayátí*" (for thy *hayát* or life), "and when thou art dead it reverts to me," in which case the gift is lawful, and the condi-

---

* *Vide* Revocation of Gifts, p. 28 *et seq.*

† Fatáwá Alamgírí, vol. iv, p. 521.—B. Dig., pp. 508 & 509.

tion void. *Third*, words which bear equally the construction of gift and of *áríat*, or commodate loan, as, "I have mounted thee on this beast," which would be a loan, unless gift were intended. The principle in cases of this kind is, that when a word is employed which has reference to the body of the thing, it is a gift; and when a word is employed which has reference to the profits of the thing, it is a loan; and when the word may be understood in either sense, the meaning is to be determined by intention.*

DCLXXVII. A gift must not depend on any thing contingent (*c*), nor must it be referred to a future time (*d*).* *Principle.*

(*c.*) As the entrance of *Zayid*, or the arrival of *Khálid.**

(*d.*) As, for instance, by saying,—"I give (or I will give) this thing to thee to-morrow."*

DCLXXVIII. The giver must be free, sane, and adult, and also the owner of the thing given.* *Principle.*

Moreover,—

DCLXXIX. The subject of gift must be in existence at the time of the gift (*e*), and must have legal value, and possession must be taken of it to establish therein the right of the donee (*f*); and if in its nature divisible, it must be actually divided from, so as not to be joined to, or involved in, any thing else that is not given. *Principle.*

ANNOTATIONS.

dclxxvii. A gift cannot be made to depend on a contingency, nor can it be referred to take effect at any future definite period.—Macn. M. L., chap. v, princ. 3.

dclxxix. It is requisite that the gift should be accompanied by delivery of possession, and that seizin should take effect immediately, or, if at a subsequent period, by the desire of the donor. A gift cannot be made of anything to be produced *in futuro*; although the means of its production be in the possession of the donee. The subject must be actually in existence at the time of the donation.—Macn. M. L., chap. v., princ. 4 & 5.

---

* Fatáwá Alamgírí, vol. iv, pp. 520, 521.—B. Dig., pp. 507—509.

(*e*). So that, if a man should give "the fruit that may be produced by his palm-tree," or "what is in the womb of this slave," or "of this sheep," or "in its udder," the gift is unlawful, though power be given to take possession at the time of production, as of birth, or of milking. The subject also must have a legal value; and possession must be taken of it, to establish therein the right of the donee, and if in its nature divisible, it must be actually divided from, so as not to be joined to, or involved in, anything else that is not given.*

Illustration. Hence the gift of a land without the crop then standing on it, or of a palm-tree in bearing without its fruit, and *vice versâ*, is unlawful. So also of a house or vessel in which there is something belonging to the donor, without its contents.*

(*f.*) If the donee take possession of the gift, in the meeting of the contract of gift,† without the order of the giver, it is lawful, upon a favorable construction. If, on the contrary, he should take possession of the gift after the breaking up of the meeting, it is not lawful, unless he have had the consent of the giver so to do. Analogy would suggest that the seizin is not valid in either case, as it is an act with respect to what is still the property of the giver; for, as his right of property continues in force until seizin, *that* is consequently invalid without his consent.—Hidáyah, vol. iii, p. 292.

Illustration. If a man should make a gift of a mansion in which there are some effects belonging to him, and should deliver the mansion to the donee, or deliver it with the effects, the gift would not be valid. But there is a device by which a valid gift can be made of the mansion; and it is by first making a deposit of the effects with the donee, vacating them for him, and then making delivery of the mansion. And, in the opposite case, if he should make a gift of the effects without the mansion, and vacate them for the donee, and then make delivery of the mansion, the gift would be valid; and if he should make a gift of the mansion and effects together, and vacate them both for the donee, the gift would be valid.‡

Precedent. If a person should give a mansion with its effects and deliver them both, and a right is subsequently established to the effects, the gift of the mansion is valid.‡

The gift of a thing not in the possession of the donor during his lifetime is null and void, and the deed containing such gift is

---

* Fatáwá Alamgírí, vol. iv, pp. 520, 521.—B. Dig., pp. 508, 509.

† Arab. "*Fi majlisi akd-ul-hibah*," which means "in the meeting where the contract of gift takes place."

‡ Fatáwá Alamgírí, vol. iv, p. 528.—B. Dig., pp. 518—520.

of no effect, because, in cases of gift, seizin is a condition. Gift is rendered valid by tender, acceptance and seizin; but in gift, seizin is necessary and absolutely indispensable to the establishment of proprietary right. According to the Hidáyah, "gifts are rendered valid by tender," acceptance and seizin. The Prophet has said, "a gift is not valid without seizin; so also if the thing given be pawned to, or usurped by, a stranger." So also in the *Sharh-i-Vikáyah*,—"A gift is perfected by complete seizin." As the gift, therefore, is null, the claim of the donee is inadmissible, and the deed is invalid, as far as regards the lands of which the donor was never possessed. But, with respect to the other lands conveyed at the same time, the donee is entitled to them, if the donor put him into possession. If, however, the donor died without conferring possession, the claim of the donee to them also is inadmissible.—Macn. Prec., M. L., chap. iv, case 6.

The gift, whether with or without a consideration, of undefined property, provided it admit of being rendered distinct and separate, is invalid; but the sale of such property is allowable, and holds good as far as the right and title of the seller is concerned; but it cannot affect the interests of parties not privy to the contract.—Macn. Prec., M. L., chap. iv, case 3. **Precedent.**

DCLXXX. A gift of (a known) part of a thing which is capable of division is not valid, unless the said part be divided off, and separated from, the property of the donor; but the gift of part of an indivisible thing is valid.—Hidáyah, vol. iii, p. 293. *Principle.*

When a gift is made of a *musháa** in property that does not admit of partition, it is a condition of the validity of the gift that the quantity be known; for if one were to give his share in a slave, the share being unknown, the gift would not be lawful, as ignorance of the share might lead to disputes.†

If a person make a gift of the flour of wheat, which is yet in grain, or of oil of *sessamé*, which is not yet expressed from the seeds, such gift is invalid; and if he afterwards grind the wheat into flour, or extract the oil from the *sessamé* seeds, and so deliver them to the donee, still the gift is not thereby rendered valid. The same rule also holds with respect to butter which is yet in milk.—Hidáyah, vol. iii, p. 295. **Illustration.**

If a person make a gift, to his partner, of his share in the partnership stock, capable of division, it is invalid, because of the **Illustration.**

* *Musháa* is the passive participle of *Shuáa*—the infinitive or rather the root—and means confused, whence undivided.

† Fatáwá Alamgírí, vol. iv, p. 531.—B. Dig., p. 521.

invalidity of the gift of an undefined part of a divisible subject, as before explained.—Hidáyah, vol. iii, p. 294.

The gift by one partner to another of a share in the profits is not lawful.—*Vide* Fatáwá Alamgírí, vol. iv, p. 531.—B. Dig., p. 521.

Principle.

DCLXXXI. The gift of a *musháa*, or undivided (but known) part of what does not admit of partition, is lawful—to a partner or to a stranger. The gift of a *musháa* in what does admit of partition is not lawful—either to a partner or one who is not a partner; and if possession is taken of it, Hasám-ud-Dín has reported that it will not avail to establish property in the donee; but he has said in another place that it will avail to establish it invalidly, and so it has been decided.*

ANNOTATIONS.

dclxxxi. The gift of a *musháa* or undivided part of a thing that admits of partition to two men or to a group, is valid according to the two disciples, and invalid according to *Abú Hanífah.* But it is not void, so that it is of avail to the establishment of property by possession. Sadar Ush-Shuhíd has remarked, that when a person has given what admits of partition to two men, so that the gift is invalid according to *Abú Hanífah*, and possession is then taken, the right of property is established in them *invalidly;* and so it has been decreed. Confusion on both sides in property susceptible of partition prevents the legality of gift, according to them all; and when the confusion is only on the side of the donee, it prevents the legality of the gift, according to Abú Hanífah, though it has not that effect in the opinion of the disciples. And if one should make a gift to two persons who are poor, it would be lawful according to them all, as in the case of *sadakah*, or alms. But if they are rich, and the gift is made to each of them in halves, or if it is made vaguely by saying, "I have given to you both," or with an excess in favor of one, as by saying, "To this one a third, and to this one two-thirds;" it is unlawful in the three cases, according to Abú Hanífah; while, according to Muhammad, it is lawful in them all; and according to Abú Yusuf, it is lawful in the two cases where the gift is made indefinitely, or in halves. When two persons have given a mansion to one person, the gift is valid, according to all opinions.—Fatáwá Alamgírí, vol. iv, p. 525.—B. Dig., pp. 515 & 516.

* Fatáwá Alamgírí, vol. iv, p. 525.—B. Dig., p. 515.

It appears from all the circumstances connected with this case, that the gift in question is invalid, and that it is, after the death of the donor, absolutely null and void; and the property so transferred will revert to the heirs of the donor, because it is evident that the produce only was transferred, the ground itself being the common property of all the heirs, it not having undergone division; and according to law, the gift of unrealized produce without the land is wholly invalid. It is immaterial whether the donee was or was not put into possession of the produce of the common lands; for, in both cases, the gift is invalid, an undefined seizin not being held to constitute legal seizin. Under these circumstances, either the mother, or any other heir of the donor, is at liberty to dispossess the donee. The mother was not competent to make over by gift to the donee all the property belonging to her husband, because the estate of her husband was the joint property of all the heirs. A gift even of her own portion is invalid, that being undefined and not admitting of legal seizin; so that in every view of the case the gift is entirely null and void. *Sharh-i-Vikáyah*,—"The gift of milk" in the udder, of wool upon the back of a goat, of grain or trees upon the ground, or of fruit upon trees, is in the nature of the gift of an undefined part of a thing; and such gifts are prohibited unless separated from the property of the donor, and seizin be subsequently made of them." But, as in this case, the trees were not cut down, and the donee did not make regular seizin during the lifetime of the donor, the heir of such donee is not competent to come in and establish the validity of the donation by the performance of any act on his own part; because he is quite a stranger to the transaction. The acceptance was not expressed by the heir, but by the ancestor, who died before separation and seizin. In the *Hidáyah*, in the Chapter treating of retraction of gifts, it is stated,—"If the donor should die, his heirs are strangers with respect to the contract, since they made no tender of the thing given. It

---

ANNOTATIONS.

The gift of property which is undivided, and mixed with other property, admitting at the same time of division or separation, is null and void, unless it be defined previously to delivery; for delivery of the gift cannot in that case be made without including something which forms no part of the gift.—Macn. M. L., chap. v, princ. 6.

appearing, therefore, that the property was not separated and delivered into the possession of the donee, the right was not transferred from the donor during his lifetime, and after his death it devolves on his heirs. It is laid down also in the *Hidáyah*,—"Seizin in cases of gift is expressly ordained, and consequently a complete seizin is a necessary condition, but a complete seizin is impracticable with respect to an indefinite part of *divisible* things, as it is impossible, in such, to make seizin of the thing given without its conjunction with some thing that is not given, and that is a defective seizin." So also in the *Vikáyah*,—"Gift is perfected by complete seizin." And in the *Sharh-i-Vikáyah*,—"A gift of part of a thing which is capable of division is not valid unless such part be divided off, so that seizin may be definite and not included in anything else." It is evident, therefore, that a seizin of undefined property is itself indefinite; and cannot be considered valid.—Macn. Prec., M. L., chap. iv, case 8.

However,—

Principle. DCLXXXII. If a person should give an undivided part of a thing which admits of division, and then make a partition and deliver the part, the gift would be valid.*

But if he give a half and deliver the whole, the gift is not lawful; while if he give the whole, and deliver it separately, the gift is lawful.*

Illustration. If a person make a gift, to another, of an undefined portion of land (such as a *half* or a *fourth*,) such gift is null for the reasons already set forth. If, however, he afterwards divided it off, and made a delivery of it, the gift becomes valid; because a gift is rendered complete by seizin, and in this case nothing else remains indefinitely involved with the gift at the time of the seizin.—Hidáyah, vol. iii, p 295.

Precedent. Under these circumstances, if the donor separated the landed property disposed of by gift, and put his wife into complete possession and enjoyment thereof, the gift will be good and valid according to law. Again, if the donee make

---

* Fatáwá Alamgírí. vol. iv, p. 527.—B. Dig., p. 517.

a verbal gift of the property which she had so acquired, to her grandson's wife, and put her into possession, such gift must also be upheld as good and valid, provided it be established by the evidence of two men, or one man and two women.—Macn. Prec., M. L., chap. iv, case 2.

The law requires that anything which is capable of division, when given to two persons, should be divided by the donor, at the time of the gift, or immediately subsequent to the transfer and prior to the delivery to the donees, in order that the objection of confusion may be avoided and full and complete seizin obtained, which is essential to the validity of a gift. It appears, in this case, that the property given was divided by the donees with the consent of the donor, two or three months subsequent to the date of the deed of transfer. Such a proceeding is not legal. To render it valid, it was essential that the delivery and the division should have been simultaneous.—*Ibid*, case 5.

DCLXXXIII. The gift of a thing then in the hands of the donee, or his guardian, either as a deposit, or in any other way, is valid without a formal delivery and seizin. *Principle.*

When the subject of gift is in the hands of the donee, either as a deposit or commodate loan (*âríat*), or trust (*amánat*), he becomes the proprietor of it by the gift and acceptance, though his taking formal possession of it should not be renewed. And if the owner of property, let to hire or usurped, should give it to the tenant or usurper, the gift would be lawful; and the receiver of it freed from all responsibility. Or if a thing were in any other way in the hands of a person on his responsibility, as, for instance, a thing on an offer of sale, and it were given to him, the gift would be valid, and the property be established in him by the mere contract. If the thing given were in pledge in the donee's hands, it is reported in the "*Jáma*" that he would become possessed of it under the gift; the previous possession under the pledge being converted into a possession under the gift; and as the gift would Illustrations.

ANNOTATIONS.

dclxxxiii. A formal delivery and seizin are not necessary in the case of a gift to a trustee having the custody of the article given, nor in the case of a gift to a minor. The seizin of the guardian in the latter case is sufficient.—Macn. M. L., chap. v, princ. 10.

To perfect the gift of a thing which is in possession of the donee, new seizin is not requisite. Sharah-i-Vikáyah.—*Vide* Macn. Prec., M. L., chap. iv, case 19.

be completed by possession, the pledge would be cancelled, and the pledgee entitled to have recourse to the pledger for his debt.*

If a thing be in the hands of the donee in virtue of a trust, the gift is in that case complete, although there be no formal seizin, since the actual article is already in the donee's hands, whence his seizin is not requisite. It is otherwise, where a depositor *sells* the deposit to his trustee, for in this case the original seizin does not suffice, because seizin in virtue of purchase is a seizin inducing responsibility, and, therefore, cannot be substituted by a seizin in virtue of a *trust;* but seizin in virtue of *gift*, on the contrary, as not being a seizin inducing reponsibility, may be substituted by a seizin in virtue of a trust.—Hidáyah, vol. iii, pp. 295 & 296.

The general principle in these cases is, that when two possessions are of the same kind, one may be substituted for the other; and that when they differ, that which is under responsibility may be substituted for that which is not; but that which is not under responsibility cannot be substituted for that which is. To renew possession when required, the donee must go to the place where the subject of gift may happen to be, and a sufficient time must elapse to enable him to do so.*

Precedents. The law requires seizin by the donee, except in the case of a gift made by a father to his minor son, and a few other specially excepted instances.—Macn. Prec., M. L., chap. iv, case 13.

If the donee made over all her property by gift to the son of her uncle, who did not however make complete seizin of it during her lifetime; on which account her gift in favor of him is null and void, as is laid down in the *Ibráhím Sháhí*,—"A gift cannot be perfected but by the complete seizin of the donee."—*Ibid*, case 14.

Principle. DCLXXXIV. The gift by one or more persons to a *single person* of a property susceptible of division is valid according to all.

Thus,—

Illustrations. If two persons jointly make the gift of a house to *one* man, it is valid; because, as they deliver it over to him wholly, and he receives it wholly, no mixture of property can be said to exist at the time of seizin.—Hidáyah, vol. iii, p. 298.

If two persons jointly make a gift of a house to one man, it is valid.—*Vikáyah. Vide* Macn. Prec., M. L., chap. iv, case 14.

---

* Fatáwá Alamgírí, vol. iv, p. 525.—B. Dig., pp. 514, 515.

When two persons have given a mansion to *one* person, the gift is valid according to all opinions.—Fatáwá Alamgírí, vol. iv, p. 527.—B. Dig., p. 517.

The gift by two persons to a minor, one of whom being his father and the other his uncle, of their joint property, is valid, provided that there was the complete seizin that is requisite, that is to say, provided the uncle relinquished all participation in the property conveyed, resigning it to the father, who is empowered to make seizin on behalf of his minor son; but the gift is invalid if the uncle continued associated with the father in possession.—Macn. Prec., M. L., chap. iv, case 20. Precedent.

But there is a difference of opinion with respect to the gift of such property to two or more persons; for it is invalid according to Abú Hanífah, but valid according to his disciples Abú Yusuf and Muhammad. The author of the Hidáyah, by citing the argument of Abú Hanífah after that of the two disciples, appears to have acquiesced in the opinion of the former.* The Durr-ul-Mukhtár, Fatáwá Kází Khán, Sharh-ul-Vikáyah, and other authorities have cited only the opinion of Abú Hanífah, and thereby they appear to have acquiesced in his opinion. The Fatáwá Alamgírí, however, cites both the opinions, with remarks thereupon. These are as follows:—"The gift of a *musháa* in property that admits of partition, to two men, or to a group, is valid according to the two disciples, and invalid according to *Abú Hanífah.*† But it is not void; so that it avails to the establishment of property by *possession.*‡— Remarks.

---

* *Vide* page 42 of Lecture I. for 1872-73, and Hidáyah, vol. iii, page 298.

† The authorities on Muhammadan law differ on this question (*i.e.*, the validity of a joint gift without determination of shares); but the prevailing authorities admit the validity of the gift (Reports, Sudder Dewanny Adawlut, Calcutta, vol. i, p. 115). In a subsequent case, however (Reports, Sudder Dewanny Adawlut, Calcutta, vol. iv, page 210), the Law Officer of the Provincial Court of Patna gave his fatwá against the validity of the gift. The fatwá being confirmed by that of the Law Officers of the Sudder Dewanny Adawlut, it was adopted by both Courts, in opposition to the fatwá of the law officer of the Zillah of *Sháhábad*, which was in favour of its validity.—B. Dig., p. 516.

‡ In the case referred to in the preceding note, the Law Officers were not asked their opinion as to the effect of possession under an invalid gift; and it does not appear that this part of Abú Hanífah's opinion was brought to the notice of the Court. The decision, therefore, which set aside the gift though possession had been formally given by the donor, and was never revoked by her, and could not then be revoked as she was dead, seems to have been passed on an imperfect representation of the Muhammadan law.—*Ibid.*

In the case of a gift made to two or more donees, the interest of each donee must be defined, either at the time of making the gift, or on delivery.—Macn. M. L., chap. v, princ. 7.

Sadr ush-Shahíd has remarked that when a person has given what admits of partition to two men, so that the gift is invalid according to Abú Hanífah, and possession is then taken, the right of property is established in them invalidly; and so it has been *decreed.** Confusion (*shuáa*) on both sides in property susceptible of partition prevents the legality of gift according to them all; and when the confusion is only on the side of the donee, it prevents the legality of the gift, according to *Abú Hanífah,* though it has not that effect in the opinion of the disciples. And if one should make a gift to two persons who are poor, it would be lawful according to them all, as in the case of *sadakuh,* or alms. But if they are rich, and the gift is made to each of them in halves, or if it is made vaguely by saying, "I have given to you both," or with an excess in favor of one, as by saying, "to this one a third, and to this one two-thirds;" it is unlawful in the three cases according to *Abú Hanífah;* while, according to Muhammad, it is lawful in them; and according to Abú Yusuf it is lawful in two cases where the gift is made indefinitely, or in halves. When two persons have given a mansion to one person, the gift is valid according to all opinions.†

The conclusion therefore is, that—

Principle. DCLXXXV. **The gift of a property susceptible of division is valid if made to two or more poor persons, and invalid, but not void, if made to two or more rich persons; the right of the latter is notwithstanding established in the subject of such gift upon their taking formal possession unrevoked by the donor.**

An invalid gift is on the donee's responsibility, after possession has been taken of it.†

---

* The remark of *Sadr ush-Shahid* aggravates the difference between the master and his disciples. In the preceding sentence, which is from another authority, it is said that possession avails to the establishment of property absolutely, which agrees with the report of Hisám's opinion in the *Kifáyah,* referred to in a previous note.—B. Dig., p. 516, n.

† Fatáwá Alamgírí, vol. iv, pp. 520 & 521.—B. Dig., pp. 515, 516, & 518.

A gift of *mushâa* may be made in three different ways: *First*, a person having the whole of a thing may give an undivided half or other share in it to another. Here there is confusion on both sides, and the gift unlawful, without difference of opinion. *Second*, a person having the whole of a thing may give it entire to two or more persons undividedly. Here there is confusion on the side of the donee only, and there is the difference of opinion noticed in the text. And *third*, two or more persons having a thing in undivided shares may combine in making a gift of it entire to one person. Here the confusion is only on the side of the donor, and the gift is valid without any difference of opinion.—B. Dig., p. 517, n.

But it is said in other authorities that possession under an invalid gift avails to the establishment of property, and that it has been so decided contrary to what is stated to be valid in *Amadíah*; and the word *Fatwá*, or decision, is stronger than the word valid.—Durr-ul-Mukhtár, p. 634.—*Vide* B. Dig., p. 518.

Gift to a Minor.

DCLXXXVI. The gift by a father to his infant child is valid, provided the subject of the gift is in his possession or in deposit with another; so also is the gift by a mother of a thing which is in her own possession, or remains so in default of the father or his executor. Such is also the case with the gift made by another person who has the care of the child or with whom the child lives. *Principle.*

If a father make a gift of something to his infant son, the infant, in virtue of the gift, becomes proprietor of the same, provided the thing given be, at that time, in the possession either of the father or of his trustee; because the possession of the father is capable of becoming possession in virtue of gift, and the possession of the trustee is equivalent to that of the father.—Hidáyah, vol. iii, p. 296. Illustrations.

The same rule holds when a *mother* gives something to her infant son whom she maintains, and of whom the father is dead, and no guardian provided: and so also with respect to the gift of any other person maintaining a child under these circumstances.—*Ibid.*

If a fatherless child be under the charge of his mother, and she take possession of a gift made to him, it is valid; because she has an authority for the preservation of him and his property; and the seizin of a gift made to him is in the nature of a preservation of *himself*, since a child could not be maintained without property. The same rule also holds with respect to a *stranger* who has the charge of an orphan, because as his seizin is of legal force, (whence it is that another stranger has not a right to take the orphan from him), he is consequently competent to all such things as are purely for the advantage of the orphan.—*Ibid*, p. 297.

Annotations.

dclxxxvi. Formal delivery and seizin are not necessary in the case of a gift to a trustee having the custody of the article given, nor in the case of a gift to a minor. The seizin of the guardian in the latter case is sufficient.—Macn. M. L., chap. v, princ. 10.

If a *stranger* make a gift of a thing to an infant, the gift is rendered complete by the seizin of the father of the infant; for, as he is master of deeds with respect to the child, liable to both good and evil (such as sale), he is consequently, in a superior degree, master of gift, which is purely advantageous.—Hidáyah, vol. iii, pp. 296 & 297.

The gift of a father to his infant child is completed by the contract; and it makes no difference whether the subject of the gift be in his own hands, or in deposit with another. But if it be in the hands of a usurper, or of a pledgee, or of a tenant who has hired it, the gift is not lawful for want of possession. In like manner, as to gifts by a mother, when the thing given is in her own hands, and the father is dead without having appointed an executor. And so also as to gifts by every other person who has the care of the child. When a father has given a mansion to his little son, in which there are goods belonging to himself, the gift is lawful and approved.—Fatáwá Alamgírí, vol. iv, p. 546.—B. Dig., pp. 529 & 530.

The gift of a father to his child is perfected by his mere declaration. Whatever gift is made by a stranger to him, he should take possession of, if possessed of suffieient discretion to do so, or his father, or grandfather should take possession of it on his behalf, or the guardian appointed by either of them, or his mother, provided he be residing with her, or a stranger in whose house he is educated.—Sharh-i Vikáyah. *Vide* Macn. Prec., M. L., chap. iv, case 19.

Precedents.

If a mother make a gift to her infant daughter, who is residing with her, of property which is distinctly her own;—if, by reason of the minority of the daughter, acceptance did not take place on her part, and the property, from the same cause, continued in the possession of the donor, and if the father was, at the time of the gift, at a remote distance, the gift is legally valid and binding. The seizin of the mother will, under such circumstances, be equivalent to that of her daughter, and, on her signifying her consent, the gift is complete without the donee's seizin. This doctrine is maintained in the Hidáyah and various other legal authorities.—Macn. Prec., M. L., chap. iv, case 9.

The law requires seizin by the donee, except in the case of a gift made by a father to his minor son, and a few other specially excepted instances.—*Ibid*, case 13.

The gift of those parts of the estate of which the minor was registered as proprietor, and of which he took *bonâ fide* possession, is undoubtedly valid; but there is a difference of opinion among lawyers concerning his right to those parts of which the donor continued in possession as ostensible proprietor. By some, the doctrine maintained is that the seizin by the donor on behalf of a minor donee, who is living in his family, but with whom he has no relation, is not sufficient to establish the validity of a gift, if the father of the minor be alive and present; but that it is sufficient if he be not alive and present. Others contend that the seizin of the donor (not being related to the donee) is sufficient to perfect the gift made to a minor, and this is the opinion of modern lawyers, such as the authors of the *Jámai-ur-ramúz, Barjundí, Durr-ul-Mukhtár, Ibráhím-Sháhí, Kohistání, Multakit*, &c., who have declared that the decisions are conformable to the doctrine of the sufficiency of seizin by a stranger in whose house the minor donee resides. Those lawyers who maintain the opposite opinion do not pretend that it is followed in practice.—Macn. Prec., M. L., chap. iv, case 21.

The donee, when competent to take possession, has the right to take it. When he is a minor, or insane, the right to take possession for him belongs to his guardian, who is first his father, then his father's executor, then his grandfather, then his executor, and next the judge, and the person appointed by him. It is alike whether the minor be in the family of any of these persons or not. If the father or his executor, or paternal grandfather or his executor, be absent at a precluding distance, possession may be taken for a minor by any person in whose family he is living. And with regard to others, besides the father and grandfather, such as the brother, paternal uncle, mother, and other relatives, they have all, on a favorable construction, the power to take possession of a gift for a minor when he is in their family. In like manner, the executors of all these have the like power, on a favorable construction, when the minor is in their family; and so also a stranger who nourishes and protects an orphan who has none other besides himself, may lawfully take possession of a gift on his behalf on a favorable construction. In all these cases, it is alike whether the minor have or have not understanding to know what "taking possession" is. But in all it is assumed that the father is dead, or, if alive, is absent at a precluding distance. For, if the father were alive and present, though there is no express authority on the subject, it would seem, from the case of the stranger, and orphan, that if possession were taken by any of the persons above mentioned and the father were present, the possession would not be valid.*

DCLXXXVII. The gift to an orphan is rendered valid by the seizin of his guardian. *Principle.*

If a person make a gift of a thing to an orphan, and it be seized on his behalf by his guardian,—being either the executor Illustrations.

* Fatáwá Alamgírí, vol. iv, pp. 547 & 548.—B. Dig., pp. 530 & 531.

appointed by his father, or his grandfather, or the executor appointed by his grandfather,—it is valid: because all these relatives have an authority over the orphan, as they stand in the place of his father.—Hidáyah, vol. iii, p. 297.

Principle.

DCLXXXVIII. A gift to a discreet minor, however, is rendered valid by the seizin of the minor himself.

Illustrations.

If an infant himself should take possession of the thing given to him, it is valid, provided he be endowed with reason; because such an act is for his advantage; and he has a capability of performing it, as capability depends on reason and understanding, which he possesses.—Hidáyah, vol. iii, p. 297.

If a youth has understanding, and takes possession of a gift, it is lawful though his father be alive; and upon this point "our"* three masters were agreed. But not so if the youth be without understanding.†

Precedent.

But if a stranger make a gift to a child, such gift will be perfected on the seizin by the donee, if he have discretion, or by seizin made on his behalf by his father or grandfather, or guardian appointed by them, or failing those persons, by his mother, or by the seizin, on his part, of a stranger who has the care of his education and under whose protection he lives. The seizin, therefore, by the grandfather's brother will not be legally sufficient, unless the donee, during his minority, was living under the protection of that relation.—Macn. Prec., M. L., chap. iv, case 13.

Principle.

DCLXXXIX. A husband's taking possession of the thing given to his young wife, whether old enough or not for conjugal intercourse, renders the gift valid, provided she then lived in the house of her husband, and under his power and protection.

Illustrations.

It is lawful for a husband to take possession of anything given to his wife, she being then an infant, provided she have been sent from her father's house to his; and this although the father be present; because he is held, by implication, to have resigned the management of her concerns to the husband. It is otherwise where she has not been sent from her father's house, because then the father is not held to have resigned the management of her concerns. It is also otherwise with respect to a *mother*, or any *others* having charge of her, because they are not entitled to possess themselves of a gift on her behalf, unless the father be

---

* So say the Compilers of the Fatáwá Alamgírí.

† Fatáwá Alamgírí, vol. iv, p. 547.—B. Dig., p. 530.

dead, or absent, and his place of residence unknown; for their power is in virtue of necessity and not from any supposed authority; and this necessity cannot exist whilst the father is present.—Hidáyah, vol. iii, pp. 297 & 298.

When a young girl, who is old enough for conjugal intercourse, is living with her husband, and a gift is made to her, possession by herself or by him is lawful. And even when she is not old enough for such intercourse, possession taken for her by her husband is valid, if she be living under his power and protection. But if she is not living under his power and protection, possession taken by him on her behalf is not lawful, and her guardian should take possession of the gift.*

Gift in Health.

DCXC. A man in health and of sound disposing mind may give any portion or the whole of his property to any of his heirs or to a stranger, and the gift, though considered immoral, is judicially valid. *Principle.*

If a man in health should give the whole of his property to one child, it is lawful judicially, though sinful for so doing, while, if he has a son given to learning instead of business, he may lawfully give more to him than to the rest.*

A superiority of affection manifested to one child above others is not blameable, because that is a natural impulse. So also in the case of gifts, unless injury (to the others) be intended. If such was intended, an impartial distribution should be made.†—Durr-ul-Mukhtár, p. 638.

If a man in health making gifts to his children, should desire to give to some of them more than to others, he may lawfully do so, according to Abú Hanífah, when the child in whose favor the distinction is made is superior to others as regards religion, but when they are all equal it is abominable to make any distinction. According to Abú Yusuf, an unequal distribution may be lawfully made when there is no intention of injuring any of the children, and as much should be given to a daughter as to a son. The *Fatwá* is in accordance with this, and it is approved.*

If, during the period of health, a person make a gift of all his property to one child, the gift is valid.†—Sharah-i-Vikáyah.

---

* Fatáwá Alamgírí, vol. iv, pp. 445 & 448.—B. Dig., pp. 529—531.

† *Vide* Macn. Prec., M. L., chap. iv, case 20.

Precedents. It is allowable for a person to make over all his property by gift to one of his heirs, if, at the time of making the gift, the donor was in a state of health and sound disposing mind; and, even though at the time he was sick, the gift is valid, provided he subsequently recover from the sickness. But if he died in consequence of such sickness, the disposition holds good to the extent of a third only of the donor's property,—that is to say, the donee will be entitled to one-third only, and the remaining two-thirds will be distributed among the other heirs.—Macn. Prec., M. L., chap. iv, case 1.

The gift of the entire property to one heir to the exclusion of all the rest, supposing the existence of the conditions noticed in the answer to the preceding question, is good and valid, notwithstanding the immorality of the act, according to the tenets of Abú Hanífah. But *Nuamán*, son of *Bashír*, the Reporter of the traditions, and *Imám Abú Yusuf*, according to the opinion reported of him, and *Muhammad Amjad*, the author of the *Fatáwá Kinojí*, deeming such gift to be an act of cruelty and oppression, have declared it inadmissible, and have pronounced that, in such a case, an equal distribution should be made among the heirs generally. Authorities for the above doctrines: In the *Fatáwá Sirájul Munír*,—"A gift by two or more persons of a house to one individual is valid." In the Hidáyah,—"If two persons jointly make a gift of a house to one man, it is valid." In the *Fatáwá Sirájul Munír*,—"It is necessary that the gift should be divided off, and distinguished, at the time of seizin." In the *Durar-i-Mukhtár*,—"If, during a period of *health*, a person make a gift of all his property to one child, the gift is valid, but the donor has acted sinfully."—Macn. Prec., M. L., chap. iv, case 20.

If the father was in sound disposing mind when he divided his property, giving distinct portions to each of his two sons, and they retained separate possession of their respective portions, the third son will not be entitled to any part of the property.—Macn. Prec., M. L., chap. i, case 1.

Gift in death-illness.

Principle. **DCXCI. A gift by a person, during his illness, of which he died, is lawful to the extent of one-third of his estate, provided the donee was not an heir, and he took possession in the donor's lifetime.**

Illustrations. If the subject of the gift be a mansion, and the donee takes possession of it, after which the donor dies without leaving any other property, the gift is lawful as to a third of the mansion, and the other two-thirds of it must be restored to the heirs. So also as to all other things, whether they do or do not admit of division.*

It is stated in the *Asal* that neither a gift, nor a *sadakah*, or charitable disposal of property, by a sick person, is lawful, except when possession has been taken of the subjects of them; that, when such possession has been taken, they are both lawful to the extent of one-third part of the sick person's estate ; and that if he should die without making delivery, they are both void.*

It is to be observed, as a general rule, that when a person performs, with his property, any gratuitous deed, of immediate operation, (that is, not restricted to his death,) if he be in health at the time, such deed is valid to the extent of all his property ; or, if he be sick, it takes effect to the extent of one-third of his property ; and where a person performs such deed, with his property, restricted to the circumstance of his decease, it takes effect to the extent of a third of his property, whether at the time he be sick or in health. If, on the contrary, a person make an acknowledgment of debt, such acknowledgment is of effect to the whole extent of his property, notwithstanding it be made during sickness, as this is not a *gratuitous* deed. Still, however, a declaration of this nature, made in health, precedes a declaration of the same nature made in sickness. It is also to be remarked, that a sickness of which a person afterwards recovers is considered, in law, as health.—Hidáyah, vol. iv, pp. 503 & 504.

If a father make a gift, during his last sickness, of all his property to one child, to the exclusion of the others, it is wholly illegal, because, in such a state, the heirs in general have an inchoate right to his property, and consequently such disposition is unauthorized. If he make the gift when in health, the donor acts immorally and oppressively, and it is sinful in an ancestor to act injuriously towards his heirs.—Macn. Prec., M. L., chap. iv, case 20. **Precedent.**

DCXCII. The gift by a person in his death-illness to the extent of more than one-third of his estate can only hold good if the donor's heir or heirs (as the case may be) consent to it after his death.—*Vide* Wills. *Principle.*

---

* Fatáwá Alamgírí, pp. 559 & 560.—B. Dig., p. 542.

DCXCIII. A gift made during illness is valid as to the whole, if the donor recovers; or even though

Principle. he die, if the sickness were not death-illness (*a*).

Principle. **DCXCIV.** As respects the gift to an heir by a person in his death-illness, it is not valid even to the extent of one-third of his estate, if the rest of the heirs do not consent to it after the donor's death.

(*a*.) As to the definition of a death-illness, it has been said, (and this is approved for the *fatwá*), that when the illness is such that it is highly probable that death will be the result, it is a death-illness, whether she has taken to her bed or not.—Fatáwá Alamgírí, vol. iv, p. 562.—B. Dig., p. 543.

The most valid definition of death-illness is, that it is one which it is highly probable will issue fatally, whether, in the case of a man, it disables him from getting up for necessary avocations, out of his house or not, or whether, in the case of a woman, it does or does not disable her from necessary avocations within doors.—*Ibid.*

Illustrations. When a sick woman has given her dower to her husband, the gift is valid if she recovers from her illness; and even though she should die of that illness, yet if it were not a death-illness, the answer would be the same; but if it were a death-illness the gift would not be valid without the sanction of the heirs.—Fatáwá Alamgírí, vol. iv, p. 561.—B. Dig., p. 543.

A woman gives her dower to her husband during her death-illness, and he dies before her: she has no claim against him, because the release is valid till she dies. But if she should die of the same disease, her heirs may claim the dower.—Fatáwá Alamgírí, vol. iv, p. 562.—B. Dig., p. 544.

If a man make a bequest in favor of a part (*i.e.*, to one or more) of his heirs, it is not valid; because of a traditional saying of the Prophet,—"*God has allotted to every heir his particular right;*" and also, because a will in favor of a part of the heirs is an injury to the rest: and, therefore, if it were deemed legal, would induce a

---

ANNOTATIONS.

dcxciv. A gift on a death-bed is viewed in the light of a legacy, and cannot take effect for more than a third of the property; consequently, no person can make a gift of any part of property on his death-bed to one of his heirs, it not being lawful for one heir to take a legacy without the consent of the rest.—Macn. M. L., chap. v, princ. 11.

breach of the ties of kindred. Besides, it is said in the traditions, "*a bequest to particular heirs is unjust.*"—Hidáyah, vol. iv, p. 472.

It is to be observed that in judging whether the legatee be an heir or otherwise, regard is paid to the time of the testator's death, *not* to the period of making the will; because the efficacy of the will is established after the death of the testator. *The gift of a dying person* (to an heir†) is, in this respect, of the same nature with a legacy, both being the same in effect, and is, therefore,* to the amount *of a third of the property*‡ (with respect to a stranger).§—Hidáyah, vol. iv, p. 472.

A bequest to an heir is not lawful, according to "*us*," without the assent of the other heirs. If it be made to an heir and to a stranger, it is valid as to the share of the stranger, and dependent as to the share of the heir on the permission of the other heirs. If permitted by them it is lawful; and if not permitted by them, it is void—no regard being had to a permission granted in the life-time of the testator; so that they may afterwards retract.—Fatáwá Alamgírí, vol. vi, p. 139.—B. Dig., p. 615.

It is also to be remarked, that a sickness from which a person afterwards recovers is considered in law as health; because upon his recovery it is evident that no one else has any right to his property.—Macn. Prec., M. L., chap. iv, case 1. **Precedents.**

If a father make a gift, during his last sickness, of all his property to one child, to the exclusion of the others, it is wholly illegal, because, in such state, the heirs in general have an inchoate right to his property, and consequently such disposition is unauthorized. If he make the gift when in health, the owner acts immorally and oppressively, and it is sinful in an ancestor to act injuriously towards his heirs.—Macn. Prec., M. L., chap. iv, case 20.

---

* Arab. "*Mariz*," which literally signifies "sick;" means here, as well as in the Chapter of Wills, "a person *sick of a mortal illness*."

† The words "to an heir," though to be found in some Editions of the Hidáyah in Arabic, are not in Hamilton's Hidáyah. The words in question are quite incompatible with the author's subsequent expression—"to the extent of a third of the property;" inasmuch as a dying person's gift to the extent of a third of his property is valid without his heir's consent with respect to a stranger, and not with respect to an *heir*, to whom a gift cannot be valid even to the extent of a third of the donor's property unless the rest of the heirs consent to it after his death.

‡ The words italicised are, in Hamilton's translation of the Hidáyah, placed within parentheses; but are not so in the Hidáyah in Arabic.

§ The words "with respect to a stranger" are supplied by a Commentator as being left to implication by the author of the Hidáyah.—*Vide* Lucknow Edition of the Hidáyah.

Lawful and Unlawful Gifts.

The lawful and unlawful gifts are defined and distinguished in the Fatáwá Alamgírí. Its passages to that effect are as follow:—

The gift of a thing which is separated from, and emptied of, the property and rights of the donor, is lawful; so also of a *musháa*, or undivided part of a thing that does not admit of partition, or is of such a nature that some kind of benefit or advantage that can be derived from it, while whole or undivided, cannot be derived from it after partition; as, for instance, a small house, or small bath. But the gift of a *musháa* in a thing that admits of partition consistently with the preservation of all the uses which might be made of it before partition, is not valid. What is required is, that the thing given be partitioned and separated at the time of taking possession, not at the time of gift, as is evidenced by the fact that if one person should give another the half of a mansion undividedly, and should not make delivery till he has given the other half, and should then make delivery of the whole, the gift is lawful; though if half the mansion were given and delivered, and then the remaining half were given and delivered, the transaction would not be lawful, but both gifts would be invalid.—Fatáwá Alamgírí, vol. iv, p. 524.—B. Dig., p. 512.

Principle.

DCXCV. The legal effect of gift is not complete until possession is taken of the thing given;* and in this respect, a stranger and the child of the donor are on the same footing when the child is adult.†

The possession on which the completion of the gift and the establishment of its legal effect are dependent, is possession taken with the permission of the owner—a permission which is sometimes express, but at others has to be established by evidence.†

---

* For this purpose the possession must be *kámil*, or perfect.—Durr-ul-Mukhtár, p. 634.

There are three obstructions to a perfect possession:—*First*, the subject of gift may be joined to something that is not given, as fruit on a tree or crops on the ground—when either is given without the other. *Second*, it may be *mushghal*, or occupied with something that is not given. *Third*, it may be *musháa*, or confused with something else by being *mashtarrak*, or held in copartnership with another. The first is obviated by the gift being *muhawwuz*, or separated (*Ináyah*, vol. iv, p. 23); the second by its being *mufarragh*, or emptied; and the third by the gift being declared to be unlawful when the property is susceptible of partition without injury.—B. Dig., pp. 512 & 513, n.

† Fatáwá Alamgírí, vol. iv, p. 524.—B. Dig., pp. 512 & 513.

It is express when a person says, "Take possession of it," when the subject of gift is produced at the meeting; or "Go and take possession of it," when it is not produced at the meeting. In the former case, if possession is taken either at the meeting, or after the parties have separated, it is valid, and the donee becomes the proprietor of the thing given, both by analogy and on a liberal construction of law. But if after the gift, he is forbidden to take possession and does so notwithstanding, the possession is not valid, whether taken at the meeting or after separation from it. When the donee is neither expressly permitted nor forbidden to take possession, and does so at the meeting, the possession is valid on a favorable construction of law, though not so by analogy. But if possession is not taken till after separation from the meeting, the possession is not valid, either by analogy or on a favorable construction. When, again, the subject of gift is not produced at the meeting, and the donee goes and takes possession, the possession is lawful on a favorable construction, though not by analogy, if taken with the permission of the donor; but if taken without his permission, it is not lawful either by analogy or on a favorable construction. If a person should say, "I have given thee this slave," the slave being present, and possession being taken, the gift is lawful, though the donee should not have said, "I have accepted." And though the slave were absent, yet if the donor should say, "I have given to thee my slave, such an one: go and take possession of him," and the person addressed should take possession, the gift would be lawful, though he should not have said, "I have accepted." When a person has given his slave to another, all three being present together, without saying "Take possession of him," and the donee goes away leaving the slave, he cannot afterwards take possession of him without a direction to that effect.*

Being enabled to take possession is like taking it; and if one should give another a piece of cloth in a locked box, and should deliver the box to him, it would not be possession, for want of ability to take the cloth out of it; but if the box were open it would be possession by the party being able to take it, as in the case of vacating in sale. It is only, however, when a gift is valid that vacating is effectual; for it is not so with an invalid gift.*

Umrá or life-grant.

DCXCVI. An *Umrá*, or life-grant, is lawful to the grantee during his life, and descends to his heirs.—Hidáyah, vol. iii, p. 309. *Principle.*

---

* Fatáwá Alamgírí, vol. iv, pp. 524 & 525—B. Dig., pp. 512, 513 & 514.

Because of the tradition before quoted.*—Besides, the meaning of *Umrá* is a gift of a *house* (for example) during the life of the donee, on condition of its being returned upon his death.—The conveyance of the house, therefore, is valid without any return; and the condition annexed is null, because the Prophet has sanctioned the gift, in this instance, and annulled the condition, as before mentioned. An *Umrá*, moreover, is nothing but a gift and a condition; and the condition is invalid; but a gift is not rendered null by involving an invalid condition, as has been already demonstrated.—Hidáyah, vol. iii, p. 309.

If he (the grantor) said, "This mansion is to thee *Umrá* (for thy age), or *hayátí* (for thy life), and when thou art dead it reverts to me," in which the gift is lawful, and the condition void.†

Principle.

DCXCVII. A gift by way of *rakbah* is null according to *Hanífah* and Muhammad (*a*).—Hidáyah, vol. iii, p. 309.

(*a.*) Hence *rakbah* is void;—as when a person says to another, "my mansion is thine *rakbah*;" meaning, "if thou diest it is mine; if I die, it is thine."†

The arguments of *Hanífah* and *Muhammad* upon this point are two-fold. First, the Prophet has legalized *Umrá* and annulled *Rakbah*. Secondly, the meaning of "my house is yours by way of *Rakbah*," is, "if I die before you, my house is yours," which is a suspension of the conveyance of property upon the decease of the donor previous to that of the donee: and this is a matter of doubt and uncertainty, and consequently null. It is to be observed that *Rakbah* is derived from *Irtikáb*, which means expectation: for the donor is, as it were, an *expectant* of the death of the donee.—Hidáyah, vol. iii, pp. 309 & 310.

Sadakah, or Alms-deed.

Principle.

DCXCVIII. Like gift, alms-deed (*sadakah*) is not valid unless attended with seizin, and it is

---

* By this the author appears to have alluded to the following passage:—"Because the Prophet approved of *Umrás* (gifts for life), but held the condition annexed to them by the grantor to be void."—*Vide* Hidáyah, vol. iii, p. 308.

† Fatáwá Alamgírí, vol. iv, pp. 520 & 521.—B. Dig., pp. 508 & 509.

gratuitous, in the same manner as a gift.* Neither is an alms lawful where it consists of an undivided part of a thing capable of division, for the reasons already explained in the case of a gift under these circumstances.—Hidáyah, vol. iii, p. 310.

DCXCIX. A gift is not valid without verbal acceptance, but charity is valid without it, on a favorable construction from a regard to custom.† *Principle.*

DCC. A charitable gift made by one, to one, two or more poor persons is valid according to all.† *Principle.*

But such gift made to two or more rich persons is invalid according to one report from Abú Hanífah, and valid according to another report from him, as well as according to the other two lawyers.†

An invalid *sadakah* (or charitable gift) is like an invalid *hibah*, yet if one were to give a *sadakah* to two rich persons, it would be lawful even according to Abú Hanífah by one report, which was the opinion of the other two; while, if it were bestowed on two Fakeers, or beggars, the *sadakah* would be valid according to them all.†

It is recorded in the *Jámi Saghír*, that if a rich man bestow ten *dirms* in alms upon two poor men, or make a gift of that sum to them, it is valid; but that, if the said charity or gift be made to two rich men, it is invalid. (The two disciples maintain that in this last instance both gift and alms are valid.) From this it appears that *Hanífah* has construed a gift into *alms*, when the object is a *poor* man; and alms into a *gift*, when the object is a

---

* If a person vow to devote his *property* [*Mál*] in charity, let him give of that kind on which it is incumbent upon him to pay *Zakát*. If, on the other hand, he vow to devote his *possessions* [*Milk*], he must give the *whole* of his property. It is related that there is no difference between these two cases. We have, however, in treating of the duties of the *Kázi*, shown the difference between *Mál* and *Milk*; and also the principles on which both these traditions proceed. It is to be observed that, in this case, the person that made the vow must be told to reserve for himself and his family as much of his property as may suffice for their maintenance until he be able to acquire more. The remainder, after such reservation, must be bestowed in charity; and after he has acquired more, he must then give in charity a portion equal to what he had reserved for the subsistence of himself and his family. An explanation of this has already been given in treating of inheritance, under the head of *Duties of the Kázi.*—Hidáyah, vol. iii, pp. 310 & 311.

† Fatáwá Alamgírí, vol. iv, p. 569.—*Vide* B. Dig., p. 545.

rich man,—because of the similarity betwixt these deeds, as each is a conveyance of property without an exchange. Hence, *Hanífah* has made a difference with respect to them, as appears by the case recited in the *Jámi Saghír*, since he has admitted of charity to two poor men, but not of a gift to two *rich* men; whilst in the *Mabsút* he has made no difference between them, but on the contrary has declared them to be equal, as he there declares "neither a gift nor alms to *two* men is valid, because the mixture of property is a bar in both cases, as both are dependent on a perfect seizin." The reason of the distinction in the *Jámi Saghír* is that the end of alms is *to give to God*, who is one; and the alms comes not to the poor men, but as their daily food from God Almighty; whereas the *gift* goes directly to the object of it, namely, *the two men*. Some have said that the recital in the *Jámi Saghír* is the most approved doctrine; and that the meaning of the doctrine in the *Mabsút* is that charity to two *rich* men is invalid, in the same manner as a *gift* to two men of *any* description.—Hidáyah, vol. iii, p. 299.

Iskát, or Cancellation.

Principle. DCCI. The gift of a debt to the debtor is a release, and it is lawful, both by analogy and on a liberal construction of law.*

The gift of a debt, or release of it to the debtor, is complete without his acceptance, though it is reversed by his rejection (*a*).†

(*a.*) But this is true only with respect to the principal debtor; for the gift of a debt to the surety is not complete without his acceptance, though it is reversed by his rejection. If the creditor releases the principal debtor from his debt, or gives it to him, and he accepts, both he and the surety are released; but if he do not accept, he is not released.*

Principle. DCCII. The gift of a debt can be made not only to the debtor himself, but also, on his death, to his heir.

Illustrations. A man, who is in debt, dies before payment, and the creditor makes a gift of the debt to the heir—the gift is valid; and if it

---

* Fatáwá Alamgírí, vol. iv, pp. 535 & 536.—B. Dig., pp. 522 & 523.

† A debt considered with reference to the prospect of payment is *mál*, or corporeal property, and is susceptible of *tamlik*. Considered with reference to its present state, it is a *wasf*, or quality (indebtedness), and is susceptible of *iskát*, or extinction. Hence a gift of it to the debtor himself, which is an extinction, is valid, both by analogy and on a favorable construction; but a gift of it to another, which is *tamlik*, is valid only on the latter ground.—*Hidáyah* and *Kifáyah*.—B. Dig., p. 522, n.

is to some of the heirs, it accrues to the benefit of all. If a debtor should say to his creditor, "Release me from what I owe thee," and he should say, "I have released thee from my debt against thee," and the other should then reply, "I will not accept," he is released notwithstanding. One of the heirs of a creditor gives his share in a debt to the debtor before partition, and in the deceased's estate there are both money and goods—the gift is good on a liberal construction, like a composition. And the gift by a creditor of his share in a specific thing to an heir of the debtor, or to any other person, is valid, if the thing does not admit of partition; but if it does admit of partition, the gift is not valid.*

A creditor makes a gift of his debt to his debtor, who neither accepts nor rejects it at the meeting, and then comes after the lapse of some days, and rejects the gift; there is some difference of opinion on the point, but the sound doctrine is that the gift is not reversed.*

DCCIII. The gift of a debt to any other than the debtor is lawful on a liberal construction when the donee is directed to take possession of the debt.* *Principle.*

DCCIV. The gift of a debt suspended on a condition, or made to take effect at a future time, is not, however, valid. *Principle.*

If a person, having a debt due to him of one thousand *dirms*, should say to the debtor "when to-morrow arrives, the said thousand *dirms* are your property," or "you are exempted from the debt," or if he should say, "whenever you pay me *one half* of the said thousand, the other half is *your property*," or "you are *exempted* from the debt of the other half,"—the gift so made is null. The reason of this is, that the gift of a debt to a debtor is an *exemption:* but an exemption has two meanings: 1.—It is a *conveyance of property* on the principle of debts being property, on which account lawyers have held that "an exemption may be undone by a rejection:" 2.—It is an *annulment,* since debt is in the nature of a quality, on which account an exemption does not rest upon acceptance. Now nothing can be suspended on a condition excepting an *utter* annulment, such as a divorce or an emancipation;—and an exemption (as has been already said) is not an *utter* annulment, and therefore cannot be suspended on a condition, but on the contrary is perfectly nugatory.—Hidáyah, vol. iii, pp. 308 & 309. Illustration.

---

* Fatáwá Alamgírí, vol. iv, pp. 535 & 536.—B. Dig., pp. 522 & 523.

Revocation or Retraction of Gifts.

Principle. DCCV. Gifts are of several kinds, some being to relations within the prohibited degrees, some to strangers, and some to relatives who are not within the prohibited degrees. All may be revoked *before* delivery to the donee, whether he were present or absent at the time of the gift, and whether permitted to take possession or not. But *after* delivery, the donor cannot revoke of himself without the decree of a judge or the consent of the donee, even though the gift be to others than to the relations within the prohibited degrees.—*Vide* Fatáwá Alamgírí, vol. iv, p. 537.—B. Dig., p. 524.

A gift cannot lawfully be retracted but with the consent of both parties, or by a decree of the *Kází*, because the retraction of a gift is a disputed point amongst the learned. There is, moreover, a degree of weakness in a retraction, because the admission of it is contrary to analogy, since it is a power over the property of another, as the right of property in a gift is established in the donee. Besides, as there may arise a contention with respect to the object in lieu of it, (since the donor may claim something which the donee may refuse,) the contention, therefore, cannot possibly be settled but by the consent of the parties, or by a decree of the *Kází*.—Hidáyah, vol. iii, p. 304.

It is lawful for a donor to retract the gift he may have made to a stranger.—Hidáyah, vol. iii, p. 300.

Principle. DCCVI. Revocation (or retraction) of a gift is abominable under any circumstances, but it is valid nevertheless.*

Principle. DCCVII. There are, however, several causes each of which prevents revocation of gifts (*viz.*),— 1, the loss of the thing given (*a*); 2, the passing

ANNOTATIONS.

dccvi. It is to be observed, however, that although a retraction of a gift be agreeable to the letter of the law, still it induces abomination; for the Prophet has said "*The retraction of a gift is like eating one's spittle.*"—Hidáyah, vol. iii, p. 301.

*** Fatáwá Alamgírí, vol. iv, pp. 537.—B. Dig., p. 524.**

of it from the property of the donee (*b*); 3, the death of the donor; 4, increase of the thing given (*c*); 5, a change in the subject of it (*d*); 6, the marriage relation between the donor and donee (*e*); 7, relationship within the prohibited degrees (*f*);* and 8, an exchange or return received for the gift (*g*).

ANNOTATIONS.

dccvii. The obstacles to the resumption of gifts are stated to be seven. 1st. The incorporation of an increase with the gift. 2nd. The death of the donee. 3rd. The donee giving a return or consideration. 4th. Alienation of the gift. 5th. The parties being husband and wife. 6th. Relation within the prohibited degrees. 7th. Destruction of the thing given.—Sharah-ul-Vikáyah. *Vide* Macn. Prec., M. L., chap. iv, case 19.

The bars to a retraction of a gift are many, amongst which are the following: 1. The donee giving the donor a return or consideration; because this fulfils the donor's object. 2. The incorporation of an increase with the gift; because in that instance a retraction cannot take place without including the increase, as that is implicated; and it cannot take place so as to include the increase, since that was not included in the deed of gift. 3. The death of one of the parties; for if the *donee* should die, his property shifts to his heir, and becomes the same as if it had shifted during his lifetime; and if the *donor* should die, his heirs are strangers with respect to the contract, since they made no tender of the thing given. 4. The alienation of the gift from the donee's property during his lifetime; because this is a consequence of the power vested in him by the gift, which power, therefore, cannot then be retracted; and also because the right of property has regenerated in another person, in virtue of a fresh cause, namely, conveyance to a second donee; and as a regeneration of the right of property is equivalent to an essential change in the thing, the case is therefore the same as if the gift were to become, in effect, a different thing from what it was, and consequently not liable to retraction.—Hidáyah, vol. iii, pp. 301 & 302.

A donor is at liberty to resume his gift, except in the following instances:—

A gift cannot be resumed where the donee is a relation, nor where anything has been received in return, nor where it has received any accession, nor where it has come into the possession of a second donee, or into that of the heirs of the first.—Macn. Prec., M. L., chap. v, princ. 12 & 13.

* Fatáwá Alamgírí, vol. iv, p. 537.—B. Dig., p. 524.

(*a.*) "The loss of the thing given,"—for there is no means of having recourse for its value, since the contract was not for value.*

(*b.*) "The passing of it from the property of the donee,"—by whatever means that may be effected, as by sale, gift, or the like, or by his death; for what is established to an heir is different from what is established to an ancestor.*

(*c.*) An increase of the thing given, of such a nature as to be united to it; and it makes no difference whether the increase be in consequence of an act of the donee, or without such act, and whether it have issued from the thing itself, or be an accession to it. But it must be incorporated with the body of the gift, and be an addition to its value, such as dyeing, sewing, carrying, or the like. Mere transfer from one place to another, when it adds to the value of a thing, is sufficient to prevent revocation, according to Abú Hanífah and Muhammad. A separate increase does not prevent the revocation of a gift, nor does damage or loss sustained by the subject of gift, though the donee is not responsible for the loss.*

(*d.*) A change in the subject of it, as grinding when it is wheat, baking when it is flour, and churning into butter when it is milk.*

(*e.*) The marriage relation prevents the revocation of a gift; and it has that effect though one of the parties be a Mooslim and the other an infidel. And when one of the married parties has made a gift to the other, it cannot be revoked, though the marriage should afterwards be dissolved. But if a man should make a gift to a stranger and then marry her, or a woman should make a gift to a stranger and then unite herself to him in marriage, the giver might recall the gift.*

(*f.*) Relationship within the forbidden degrees prevents the revocation of a gift, whether the relative be a Mooslim or an infidel; and there is, consequently, no revocation of gifts to fathers and mothers, how high soever, or to children, how low soever; the children of sons and the children of daughters being in this respect alike. In the same manner there is no revocation of gifts to brothers and sisters, and paternal uncles and aunts. But where the prohibition is for some other cause than consanguinity, it does not prevent revocation; as in the case of fathers and mothers, or brothers and sisters by fosterage, and of mothers of wives, stepsons, and the wives of sons, and husbands of daughters who are prohibited by affinity.*

If a person make a gift of anything to his relation within the prohibited degrees, it is not lawful for him to resume it, because

* Fatáwá Alamgírí, vol. iv, pp. 537 & 538.—B. Dig., pp. 524—526.

the Prophet has said, "*When a gift is made to a prohibited relation, it must not be resumed*;"—and also because the object of the gift is an increase of the ties of affinity, which is thereby obtained.—Hidáyah, vol. iii, p. 302.

If a husband make a gift of anything to his wife, or a wife to her husband, it cannot be retracted, because the object of the gift is an improvement of affection (in the same manner as in the case of presents to relations); and as the object is obtained, the gift cannot be retracted. This object, however, is to be regarded only during the existent period of the contract; insomuch that, if a person give something to a strange woman, and afterwards marry her, he may retract the gift;—whereas, if a man give something to his wife, and afterwards divorce her three times, he is not entitled to retract the gift.—Hidáyah, vol. iii, pp. 302 & 303. **Illustrations.**

The donor is not entitled to revoke the gift which she made in favor of her daughter, because, in this case, there are two obstacles to resumption: first, the death of the donee, agreeably to the doctrine laid down in the *Kanz-ud-dakáik*,—"one obstacle to the resumption of a gift is the death of one of the parties;" and, secondly, relation within the prohibited degrees, as is stated in the Hidáyah,—"If a person make a gift of anything to his relation within the prohibited degrees, it is not lawful for him to resume it."—Macn. Prec., M. L., chap. iv, case 14. **Precedents.**

The gift by a grandmother to her grandson is legal and valid, and does not admit of resumption, because, between the grandmother and her grandson, there exists a relationship within the prohibited degrees, and such relationship is an obstacle to resumption. Her distribution of the property among the heirs generally, five years after the gift, is null and void, and the former gift will remain in full force. According to the *Sharh-i-Vikáyah*,—"To perfect the gift of a thing which is in possession of the donee, new seizin is not requisite."—Macn. Prec., M. L., chap. iv, case 19.

(*g.*) "An exchange (or return) received for the gift," prevents its revocation.—Fatáwá Alamgírí, p. 537.—B. Dig. p. 525.

DCCVIII. When, however, the return or change is opposed only to a part, the remainder of the gift may be resumed. *Principle.*

If a person make a gift of a *house* to another, and the donee give a return to the donor for a *half* only of the house so given, the donor may in that case resume the half of the house for which he received no exchange, since a bar to his retraction existed only with respect to the *other* half.—Hidáyah, vol. iii, p. 304. **Illustration.**

Principle. **DCCIX. When the donee has sold any part of the granted land undivided, the donor may resume the unsold part.**

Illustration. If the donee sell one-half of granted land undivided, the donor may in that case resume the other half; as to the resumption of that no bar exists. If, on the other hand, the donee should *not* have sold any part of the land, the donor may resume one-half of it, for as he is entitled to resume the whole, it follows that he is entitled to resume the half, *a fortiori.*—Hidáyah, vol. iii, p. 302.

Principle. DCCX. The gift of land cannot be retracted after the donee has erected buildings or planted trees thereon.

Illustration. If a person make a gift to another of a piece of land destitute of buildings or plantations, and the donee plant trees in it, or build a house, a stable, or a shop of such a size as to be deemed an increase, in that case the donor is not entitled to retract the gift, because of the increase which it has received. The restriction is stated with respect to the shop, because shops are sometimes so small as not to be deemed an increase, and sometimes the land is very extensive, the shop occupying only one particular part of it; in which case the bar operates only with respect to that part.—Hidáyah, vol. iii, p. 302.

Principle. DCCXI. The gift of debt to one's debtor is not revocable.

Illustration. When a man gives a debt to his debtor, the gift is not revocable; but when he gives fruit on a tree, with permission to take possession, and it is taken, he may revoke the gift.—Fatáwá Alamgírí, vol. iv, p. 544.—B. Dig., p. 527.

Principle. DCCXII. The donor's repossession of the thing given in gift is not requisite to the validity of retraction.

Illustration. When a person retracts his gift, either in virtue of a decree of the *Kází*, or of the mutual consent of the parties, it is an annulment of the original gift, and not a gift *de novo* on the part of the *donee*, and therefore seizin by the donor is not in such a case a requisite condition. Retraction, moreover, is lawful with respect to an undivided portion; but if a retraction were a gift *de novo*, seizin would be a requisite condition, and consequently retraction with respect to an undivided portion would not be lawful.—Hidáyah, vol. iii, p. 305.

Principle. DCCXIII. Revocation under a judge's decree is a cancellation, without any difference of opinion; but there is some difference as to revocation by mutual consent being so. The tendency of precedents, however, is in favor of its being a cancellation also.*

Thus, when one person has given a thing to another, who, after giving it to a third party, revokes the gift, the first donor is entitled to revoke also; but this could not be the case if the revocation by the first donee were a mere gift.*

DCCXIV. Revocation being a cancellation, it follows that the thing given returns to the former state of property, and that the donor repossesses it without any necessity for renewing his taking of possession.* *Principle.*

DCCXV. The thing given is also, after revocation of the gift, an *amánat,* or trust in the hands of the donee; so that, if it should perish, he is not responsible for the loss.* *Principle.*

DCCXVI. But when revocation is neither by a judge's decree nor by mutual consent, and the donee gives back the subject of the gift to the donor, and he accepts it, he does not again become the proprietor of it till he has taken possession. When he does take possession, the gift by the donee comes into the place of a revocation by a judge's decree or mutual consent, and the donee has no power to revoke it.* *Principle.*

It is reported as from Abú Yusuf, that—

DCCXVII. Until an order has been passed by a judge for cancelling a gift, the donee may use, and dispose of, the subject of it; but any such use or disposal, after the judge has given his order, is unlawful. And the opinions of Abú Hanífah and Muhammad were of the same effect.* *Principle.*

DCCXVIII. If the subject of gift should perish in the hands of the donee after the passing of the judge's order, and previous to the donor's retaking possession, the donee is not responsible for the loss, unless possession had been demanded of him, and he had refused to give it.* *Principle.*

DCCXIX. Retraction of alms (*sadakah*) is not lawful. *Principle.*

ANNOTATIONS.

dccxix. There is no revocation of a *sadakah* after it has been completed; and it makes no difference whether it be bestowed on the rich

---

* Fatáwá Alamgírí, vol. iv, pp. 544, 545, 549, & 569.—B. Dig.. pp. 527, 528, 532, & 546.

Because the object, in alms, is *merit in the sight of* God, and that has been obtained. If, also, a person bestows alms upon a *rich* man, it is not lawful to retract therefrom, on a favorable construction of the law, because to acquire merit in the sight of God may sometimes be the object in bestowing alms upon the rich. In the same manner also, if a person make a *gift* of anything to a poor man, it is not lawful to retract it, because the object in such gift is *merit,* and that has been obtained.—Hidáyah, vol. iii, p. 310

Principle. DCCXX. When he (the donor) gives to one who asks of him, or is needy, without saying expressly that it is charity, he has no power to revoke on a favorable construction.*

Hibah bil-iwaz and *Hibah ba-shart ul-iwaz.*

Besides the ordinary gift, there are two other contracts termed "*Hibah bil-iwaz,*" or gift for an exchange; and "*Hibah ba-shart ul-iwaz,*" or gift on condition of an exchange.†

Principle. DCCXXI. In the transaction of *hibah bil-iwaz,* the *iwaz* (exchange) must be distinctly opposed to the prior gift by words clearly expressive of such opposition (*a*).*

(*a.*) As, for instance, by saying—"This is the *iwaz,*" or "the *badal,*" or "in the place of thy gift," or "I have made a donation of this for thy gift," or "I have made it lawful to thee," or "established it to thee," or words of similar import.*

So that if one should give a thing to another, and the donee should take possession, and then make a gift of something to the

ANNOTATIONS.

or on the poor, for it cannot be revoked in either case. When a man has bestowed a mansion in charity on another, he cannot revoke, whether the person on whom it has been bestowed is rich or poor.—Fatáwá Alamgírí, vol. iv, p. 569.—B. Dig., p. 545.

* Fatáwá Alamgírí, vol. iv, pp. 544, 545, 549, & 569.—B. Dig., pp. 528, 532, & 546.

† Besides the ordinary species of gift, the law enumerates two contracts under the head of gifts, which, however, more nearly resemble exchange or sale. They are technically termed "*Hibah bil-iwaz,*" mutual gift or gift for a consideration, and the "*Hibah ba-shart ul-iwaz,*" gift on stipulation or promise of a consideration.—Macn. M. L., chap. v, princ. 14.

donor, without saying "in *iwaz* of thy gift," or using some other of the forms of expression above-mentioned, the second gift would not be an exchange for the first, but a new gift, and each of the parties would have the right to revoke.*

It appears that the gift in this case was that of the description of gift which is technically termed in law "*a hibah bil-iwaz*," or gift for a consideration, and this species of gift resembles a sale both in principle and in effect; but there is a doubt as to the legality of this transaction, from the circumstance of the articles opposed to each other consisting partly of money which constitutes a *Sirf* sale. In this description of contract, seizin on the spot is essential to its validity. If seizin was made, the transaction must be held to be valid; if not, it must be declared null and void, and both the parties have a right to recede from the contract. So also the heirs and creditors are at liberty to set it aside and resume the property parted with, on repaying the consideration for which it may have been given, until which time, the property will remain as a pledge in the hands of the purchaser, but when the consideration is restored, it will become subject to the Law of Inheritance; and in this event it should be made into forty-eight parts, of which each widow is entitled to three, and each daughter to fourteen.—Macn. Prec., M. L., chap. iv, case 17.

DCCXXII. The *iwaz* (exchange) in a contract of gift should not have come into the possession of the donee by means of the contract itself. So that, if the donee should give in exchange for the gift a part of the thing given, it would not be valid, and there would be no *iwaz*. But if such a change should take place in the thing given, as would prevent a revocation of the gift, part of it may be made an *iwaz* for the remainder.* *Principle.*

DCCXXIII. And if two things are given by different contracts, and one of the two is given back as an exchange for the other, though there is some difference of opinion on the point, yet, according to *Abú Hanífah* and *Muhammad*, it would be a good *iwaz;* and if one of them were given by way of gift, and the other as *sadakah*, and the *sadakah* were *Principle.*

---

* Fatáwá Alamgírí. vol. iv. pp. 549 & 550.—B. Dig., pp. 332—334.

exchanged for the gift, it would be an *iwaz* according to them all.*

Principle. DCCXXIV. The *iwaz* (exchange) must be secured to the giver; and if it be not secured to him, as, for instance, if a right be established to it while in his hands, it is no *iwaz*, and he may revoke the previous gift if the thing given be still subsisting in kind, undestroyed, and without any increase for the better, or anything happening in it to prevent revocation.*

Principle. DCCXXV. If part of the gift prove to be the property of another, a proportionable part of the return may be resumed. If, on the contrary, part of the exchange prove to be the property of a person other than the donee, the donor is not, in that case, entitled to take back a particular part of the gift; but he may restore the remaining part of the return, and resume the whole of the gift from the donee.

If half of a gift prove the property of some other than the donor, the donee is in that case entitled to take back from the donor half of the return he may have made him for the gift, since the thing opposed to that half was not secured and rendered safe to him. If, on the contrary, half the return prove the property of some other than the donee, the donor is not, in that case, entitled to take back from the donee a particular part of the gift; but he may restore the remaining part of the return, and then resume the whole of the gift from the donee.—Hidáyah, vol. iii, p. 303.

Principle. DCCXXVI. When the subject of the gift, or the *iwaz*, is a thing that does not admit of partition, a right is established in part of it; but when it admits of partition, and a right is established in part of one of them, the *iwaz* is void if the right be established in it; and in like manner the gift is void if the right be established in it; and when the *iwaz* is void, the gift may be revoked, and when the gift is void, the *iwaz* may be revoked.*

---

* Fatáwá Alamgírí, vol. iv, pp. 549 & 550.—B. Dig., pp. 332—334.

DCCXXVII. When the exchanging takes place subsequently to the gift, the *iwaz* is, without any difference of opinion between *our** masters, a gift *ab initio*. So that it is valid where gift is valid, and void where gift is void; there being no difference between them except as to the dropping of the power of revocation in the case of the *iwaz*, while it is established in that of the gift.† *Principle.*

DCCXXVIII. After possession has been taken of the *iwaz* (exchange), the power to revoke drops also with respect to the gift.—Durr-ul-Mukhtár, p. 637. *Principle.*

So that neither party can reclaim from his fellow what he has become possessed of, whether the *iwaz* were given by the donee or by a stranger, with or without his direction.†

DCCXXIX. All the conditions of gift are applicable to the *iwaz;* the transaction does not come within the contract of *muávazat*, or mutual exchange, either in its inception or completion.‡ Hence, it is *Principle.*

ANNOTATIONS.

dccxxvi, dccxxvii. If a right be established to a part of the *iwaz*, the remainder is still an exchange for the whole gift; but the donor may, if he please, return what remains of the *iwaz* in his hands, and revoke the whole of his gift, if it be stiil in existence without any increase in its substance, and have not passed out of his property. As to the security of the thing given, that also is a condition of the exchanging; so that, if a right be established in it, the donee under the original gift may revoke the *iwaz*, and if the right be to a half, he may revoke a half of the *iwaz*, when the thing given is of such a nature as to admit of partition; and it matters not whether the *iwaz* itself have increased or diminished in price or in substance, he takes half the increase or the loss, as the case may be.—Fatáwá Alamgírí, page 549.—B. Dig., page 533.

* So say the Compilers of the Fatáwá Alamgírí.

† Fatáwá Alamgírí, vol. iv, pp. 549 & 550.—B. Dig., pp. 332, 334 & 535.

‡ Sir William Macnaghten, however, says—"*Hibah bil-iwaz* is said to resemble a sale in its proper ties. The same conditions attach to it, and the mutual seizin of the donees is not, in all cases, necessary."—Macn. M. L., chap. v, princ. 15.

not exposed to *shufáa*, or the right of pre-emption, nor can the thing given be rejected on either side on account of defect.*

Principle.

DCCXXX. When a gift is made on condition of an *iwaz*, or exchange, all the conditions of gift attach to the *iwaz* in the beginning.*

So that it is not valid in *Musháa*,† or anything that admits of partition. Property is not established in it before possession; and each of the parties may refuse delivery. But after mutual possession has been taken, the effect is that of sale. Hence neither of the parties can recall what was his. *Shufáa*, or the right of pre-emption, is established by the transaction; and each of the parties may return for a fault the thing of which he took possession.*

According to analogy, a gift on condition of an exchange ought to be a sale† in its inception as well as in its completion.*

When a man gives a mansion to two men on condition of an *iwaz*, or exchange, of a thousand *dirms*, the transaction becomes a lawful sale† after mutual possession.*

A gift is invalid by confusion.—Mír Niár Alí *v.* Májidah and others, 30th July 1831, S. D. A. Rep., vol. v, p. 136.

Precedents.

But the court will consider that a gift for a consideration is, in effect, a sale and purchase, and is not vitiated by confusion of property, or defect of possession, according to the Muhammadan law.—Sayyid Hosain Alí Khán *v.* Fayyáz-ud-dín Haydar, 28th November 1832, S. D. A. Rep., vol. vi, p. 239.

The Muhammadan law recognizes a distinction between a gift for a consideration (*hibah bil-iwaz*), and a gift on consideration of a return (*hibah ba shart ul-iwaz*); the latter is, the former is not, vitiated by confusion and non-possession.—Imdád Alí *v.* Kádir Buksh and others, 24th April 1833, S. D. A. Rep., p. 296.

Seizin of the donee is not requisite by the Muhammadan law, in order to render a *hibah bil-iwaz*, or gift for consideration, valid. —Mír Najíbullah *v.* Mussamut Kasíma, 8th November 1795, S. D. A. Rep., vol. i, p. 10.—Morl. Dig., vol. i, p. 268.

---

* Fatáwá Alamgírí, vol iv, p. 550.—B. Dig., pp. 534 & 535.

† "*Hiba ba-shart ul-iwaz*, on the other hand," says Sir William Macnaghten, "is said to resemble a sale in the first stage only," that is, before the consideration, for which the gift is made, has been received, and the seizin of the donor and donee is therefore a requisite condition.—M. L., chap. v, princ. 16, p. 51.

DCCXXXI. If an exchange, be it much or little, be given for the whole of a gift, it would prevent revocation of the gift; but if the exchange be given for part of the gift, the other part, for which no exchange is given, may be revoked. *Principle.*

If a person should give an *iwaz* for the whole of a gift, it would prevent revocation, whether the *iwaz* be much or little; if the *iwaz* be for part of the gift, the part for which there is no *iwaz* may be revoked, but not that part to which the *iwaz* is opposed.*

DCCXXXII. An *iwaz*, or exchange, made by a stranger, is lawful, whether by the direction of the donee or not.* *Principle.*

The general principle in cases of this kind is, that when anything is demandable of a person in *specie*, and is obligatory upon him, his direction to another to pay it is a cause of recourse against himself without any condition for responsibility; and that when a thing is not demandable from a person in *specie*, and is not obligatory on him, his direction to another to pay it is not a cause of recourse against him, unless his responsibility is made a condition of the payment.—Fatáwá Alamgírí, p. 551.—B. Dig., p. 535.

---

* Fatáwá Alamgírí, vol. iv, p. 550 —B. Dig., pp. 534 & 535.

LECTURE II.

ON WASÁYAH, OR WILLS.

Definition—Constitution—Conditions and legal effects of Wills—Who are, and who are not, competent to make Wills—Proper subjects and objects of Legacies—Usufructuary Wills—Will for charitable purposes—Revocation of Wills.

WASAYAH is the plural of *wasiyat*. *Wasiyat* means an endowment with the property of anything after death, as if one person should say to another, "give this article of mine after my death to a particular person."*

The thing so given is termed "*músá bi-hi*," or subject of the bequest; the person who wills that it be given is denominated the "*músí*," or testator; the person in whose favor the will is made, is called "the *músá la-hu*," or the legatee; and the person appointed to carry the will into execution is called "the *wasí*," or executor.*

Wills are declared to be lawful in the *Kurán* and the traditions (*ahádís*), and all our doctors, moreover, have concurred in this opinion.—Hidáyah, vol. vi, p. 468.

Principle. DCCXXXIII. A will (*wasiyat*) is constituted by saying—"I have bequeathed such a thing *to*† such an one," or "I have bequeathed *towards*† such an one," or by any other words that are commonly used instead of these.‡

---

* *Vide* Hamilton's Hidáyah, vol. iv, pp. 466 & 467.

To bequeath, in the language of law, is to confer a right of property in a specific thing, or in a profit or advantage in the manner of a gratuity, postponed till after the death of the testator.—Fatáwá Alamgírí, vol. vi, p. 139.—B. Dig., p. 613.

† The difference between the two expressions lies in the prepositions; the first being "*la-hu*," which signifies that the bequest is made for the legatee's own benefit; and the second being "*ilá*," which indicates that the party to whom the bequest is made is executor.—*Ibid.*

‡ Fatáwá Alamgírí, vol. vi, p. 149.—B. Dig., p. 13. Durr-ul-mukhtár, p. 818.

DCCXXXIV. A will may be made verbally as well as by writing.*

DCCXXXV. A bequest may also be made by a sign or signs, if the person bequeathing is so sick as to be unable to speak, provided the meaning of the sign or signs made by him is intelligible, and he died without regaining the power of speech. *Principle.*

A sick man makes a bequest, and, being unable to speak, gives a nod with his head, and it is known that he comprehends what he is about; in these circumstances, if his meaning be understood, the bequest is lawful; but not otherwise. And it is implied that he dies without regaining the power of speech; for then it is evident that there was no hope at the time of the bequest of his being able to speak, and his condition was therefore the same as that of a dumb man.—Fatáwá Alamgírí, vol. vi, p. 168—B. Dig., p. 641. Illustration.

DCCXXXVI. The conditions of a valid bequest or will are—that the testator be competent to make a transfer of the property; that the legatee be competent to receive it, and that the subject of the bequest be a thing susceptible of being transferred *after* the testator's death, whether it were in existence at the time of bequeathing or not.† *Principle.*

It is essential to the validity of a will that the property willed away should exist in the possession of the testator at the time of his death, otherwise the legacy will have Precedent.

ANNOTATIONS.

dccxxxiv. There is no preference shown to a written over a nuncupative will, and they are entitled to equal weight, whether the property which is the subject of the will be real or personal.—Macn. M. L., chap. vi, princ 1.

dccxxxvi. It is not necessary that the subject of the legacy should exist at the time of the execution of the will. It is sufficient for its validity that it should be in existence at the time of the death of the testator.—Macn. M. L., chap. vi, prine. 8.

* A written will is in this country termed "*Wasiyat-námah*," while a nuncupative will is called simply "*Wasiyat*," and sometimes "*Wasiyat-i zabáni*."

† Fatáwá Alamgírí, vol. vi, p. 139.—B. Dig., p. 614. Durr-ul-Mukhtár, p. 818.

no effect. For instance, if a person leave by will one-third of his flock of sheep to another, and it appear that, at the time of his death, he had no animal of this description, the legacy will be void, on the principle of its being necessary, that the property should exist in the possession of the testator at the time of his death.—Macn. Prec., chap. v, case i, p. 242.

Principle. DCCXXXVII. It is also a condition that the bequest be accepted, either expressly or by implication (*a*), which is by the legatee's dying before rejection or acceptance, whereupon his death becomes an acceptance, and his heirs inherit the legacy.*

(*a.*) Acceptance may be inferred from conduct, as by giving operation to a bequest, or purchasing something on account of the heirs, or paying debts; in which case the acceptance is good as if made in express terms.—Fatáwá Alamgírí, vol. vi, p. 139.—B. Dig., p. 614.

The property of a legatee in a legacy is established by his acceptance of it.—Hidáyah, vol. iv, p. 474.

Our doctors argue that a legacy establishes the property in the legatee *de novo*, and does not vest by succession and descent as in the case of inheritance; and such being the case, it rests, therefore, entirely on his acceptance, as no person can be made proprietor of anything against his will.—Hidáyah, vol. iv, pp. 474 & 475.

Principle. DCCXXXVIII. Acceptance of a bequest must be made *after* the death of the testator, in so much that if it be accepted or rejected during his life, either act is void, and the rejector is still at liberty to accept after his death.*

Acceptance or rejection of a bequest is not established until after the death of the testator; for as the bequest does not take

ANNOTATIONS.

dccxxxvii. There is this difference between the property which is the subject of inheritance and that which is the subject of legacy. The former becomes the property of the heir by the mere operation of law; the latter does not become the property of the legatee until his consent shall have been obtained either expressly or impliedly.—Macn. M. L., chap. vi, princ. 4.

* Fatáwá Alamgírí, vol. vi, p. 139.—B. Dig., p. 614.

effect before that event, those cannot be previously regarded. Hence the acceptance or rejection during the life of the testator has no effect, in the same manner as an acceptance declared before the existence of a contract. If, therefore, a legatee accept a bequest *after* the death of the testator, it is valid, notwithstanding that he may have rejected it during his lifetime.—Hidáyah, vol. iv, p. 473.

It is to be observed that acceptance, in cases of bequest, is of two kinds :—1. *Express*, which needs not to be explained. 2. *Implied*, which is where the legatee dies without having either declared his acceptance or refusal ; for this also is an acceptance in effect ; because the bequest is rendered complete on the part of the testator by his death (in other words, it cannot be rescinded after that event) ; and as it was suspended in its effect purely in deference to his right of rejection, it of course falls into his property upon his demise ;—in the same manner as holds in a case of sale with a reserve of option to the purchaser, in which instance, if the purchaser die without formally signifying his assent to the sale, it is then regarded as complete, and the article sold is considered as part of his estate.—Hidáyah, vol. iv, p. 475. Illustration.

DCCXXXIX. The legal effect of a bequest is to confer on the legatee a new right of property, in the same way as in the case of gift, and the bequest becomes vested in him by acceptance; so that, if he accept after the death of the testator, his ownership of the thing bequeathed is established, whether he takes possession of it or not. If the legatee reject a bequest, it is cancelled.* *Principle.*

DCCXL. A bequest to a stranger to the amount of a third of one's property is valid even without the consent of his heir or heirs, but a bequest to him of more than a third is not valid unless consent is given to it by all the heirs of the testator after his death. *Principle.*

ANNOTATIONS.

dccxl. Legacies cannot be made to a larger amount than one-third of the testator's estate, without the consent of the heirs.—Macn. M. L., chap. vi, princ. 2.

* Fatáwá Alamgírí, vol. vi., p. 139.—B. Dig., p. 614.

A bequest to a stranger is valid without the consent of the heirs, but *not* beyond a third of the estate, unless assented to by them *after* the testator's death. It is implied that they are of full age, and no regard is had to their permission granted during the lifetime of the testator.—Fatáwá Alamgírí, vol. vi, p. 139.—B. Dig., p. 614.

It is to be observed, as a general rule, that where a person performs, with his property, any gratuitous deed, of immediate operation, (that is, not restricted to his death,) if he be in health at the time, such deed is valid to the extent of all his property,—or, if he be sick,* it takes effect to the extent of one-third of his property; and where a person performs such deed, with his property, restricted to the circumstance of his decease, it takes effect to the extent of a third of his property, whether, at the time, he be sick or in health.—Hidáyah, vol. iv, pp. 503 & 504.

Still, however, a declaration of this nature, made in health, precedes a declaration of the same nature made in sickness. It is also to be remarked, that a sickness of which a person afterwards recovers is considered, in law, as health.†—Hidáyah, vol. iv, p. 504.

If a person make a will in favor of a stranger to the amount of a third of his property, it is valid, although the *heirs* of the testator should not be consenting thereto, for it is so recorded in the traditions.—Hidáyah, vol. iv, p. 468.

It is to be observed, however, that although a will, bequeathing more than a third of the testator's property, be not lawful, yet if the heirs, being arrived at the age of maturity, should give their consent to it, *after* the death of the testator, it then becomes valid; for the objection to its validity is founded merely on a regard to their right, and therefore does not operate any longer, after they themselves agree to forego such right. Their consent, indeed, during the lifetime of the testator, is not regarded; for this is an assent previous to the establishment of their right, they are, therefore, at liberty to annul it upon the death of the testator. It is otherwise where the consent is given *after* that event; for as this is an assent subsequent to the establishment of their right, they

---

* Arab "*Mariz*."—This term literally means "sick." But in the language of the law, it is used to signify death-illness.

† This passage has no place in the Arabic copy. It has been introduced from other authorities in the Persian version as a premiss necessary to the completely understanding of what follows.—Note by Mr. Hamilton.

The above is to be found in the Jámi ur-Ramúz in which it is also laid down, that if an illness continues for more than a year, then although the patient should afterwards die of that illness, yet the same must be considered as *health* for the space of one year from its commencement.

are not afterwards at liberty to annul it.—Hidáyah, vol. iv; pp. 469 & 470.

DCCXLI. A bequest by a person having no heir is valid even to the extent of his or her whole property. *Principle.*

When a man bequeaths his whole estate having no heirs, the bequest takes effect, and there is no occasion for any assent on the part of the public treasury (*Bayit-ul-mál*).*

Where a person makes a will in favor of part of his heirs, the same rule holds as in the case of bequeathing more than a third to a stranger;—in other words, the deed is not valid, unless the other heirs give their consent to the disposition *after* the death of the testator; and their consent *previous* to his death will have no effect. It is to be observed that, in every instance where a will is rendered valid by the consent of the heirs, the legatee derives his property from the *testator*, not from the *heirs*. This is the opinion of our doctors.—Hidáyah, vol. iv, p. 470. Illustration.

Consequently,—

DCCXLII. A bequest of any portion of one's estate to one or some of the heirs is not valid except when consented to by the rest of the heirs. *Principle.*

A bequest to an heir is not lawful according to us‡ without the consent of the other heirs.†

If a man make a bequest in favor of part of his heirs, it is not valid; because of a traditional saying of the Prophet, "God has allotted to every heir his particular right;" and, also, because a will in favor of part only of the heirs is an injury to the rest; and, therefore, if it were deemed legal, would induce a breach of the ties of kindred. Besides, it is said in the traditions, "a bequest to particular heirs is unjust."—Hidáyah, vol. iv, p. 472. Illustration.

It is to be observed that in judging whether the legatee be an heir, or otherwise, regard is paid to the time of the testator's death,

---

ANNOTATIONS.

dccxlii. A legacy cannot be left to one of the heirs without the consent of the rest.—Macn. M. L., chap. vi, princ. 3.

---

* Though it is *ultimus hæres*.—B. Dig., p. 615.

† Fatáwá Alamgírí, vol. vi, pp. 140 & 164.—B. Dig., pp. 615 & 636.

‡ So say the Compilers of the Fatáwá Alamgírí.

not to the period of making the will; because the efficacy of the will is established *after* the death of the testator.* So,—

In determining whether a person is an heir or not, regard is to be had to the time of the testator's death. Thus, if a man makes a bequest in favor of his brother, who is his heir at the time, and a son is afterwards born to him, the bequest to the brother is valid; but if at the time of the bequest to his brother the testator has a son who afterwards dies before himself, the bequest to the brother is cancelled.*

Principle. DCCXLIII. If a bequest is made to an heir and also to a stranger, the bequest with respect to the heir's portion, even if it were less than a third, is not valid without the consent of the other heirs, while that which respects the portion of the stranger is valid without such consent, provided the portion bequeathed to him does not exceed a third of the testator's estate; otherwise the consent of the heirs is requisite to the validity of such bequest.

Illustrations. If a person bequeath any article jointly to one of his heirs and a stranger; in this case the bequest in favor of the heir is not admitted, and a moiety only of the legacy is given to the stranger; because, as an heir possesses the capacity of being a legatee, he therefore obstructs the stranger in the title which he would otherwise have to the complete legacy. It is not so where a legacy is left between one person living and another dead, for here the whole goes to the living legatee, since as a dead person is incapable of succeeding to a bequest; there is no obstruction in this instance.—Hidáyah, vol. iv, pp. 495 & 496.

When a man makes a bequest to a stranger and his heir, the stranger takes half the bequest, and the remainder is void, and, in like manner, if the bequest be to a homicide and a stranger. This is contrary to the case of an acknowledgment; for if one were to acknowledge a specific thing or a debt in favor of his heir and a stranger, the acknowledgmeut would be void as to the stranger also.*

If it be made to an heir and a stranger, it is valid, as to the share of the stranger, and dependent as to the share of the heir on the permission of the other heirs. If permitted by them, it is lawful; and, if not permitted by them, it is void—no regard being had to a permission granted in the lifetime of the testator; so that they may afterwards retract.*

* Fatáwá Alamgírí, vol. vi, pp. 140 & 164.—B. Dig., pp. 615, 616 & 636.

DCCXLIV. It is, however, lawful to make a bequest to the son of one's heir, and the bequest is valid to the extent of one-third without the consent of the heirs.

It is lawful to make a bequest to the son of one's heir, or to one's own *mukátab,** or *muddabar,** on a favorable construction of law.†

DCCXLV. In all cases where there is any occasion for the assent of the heirs, the assent is lawful only where the person who grants it is competent to grant,—as for instance, when he is of mature age, and of sane mind.† *Principle.*

DCCXLVI. If the assenting heir, being of mature age, is sick, but afterwards recovers from his illness, the assent is valid; and if he die of the illness, the assent is to be treated in the same way as if it were a bequest; so that, if the original legatee be an heir of the assenting heir, the assent is not lawful unless concurred in by the other heirs of the sick person; but if the original legatee be in the position of a stranger to the sick person, the assent is lawful to the extent of a third of his estate.† *Principle.*

DCCXLVII. After the heirs have once assented to a legacy in excess of a third of the estate, or in favor of an heir of the testator, or of his slayer, they cannot refuse to deliver the subject of bequest, and may be compelled to make delivery, as the legatee does not take from them, but from the testator.† *Principle.*

DCCXLVIII. If not consented to, by all the heirs of the testator, his bequests, though made to several persons, are valid only to the extent of one-third of his estate, and this one-third is to be proportionately divided among them all. *Principle.*

If a man bequeath a third of his property to one man, and a third to another, and the heirs refuse their consent to the execu- *Illustrations.*

---

* *Vide* page 275 of Lecture viii delivered in 1873.

† Fatáwá Alamgírí, vol. vi, p. 140.—B. Dig., pp. 615 & 616.

tion of both bequests, one-third is, in that case, divided equally between the two legatees. For where the will exceeds a third of the estate, and the heirs refuse their consent to the execution of the whole, it is then restricted to one-third, as has been already explained; and as, in the present instance, the right of both claimants is equally good, and the third is capable of division, it is therefore divided equally between them.—Hidáyah, vol. iv, p. 482.

If a man bequeath a third of his property to one person and a sixth to another, and the heirs refuse to confirm the whole, in that case one-third of the property is to be divided between the legatees in three equal lots; two to the legatee of the *third*, and one to the legatee of the sixth.—Hidáyah, vol. iv, p. 482.

Principle.

DCCXLIX. But if consented to, or allowed, by all his heirs, the testator can lawfully bequeath any portion or even the whole of his estate.

Illustrations.

If a person bequeath a particular number of *dirms*, without specifying the relative proportion they bear to his estate,—such as a half, a third, a fourth, or the like,—it is valid, but is executed only to the extent of a *third* of his whole property, unless the heirs be willing to confirm the whole.—Hidáyah, vol. iv, p. 484.

When a man has bequeathed a third of his property to one man, and a third of it to another, and both bequests are allowed by the heirs, the legatees have two-thirds, and the heirs one-third; and if the bequests are not allowed by them, the legatees have the third between them in halves.*

When a man has bequeathed a fourth of his property to one person, and a half of it to another, and both bequests are allowed by the heirs, the legatee of the half takes a half, and the legatee of the fourth takes a fourth, and the residue goes to the heirs, in proportion to the shares appointed for them by Almighty God. When the heirs do not allow the legacies, they are valid from the testator's third, which is to be divided among the legatees in seven parts, four of which are for the legatee of the half, and three for the legatee of the third. This was the opinion of Abú Hanífah. But, according to Abú Yusuf and Muhammad, the third of the property should be divided into three equal parts, and two of them given to the legatee of the half, and one to the legatee of the fourth.*

---

* Fatáwá Alamgírí, vol. vi, p. 150.—B. Dig., pp. 126, 127.

If a person first bequeathed the whole of his estate to one man, and then a third of it to another, and the heirs refuse their assent, in that case, one-third of his estate is divided into four shares, of which three are given to the legatee of the whole, and one to the legatee of the third. This is according to the two disciples. Hanífah alleges that the third of the estate must be divided equally between the legatees.*—Hidáyah, vol. iv, p. 484. Illustrations.

If a person bequeath a portion of his estate, the legatee is, in that case, entitled to the smallest portion allotted to any of the heirs,—provided, however, that such portion be not less than a sixth, for then a complete sixth must be given to him.—Hidáyah, vol. vi, p. 488.

When a person has bequeathed to another something, or a portion out of his property, or some of his property, the explanation of this rests with himself while he is alive, and with his heirs after his death. And if he should bequeath a share *(saham)*, or part *(juz)*, the heirs are to be told to give what they please. This is founded on the common acceptation of the word *saham*; but it is said in the Mabsút that the legatee of a *saham* should have an equivalent to the smallest share of the heirs, provided, according to the disciples, that it does not exceed a third, the reports of Abú Hanífah's opinion being contradictory. When a person has bequeathed a *saham* of his property, and has no heirs, the legatee takes a half; for the *bayit-ul-mál*, or public treasury, is in the place of a son, and the case is as if he had left two sons, when the estate would be equally divided between them.—Fatáwá 'Alamgírí, vol. vi, p. 152.—B. Dig., pp. 628 & 629.

DCCL. If a person bequeath a part of his property to another without specifying the amount, the heirs are at liberty to give whatever they please to the legatee. *Principle.*

For here the amount of the bequest is unknown; but as the uncertainty with respect to that is no bar to its validity, it is therefore valid; and such being the case, and the heirs being the representatives of the testator, it is consequently at their discretion to fix the amount, in the same manner as the testator himself might do if he were living.—Hidáyah, vol. iv, p. 488. Reason.

DCCLI. If a person bequeath a *sixth* of his property to another, and afterwards before the same or another company, bequeath *a third* of his property to that same person, in *Principle.*

---

* **The author of the Hidáyah by citing the argument of Hanífah *after* that of the two disciples, appears to have adopted the opinion of Hanífah alone.—*Vide* Hidáyah, vol. iv, pp. 484 & 485.**

this case, the legatee is entitled to a *third* of the testator's estate, whether the heirs be consenting parties or not, the sixth being included in the latter bequest of the third.—Hidáyah, vol. iv, p. 488.

Principle.

DCCLII. If a person bequeath a third of any particular property, and two-thirds thereof be lost, and the remainder come within a third of the testator's estate, the legatee is entitled to the whole of such remainder.

Illustrations.

If a person bequeath to another "*a third of his dirms,*" amounting in all to three thousand, or "*a third of his goats,*" amounting in all to three, and afterwards two-thirds of the *dirms* or goats be lost or destroyed, so that only one-third remains, and the remaining third does not amount to a third of the whole of the testator's property (he having been in possession of *other* things besides the *dirms* or goats), the legatee is entitled to the complete remaining third; that is, to a thousand *dirms* in the first case, and to one goat in the second.—Hidáyah, vol. iv, pp. 488 & 489.

If a man bequeaths a third of his *dirms*, or a third of his flocks, and two-thirds of them happen to perish, leaving what remain no more than a third of his property, the legatee is entitled to the whole of the remainder. But if the bequest were of a third of his clothes, and two-thirds were to perish, still leaving the remainder less than a third of the whole property, the legatee would be entitled to no more than a third of the remainder. It is said, however, that this applies only to clothes of different kinds; for if all the clothes be of one kind, the case is to be treated in the same way as that of the *dirms*. In like manner all things estimated by weight or measure of capacity are to be treated in the same way as *dirms*, but mansions of different kinds are like clothes of different kinds, according to Abú Hanífah.—Fatáwá Alamgírí, vol. vi, p. 161.—B. Dig., p. 631.

Principle.

DCCLIII. If a person bequeath to another "*his son's portion of inheritance,*" such bequest is null; whereas, if he bequeath "*an equivalent to his son's portion,*" such bequest is valid.

Illustration.

For the first is a bequest of what is the property of another, whereas the second is merely a bequest of something similar; and the semblance of a thing is different from the thing itself, notwithstanding its rate be determined thereby. *Ziffer* is of opinion that a bequest of the former nature is likewise valid; because at the time of making it the portion belonged evidently to the testator. In reply to this, however, it is to be observed, that the legacy does not take place until after the death of the testator, when the property does not belong to him, and hence his bequest of his son's portion is a bequest of property not his own.—Hidáyah, vol. iv, p. 486.

DCCLIV. A will made by a Musalmán in favor of a *Zimmí*,* is lawful, and *vice versâ*,† but a bequest in favor of an alien* who is not a *Mustámin* is not lawful. *Principle.*

Illustrations. A bequest of a Musalmán in favor of a *Zimmí*, or of a Zimmí in favor of a Musalmán, is valid: the former, because God has said in the *Kurán*, "Ye are not prohibited, O believers, from acts of benevolence towards those who subject themselves to you, and refrain from battles and contentions;"—and the latter, because *Zimmís* in virtue of their compact with the *Musalmáns*, are considered in the same light with them in all temporal concerns; and, as on this principle, an intercourse of good offices towards each other is held lawful during life, they are therefore in the same manner permitted to extend beyond the grave. It is related in the *Jámi Saghír* that a will in favor of a hostile infidel is not valid, as God has prohibited in the *Kurán* the exercise of benevolence towards them.—Hidáyah, vol. vi, p. 473.

A Musalmán may lawfully make a bequest to a *Zimmí*, or *vice versâ*; but a bequest to an alien who is not a *Mustámin* is not lawful. If a Muslim make a bequest to an alien living in a *dár-ul-harb*, or foreign country, the bequest is not lawful, though the heirs should give their consent. And if the alien should come into the Muslim territory under protection, with the intention of taking his legacy, still he cannot do so even with the consent of the heirs. This is when the *Muslim* who made the bequest was in the *dár-ul-Islám* at the time. If he were also residing in the *dár-ul-harb*, "our" doctors differ as to the legality of the bequest. When the alien is a *Mustámin*, residing in the Muslim territory, it seems, on the authority of the Záhir Rawáyet, that a bequest to him would be lawful to the extent of a third of the testator's property without the consent of the heirs, and beyond that amount with their consent. But a bequest by a Muslim to an apostate is not lawful.—Fatáwá Alamgírí, vol. vi, p. 141.—B. Dig., pp. 616 & 617.

DCCLV. A will in favor of a fœtus in the womb, and a will bequeathing a fœtus, are both *Principle.*

ANNOTATIONS.

dcclv. The ground on which the first case proceeds is, that a legacy is, in a manner, a succession to property; and as a fœtus is capable to

* *Vide* Lecture viii of 1873, pp. 280—282.

† Though difference of religion is an impediment to succession. *Vide* Lecture viii of 1873.

valid, provided the birth happens in less than six months from the date of the will.—Hidáyah, vol. iv, p. 417.—*Vide* Fatáwá Alamgírí, vol. vi, pp. 140 & 141.—B. Dig., p. 617.

Principle.

DCCLVI. A bequest to the person from whom the testator had received a mortal wound is not valid; and if the legatee slay his testator, the bequest in his favor is rendered void, unless, however, the heirs consent to such bequest.

Illustrations.

If a person make a bequest in favor of another from whom he has received a mortal wound, it is not valid; whether the murderer be one of his heirs, or a stranger, or whether he may have wounded him wilfully or by misadventure, provided he be the actual perpetrator of the deed; because it is recorded in the traditions, that "there is no *legacy* for a murderer;" and also, because, as the person who gave the wound has hastened the death of the testator, he is, by way of punishment, excluded from the benefit of the will, in the same manner as a person under similar circumstances is excluded from inheritance. So likewise, where a man, having made a bequest in favor of a particular person, is afterwards killed by that person, such bequest is invalid. If, however, in these cases, the heirs should give their consent, the bequest then becomes valid, according to *Hanífah* and Muhammad.—Hidáyah, vol. iv, p. 471.

A bequest to a person who slays the testator, either intentionally or by accident, is not lawful, whether the bequest were made before the deathwound or after it. But if the heirs assent to the bequest, it is lawful, according to Abú Hanífah and Muhammad.*

ANNOTATIONS.

succeed in the case of inheritance, it is so likewise in the case of a legacy, that being analogous to inheritance.—Hidáyah, vol. iv, p. 477.

The ground, on the other hand, on which the second case proceeds is, that the existence of the fœtus is understood at the period of making the will; and as the legacy of things not yet in being, (such as the fruit a tree may hereafter yield) is valid, it follows that a legacy of a thing actually existing is valid *a fortiori*.—*Ibid.*, p. 478.

---

* Fatáwá Alamgírí, vol. vi, p. 140.—B. Dig., p. 616.

DCCLVII. If, however, the slayer be a youth under puberty, or insane, the bequest to him is lawful without the consent of the heirs; or if the slayer be himself the sole heir, a bequest to him is lawful, according to Abú Hanífah and Muhammad.* *Principle.*

A bequest to the *mukátab*, or *mudabbar*, or *um-i-walad*† of the slayer is also unlawful without the consent of the heirs.*

DCCLVIII. A bequest to the parent or other ancestor, or child, or other descendant of one's slayer is valid. *Principle.*

It is lawful to make a bequest to the son of one's heir, or to one's own *mukátab*, or *mudabbar*,† on a favorable construction of law; so also to the parent or other ancestor, or child, or other descendant of one's slayer, and to the *mukátabs*, *mudabbars*, and absolute slaves of all these.‡

DCCLIX. When a person makes a bequest, being in debt to the full amount of his property, the bequest is not lawful, unless the creditors agree to release the property *pro tanto*.‡ *Principle.*

If a person deeply involved in debt bequeath any legacies, such bequest is unlawful and of no effect; because debts have a preference to bequests, as the discharge of debts is an absolute duty, whereas bequests are gratuitous and voluntary; and that which is most indispensable must be first considered. If, however, the creditors of the deceased relinquish their claims, the bequest is then valid, the obstacle to it being removed, and the legatee being supposed to stand in need of his legacy.—Hidáyah, vol. iv, p. 475.

DCCLX. A bequest by a person who is free and sane, whether a man or woman, is lawful; so also is the bequest by a person who is travelling and is separated from his property lawful.‡ *Principle.*

DCCLXI. A bequest by any one who is incompetent to do a gratuitous act is invalid.‡ *Principle.*

---

* Fatáwá Alamgírí, vol. vi, pp. 140 & 141.—B. Dig., pp. 616 & 617.

† *Vide* Lecture viii of 1873, pp. 280—282.

‡ Fatáwá Alamgírí, vol. vi, pp. 141 & 142.—B. Dig., pp. 616 & 617.

Hence,—

Principle. DCCLXII. A bequest by an insane person, or a *mukátab* or a *mázún*,* is not valid. And if a person is insane at the time of making his will, but afterwards recovers from his insanity and then dies, still the bequest is unlawful for want of competency at the time of making it.†

Principle. **DCCLXIII. A bequest by a minor at any stage or age of his infancy is invalid.**

Illustrations. A bequest by a youth under puberty, whether he be a *muráhik* (that is, approaching to puberty), or not, is unlawful according to "us."‡ And it makes no difference whether the youth be permitted to trade or be under inhibition, or whether he die before puberty or after it. So also, though he should say, "If I arrive at majority, a third of my property is to such an one," the bequest is not valid for want of competency at the time of making it. But with regard to an absolute slave or a *mukátab*, when they refer a bequest to a time subsequent to their becoming free, it is valid.†

A bequest by an infant is not valid. *Sháfeí* maintains that it is valid, provided it be made to a discreet and advisable purpose. The arguments of *our* doctors, in support of their opinion upon this point, are twofold. First, a will is a voluntary act, concerning which an infant has not a capacity of forming a proper judgment. Secondly, the declaration of an infant is not of a binding nature; but if the validity of a bequest by such were admitted, that effect would follow of course.—Hidáyah, vol. iv, p. 476.

Principle. **DCCLXIV. A bequest made by a minor becomes, however, effective *ab initio* upon his confirming or ratifying the same after attaining majority.**

If a youth or a *mukátab* make a bequest, and the former after attaining his majority, or the latter after obtaining his freedom, allows it, the bequest is valid, *ab initio*.†

Principle. DCCLXV. If a person who is poor bequeath to another "*a third of his property*," and afterwards become rich, the legatee is in that case entitled to a third of his estate, whatever the same may amount to; for the bequest does not take effect until after the death of the testator; and there-

---

* A *Mázún* is a slave who is permitted by his master to earn for his emancipation.

† Fatáwá Alamgírí, vol. vi, pp. 141 & 142.—B. Dig., pp. 616 & 617.

‡ So say the Compilers of the Fatáwá Alamgírí.

fore the condition of its validity is, his being possessed of property *at the time of his decease.* The law is also the same, in case the testator, being rich at the time of making the will, should afterwards become poor, and again acquire wealth.—Hidáyah, vol. iv, p. 492.

DCCLXVI. A will made by a person in jest, or under compulsion or mistake, is not valid.* *Principle.*

DCCLXVII. A legacy left to two persons, one of them being *at that time dead*, goes entire to the living legatee. *Principle.*

If a person leave a third of his property to "*Zayid* and *Umar*," and *Umar* be at that time dead, the whole of the third is given to *Zayid*, whether the testator, at the time of making the will, may have been acquainted with the death of *Umar* or not; for as a defunct is not capable of becoming a legatee, he therefore cannot prevent a living person from being so;—in the same manner as where, for instance, a person bequeaths something "*to Zayid and to a wall.*" According to one tradition from *Abú Yusuf* it is said, that if the testator were not acquainted with the death of *Umar*, *Zayid* is then entitled only to one-half of the third; for on such a supposition the will in favor of *Umar* was valid in the opinion of the testator; which sufficiently indicates his will and intention to have been that *Zayid* should receive only one-half of the third. But if, on the other hand, he was acquainted with the circumstance of *Umar's* death, it is evident that he intended that *Zayid* should receive the whole; as a will in favor of a dead man is vain and useless.—Hidáyah, vol. iv, p. 491. Illustrations.

If a man should bequeath a third of his property to *Zayid* and *Bakr*, *Bakr* being dead at the time, whether with or without the knowledge of the testator, or to *Zayid* and *Bakr* if he be alive, he being in fact dead, or to him and to the person in this house, no one being in the house, or to him and to his posterity (*akab*), or to him and to a child of *Bakr*, and his child dies before the testator, or to him and to the poor of his children, or to him who may become poor of his children, and the condition fails at the time of his death, the whole legacy is to *Zayid*, in all of these cases; for the non-existing or the dead can have no right, and, there being no one to contend with *Zayid*, the legacy is the same as if it were to him alone. With regard to the case of *Zayid* and his posterity,

* Fatáwá Alamgírí, vol. vi, p. 142.—B. Dig., p. 617.

as they are to follow him after his death, they are to be considered as non-existing at present. In all these cases, the competitor with *Zayid* is out of the contest from the beginning; but if he were at first competent to contend with him, and should subsequently become disqualified by failure of a condition, *Zayid* would have only a half. Thus, if a person should say, "A third of my property to *Zayid* and *Bakr*, if I die, he being alive or poor," and the testator dies when *Bakr* is dead or rich, or if he should say, "to him and to *Bakr* if he be in the house," and he is not in it; or, "to him and the children of such an one if they become poor," and they do not become poor till the testator dies, or "to him and to his heir,"—in all these cases, the legatee has only half of the third. The principle in these cases is that when the person conjoined with another enters into a bequest, and then comes out of it by the failure of a condition, he does not occasion any cessation to the right of the other, and that when he does not enter into the bequest for want of personality or competence (*ahlíat*), the other takes the whole. And if one should say, "A third of my property between *Zayid* and *Bakr*," *Bakr* being dead at the time, *Zayid* would have only a half of the third, because the word "between" implies a division in half, insomuch that if he were to say, "betwe n *Zayid*," and then stop, *Zayid* would have a half also. Yet if one should say, "A third of my property between the sons of *Zayid* and the sons of *Bakr*," and one of them has no sons, the whole third belongs to the sons of the other. If one should bequeath a third of his property "to *Zayid* and to *Amr*," or should say, "between *Zayid* and *Amar*," and should then die, and one of the legatees should die after him, half of the third would belong to the survivor, and the other half of it to the heirs of the deceased legatee. So, also, if one of them should die after the testator, but before acceptance of the legacy, and the survivor should then accept, both legatees would be entitled to the bequest. But if one of them should die before the testator, the share of the legatee so dying would revert to the testator.—Fatáwá Alamgírí, vol. vi, p. 161.—B. Dig., pp. 631—633.

Principle.

DCCLXVIII. A legacy being bequeathed to two persons, if one of them, subsequently dies, only a moiety thereof goes to the other.

Illustrations.

If a person will that one-third of his property *"be divided" as a legacy*, between *"Zayid and Umar,"* and *Umar* be at that time dead, *Zayid* is entitled to only one-half of the third; for the words used by the testator clearly denote his intention that each should have a half; but *Umar* being at that time dead, the will with respect to him is void.—Hidáyah, vol. iv, p. 491.

DCCLXIX. When a man bequeaths a third of his property to the sons of "such an one," and the person has no son at the date of the bequest, but sons are subsequently born to him, after which the testator dies, these sons are entitled to the third. And even though the person had sons at the date of the bequest, yet if they were not mentioned by their names, as *Ahmad, Zayid,* and *Bakr,* or otherwise distinctly indicated by saying "*these,*" the bequest would be to the sons existing at the time of the testator's death.* *Principle.*

So that if those in existence at the date of the bequest should die, and others are subsequently born, who are living at the time of the testator's death, these also are entitled to the third of the property. If, however, the existing sons are mentioned by name, or are otherwise distinctly indicated, the bequest is only to them, and becomes void in the event of their death. Thus, when legatees are named, or otherwise distinctly indicated, the bequest to them is said to be special, and regard must be had to the time at which it was made.* Illustration.

DCCLXX. A bequest of any article not existing in the possession or disposal of the testator at his decease, is null (*a*), unless it was referred to his property, in which case it must be discharged by a payment of the value (*b*). *Principle.*

(*a*.) If a person bequeath "*a third of his goats*" to another, and it happen either that he has no goats, or that such as he had were destroyed before his death, the bequest is null; for the condition of its validity is, the testator being possessed of the property *at the time of his decease,* which is not here the case. If, on the contrary, having no goats at the time of making the will, he should afterwards acquire goats, so as to leave some at his death, one-third of them goes as a legacy to *Zayid* (according to the *Rawáyet-i Sahíh*); for here the condition of validity (namely, that the testator die possessed of the property) exists.—Hidáyah, vol. iv, p. 492. Illustrations.

(*b*.) If a person bequeath "*a goat of his property*" to *Zayid,* and afterwards die without leaving any goats, the price of a goat must, in that case, be paid to *Zayid;* for the testator's expression, "*a goat of his property,*" denotes his intention to bequeath the *worth* of the animal. If, on the contrary, he neither bequeath "*a goat*

---

* Fatáwá Alamgírí, vol. vi, p. 162—B. Dig., pp. 634 & 635.

of his property," nor "one of his goats," but simply a "goat," (to *Zayid*), without any relation to his property or herd of goats, in that case there is a difference of opinion, some saying that the bequest is not valid, as the absolute expression of the testator denotes his intention to have been, a legacy of the animal itself, of which he had none,—whilst others maintain it to be valid, for this reason, that the testator having specified a *goat*, of which he had none, must be supposed to have intended the *worth* of it. If, on the other hand, the words of the testator were "*I bequeath one of my goats*," in that case the bequest is evidently invalid; because the relation to his herd of goats determines the legacy to have been restricted to the animal itself. (A variety of cases of this nature occur, and are determined on the principle now stated.)—Hidáyah, vol. iv, pp, 492 & 493.

Principle. DCCLXXI. When a man who bequeaths a third of his property has no property at the time of such bequest, the legatee is entitled to a third of whatever he may be possessed of at the time of his death. But if the bequest be specific, or of some particular kind of property, as a third of his flocks, and they all perish before his death, the legacy is void.*

Illustrations. Insomuch that if he should afterwards become possessed of other flocks or another specific thing of the same kind, the right of the legatee would not attach to the subsequent acquisition; yet if he had no flocks at the date of the bequest, but afterwards acquires them, and then dies, it would seem that the bequest is valid. And if he should say, "a sheep from my property," and have none, the value of a sheep must be given. If the bequest were only of a sheep, without the addition of words referring it to his property, the bequest, according to some, would be valid, while according to others it would be invalid. But if the expression were "a sheep from my flocks," and the testator had no flocks, there is no doubt that the bequest would be void. And in like manner with regard to other kinds of property, such as cows, camels, and the like. When a person says, "I have bequeathed to thee a sheep from my property," the bequest is not confined to the sheep that he may have at its date, but applies to the sheep that may be among his property at his death; and since this is the case, if the testator should afterwards die, leaving property, comprehending sheep, with other things, the heirs are at liberty to give one of the sheep or its value. There is nothing in the books as to the sheep's being of the best, worst, or medium quality; but accord-

* Fatáwá Alamgírí, vol. iv, p. 163.—B. Dig., p. 635.

ing to a report of Hasn-bin-Zayid, the companions (of the Prophet) were of opinion that the heirs might, in such a case, either give a sheep of medium quality or its value. When a person says, "My Roan Turkish horse is a bequest to such an one,"—these words are held to refer to a horse then in his possession, not to one which he may afterwards acquire. So, also, if the expressions were, "my blind slave," or, "my Sindian or Abyssinian slave;" while if the terms of the bequest were only, "my Turkish horse to such an one," without further addition or qualification, it would include his property at the time and his subsequent acquisitions.—Fatáwá Alamgírí, vol. vi, p. 163.—B. Dig., pp. 635 & 636.

DCCLXXII. If a third person is declared by the testator to be a participator in the bequest already made by him to two persons, he (the third person) is entitled to participate with the other two legatees. *Principle.*

If a person bequeath one hundred *dirms* to *Zayid*, and one hundred to *Umar*, and afterwards declare *Bakr* to be a participator with them, by saying "I have made *Bakr* a sharer with *Zayid* and *Umar*," *Bakr* is in that case entitled to a third of each of their portions, in order that he may be put on an equality, as the words of the testator evidently imply *that* intention; for the term [*Shirkat*] used by him literally means equality which it is here possible to preserve, and there is no impracticability in the execution of the bequest. It is otherwise, where the portions of the legatees are unequal, as if the legacy of *Zayid* were four hundred *dirms* and that of *Umar* two hundred, and *Bakr* were declared by the testator to be a sharer with them; for in that case the establishment of an equality is impracticable, and therefore *Bakr* is entitled to receive a moiety of each of their shares, that they may be brought as nearly on an equality as possible.—Hidáyah, vol. iv, pp. 493 & 494. Illustrations.

When a person bequeaths a third of his property to one man, and then says to another, "I have made you a partner and joined you with him," the third belongs to them both. And if, after bequeathing to one man a hundred, and to another a hundred, he should say to a third, "I have made you a partner with them," the person addressed would be entitled to a third of each hundred.—Fatáwá Alamgírí, vol. vi, p. 664.—B. Dig., p. 636.

DCCLXXIII. If a person, whose estate consists partly of ready money, and partly of debts due to him from others, *Principle.*

ANNOTATIONS.

dcclxxiii. **When a man bequeaths a thousand *dirms*, and leaves actual property and outstanding debts due to him, the legacy is to be imme-**

bequeath to another one thousan *dirms*, and if that sum do not exceed a third of the *existen* property, it is paid to the legatee without any deduction. If, on the contrary, it exceed a third of the ready property, he is only to receive a third of the amount in hand; and afterwards a third must be paid him, of whatever sums may occasionally be recovered by the heirs, until in this manner the amount of the legacy be completely discharged.—Hidáyah, vol. iv, pp. 490 & 491.

Reason. The reason of this is, that the legatee is (as if it were) a partner with the heirs; and, therefore, if his claim in particular were discharged with the ready property (by its being applied to the payment of the whole of his legacy), an injury would be occasioned to the right of the heirs, as ready money is allowed to be preferable to money that is due.—Hidáyah, vol. iv, p. 491.

Principle. DCCLXXIV. The validity of a bequest of property belonging to another rests upon the proprietor's consent.

Illustration. If a person bequeath a thousand *dirms* belonging to another, the execution of the bequest rests entirely on the consent of the proprietor, and it is optional with him to confirm it or not as he pleases. If he, therefore, after the death of the testator, give his consent, the bequest is valid, and the money paid to the legatee accordingly. This consent, however, is purely voluntary and gratuitous; whence if, after having signified it, the person refuse to pay the money, it is lawful.—Hidáyah, vol. iv, p. 501.

Principle. **DCCLXXV. Any accident, occasioning uncertainty with respect to the legacies or legatees, generally annuls the will.**

Illustrations. If a person bequeath three garments of different prices, leaving the best to *Zayid*, the next in value to *Umar*, and the worst to *Bakr*, and one of these garments be afterwards lost, without its being known which of them it was, and the heirs of the testator declare, to each legatee in particular, that "his share is lost," the bequest is null *in toto*, as it is in this case uncertain who are the legatees, and such uncertainty occasions an annulment of the will,

---

ANNOTATIONS.

diately paid if it do not exceed a third of the actual property; but if it exceed a third, one-third is to be delivered to him, and, as the debts come in, he is entitled to take a third out of every payment until his legacy is paid up in full.—Fatáwá Alamgírí, vol. vi, p. 161.—B. Dig., p. 631.

since the *Kází* cannot pass a decrèe concerning a thing unknown. If, on the contrary, the heirs make over the two remaining garments to the legatees, the bequest is not null, but still continues in force, and those two garments are divided among them, by two-thirds of the best being given to *Zayid*, two-thirds of the worst to *Bakr*, and the remaining third of each to *Umar* — Hidáyah, vol. iv, pp. 496 & 497.

A person having three garments, one good, the other middling, and the third bad, bequeaths them to three different legatees : one of the garments is then lost or destroyed, but which of them is not known, and the heirs refuse to make delivery of the remaining garments to any of the legatees, saying, to each of them, "the garment in which you had a right has been destroyed,"—in these circumstances, since the parties entitled are unknown, and ignorance of this fact prevents the validity of any judgment that may be pronounced in the matter, and the attainment of the testator's object, the bequests must be pronounced to be void, unless the heirs will deliver up the remaining garments.—Fatáwá Alamgírí. vol. vi, p. 164.—B. Dig., p. 637.

Wills in favor of Relations (akárib) or others, and construction of such Wills.*

DCCLXXVI. If a man make a will in favor of his next of kin (*akárib**) without mentioning the name of any, it is to be construed to be in favor of the nearest of kin within the prohibited degrees, failing them, in favor of the next in propinquity, on their failure, it is for the rest within the prohibited degrees in the order of proximity. The testator's father, mother, or children, or other immediate heirs are not, however, to be included among the legatees. *Principle.*

If a person make a will in favor of his relations [*Akrabah**], it is executed in favor of the nearest of kin within the prohibited degrees, and failing them, in favor of the next in proximity, and so on, with respect to the rest within the prohibited degrees, in regular succession. The will, in this case, includes two or more ; but the father, mother, or children of the testator are not comprehended in it. This is the opinion of *Hanífah.*—Hidáyah, vol. iv, p. 519. Illustration.

* ***Akárib*** **or** ***akrabah*** **is the plural of** ***karib*** **(near), and signifies kindred.**

In the case of a bequest to *akárib,* four conditions are required by Abú Hanífah to give a right to it. *First,* the parties must be two or more. *Second,* regard is to be had to the nearest, so that the nearer excludes the more remote, as in cases of inheritance. *Third,* the claimant must be within the prohibited degrees to the testator, so that the son of a paternal uncle is not entitled to participate in such a bequest. *Fourth,* the claimant must not be an heir of the testator. Subject to these conditions, infidels and Muslims, males and females, free and slaves, children and adults, are all equal.*

According to the other two,† every one of kin to the testator has an interest in the legacy, whether the relation be on the father's or on the mother's side, up to his most remote ancestor in *Islám;* and there is no difference between the nearer and the more remote, one and many, infidel and Muslim.*

According to the two disciples (Abú Yusuf and Muhammad), the will includes such as are descended from the most distant progenitor of the testator, professing the Musalmán faith. The argument of the two disciples is, that the term *relations* being in general applied to all of the *same blood,* the will, therefore, extends to all such as fall under this description to whatever degree removed. The arguments of Hanífah are, that legacies are a species of inheritance; and, as in inheritance, the arrangement here described is observed with respect to the heirs, it is also observed in the payment of legacies.—As, moreover, the plural term *(akrabah)* mentioned in inheritance means *two,*‡ so likewise in bequest. Besides, the object of the testator in this bequest is to compensate for his deficiencies, during life, with respect to the ties of kindred,§ which affects only his relations within the prohibited degrees. The parents or children, moreover, are not styled relations *(akrabah),* insomuch that if a person were to call his father "*his* relation," *(karíb),* he would be considered as denying his parentage. The reason of this is that,

---

* Fatáwá Alamgírí, vol. vi, p. 179.—B. Dig., p. 644.

† That is, the two disciples, Abú Yusuf and Muhammad.

‡ Here is something like a contradiction, for it was before said that "the will includes *two* or *more.*" This, however, is not to be taken as excluding any number *above two,* but merely as comprehending the dual as well as any higher number. Note by the Translator of the Hidáyah.

§ Arab. "*Silái Rihm.*"—This is a technical term, comprehending in its application the kindred within the prohibited degrees only.—*Ibid.*

in common usage, by the term relation *(karíb)* is understood one related to a person by means of another; but the relation of parent and child is personal, and not by means of another. In short, according to *Haníjah,* the will in question is restricted in its operation to the prohibited relations of the testator; whereas, according to the two disciples, it extends to [all the descendants of] the most distant progenitor professing the faith.—Hidáyah, vol. iv, pp. 519 & 520.

The opinion of Abú Haníjah having been first cited in the Fatáwá Alamgírí, it must be concluded that preference is given by that authority to the said opinion of Abú Haníjah over that of his disciples Abú Yusuf and Muhammad. The author of the Hidáyah, too, seems to have adopted the above opinion of Abú Haníjah as being the law on the subject, inasmuch as he has cited *Haníjah's* arguments *after* those of the two disciples, and it is his invariable practice to cite at the last the argument of that lawyer whose doctrine he adopts.* In fact the above opinion of Abú Haníjah appears to be the prevalent one and received as law.

All are agreed that an heir has no right to the legacy.†

DCCLXXVII. The nullity of a bequest in favor of an heir depends, however, on the legatee's being so at the time of the testator's death, as well as upon the non-consent of the other heir or heirs.‡ *Principle.*

If a person, having two paternal and two maternal uncles, make a will in favor of "his relations" *(akrabah),* it is in favor of the *paternal* uncles only, according to Haníjah; he holding that regard is to be paid to the order of relationship;—whereas, according to the two disciples, all the four uncles are included, they holding that no regard is to be paid to the order of relationship. If, on the other hand, the testator have only one paternal and two maternal uncles, the half of the legacy in that case goes to the paternal uncle, and the other half to the two maternal uncles, out of attention to the plural number, which, in bequests, comprehends *two* (as before observed); for as, if there were *two* paternal uncles, the whole legacy would go to them, it follows that where there is *one* only, he gets no more than a half, and the other half goes to the two maternal uncles.—Hidáyah, vol. iv, pp. 520 & 521. Illustrations.

* See the Annotations at p. 42 of Lecture I, delivered in 1873.

† Fatáwá Alamgírí, vol. vi, p. 179—B. Dig., pp. 644 & 646.

‡ See *ante*, pp. 43, 45 & 46; and Hidáyah, vol. iv, p. 504.

It would be otherwise if the person had expressed his bequest for "his *kinsman;*" for in this case the whole legacy would go to the paternal uncle, and nothing whatever to the two maternal uncles; because, as the term *kinsman* expresses a *singular*, not a *plural* number, the paternal uncle therefore takes the whole, he being next of kin. If (in the case of a bequest to "*relations*") the testator have a paternal uncle only [and no maternal uncles], he is entitled to no more than a moiety of the third of the estate; for as, if there had been *two* paternal uncles, they would have had the whole between them, one consequently gets only a half.—Hidáyah, vol. iv, p. 521.

Thus, according to Abú Hanífah—

Principle.

DCCLXXVIII. If there be one relative, he is entitled to half the legacy.*

If, on the contrary, he have a paternal uncle and aunt, and a maternal uncle and aunt, the legacy goes in equal shares between the paternal uncle and aunt, both being related to the testator within an equal degree of affinity,—and their connexion being of a stronger nature than that of the *maternal* uncle or aunt. A paternal aunt, moreover, although she be not entitled to inherit, is nevertheless capable of succeeding to a legacy in the same manner as holds with respect to a relation who is a *slave* or an *infidel.* It is to be observed that, in all these cases, if the testator have no prohibited relation, the bequest is null, because it is restricted in its operation to those within the prohibited degrees as before noticed.—Hidáyah, vol. iv, p. 521.

If a testator have left two paternal and two maternal uncles, none of whom is an heir, as for instance when he has left them and a son, the legacy is to the paternal, and not to the maternal, uncles, according to Abú Hanífah; while, according to the other two, it is to be divided among them in four equal parts. If he have left one paternal uncle and two maternal uncles, the paternal uncle, according to the former, has a half of the third (that is, the legacy), and the maternal uncles have the other half between them; while, according to the latter, it is to be divided among them in thirds. And if there were only one paternal uncle and no other relative within the prohibited degrees, half the third would go to the paternal uncle, while the other half of it would revert to the heirs of the testator, according to Abú Hanífah, while, according to the disciples, the other half of the third would pass

---

* Fatáwá Alamgírí, vol. iv, p. 179.—B. Dig., p. 644.

to a relative not within the prohibited degrees. When the testator has left a paternal uncle and aunt, and a maternal uncle and aunt, the legacy is to the paternal uncle and aunt equally, by reason of their being equally near to the deceased.—Fatáwá Alamgírí, vol. vi, p. 179.—B. Dig., p. 644.

If a person make a bequest to the *ahl* of such an one, it is, according to Abú Hanífah, a bequest to the *wife* of the person mentioned; but the two disciples maintain that the bequest comprehends every individual of the family entitled to maintenance from that person. Remarks.

The author of the Hidáyah, by citing the argument of Abú Hanífah alone, has adopted the doctrine of Abú Hanífah, whose argument is that—"*ahl*," in its literal sense, signifies a wife, a proof of which is drawn from this sentence of the *Kurán*, "*Moses* walked with his *ahl* [wife]," whence also the common mode of expression "such a person made *taáhul* (married) in a particular city;"—and as the word "*ahl*," in its literal sense, means a *wife*, it follows that, whenever it is used absolutely, it must be resolved into its *literal* sense, which is the *true* one.—*Vide* Hidáyah, vol. iv, pp. 521 & 522.

The compilers of the Fatáwá Alamgírí, the latest authority on the subject, have, on the other hand, adopted the opinion of the two disciples. They (the learned compilers) say—"When a person has bequeathed a third of his property to his '*ahl*,' or to the *ahl* of such an one, though by analogy a wife, and none other, should have any interest in the legacy, yet it is applied, on a favorable construction, to all who are living in his family, and are maintained by him, with the exception of his slaves; and though his *ahl* are in two cities, or in two houses, they are all included, on account of the generality of the word employed."—*Vide* Fatáwá Alamgírí, vol. vi, p. 170.—B. Dig., p. 646.

The above opinion of the two disciples appears to be more prevalent than that of their master Abú Hanífah.

DCCLXXIX. If a person make a bequest to the *ahl* of the *house* of such an one, the father and grandfather of the person named are included in such bequest, as well as all the descendants from the remotest progenitor on the paternal side, professing the *Musalmán* faith.—Hidáyah, vol. iv, p. 522. *Principl*

K

So also the Fatáwá Alamgírí, which says—"When a person has made a bequest to the people of his house *(ahl-ul-bayit)*, all are included who are connected with his fathers, to the most remote of them in *Islám*, whether the individual be male or female, provided that the connection with the testator be on the side of his fathers; and no one who is related to him only on the side of the mother participates in the benefit of it."*

Principle. DCCLXXX. If a person make a bequest to the *ahl* of such a person's *nasab* (race) or *jins* (generation),†—by the former is understood all those descended from his ancestors in general,—but by the latter those only descended from the *paternal* stock, not from the maternal, because men are said to be of the generation *(jins)* of their *fathers*, not of their *mothers*. It is otherwise when the term *karábat* (affinity) is used; for that appertains both to father and mother.—Hidáyah, vol. iv, p. 522.

Principle. DCCLXXXI. A bequest "to the *ál*† of such an one" comes into the place of a bequest to the people of his *bayit*, none of the kindred of the mother having any interest therein.*

Annotations.

dcclxxx. In like manner, when one has made a bequest to his *nasab*, or *hasab*,† it is for the benefit of his kindred who are related to him through his fathers, up to the most remote of them in *Islám*.—Fatáwá Alamgírí, vol. vi, p. 180.—B. Dig., pp. 645 & 646.

So, also, when the bequest is to the *jins*, or *luhmah*† of such an one, it is to the children of his fathers; and a bequest to the *ál* of such an one comes into the place of a bequest to the people of his *bayit*, none of the kindred of the mother having any interest in it.—*Ibid.*

dcclxxxi. If a person make a bequest "to the *ál* of such an one," it is a bequest "to the *ahl* of his house," the term *ál* applying to the tribe from which he is descended.—Hidáyah, vol. iv, p. 522.

---

* Fatáwá Alamgírí, vol. vi, p. 180.—B. Dig., pp. 645 & 646.

† The lexicographical meanings of the above Arabic words are as follow:—

"*Nasab*."—Genealogy (especially in the paternal line), lineage, race, stock, family, house.

"*Jins*."—A generation.

"*Al*."—Offspring, posterity, progeny, descendants, family, house, race.

"*Hasab*,"—A family, a tribe.

"*Luhmah*" or "*Luhmat*,"—Propinquity, relationship.

DCCLXXXII. If a woman should make a bequest to her *jins* or the people of her *bayil*, her own child would have no interest in it; for he is of the *nasab* of his father, and not of his mother, except when her husband was of her *ashírah* or paternal relatives.* *Principle.*

DCCLXXXIII. When a man has made a bequest to his three brothers, of different kinds, and has left a son, the legacy is lawful, and belongs to them equally, because none of them inherits with a son. But if there were a daughter, the legacy would be lawful only with regard to the half-brother on the father's side and the half-brother on the mother's side, but not to the full brother, because he participates in the inheritance with the daughter; while, if the testator has left neither son nor daughter, the whole of the legacy belongs to the half-brother on the father's side, for he is not an heir, and is void as to the full brother and the half-brother by the mother, because both of them inherit from the testator.* *Principle.*

DCCLXXXIV. If a man should make a bequest to his *hasham*,† all who are in the family with him, or are maintained by him, are entitled to participate, to the exclusion, however, of his child, parent, wife, and slave; but all of his *Karábat*, or kindred, are included.* *Principle.*

DCCLXXXV. If one should make a bequest to his *kowm* (tribe) or *átrat*, it is not lawful,‡ unless he say, "to the poor of them." *Principle.*

DCCLXXXVI. A bequest to one's *kudama*§ is to all those who have associated with him for thirty years.* *Principle.*

DCCLXXXVII. If a person make a bequest to the children *(aulád)* of the race of such an one, the males and *Principle.*

* Fatáwá Alamgírí, vol. vi, pp. 180 & 181.—B. Dig., pp. 646 & 647.

† "*Hasham*,"—Train, equipage, suite, neighbours.

"*Hashmat*" (from *Hasham*.) A woman, patronage, propinquity, affinity, neighbourhood.

‡ Perhaps on account of their number not being ascertained.

§ "*Kudama*" (plural of *kadim*), ancients, excellent (men).

female have equal right in such bequest, as the term *aulád* comprehends the whole.—Hidáyah, vol. iv, p. 524.

Principle. DCCLXXXVIII. If a person make a bequest "to the race of such an one," in that case, according to the two disciples, and also according to the first opinion of Abú Hanífah, the women of the said race are included, the plural term *baní* extending to females as well as to males.—Hidáyah, vol. iv, p. 523.

Hanífah, however, afterwards retracted this opinion, and maintained the males of the race only to be included, not the females; because the term *Baní* applies to men *literally*, but to women only *metaphorically;* and a word must be taken in its *literal*, not its *figurative*, acceptation. It is otherwise where "*the race of such a person*" is the proper name of any particular tribe; for in that case the bequest includes the women also, as the term *Baní*, in such instance, comprehends the females of the tribe along with the males,—in the same manner as the general expression *Baní-Adam* (the sons of *Adam*),—whence the bequest includes the freedmen, the sworn confederates [Halífs], the slaves, and the *Mawálát* confederates of the tribe named.—Hidáyah, vol. iv, p. 524.

Principle. DCCLXXXIX. If a person make a bequest "to the heirs of such an one," the legacy is, in that case, divided among the heirs of the person named, in the manner of inheritance, a male getting as much as two females.—Hidáyah, vol. iv, p. 524.

Reason. Because there is reason to imagine that the object of the testator, in using the word "heirs," was, that the same distinction might be observed in the partition of the legacies as obtains in the case of inheritance.—Hidáyah, vol. iv, p. 524.

Annotations.

dcclxxxviii. If a person should bequeath a third of his property to the *baní* of such an one, and the person referred to was the father or ancestor of a *kabílah*, or large collection of persons like Tamím to the Baní Tamím, and there are *aulád*, or descendants, both male and female, the third is to be divided among them all equally, when they can be numbered, according to all opinions; and the division is to be in like manner when they are all males.—Fatáwá Alamgírí, vol. vi, p. 182.—B. Dig., p. 647.

dcclxxxix. When there is a bequest to the heirs of such an one, it is to them in the proportion of a double share to males over females.—*Ibid.*—B. Dig., p. 648.

DCCXC. When one has made a bequest "to the daughters of such an one," and he has sons and daughters, the legacy is to the latter exclusively; and if he have sons and daughters of other sons, it is to these daughters only; but if there be only daughter's daughters, they are not included in the legacy, unless there is anything to indicate that the testator intended it for them, when they would be included.* *Principle.*

If one should say, "I have bequeathed a third of my property to the *baní* of such an one, and they are five;" when they are only three or two, these take the whole legacy. But if he should say "to the two sons of such an one," when there is only one, he has but a half of the legacy. While if he name them, saying, "to the two sons of such an one, *Zayid* and *Umar*," when there is only one son, he takes the whole. If the words are, "to the *baní* of such an one, and they are three, a third of my property," when there are five, the legacy is to three of them, and the choice is with the heirs; and if another be joined with them in the bequest, he has a fourth of the third. If he should say, "I have bequeathed a third of my property to the *baní* of such an one, and they are five, and to such an one a third of my property," when there are only three sons of the first, the other is their partner for a fourth.* **Illustration.**

DCCXCI. When a bequest is "to the fathers of so and so, and the fathers of so and so," and the persons indicated have fathers and mothers, they are all included in the legacy; but if there are no fathers nor mothers, and only grandfathers and grandmothers, these have no interest in the legacy.* *Principle.*

DCCXCII. If a person make a bequest "to the orphans, the blind, lame, or the widows" of the *race* of such an one, and the individuals of the *race* named can be enumerated, the bequest includes them indiscriminately, whether rich or poor, males or females.—Hidáyah, vol. iv, p. 522. *Principle.*

For the execution of the bequest is practicable in this instance, because of the ascertainment of the legatees.—*Ibid*, p. 523.

DCCXCIII. But if the individuals of the race named be incapable of enumeration, the *poor* only are in that case included in the bequest, not the *rich*. *Principle.*

For, it (the bequest) is of a pious nature, and the object of it (namely, the good will of God) is best attainable by removing the

---

* **Fatáwá Alamgírí, vol. vi, p. 182.—B. Dig., p. 648.**

wants of the poor. Besides, as the very descriptions used indicate a degree of want and distress in the legatee, it is therefore proper to admit this to have been the testator's meaning. It is otherwise where a person makes a bequest "to the *youths* (or the *virgins*) of a particular race," who are innumerable; for in such case the bequest is void, because, as the description used does not indicate want, the words of the testator cannot be construed to apply to the *poor:* neither can the bequest possibly hold valid in favor of all the individuals of the class named, since, as they are not to be enumerated, it is impracticable to define them, and a bequest to unknown legatees is null, for bequest is an act of endowment, and it is impossible to endow persons unknown.—Hidáyah, vol. iv, p. 523.

Muhammad has said that when a bequest is made to the *orphans* of the *baní* of such an one, and they can be numbered, and is to be expended on all in the same way as if it were on the orphans of this street, or of this mansion, rich and poor participating alike; but if they cannot be numbered, the legacy is to be expended on the poor among them.*

Principle. DCCXCIV. If a person make a bequest in favor of his *as-hár,** all the relations of his wife within the prohibited degrees (such as her father, brother, and so forth) are therein included; and likewise, all the relations of his father's wife (his step-mother), and of his son's wife (his daughter-in-law) within the prohibited degrees, as these all stand in the relation of *as-hár* to the testator (*a*).—Hidáyah, vol. iv, p. 518.

Annotations.

dccxciv. When a man has made a bequest to his *as-hár*, it is for every one within the prohibited degrees to his wife, or to his father's wife, and the wife of every one within the prohibited degrees to himself, for all these come within the meaning of the term; and every one is comprehended who is *sahar* (singular of *as-hár*) to the testator at the time of his death, by being so connected with a woman who is then actually his wife, or in her *iddat*, for a revocable divorce; but if the *iddat* be for one that is absolute, or for three repudiations, the person connected with her has no right.—Fatáwá Alamgírí, vol. vi, p. 186.—B. Dig., p. 650.

* "*As-hár*" is the plural of "*sahr*" (pronounced in *Arabia* as "*dahr*") which is a general term for all relations by marriage.

(*a.*) This explanation of *As-hár* has been followed by *Muhammad Abú Ubaydah.* It is to be observed that all the kindred of the wife within the prohibited degrees are included in the bequest, notwithstanding she were, at the time of the death of the testator, in her *iddat* from a reversible divorce. But if the divorce was irreversible, her relations are not to be included, as the existence of that degree of relation, entitled *As-hár*, depends on the actual existence of the marriage at the time of the testator's death; and by an irreversible divorce marriage is utterly annulled.—Hidáyah, vol. iv, p. 518.

DCCXCV. When a man has made a bequest to his *akhtan* (plural of *khatan*), it belongs to the husbands of his female relatives within the prohibited degrees, such as the husbands of his daughters, sisters, paternal and maternal aunts, for all come within the meaning of the term.* *Principle.*

DCCXCVI. A bequest to the husbands of one's daughters includes the husband of every daughter that is a wife at the time of the testator's death, or a *mutadda* for a revocable divorce, but not one who has been divorced absolutely.* *Principle.*

DCCXCVII. If a person make a bequest in favor of his *neighbour*, this according to *Hanífah*, is a bequest to the person who is immediately adjoining to that of the testator. —Hidáyah, vol. iv, p. 517. *Principle.*

The two disciples, on the contrary, maintain that it comprehends all the inhabitants of the vicinity, who belong to the same *mosque*, without any regard to the immediate adjunction of the houses; since, according to the common acceptation of the word,

ANNOTATIONS.

dccxcv. If a man make a bequest in favor of his *khatn*, it is a bequest to the husbands of his female relations within the prohibited degrees, and in it are likewise included all the relations of these husbands within the prohibited degrees; these also falling under the description of *khatn*. (Some Commentators remark, that this explanation is agreeable to the ancient custom; but that in the present times *khatn* comprehends only the husbands, as above.) It is also to be observed that in this respect freemen and slaves and the near and the distant relations are all upon a footing, because the term *khatn* comprehends the whole of these.—Hidáyah, vol. iv, p. 519.

* Fatáwá Alamgírí, vol. vi, p. 184.—B. Dig., pp. 649 & 650.

they all fall equally under the description of *neighbours*. The arguments adduced by Hanífah in support of his opinion upon this point are two-fold. *First*, the person whose house adjoins to that of the testator is in reality the *neighbour*. *Secondly*, the modes and descriptions of *neighbourhood* are many; and as it would be impracticable to carry the will into execution with respect to the *whole*, it is therefore necessary to restrict it to him whose title, from the circumstance of adjunction, is the most perfect and indisputable. It is to be observed that the learned in the law are of opinion that every person may be included under this description of neighbour, whether the proprietor of a house or not, or, whether a man or a woman, a *Musalmán* or a *Zimmí*, the term *neighbour* being equally applicable to all these. Hanífah also holds that an absolute slave, possessed of a house in the neighbourhood, is entitled to the benefit of the will. The two disciples hold a different opinion; because, in such case, the benefit of the will would ultimately revert to the master of the slave, who is not supposed to be a neighbour. The argument of *Hanífah* is, that the term *neighbour* applies indiscriminately to all.—Hidáyah, vol. iv, pp. 517 & 518.

When a person bequeaths a third of his property to his neighbours, some say, that if they can be numbered, the third is to be divided among them all, rich and poor. And it is to be divided in like manner if he should say to the people of the *masjid* (*a*). Others, however, have said that the matter should be left to the discretion of the judge, and the *fatwá* is to that effect; though Muhammad's rule is easier.—Fatáwá Alamgírí, vol. vi, p. 184.—B. Dig., p. 649.

(*a*.) The definition, or meaning of (the expression), "cannot be numbered," according to Abú Yusuf, is when the persons cannot be computed without the aid of a written account; but, according to Muhammad, it is when they are more than a hundred.—*Ibid.*—B. Dig., p. 649.

If the neighbours cannot e numbered, the legacy is void, and so also when the legacy is to the people of the *masjid* or of the *sijn* or prison, and they cannot be numbered.—Fatáwá Alamgírí, vol. vi, p. 184.—*Ibid.*

Principle. DCCXCVIII. A bequest to the blind, or infirm, or debtors, travellers, prisoners, warriors, or *árámil* (*b*), if they can be numbered, is for the rich and poor of them, and if they cannot be numbered, for their poor.*

---

* Fatáwá Alamgírí, vol. vi, pp. 154 & 157.—B. Dig., pp. 650 & 651.

If one should make a bequest to the *árámil* (*a*) of the *baní* of such an one, it is lawful, whether they can be numbered or not, and is to be expended on as many of them as possible, down to two, according to Muhammad, or even one, according to the other two.*

(*b.*) "*Arámil*" is plural of *armalat*, which signifies an adult female who has had connection, but has no husband. *Sháb* and *Fatá* are persons between twenty-five and thirty or forty years of age, unless whiteness (of the hair) predominates sooner. *Kuhl* is a person from thirty or forty years of age to sixty, unless whiteness predominates sooner; *Shaikh* is a person above fifty; and *Ghulám*, a youth under fifteen years of age, unless he arrives sooner at puberty. *Akab* is one who succeeds his father after his death; and so also as to *warásat.**

DCCXCIX. A bequest to the poor *sayyids* or descendants of the Prophet would be lawful (*c*). According to this, a legacy to lawyers or to students of learning would not be lawful, but to their poor would be so; and by analogy a legacy to the students of a particular place or particular kind of knowledge would also be lawful.* *Principle.*

(*c.*) The lawyer Abú Jaafar, being asked as to a bequest to the *aulád* of the Prophet, is reported to have answered, that it was for the *aulád* of Hasan and Husain, and none other. And when one made a bequest to *Alyites* (descendants of Alí), the same Abú Jaafar is reported to have said that it was not lawful, because they cannot be numbered, and there is nothing in the term that has reference to the poor or necessitous. But a bequest to the poor of them would be lawful.*

DCCC. A bequest to the *ahl-ul-ilm*, or learned, of such a city, includes lawyers and traditionists, but not those who discourse with wisdom.* *Principle.*

But do rhetoricians *(mutakullimán)* participate? There is no express *dictum* in the books on this subject; but it has been said by Abú Kásim, that books on rhetoric are not accounted books of knowledge; and, therefore, by analogy, rhetoricians should not be included. It is reported, as from Muhammad, that when a man has made a bequest to "such an one and to the Baní Tamím," the whole belongs to such an one, and there is nothing for the Baní Tamím; for it is as if he had said "to such an one and

---

* Fatáwá Alamgírí. vol. vi. pp. 151 & 157.—B. Dig., pp. 649—651.

the dead," since they cannot be numbered; and the legacy to them is void. If the legacy were, "A third of my property to such an one, and to a man of the Musalmáns," such an one would have a half of it and nothing more. In like manner, if he were to say, "A third of my property to such an one and to ten Musalmáns," such an one would have one part out of eleven, and there would be nothing for Musalmáns.—Fatáwá Alamgírí, vol. vi, p. 187.—B. Dig., p. 651.

Of Bequests for Pious Purposes.

Principle. DCCCI. If a person make several bequests, for the performance of sundry religious duties, such as *pilgrimage*, *prayers*, and so forth, it is requisite to execute first such as are absolutely incumbent and ordained; and this, whether the testator have mentioned them first or not; for the discharge of the *ordained* duties is of more importance than that of acts which are merely voluntary; and the law therefore supposes that the object of the testator was to begin with the performance of them.*

But if the several duties, the objects of the will, be all of the same importance, and of similar force, and the third of the estate suffice not for the discharge of the whole, they must in that case be executed agreeably to the order in which they have been specified by the testator, as it may be inferred that those to which he gave the precedence were, in his opinion, the most urgent.* Hence,—

Principle. DCCCII. In the execution of all pious wills, where the objects of them are not incumbent duties,† it is requisite to follow the arrangement of the testator.—Hidáyah, vol. iv, p. 515.

Since it may be inferred that he considered those first mentioned as the most urgent. · Lawyers, moreover, have remarked that if a person make several bequests, some for the performance of religious duties immediately enjoined by God, and others for benevolent purposes amongst mankind, in that case a third of his property must be set aside for the execution of them; and whatever may be the share appropriated for the performance of the

---

* Hidáyah, vol. iv, p. 514.

† Such as the erection of a mosque, of a receptacle for travellers, or of a bridge.—Hamilton's Hidáyah, vol. iv, p. 515.

duties belonging to God, it must be applied agreeably to the order of arrangement, as already explained. It is to be observed, also, that every different duty is to be considered in the nature of a distinct legacy, for the object of each being the attainment of the good will of the Almighty, every several duty has an object in itself, and each is therefore to be considered in the nature of a legacy left to a different person.—Hidáyah, vol. iv, p. 514.

DCCCIII. When the legacies are partly to Almighty God, and partly to mankind, as for instance, to a class of persons, the portion of the latter is to be taken out of the third, to be divided among them without preference of any over the others.* *Principle.*

DCCCIV. When the legacies have been added up, and a third of the estate is sufficient to meet them all, they are all to be paid out of it, whether they be bequests to Almighty God (*d*) or to mankind (*e*). *Principle.*

(*d*.) By bequests to Almighty God are to be understood "bequests of approach," or which are the means of drawing nigh to him, such as the prescribed *hajj* or pilgrimage to Mecca, the *zakát*, or poor's rate, fasting, prayers, expiations, the erection of masjids, and the like.*

(*e*.) By bequests to mankind are to be understood such as bequests "to Zayid, Bakr, and Khálid."*

DCCCV. All the legacies are to be paid in like manner, when, though the third of the estate is insufficient to meet them, they are allowed by the heirs.* *Principle.*

If the third of the estate be insufficient to meet all the legacies, and they are not allowed by the heirs, then it is to be considered whether they are all *faráyiz*,—that is, actually prescribed or appointed duties; or *wájibát*,—that is, things which, though not actually prescribed, are yet, in themselves, necessary and proper; r *nawáfil*, which are voluntarily assumed obligations; or whether they are partly of one kind and partly of another.* Illustration.

DCCCVI. When they are all *equally* prescribed or appointed duties, a beginning is to be made with that *Principle.*

---

* Fatáwá Alamgírí, vol. vi, pp. 177 & 178.—B. Dig., pp. 642 & 643.

which the testator began with. When they are not so, the *faráyiz* is to begin, then the *wájibát*, and then the *nawáfil.**

Principle. DCCCVII. With regard to the portion of Almighty God, it is to be applied first to *faráyiz*, next to *wájibát*, and then to *nawáfil.**

Principle. DCCCVIII. When the bequest is for *hajj* and *zakát*, a commencement is to be made with the former, though it were verbally last.*

Usufructuary Wills.

Principle. DCCCIX. The bequest of the service of a slave, or the occupation of a mansion, or the produce (*ghallat*) of both, or of lands and gardens, is lawful. And it is valid for a limited time or for ever.

Illustrations. For, as the profits of a thing may be transferred by a person during his lifetime, with or without a consideration, so they may, in like manner, be transferred after his death; the thing itself being, in a manner, detained in his ownership, that the legatee may enjoy its profits, in the same way, as a person in whose favor a *wakf*, or appropriation, has been made, enjoys its profits, by virtue of the ownership of the proprietor.†—Fatáwá Alamgírí, vol. vi, p. 188.—B. Dig., p. 652.

If a person bequeath the service of his slave, or the use of his house, either for a definite or indefinite period, such bequest is valid; because as an endowment with usufruct, either gratuitous or for an equivalent, is valid during life, it is consequently so after death; and also because men have occasion to make bequests of this nature as well as bequests of actual property. So,

* Fatáwá Alamgírí, vol. vi, pp. 177 & 178.—B. Dig., pp. 642 & 643.

† This being so, we may say that when the service of a slave has been bequeathed for a limited time, as, for instance, for a year, the bequest may either be for a particular year, as when one says, "I have bequeathed for the year 460 (A. H.)," or without any specification of a particular year, as when he does not say, "for such a year," and in each case the slave may or may not fall within a third of the property. When the bequest is for a particular year, which is past at the time of the testator's death, it is void. If a part only of the year has expired, or if it has not commenced, at the time of the testator's death, and the slave comes within the third of his property, or the heirs allow the legacy, the slave is to be delivered to the legatee, to serve him during the remainder, or the whole, of the specified year, as the case may be.—Fatáwá Alamgírí, vol. vi, p. 188.—B. Dig., pp. 642 & 643.

likewise, if a person bequeath the wages of his slave, or the rent of his house, for a definite or indefinite term, it is valid for the same reason. In both cases, moreover, it is necessary to consign over the house or the slave to the legatee, provided they do not exceed the third of the property, in order that he may enjoy the wages or service of the slave or the rent or use of the house during the term prescribed, and afterwards restore it to the heirs.—Hidáyah, vol. iv, p. 527. So,—

DCCCX. If the property of the testator consist of things, the use of the produce of which has been bequeathed, in that case, the legatee is entitled to enjoyment or appropriation only *of one-third*, and the heir of the testator to two-thirds of the same. *Principle.*

If the whole property of the testator consist of a slave or a house, in that case, the slave is to be possessed one day by the legatee, and two by the heirs, alternately ; but the house, on the contrary, is to be portioned into three equal parts, of which one is given to the legatee, and two to the heirs,—the legatee being entitled to one-third of the estate, and the heirs to two-thirds. The reason of the distinction here made between a house and a slave is, that a slave is incapable of being divided, and therefore an alternate use of him is established from necessity ; whereas a house, on the contrary, is capable of division, and as division is the most fair and equitable mode (since retaliation necessarily induces a preference of one over the other in point of time), it ought to be adopted where it is practicable. Still, however, if the parties agree to enjoy the house by turns, it is lawful, as the right rests entirely with them ; but division is the most equitable mode.—Hidáyah, vol. iv, pp. 527 & 528. Illustration.

DCCCXI. If the legatee die before the expiration of the limited term of the usufruct, the article bequeathed in usufruct immediately reverts to the heirs of the testator, the bequest being rendered void by the legatee's death. *Principle.*

For the bequest was made with a view that the legatee might derive a benefit from the testator's property ; but if the article were to devolve to the legatee's heirs, it induces the consequence of their being entitled to the use of the testator's property without his consent, which is contrary to law.—Hidáyah, vol. iv, p. 528. **Reason.**

DCCCXII. If the legatee die during the testator's lifetime, the bequest is void; because the acceptance of it is suspended upon the death of the *Principle.*

testator, as has been already explained.—Hidáyah, vol. iv, p. 528.

Principle. DCCCXIII. A bequest of the *produce* of an article does not entitle the legatee to the personal use of *that* article, nor does a bequest of the use entitle him to let it out on hire.

Illustration. If a person bequeath the *produce* of his house or of his slave to *Zayid*, in that case some are of opinion that it is lawful for *Zayid* to reside in the said house himself, or to use the slave for his own service, because an equivalent for the use is in fact the same as the use itself, so far as relates to the accomplishment of the testator's object. The more approved opinion, however, is, that it is not lawful; for a bequest of produce is a bequest of money, as it is that which constitutes produce; whereas residence or service is an enjoyment of the use; and the effect of these is different with respect to the heirs; for if any just debt should afterwards appear against the testator, it might be repaid by means of a restitution of the rent by the legatee, which could not be done in case of his having had the actual use.—Hidáyah, vol. iv, pp. 528 & 529.

It is not lawful for the usufructuary legatee of a slave or of a house to let them out for hire.—*Ibid*, p. 529.

DCCCXIV. A bequest of a year's product, if the article exceed a third of the estate, does not entitle the legatee to a consignment of it.

Illustration. If a person leave one year's product of his slave, or house, to another, and he have no other property, except such house or slave, the legatee in that case receives one-third of a year's product; because product, as being property, is capable of division. If, therefore, the legatee require the heirs to make a division of the house, in order that he may himself collect the product from his own share (being a third), it would not be admitted. *Abú Yusuf*, indeed, according to one report, holds a contrary opinion; for he argues that the legatee is a partner with the heirs; and a partner has a right to demand a division of the common property. In answer to this, however, it may be observed that this right amongst co-partners arises from their having a property in the article itself; whereas the legatee, in the present instance, has a property only in the *product* of the article, and consequently is not entitled to demand a division.—Hidáyah, vol. iv, p. 531.

Principle. DCCCXV. A bequest of produce includes the existing and future produce; but a bequest of fruit includes only the existing fruit, unless the bequest is for ever.

When a man has bequeathed the produce of his garden, the legatee is entitled to the existing and future produce. But when the bequest is of the fruit of his garden, it may be in two ways. He may either have said, "for ever," or he may not have so said, and in this last case there may or may not be fruit in existence at the time of his death. When there is fruit in the garden on the day of the testator's death, the legatee is entitled to it out of the third of his estate, but he is not entitled to the fruit that may be thereafter up to the time of his own death. When, again, there is no fruit in the garden on the day of the testator's death, the beques. tought by analogy to be void, but, on a favorable construction, it is not void, and takes effect on any fruit that there may be subsequent to the death of the testator and up to that of the legatee. All this, when it has not been expressly said that the legacy is for ever; but when the testator has said, "I have bequeathed to thee the fruit of my garden for ever," the legatee is entitled to the existing fruit and to all that there may be thereafter.—Fatáwá Alamgírí, vol. vi, p. 189.—B. Dig., pp. 654 & 655. Illustrations.

If a person bequeath to any one "the fruit of his garden," in that case the legatee gets the fruit actually in being at the time of the testator's death, not what may be produced afterwards. If, however, the testator say, "I bequeath the fruit of my garden *perpetually* to such an one," the legatee is in that case entitled to the fruit then existing, as well as to whatever may afterwards grow there during his life. But if, on the other hand, the testator bequeath the *produce* of his garden (not the *fruit*), the legatee is then entitled to the present produce and to whatever may be collected from it until his death, although the word *perpetual* should not have been expressed; for as the word *fruit*, in its common acceptation, means a thing actually in being, it cannot therefore be applied to what is *not* in being, unless by an express provision for that purpose;—whereas *produce*, in the common acceptation of the term, comprehends not only what at present exists, but also what may hereafter exist in succession; and therefore its including what may appear after the testator's decease does not depend upon the mention of any particular sion or term.—Hidáyah, vol. iv, p. 533.

When one has bequeathed the produce of his mansion or slave, and the legatee wishes to occupy the mansion himself, or make use of the service of the slave, can he lawfully do so? There is nothing on the subject in the *Asal;* and "our" Shaikhs differ, but Abú Bakr has said that he cannot; and this is valid. If the bequest be of the occupancy of a mansion, and there is no property besides, the legatee may occupy a third of the mansion, and the heirs have no right to sell the two-thirds of the mansion in their possession. Neither has a legatee of occupancy a right to let the mansion or slave to hire, according to "us," nor to remove the slave from Kúfá, for instance, unless the legatee and his people are in another place, when the slave may be taken there for the purpose of serving them.—Fatáwá Alamgírí, vol. vi, p. 189.—B. Dig., p. 654.

Principle. DCCCXVI. A bequest of produce is cancelled by the legatee's purchasing the property itself.

Illustration. When a man has bequeathed to another the produce of his garden, the legatee may purchase the garden from the heirs of the testator, but that cancels the legacy. In like manner, if they satisfy him with something else, he may surrender his third of the produce, and release them from it. So, also, the occupancy of a house, or the service of a slave, may be lawfully compounded for, though a sale of these rights is not lawful.—Fatáwá Alamgírí, vol. vi, p. 190.—B. Dig., p. 656.

Principle. DCCCXVII. A bequest of the produce of a mansion to the poor generally is lawful; but a bequest of the occupancy of a mansion to the poor is not lawful, unless the persons are known.—*Ibid*.

Muhabát.

Principle. DCCCXVIII. A will by a way of *muhabát* (a) on a death-bed, is the same in effect as a bequest of property, and is therefore executed to any amount not exceeding a third of the testator's estate.*

(*a*.) "*Muhabát*" literally signifies a "*gift*." In the language of the *law* it means a gift interwoven in some contract or deed,—as if a person should sell a part of his property to another at an inferior value.*

Illustration. If a person, having two slaves, one estimated at thirty *dirms*, and the other at sixty, should on his death-bed will, that the slave worth thirty *dirms* be sold to *Zayid* for ten, and that the other worth sixty, be sold to *Umar* for twenty,—in that case *Zayid* obtains a *muhabát* of twenty *dirms*, and *Umar* a *múhabát* of forty *dirms*; and this is what is denominated a will by *muhabát*. But if the testator should not be possessed of any other property than these two slaves, and the heirs refuse to ratify the will, in that

* Hidáyah, vol. iv. p. 483.

case the *muhabát* is executed only in the proportion of a third. Now the whole of the property is ninety *dirms*, that being the aggregate value of the two slaves: one-third of that, therefore, (being thirty *dirms*) is divided into three shares, two of which are given in *muhabát* to *Umar*, and one to *Zayid*; that is, the slave worth sixty *dirms* is sold to *Umar* for forty, and the other, worth thirty, to *Zayid*, for twenty.—Hidáyah, vol. iv, p. 483.

When a man has made a *muhabát* and emancipated a slave, and the third of his estate is not sufficient for both, the *muhabát* is to be preferred according to Abú Hanífah; but if he emancipates first and then makes a *muhabát*, both are on an equal footing. According to the two disciples, preference is to be given in both cases to the emancipation. When a sick man has sold for fifty what is worth a hundred, or has bought for a hundred what is worth fifty, the excess above the proper price in the case of the purchase, and the deficiency in the case of sale, is a *muhabát*. Emancipation and *muhabát* in a last illness are both entitled to preference over all other legacies, because they cannot be revoked by the testator, the former being like *tadbír*, and the latter a contract; while all other legacies may be revoked by him at any time.—Fatáwá Alamgírí, vol. vi, p. 168.—B. Dig., p. 641.

Revocation of Bequests.

DCCCXIX. Bequests may be revoked expressly by words of mouth, by implication or deed (*a*), or by words and deed. *Principle.*

ANNOTATIONS.

dcccxix. Bequests are of four kinds. The *first* admits of being cancelled both by word and deed; the *second* by word only; the *third* by deed only; and the *fourth* neither by word nor by deed. The first are specific legacies, which may be cancelled by word, as by the testator's saying, "I have cancelled the bequest," and by deed, as by his selling the specific thing bequeathed, or emancipating him when a slave, or otherwise parting with his property in the subject of bequest in such a manner that the parting cannot be cancelled or reversed, as, for instance, by *tadbír*. The second kind of bequest, which can be cancelled by word only, and not by deed, is a bequest of a third or a fourth of the testator's property, which may be cancelled by express words; but though the testator should part with his property in the share indicated, the legacy would not be revoked, but take effect as to another third. The third kind, which admits of revocation by deed only, and not by word, is restricted *tadbír*, which, if revoked by deed, as by selling the slave, the revocation is valid, but cannot be validly revoked by words.—Fatáwá Alamgírí, vol. vi, p. 143.—B. Dig., p. 619.

(a.) A testator may revoke his bequest, and the revocation may be either express, as when he says "I have revoked," or the like, or implied, as when he does some act from which it may be inferred.—Fatáwá Alamgírí, vol. vi, p. 143.—B. Dig., p. 618.

Illustrations. If a man should bequeath a piece of cloth, and afterwards cut it up and sew it; or cotton, and afterwards spin it into thread, or thread and weave it; or iron, and afterwards manufacture it into a vessel,—in all these cases there is a revocation of the bequest.—*Ibid.*

Upon the testator either expressly rescinding his bequest (as if he were to say "I retract what I had bequeathed"), or performing any act which argues his having rescinded it, retraction is established. It is established, in the former instance, evidently; and so likewise in the latter; for as acts are demonstrative of the inclination as much as express words, they are consequently equivalent thereto. It is to be observed, that if the testator perform, upon the article he had bequeathed, any act which, when performed on the property of another, is the cause of terminating the right of the proprietor (such as the slaughter of a goat, or the fleecing, roasting, or boiling of it, the fabrication of a vessel from a piece of copper, the grinding wheat into flour, or the fabrication cf a sword from iron),—such act is a retraction of the bequest. If, also, he perform upon it any act creating an addition to the legacy, and this addition be so connected that the legacy cannot be separately delivered (as where a person bequeaths the flour of wheat, and afterwards mixes it with oil,—or a piece of ground, and afterwards erects a building on it,—or undrest cotton, and afterwards dresses it,—or a piece of cloth, and afterwards lines or covers a gown with it),—such act is a retraction of the bequest. It is otherwise with respect to plastering the wall of a bequeathed house, or undermining the foundation of it; for these acts do not indicate a retraction of the bequest, as they affect the legacy in its *dependencies* only.—Hidáyah, vol. iv, pp. 478 & 479.

Every act or deed which occasions an extinction of the property of the testator is a retraction from his bequest (as where, for instance, a testator sells the article he had bequeathed, and afterwards purchases it,—or gives it to some person, and afterwards retracts the gift),—and consequently the legacy does not go to the legatee after his [the testator's] decease, because a will can hold good only with respect to the testator's property; and therefore, upon his property being extinguished, the bequest becomes null of course.—Hidáyah, vol. iv, p. 479.

Principle. DCCCXX. A bequest to one person is annulled by a subsequent bequest of the same article to another, unless that other be not then alive; or by the second legatee being made a partner with the first, according to the words employed.

Illustrations.

If one should say "The slave whom I have bequeathed to such an one is to such an one," that would be a revocation; for the assertion excludes the idea of partnership. It is otherwise when a man has bequeathed to one person what he had already bequeathed to another; for the subject of a bequest is susceptible of partnership, and the expression (that is, the word "bequeath") will bear that construction. And, in like manner, if the testator should say "The slave whom I have bequeathed is to such an one my heir," that would be a revocation of the first bequest, for the same reason, and be a bequest to the heir, which the other heirs may allow or reject as they please. But if the second person were dead at the time of the testator's speaking, the first bequest would remain as before, by reason of the second being void; while, if the second person were living at the time that the testator spoke, and should subsequently die before him, both legacies would be void, and the subject of them revert to the heirs of the testator.—Fatáwá Alamgírí, vol. vi, p. 144.—B. Dig., p. 620.

If a person say "I will that a particular slave, which I formerly bequeathed to *Zayid*, be given as a legacy to *Amroo*," in that case a retraction from the first will is established, as the tenor of his speech evidently shows that it was not his intention they should both partake of the legacy. It is otherwise where a person first leaves a particular article to one man, and then leaves the same thing to another;—as if he should say "I will that this thing be given to *Zayid*," and afterwards makes a bequest of the same thing in favor of *Amroo*, for in that case a retraction of the first will does not take place, the subject being capable of division, and the separate sentences bearing that construction.—Hidáyah, vol. iv, p. 481.

If a person say "The slave which I formerly left to Zayid I now bequeath to *Amroo*, and at that time *Amroo* be not alive, the first will, in favor of *Zayid*, holds good, for *that* was annulled only on account of the legacy having been completely devised to *Amroo*, and upon this no longer remaining in force, because of *Amroo's* death, the first will reverts. If, on the contrary, *Amroo* be alive at the time of the bequest in his favor, and afterwards die before the testator, the legacy [the slave] in that case passes to the heirs, both bequests being void,—the first, because of the retraction, and the last, because of the death of the legatee previous to that of the testator.—Hidáyah, vol. iv, p. 481.

If a person should say "The slave whom I bequeathed to such an one, I have also bequeathed to such another," the slave would belong to both parties in halves. So also if he should say "I have bequeathed half of him to such an one," the slave would be between them both. And if he should bequeath a third of him to such an one, and then say, "The third which I bequeathed to such an one, I have also bequeathed half of it to such another, or say "Then, I have bequeathed half of it to such an one," the third would be between them in halves. But if he should say "The third which I have bequeathed to such an one I have also bequeathed a half of it to such another," the first legatee would have only a third of the third. And if one bequeathed something, and then say "What I bequeathed to such an one I have bequeathed half of it to such another, it will be between both," that would be a revocation as to half.—Fatáwá Alamgírí, vol. vi, p. 144.—B. Dig., pp. 620 & 621.

Principle. DCCCXXI. The testator's denying his bequest is not, however, a retraction of it; nor his declaring it unlawful or usurious.

Illustration. If a testator deny his bequest, and the legatee produce witnesses to prove it, there is in that case a difference of opinion among our doctors; for, according to *Muhammad* this is not a retraction; whereas Abú Yúsuf maintains that it is so, because *retraction* signifies the testator's negativing his bequest *at the present time;* and as the denial is a negative applying both to the *present* and to the *past,* it therefore amounts to a retraction *a fortiori.* The argument of *Muhammad* is, that the denial of a bequest signifies the putting a negative upon it with respect to the *past,* of which its being negatived with respect to the *present* is a consequence; and upon the bequest being proved, by witnesses, to exist at present, the denial is of no effect. Another argument is, that as a retraction implies the former existence of a will, and the present annihilation of it, and denial (on the other hand) disavows both the former and the present existence of it, there is therefore an evident difference between a retraction and a denial; whence the latter ought not to be considered in the light of the former; and, accordingly, denial not being a retraction, if a husband deny his marriage, and the wife bring witnesses to prove it, still a separation does not take place between them.—Hidáyah, vol. iv, pp. 479 & 480.

Principle. DCCCXXII. If a testator should desire that the execution of his will be suspended for some time after his death, this is not a retraction. If, on the contrary, he say, "I depart from my will," he is then held to have retracted it.—Hidáyah, vol. iv, p. 480.

DCCCXXIII. The bequest of another's property may be revoked at any time before its actual delivery to the legatee. *Principle.*

Illustration. When a person has bequeathed a thousand *dirms*, or a slave, or a garment, belonging to another, and he allows the gift before or after the death of the testator, he may revoke it at any time up to actual delivery to the legatee. But when he has made delivery, the legacy is lawful. For the legacy of another's property is like the gift of it, and is not valid without delivery and taking possession.—Fatáwá Alamgírí, vol. vi, p. 144.—B. Dig., p. 621.

Acknowledgment of Debts.

Principle. DCCCXXIV. It is to be observed, as a general rule, that where a person performs, with his property, any gratuitous deed of immediate operation (that is not restricted to his death), if he be in health at the time, such deed is valid to the extent of all his property, or, if he be sick,* it takes effect to the extent of one-third of his property; and where a person performs such deed, with his property, restricted to the circumstance of his decease, it takes effect to the extent of a third of his property, whether, at the time, he be sick or in health.—Hidáyah, vol. iv, p. 503.

On the contrary,—

Principle. DCCCXXV. If a person make an acknowledgment of debt, such acknowledgment is of effect to the whole extent of his property, notwithstanding it be made during sickness, as this is not a *gratuitous* deed.—*Ibid.* But,—

Principle. DCCCXXVI. If a person in his death-illness (*a*) say to his heirs "I am indebted to *Zayid*, and you must credit what he says," in that case the claim of Zayid to any amount not

---

* Arab. "*Mariz.*" This term literally means sick. In the language of the law, however, it is used to signify a dying person, or a person sick of a mortal disease.

exceeding a third of the estate must be admitted, although the heirs should falsify it.*—Hidáyah, vol. iv, p. 494.

(*a.*) Paralytic, gouty, or consumptive persons, where their disorder has continued for a length of time, and they are in no immediate danger of death, do not fall under the description of sick [*Maríz*]; whence deeds of gift, executed by such, take effect to the extent of their whole property; because, when a long time has elapsed, the patient has become familiarized to his disease, which is not then accounted as *sickness.* (The length of time requisite, by its lapse, to do away the idea of *sickness* in those cases is determined at one year; and if after that time the invalid should become bed-ridden, he is then accounted as one recently sick.)† If, therefore, any of the sick persons thus described make a gift in the beginning of their illness, or after they are bed-ridden, such gift takes effect from the third of their property, because at such a time there is apprehension of death (whence medicine is then administered to them), and therefore the disorder is then considered as a *death-bed illness.*—Hidáyah, vol. iv, p. 506.

Principle. DCCCXXVII. If, therefore, besides the acknowledgment in question, the dying person had made various bequests in favor of others, one-third of his estate must be set apart for the legatees, and two-thirds for the heirs, when both parties must be required "to verify the declaration of *Zayid* to such extent as they may think proper." Now, if both parties acknowledge that there is something owing to *Zayid,* it is evident that there rests a debt upon the estate affecting the shares of each respectively; and, accordingly, a deduction is made from the legatees, to the amount of one-third of what they acknowledge to be owing to *Zayid,* and from the heirs, to the amount of two-thirds of what they have so acknowledged, in order that the acknowledgment of each party may be carried into execution in proportion to his right in the whole estate.

If *Zayid* should claim still more than what falls to him in virtue of this acknowledgment of the parties, each party (the heirs and legatees) must be respectively required to make oath, to the *best of their knowledge, or,* in other words, to this effect, that "they do

---

* An acknowledgment of debt in favor of an heir on a death-bed resembles a legacy; inasmuch as it does not avail for more than a third of the estate.—Macn. M. L., chap. vi, princ. 7.

† What is within brackets is to be found in the *Jámi ur-Ramúz.*

not *know* of any more being due to *Zayid*;"—for they cannot be required to swear *positively*, as their oath regards a matter between the claimant and the acknowledger merely, and in which they are not principals.—Hiyáyah, vol. iv, p. 495.

DCCCXXVIII. If two sons make a partition of their father's estate, and one of them then declare that "his father had bequeathed a third of his property to *Zayid*," he (the declarer) must in that case make over a third of his portion to *Zayid*. This proceeds upcn a favorable construction. *Principle.*

Muhammad, on the contrary, maintains that the declarer is to make over a *half* of his portion to *Zayid* (and such is what analogy would suggest); because when this son made the declaration that *Zayid* was entitled to a third, he then in fact declared *Zayid* to be entitled to as much as himself, whence it is requisite that he make over a moiety of his portion to him, in order that both may be placed on an equality. The reason, however, for a more favorable construction in this particular is, that the son has here made a declaration, in favor of *Zayid*, of one-third, affecting the whole estate indefinitely; and as the whole estate has gone in two portions, each falling to each son respectively, it follows that the son has made his declaration in favor of *Zayid* with respect only to a *third* of his own portion.—Hidáyah, vol. iv, pp. 501 & 502.

LECTURE III.

ON THE EXECUTOR, HIS POWERS, &c.

THE executor is termed "*wasí*," or "*músá-ilehi* ;"* and is defined to be an *amín*, or trustee,† appointed by the testator (*músí*) to superintend, protect, and take care of his property and children after his death. He is also the testator's personal representative.‡

There are three kinds of executors. The first is a trustee, who is capable of performing the duty which has been committed to him; such an one is fixed (*mukarrar*), and cannot be removed by the judge (except for misconduct§). The second is a trustee who is weak and incapable, and to whom the judge should appoint an assistant. The third is a profligate, an infidel, or a slave, whom it is proper that the judge should remove, and appoint another in his stead. The word implies that the appointment is valid in the first instance, for otherwise there could be no removal.||

Principle. DCCCXXIX. Any testator may appoint his executor according to his own choice, yet if the executor so appointed be an improper person, by misconduct or the like, and prove to be unfit for the office, and there be apprehension of danger to the estate, he is to be removed by the judge (*kází*), and a proper person appointed in his stead.§

Principle. DCCCXXX. A person may appoint a slave, a reprobate, or an infidel, to be his executor; but it is incumbent on the *kází* (judge) to annul such appointment, and nominate another person.—Hidáyah, vol. iv, p. 541.

---

* *Ináyah*, vol. iv, pp. 607, 610.

† Hidáyah, Arabic, vol. iv, p. 1496.

‡ Arabic "*Káem mukám*," which means one who stands in his place.

§ *Vide post*, pp. 90 & 91.

|| Fatáwá Alamgírí, vol. vi, p. 211.—B. Dig., p. 665.

DCCCXXXI. When a person has appointed a slave, whether his own, or that of another, to be his executor, and all his heirs are adult, or some of them are adult and some minors, the appointment is void.* *Principle.*

DCCCXXXII. The appointment of a minor, or of an insane person, whether permanently so or with lucid intervals, is unlawful. But a woman, a blind person, or one who has undergone the *hadd*, or specific punishment for slander, may lawfully be appointed an executor.* *Principle.*

When a minor has been appointed an executor, the judge should remove him. So Khassáf has ordained. But are his acts of disposal before removal valid, like those of a *zimmí* or a slave? Though authorities differ on this point, the current opinion is that the acts are not operative. Authorities also differ as to the minor's remaining an executor after he has attained to puberty, if he has not been removed by the judge; Abú Hanífah saying that he does not continue to be executor, while Abú Yusaf maintained that he does, and Muhammad agreed with him in opinion.*

DCCCXXXIII. When a Muslim has appointed an alien his *executor*, the appointment is futile (*bátil*), whether he be a fugitive (*mustámin*) or not, by which is understood that the appointment will be cancelled.* *Principle.*

For, if it be of an alien tributary (*Zimmí*), the judge may cancel it, and expel him from the office.* But,—

DCCCXXXIV. If a Muslim should appoint an alien his executor, and the alien be converted to the faith, he remains in his state of executor. So also when the appointment is of an apostate who returns to the faith.* *Principle.*

ANNOTATIONS.

dcccxxxi. If a person appoint his own slave his executor, any of the heirs being arrived at the age of maturity, it is not valid.—Hidáyah, vol. iv, p. 541.

---

* Fatáwá Alamgírí, vol. vi, pp. 112, 213.—Dig., pp. 667—669.

When a profligate has been appointed from whom danger may be apprehended to the property, it is stated in the *Asal* that the appointment is void, by which, they say, is to be understood that the judge should expel him from the office. And *Hasan* has reported, as from Abú Hanífah, that it is incumbent on the judge to expel him and appoint another in his stead, when this profligate is such an one as ought not be an executor.

Principle. **DCCCXXXV. If the judge has given operation to the appointment, and the executor has paid the debts of the deceased, or sold something, as executors usually do, before the judge expels him from the office, his acts are lawful; and if he is not expelled till he repents and becomes good, the judge should allow him to remain in his office.***

Principle. **DCCCXXXVI. If the judge is not aware that he is executor, and appoints another in his presence, who wishes to enter upon his office, he may lawfully do so; but this is not an expulsion of the first executor. And if a judge not knowing that there is an executor to the deceased, appoints another in the executor's absence, the proper executor is the nominee of the deceased, not the nominee of the judge.***

Principle. **DCCCXXXVII. If an executor be unequal to the execution of his office, it is incumbent on the judge *(kází)* to associate another with him, in order that the duties of the office may be properly executed.— Hidáyah, vol. iv, p. 542.**

Principle. **DCCCXXXVIII. If an executor represents to the judge his inability to execute the duties of his charge,**

ANNOTATIONS.

dcccxxxvii. When a person has been an executor, who is weak and insufficient, the judge should add another to him.*

dcccxxxviii. If an executor should himself represent his incapacity, the judge is not to allow it on his mere representation, nor until the ascertain the fact; but if it is manifest that he is really incompetent, the judge should appoint another in his stead.*

* Fatáwá Alamgírí, vol. vi, pp. 212, 213—B. Dig., pp. 667—669.

it is requisite, in such case, that the judge, before he attends to his representation, make particular enquiry into the truth of it. But if it shall appear to the judge, on due examination, that the executor is utterly incapable of the office, he must release him, and appoint another in his place, this being advantageous both to the executor and to the estate.—Hidáyah, vol. iv, p. 542.

DCCCXXXIX. If all, or part of the heirs, prefer a complaint against the executor, still the judge (*kází*) must not dismiss him *immediately*, nor until his guilt be ascertained, as he acts under the authority derived from the *deceased*. If, however, he prove culpable, it is incumbent on the *kází* to dismiss him, and appoint another in his place. *Principle.*

For, the deceased nominated him to the office supposing him worthy of confidence, but upon being found culpable, he no longer continues so, insomuch that if the testator were living he would himself discharge him; and as *he* is incapacitated, by death, from so doing, the *kází* must take this upon himself as his substitute.—Hidáyah, vol. iv, p. 543.

DCCCXL. If an executor be perfectly equal to the discharge of his office and trustworthy therein, the judge is not at liberty to dismiss him.—Hidáyah, vol. iv, p. 542. *Principle.*

For any person whom the *kází* may appoint in his place must be less eligible, as the deceased had particularly selected him, and signified his confidence in him. He, therefore, must be continued in preference to all others, even to the testator's father, notwithstanding his supposed tenderness; and consequently to others *a fortiori.*—*Ibid.*

DCCCXLI. An executor may decline or accept office before or after the death of the testator. But if he has once accepted, he cannot retract after the death of the testator, nor in his lifetime without his knowledge. *Principle.*

Muhammad has said in the *Jámi Saghír*, with respect to a person who had appointed another his executor, and the executor had accepted in his lifetime, that the executorship is binding on the

acceptor; so that if he should wish to withdraw from the office after the death of the testator, he is not at liberty to do so. But if he retracts in the lifetime of the testator and before his face, the retraction is valid, but if it is not made before his face, it is not valid. What is meant by saying "before his face" is with his knowledge, and "not before his face" is without his knowledge. If an executor should accept in the presence of his testator, and the testator should say when he is absent "Take witness that I have discharged him from the executorship." Hasan has reported as from Abú Hanífah, that the discharge is valid. But if an executor should reject his appointment in the testator's absence (after he has once accepted) the rejection according to "us" is void.*

If a person appoint another his executor, it remains with that other either to accept of or decline the appointment in the presence of the testator, because no one has the power of compelling another to interfere in his concerns. But if the executor accept his appointment in the presence of the testator, and afterwards, either in his absence, or after his death, decline it, such refusal is not admitted.—Hidáyah, vol. iv, p. 539.

If a man appoint another his executor, and the person so appointed remain silent until the testator's decease, and then reject the office, and afterwards declare his acceptance of it, such acceptance is valid, unless the *kázi*, during the *interim*, should have set him aside and appointed another in consequence. Because the testator had placed a reliance on his consent; and therefore, if the rejection were allowed of, either in his absence or after his decease, he would necessarily be deceived.—Hidáyah, vol. iv, pp. 539, 540.

Principle. DCCCXLII. If an executor after having accepted his office as such, or having, after the testator's death, disposed of any part of his property, wishes to relieve himself of his office, he cannot be relieved, unless the judge believe him to be unfit or overburdened with business.*

Karkhí has said that when an executor has accepted, or has, after the death of the testator, disposed of any part of his property, and then wishes to relieve himself of his office, he cannot lawfully do so, except in the presence of the *hákim*, or judge. And when he appears before the judge with this view, the judge ought not to [illegible]ieve him without considering whether he is competent to the proper discharge of its functions, and relieve him only if he believes him to be unfit or over-burdened with business.*

* Fatáwá Alamgírí, vol vi, pp. 212, 214.—B. Dig., pp. 666—669

If a person appoint another his executor, and that other remain silent, without giving any indication of his acceptance or refusal, he is in that case at liberty, after the death of the testator, to accept or refuse the appointment, as may be most agreeable to him. But if a person, under such circumstances, should, immediately after the death of the testator, dispose of any part of the effects by sale, then, as an act of this kind is a clear indication of his acceptance, the executorship becomes obligatory on him. The sale, moreover, is valid in this instance, notwithstanding the executor may not have considered himself as such at that time; for his executorship (like inheritance, bequest being a sort of succession as well as inheritance) does not depend on his knowledge; and, as being an executor, a sale transacted by him is valid. —Hidáyah, vol. iv, p. 540.

DCCCXLIII. When a person has appointed another his executor without the other's knowledge, and the executor sells some part of the estate after his death, the sale is good, and the executorship binding on the person appointed.* *Principle.*

A person having appointed two executors, one of whom accepted and the other remained silent, the acceptor says to the one that was silent, "Buy a shroud for the deceased," and he does so, or answers "Yes;"—this is acceptance of the executorship, even though the silent one be the servant of the other, unless he is a freeman working with him.* Illustration.

DCCCXLIV. When there is more than one executor appointed, none of them can alone dispose of the testator's property, and the acts done by one of them singly are not operative without the sanction of the other, except in such necessary matters as require immediate execution or are considered mere duties, or in which the interest or the advantage of the estate is concerned.* *Principle.*

DCCCXLV. When a man appoints two executors, neither of them is entitled, according to Abú *Principle.*

ANNOTATIONS.

dcccxlv. When a man has appointed two executors, one of them, according to Abú Hanífah and Muhammad, can not alone dispose of pro-

* Fatáwá Alamghírí, vol. vii, pp. 212, 213.—B. Dig., pp. 666 & 667.

Hanífah and Muhammad, to act without the other, except in particular cases (*a*).—Hidáyah, vol. iv, p. 543.

(*a*.) The cases excepted by Hanífah and Muhammad, in which they hold the acts of either executor singly to be valid, are such as require *immediate* execution. Thus,—

Exceptions.

It is lawful for either executor singly to disburse the funeral charges, as a delay in this might occasion the body to become offensive; whence it is that a similar power is vested in the neighbours. In the same manner, either of the executors, singly, may purchase victuals or clothes for the infant children of the testator, this being a matter of urgency, and which admits of no delay. So, likewise, it is lawful for either of the executors to restore a deposit, an usurped article, or a thing purchased by the testator under an invalid contract. In preserving the estate of the testator, also, and in discharging his debts, the act of either executor is lawful independent of the other. For none of these is considered as an *exercise of power*, but merely the performance of a duty.—Hidáyah, vol. iv, pp. 544 & 545.

Either of the executors has also a right singly to discharge a legacy, or emancipate a slave, if directed by the testator, because such deeds require no thought or consideration. In the same manner, either of them may institute a suit in claim of the rights of the testator.—Hidáyah, vol. iv, p. 545.

ANNOTATIONS.

perty, and acts done by either of them singly are not operative without the sanction of the other, except in some special matters.—Fatáwá Alamgírí, vol. vi, p. 213.—B. Dig., p. 669. Thus,—

One may act separately as to the washing and shrouding of the deceased's body, and its removal to the grave; the payment of the debts out of the assets of the same kind as the debts; the delivery of specific bequests; the restoration of deposits, or of things usurped by the deceased, or acquired under defective sales, the manumission of a specific slave; and the general preservation of his property. But they cannot act singly in taking possession of deposits belonging to him, nor in receiving payments of debts due to him; though they may in suing for his rights. According to the same authorities, they may also act separately in accepting a gift for a minor, sanctioning his acts, making a partition of things weighable or measurable, and selling what is liable to spoil.—*Ibid.*

* Fatáwá Alamgírí, vol. vi, pp. 212 & 213.—B. Dig., pp. 666 & 667.

The acceptance of a gift for an infant is likewise an act which either may perform singly; for in case of delay there is a possibility of the gift being rendered null by the death of the donor previous to the seizure.—Hidáyah, vol. iv, p. 545.

These acts, moreover, being permitted to a mother and nurse, are proofs that they are not *exertions of power*. It is likewise permitted to any of the executors,* singly, to sell goods where there is an apprehension of their spoiling, as in the case of fruit, and the like; and also to collect together and preserve the scattered property of the testator, as a delay might occasion the destruction of it; and such permission is, moreover, given to every person into whose hands property may fall, whence it may be inferred that this is not an exertion of power.—*Ibid*, p. 545.

DCCCXLVI. When the deceased has directed such and such parts of his property to be bestowed in charity, on beggars and indigent persons, without specifying them, one executor cannot act separately from the other, according to Abú Hanífah and Muhammad.† But if the objects of charity are specified, he may act alone according to them all.‡ *Principle.*

DCCCXLVII. But they (the executors) cannot act singly in taking possession of deposits belonging to him (the testator), nor in receiving payment of debts due to him, though they may in suing for his rights.‡ *Principle.*

DCCCXLVIII. But if every one of the executors is declared to be a complete executor, any one of them may dispose of property alone.‡ *Principle.*

If, however, two (executors) are appointed, and it has been said "each of you is a complete executor (*wasí-i támm*)," each one of them may dispose of the property alone.‡

---

* It is recorded in the *Jámi Saghir*, that none of the executors, where there are more than one, has singly the power of selling goods or receiving payment of debts, because these are exercises of power which they must perform jointly, in conformity with the will and intention of the testator.—Hamilton's Hidáyah, vol. iv, pp. 545 & 546.

† Though they may do so according to Abú Yusuf.—*Ibid.*

‡ Fatáwá Alamgírí, vol. vi, p. 214.—B. Dig., p. 670.

Principle.

DCCCXLIX. If the executors have been appointed by the testator *not* simultaneously, but one after another,* then they cannot act *separately* in disposing of property in any case whatsoever.

In what has been said, it is supposed that the two executors have been appointed together in one sentence (*kalám*). And if the testator should first appoint one, and then the other, there is a difference of opinion among our Shaikhs, according to Halwáí; one saying that here each of the executors may act separately, while another says that, according to Abú Hanífah and Muhammad, they cannot act separately in disposing of property in any case; and this has been adopted by *Sarakhsí*.†

Principle.

DCCCL. When a person has been appointed executor for a particular purpose, he becomes a general executor, unless expressly prohibited to act in any other matter with respect to which another is appointed as executor.†

ANNOTATIONS.

dcccxlix. If a person appoint two executors in a separate manner,† some allege that in this case each of them has individually a power of exercising the functions of his appointment, without consulting the other, in the same manner as two agents, where they are appointed by different commissions;—the reason of which is that the testator, in appointing the two separately, indicates his assent to each acting from his own judgment, without the other's assistance or advice. Others again say that, concerning this case, also a disagreement subsists between *Haníjah* and *Muhammad* on one side, and *Abú Yusuf* on the other; because a will is not established until the death of the testator; and at that time both are executors together, notwithstanding they had been appointed separately. It is otherwise with two agents appointed under different commissions; for the appointment of each of those still continues distinct and separate, as settled by the constituent.—Hidáyah, vol. iv, p. 546.

---

* As if the testator should first say to the one "I have appointed you my executor," and again, at a different period, to the other "I have appointed you my executor."—Hamilton's Hidáyah, vol. iv, p. 546.

† Fatáwá Alamgírí, vol. vi, p. 214.—B. Dig., p. 670.

When a person appoints an executor for a particular purpose, as by saying "I have appointed thee my executor to pay my debts," and says to another "I have appointed thee my executor in the administration of my property;" or by saying "I have appointed such an one my executor to pay my debts, and does not appoint him for anything else, and I have appointed such another my executor for all my property," each one is executor in all matters, according to Abú Hanífah and Abú Yusuf, as if he had appointed them both for all matters; but, according to Muhammad, each is restricted to the particular matter for which he has been appointed. And where it is made an express condition that one shall not be executor in the matter to which the other is appointed, it has been said by Muhammad Bin Al-fazl that the matter is as conditioned, according to all opinions; and it is only where he has not made such condition that there is the difference of opinion above-mentioned, the *fatwá* being with Abú Hanífah.* *Principle.*

DCCCLI. When one of two executors dies, the survivor cannot act without authority from the *Principle*

ANNOTATIONS.

dcccli. When a man has appointed two executors, and one of them dies, the survivor cannot, according to Abú Hanífah and Muhammad, dispose of the property, but should lay the matter before the judge, who, if he see proper, may make him sole executor, and transfer to him the power of disposal. According to Abú Yusuf, however, the survivor can act alone, as, in his opinion, he was competent to do while the other was alive. Though one of the executors should die before the testator and before acceptance by the other, the single executor is incompetent to act by himself, according to Abú Hanífah and Muhammad; while according to Abú Yusuf he is competent. If one of two executors is profligate, the judge may authorize the other to act singly, or may add another to him, when the just one cannot act without the other, according to Abú Hanífah and Muhammad; while according to Abú Yusuf he can.—Fatáwá Alamgírí, vol. vi, p. 216.—B. Dig., p. 671.

A person having appointed two executors, one of them dies, having first appointed his fellow to be his executor. This is lawful, and the fellow may dispose, of the property of the first deceased; for, as he could have done so with the sanction of his co-executor in his lifetime, so he can, in like manner, do so after his death. There is another report, however, against the legality of the disposal; but the first is correct.— *Ibid,* pp. 674 & 672.

---

* Fatáwá, Alamgírí , vol. vi pp. 214, 216, 218.— B. Dig., pp. 671 & 672.

judge, unless he is appointed by the late executor to be *his* executor also.

If one of two executors die, it is incumbent on the judge (*kází*) to appoint another in his room. This is the opinion of *Hanífah* and *Muhammad;* because, according to their doctrine, the remaining executor has not, of himself, power to act on every occasion, and the interest of the deceased therefore requires the appointment of another to operate with him; and it is also the opinion of *Abú Yusuf*, because, although the remaining executor be (according to him) empowered to act of himself, still it behoves the *kází* to appoint another as his companion; for the design of the testator evidently was to leave *two* successors for the management of his concerns; and as this may be fulfilled by the appointment of a substitute for him who dies, one must be appointed accordingly.—Hidáyah, vol. iv, p. 546.

If the deceased executor have appointed the living executor to act for him, it is in that case lawful for the latter (according to the *Záhir ur-Rawáyet*) to act alone, nor is it incumbent on the *kází* to appoint another in the room of the deceased; because here the judgment of the deceased executor virtually subsists in the living one, as it were, by succession. (There is a tradition of *Hanífah* having contradicted this doctrine, because of its repugnance to the object of the testator, namely, the agency of two persons; in opposition to the case where a dying executor appoints some other person to succeed him; for such appointment is valid, because of its being attended with the advantage of the judgment of two distinct persons, as was intended by the testator.)—Hidáyah, vol. iv, p. 547.

If an executor, previous to his death, appoint another person *his* executor, in that case, the person so appointed is entitled to act as executor both to him and also to the person to whose affairs his immediate testator had acted as executor. This is according to our doctors.—Hidáyah, vol, iv, p. 547.

Principle. DCCCLII. An executor may, on the approach of death, appoint a successor, though the *deceased* had not committed that power to him.*

Principle. DCCCLIII. If a number of persons are directed by a testator to be his executors, they all become so, if they accept; but if they remain silent till the tes-

---

* Fatáwá Alamgírí, vol. vi, pp. 214, 216, 218.—B. Dig., pp. 671 & 672.

tator's death, and then two or more of them accept the office, they become executors, and can lawfully carry the will into execution. But if only one of them accepts, though he becomes the executor, he cannot lawfully carry the will into execution without bringing the matter before the judge, who may either appoint another to act with him, or authorize him to act singly.*

DCCCLIV. If a person should appoint an executor, and say, "Act with the knowledge of such an one," the executor may act without his knowledge. But if the words were "*Do not* act *without* the knowledge of such an one," it would not be lawful for him to act without his knowledge; and the *fatwá* is to that effect.* *Principle.*

If he (the testator) should say, "Act with the opinion of such an one;" or "Do not act except with the opinion of such an one;" in the first case, the person addressed would be the executor; in the second, they are both executors, according to what is approved.*

DCCCLV. When a man appoints one person his executor, and another *mushrif*, or inspector to him, the first is the executor for the purpose of taking possession of the property, and the *mushrif* is not an executor; the effect of the appointment being that the executor cannot act without his knowledge.* *Principle.*

DCCCLVI. When a man has appointed a person his executor, and a third party has appointed the testator his executor, and the second testator *Principle.*

ANNOTATIONS.

dcccliv. Abú Nasar has said, that if the words were "Act in the matter with the orders of such an one," he is a special executor; while if the words were "Do not act without his orders," both would be executors; and this seems probable according to the doctrine of *our* masters.*

* Fatáwá Alamgírí, vol. vi, pp. 218 & 219.—B. Dig., pp. 672 & 673.

then dies, the first is his executor; and if the first should die without making another appointment, his executor is executor of both together.*

Principle. **DCCCLVII. A father's executor can, for the testator's young children, enter into a partition with the legatee or legatees of the immovable as well as movable property.***

Muhammad has said that the executor of a father may enter into a partition of property for young children, whatever the property may be, and whether movable or immovable, with a slight inadequacy in the terms *(ghabn-yusír),* but not if the inadequacy be glaring *(ghabn-fáhish)*;† the principle in these cases being, that he who has the power to sell a thing has the power to make a partition of it.*

Principle. **DCCCLVIII. When all the heirs are minors, and the executor has made a partition with a legatee, giving him his third, and holding two-thirds for the heirs, the partition is lawful; so that if what is in his hands belonging to them should happen to perish, they have no right of recourse against the legatee, nor is the executor responsible to them on account of the loss.***

ANNOTATIONS.

dccclviii, dccclix. If an executor, the legatees being present, divide off the estate of the testator from the legacies, on behalf of his heirs, who are infants, or adult absentees, and take possession of their portions, it is lawful; for an heir is successor to the deceased ; and as an executor is also a successor to him, he is of course a competent litigant on behalf of infant or absent heirs, and may, of consequence, make a division, and possess himself of their portions on their behalf,—insomuch that if those portions were to perish in his hands, still they are not at liberty to participate with the legatees in what remained to them after such division.— Hidáyah, vol. iv, p. 548.

---

* Fatáwá Alamgírí. vol. vi, pp. 218 .& 219.—B. Dig., pp. 672 & 673.

† The legatee of a third or other share of the estate is a partner with the heirs, and the executor may be called upon by either party to make a partition. But this is beyond his function; his power seems entirely to depend on the relation which the deceased bore to the heirs,—Note by Mr. Baillie.

DCCCLIX. When some of the heirs are adult and absent, it is lawful for the executor to make a partition on their behalf with the legatee, in everything except *akár*, or what is immovable, and to hold shares on account of the minors. But if the heirs are all adult, and some of them present, a partition made by the executor with the legatee is void as against the adult heirs, both with respect to movable and immovable property. And if the heirs are adult and absent, a partition of immovable property made by the executor with the legatee is void as against the heirs.* But— *Principle.*

DCCCLX. If all the heirs are adult and present, it is unlawful for the executor to divide off the legacies from the estate and hold them for the infant and absent legatees. *Principle.*

If, on the contrary, an executor, the heirs being adult and present, divide off the legacies from the estate, and take possession of them on behalf of infant or absent legatees, it is unlawful; for a legatee is not a successor to the deceased in *every* respect, he being constituted a proprietor by a new and supervenient cause; and as, therefore, the executor does not stand as litigant on his behalf, his taking his (the legatee's) portion is not valid,—insomuch that if the legacy were to perish in his (the executor's) hands, the legatee would be entitled to take a third of whatever had remained to the heirs. Neither is any compensation due from the executor in this instance, because an executor is a trustee; and as the power of conserving the effects of the testator is lodged in him, the case is, therefore, the same as if the loss had happened previous to the division of the effects.—Hidáyah, vol. iv, p. 549.

DCCCLXI. Should the executor make a partition in the absence of a secular legatee or legatees, the same is not lawful, and the legatee or legatees may still claim to participate with the heirs in a third of what remains, if the portion allotted to him or to them happen to perish. *Principle.*

---

* Fatáwa Alamgírí, vol. vi, p. 220.—B. Dig., p. 674.

If an executor should make a partition to, or in favor of, heirs, when there are legacies to mankind (that is, for secular purposes) against the estate, and the legatee is absent, the partition is not lawful, and the legatee may still claim to be a partner with the heirs, that is, for a third of what remains, if the portion allotted to him should perish.—Durr-ul-Mukhtár, p. 836.

Principle. DCCCLXII. But a partition made by the judge, and the taking possession by him of the legatee's portion, is valid; so that, if the portion should perish in the hands of the judge or his *amín*, the legatee would have no right of recourse against the heirs, neither would the judge be responsible.*

The above, however, is only when the things are weighable or movable, a partition of which is separation. But—

Principle. DCCCLXIII. With respect to things that are not so, the partition being an exchange like a sale, is unlawful, for it is not lawful to sell another person's property.*

Principle. DCCCLXIV. When the judge has appointed a guardian (*wasí*) for an orphan in all matters, and he has made a partition against him, whether of movable or immovable property, the partition is

ANNOTATIONS.

dccclxii. If a person bequeath a third of one thousand *dirms* to another who is at that time absent, and the heirs consign the said sum to the *kází*, in order to divide and set apart the share of the absent legatee, the division thus made by the *kází* is valid, because of the original validity of the will, insomuch that if the absentee should afterwards die, previous to his having declared his acceptance, the legacy nevertheless devolves to his heirs.—Hidáyah, vol. iv, p. 550.

* Fatáwá Alamgírí, vol. vi, p. 220.—B. Dig., p. 674.

lawful; but if the appointment is only for a special purpose (*a*), the partition is unlawful.*

(*a.*) As for the maintenance of the orphan, or conservation of his property.*

DCCCLXV. The executor of a mother may make a partition on account of her minor children of movable property, which they have inherited from her, when they have no father nor father's executor; but he has no such power when there is either of these; and he cannot make a partition of the immovable estate under any circumstances, nor of anything that the minor has inherited from any other than his mother, whether it be movable or immovable.* *Principle.*

DCCCLXVI. What has been said with respect to the executor of a mother, is applicable to the executor of a brother and paternal uncle.* *Principle.*

DCCCLXVII. When an executor makes a partition among heirs, and they are all minors, without any admixture of adults, the partition is unlawful. If they are all adults, but some of them absent, and a partition is made with those who are present, and their shares separated from the mass, the partition is lawful with respect to chattels, but not as to immovable property. If there are both minor and adult heirs, but the adult are present, the partition is unlawful. If the adults are present, and their share is given up to them, and the shares of the minors separated from them in a mass without partition among the individual minors, the division is lawful. When the share of each minor or adult is separated from the rest, the whole partition is invalid. But if the share of the adult is surrendered to them, and the portion of the minors retained, and then divided among them, the partition as between the adults and the minors is valid.* *Principle.*

DCCCLXVIII. The executor of a father is in the place of a father. So also the executor of the grandfather is in the *Principle.*

* Fatáwá Alamgírí, vol. vi, pp. 220—222.—B. Dig., pp. 675—678.

place of a father's executor, and the executor of a grandfather's executor in the place of a grandfather's executor.*

However,—

Principle. DCCCLXIX. The power of the father's executor, in the management of the property of his orhpans, is superior to, and precedes that of, the grandfather.—Hidáyah, vol. iv, p. 554.

Principle. **DCCCLXX. An executor cannot lawfully purchase for a minor anything at a price much above its value.***

Principle. **DCCCLXXI. An executor may accept a transfer for a debt due to his infant ward.***

If a person indebted to an orphan give a transfer on some other person, and the executor (the guardian of the orphan) accept the same, such acceptance is approved, provided it be for the interest of the orphan, because of the person on whom the transfer is made being richer (for instance) than the transferer, and also a man of probity; for the power of acting is vested in the executor, merely that he may employ it for the interest of the orphan; but if the transferer be richer than the other, the acceptance is not approved, as being, in its tendency, prejudicial to the orphan.—Hidáyah, vol. iv, pp. 552 & 553.

DCCCLXXII. When the heirs are all adult and present, the executor cannot sell any part of the estate without their consent; but if they are absent, he can sell the movable, but not the immovable, property, except in the case of falling into decay.*

When the heirs are all adult and present, the executor can sell no part of the estate except by their directions; and if they are absent, he cannot lawfully sell the *akár*, though he may sell anything but the *akár* (and let the whole to hire), because he has the power of conservation over the property of an absentee, and it may be necessary to sell chattels in order to preserve them; but *akár*, or immovable property, is secure in itself, except in the case of its falling into decay, and in that case it also may be sold.*

* Fatáwá Alamgírí, vol. vi, pp. 221 & 222.—B. Dig., pp. 676 & 677.

DCCCLXXIII. When all the heirs are adult, and one of them is absent, while the others are present, the executor may sell the share of the absentee in all that is not *akár* (immovable property) for the sake of preserving it, according to all opinions. And the shares of those who are present, according to Abú Hanífah; but according to both his companions, the sale of their shares is unlawful.*

DCCCLXXIV. An executor has the power *of* selling every species of property belonging to an adult absent heir, excepting such as is immovable (*akár*). *Principle.*

For as a father is authorized to sell the movable property of his adult absent son, but not such as is immovable, so his guardian (the executor) has the same power.—Hidáyah, vol. iv, p. 553.

An executor cannot sell immovable property *(akár)* except under the following circumstances :—

DCCCLXXV. An executor is allowed to sell immovable property, not to himself, but to a stranger, for double the value of the property, or for the benefit of the minor, or for (liquidation of) the debts of the deceased (testator), or where there are (some) general provisions in the (late incumbent's) will which cannot be carried into effect without selling (such property), or where the produce or income of the property does not exceed the expense (of keeping it), or where it is in danger of being destroyed, damaged, or decayed, or where it is in the hands of a usurper (and there is apprehension of its not being recovered*). *Durr-ul-Mukhtár,* the chapter on will and executorsbip, pp. 846 & 847; so also the Jámi-ur-Ramúz. *Principle.*

The Fatáwá, Alamgírí is almost to the same effect. It is laid down therein as follows:—

---

* *Radd-ul-Mukhtár*, a very copious commentary on the *Durr-ul-Mukhtár*. *Vide* pp. 484 & 485 of Lecture xvi delivered during the last session.

When a father's executor has sold anything belonging to the estate of the father, the case presents two aspects. The first is, when the deceased has left neither debts nor legacies; the second is, when he has left one or other of these. With regard to the first, it is said in the book,* that the executor may sell the whole property, movable and immovable, when the heirs are minors. But Halwáí has said that this was the opinion of the ancients, and that, according to the moderns, "the *akár*, or immovable property, of a minor can be sold only (that is, when there are no debts, nor general legacies), if the minor has occasion for the price of it, or a purchaser is eager to obtain it by giving double its value, or the sale is otherwise for the minor's advantage, as, for instance, when the *kharáj*, or land-tax, and expenses exceed its income; or the property, being shops or a mansion, is falling into decay. With regard to the land-tax, when a necessity arises for paying it, and there is belonging to the estate any other property besides *akár*, the other property is first to be applied to its payment; and if that is not sufficient, the *akár* may then be sold for its value, or a price not much less than its value; but the executor cannot lawfully sell it at a greater depreciation than men would usually submit to.†

Principle. DCCCLXXVI. When, however, an executor has actually sold *akár*, or immovable property, for the payment of debts while he has other property in his hands sufficient for that purpose, the sale is lawful.*

DCCCLXXVII. But if there are debts, and they cover the whole of their estate, the executor may sell the whole by general agreement; and when the debts do not cover the whole estate, he may sell as much as may be necessary for their payment.*

He may also sell the surplus according to Abú Hanífah; but this is contrary to the opinion of his companions.—*Ibid.*

Principle. DCCCLXXVIII. And if there are general legacies, the executor may sell as much of the property

* That is *Kudúri.*

† Fatáwá Alamgírí, vol. vi. pp. 221 & 222.—B. Dig., pp. 676 & 677.

as may be necessary for their liquidation (not exceeding, of course, a third of the whole after payment of the debts).*

DCCCLXXIX. If there be among the heirs one minor, and all the rest are adults, and neither debts nor legacies, the estates consisting entirely of chattels, the executor may sell the share of the minor according to all the (authorities.)* *Principle.*

And the shares of the others, according to Abú Hanífah; so that, if he should sell the whole, the sale would be lawful according to him; but it would not be lawful, according to the other two (Abú Yusuf and Muhammad), as to the shares of the adults; the principle of the former being that, whenever the executor has power to sell a part of the estate, he has power to sell the whole.*

DCCCLXXX. The executor of a mother or brother may lawfully sell movable property belonging to the estate of the deceased; but can neither sell the immovable property, nor can he buy for his ward anything but food and raiment necessary for his support. *Principle.*

With regard to the executor of a mother or a brother,—when a mother has died leaving property and a minor son and having appointed an executor, or a brother has died leaving property and a minor brother and having appointed an executor, the executor may lawfully sell anything but *akár* belonging to the estate of the deceased, but can neither sell the *akár*, nor lawfully buy anything for the minor but food and clothing, which are necessary for his preservation.*

DCCCLXXXI. The executor of a mother has no power to sell anything that a minor has inherited from his father, whether movable or immovable, and whether the property be involved in debt or be free from it. But what he has inherited from herself, when it is free from debts and legacies, the executor may sell what is the movable portion thereof, but he cannot sell *akár*.* *Principle.*

DCCCLXXXII. If the estate is involved in debt or in legacies, and the debt is such as to absorb the whole, he may sell the whole, the sale of *akár* coming within his *Principle.*

---

* Fatáwá Alamgírí, vol. vi, pp. 222 & 223.—B. Dig., pp. 677—679.

power; and if the debt does not absorb the whole, he may sell as much of it as is necessary to defray the debts. And as to his power to sell the surplus, there is the same difference of opinion as has been stated above.*

Principle. DCCCLXXXIII. If all the heirs of a mother are adult and present, and her estate is free from debt, her executor can sell no part of the same; but if the estate be in debt, he may sell as much of it as may be necessary for payment of that debt.

If all the heirs are adult and present, the estate being free from debt, the mother's executor can sell no part of her estate; and if the estate is in debt, the answer to be given as to the power of the mother's executor is like that in the case of the father's executor, both in respect of what opinions agree and of what differ.*

Principle. DCCCLXXXIV. And if there are both adult and minor sons, and the adult are absent, the estate being free from debt, the mother's executor may sell what is movable of her estate, whether it belongs to the share of the minor or the adult, but cannot sell the *akár* of her estate,—the shares of minors and adults being in this case the same.*

And if the estate be involved in debt, the answer to be given as to the power of the mother's executor is like the answer in the case of the father's executor.*

Principle. DCCCLXXXV. If the adults are present, and the estate is free from debt, the (mother's) executor may sell the minor's share of her movable estate; but whether he can sell the shares of the adults, opinions differ, while he certainly cannot sell the *akár*.*

Principle. DCCCLXXXVI. If the estate has to pay legacies, he may sell one-third of the estate to pay them; but if it be debts, he may sell as much of it as may be sufficient for the liquidation of those debts.*

---

* Fatáwá Alamgírí, vol. vi, pp. 222 & 223.—B. Dig., pp 677 679.

And if the estate be involved in debts or legacies, and the debts absorb the whole, he may sell the whole; and if they do not, he may sell the movable and as much of the *akár* as may be necessary for the payment of debts, and as to the surplus there is the difference among "our shaikhs" already mentioned.*

DCCCLXXXVII. Whatever has been said as to the executor of the mother, is true of the executor of the brother and the paternal uncle, the principle being that the power of the executor is measured by the power of his testator.* *Principle.*

According to *Muhammad* and *Abú Yusuf*,—

The executor of a brother, with respect to an infant brother, or one of mature age, who is absent, stands in the same predicament as the executor of a father with respect to his adult absent son (in other words, he is empowered to sell the movable property of the orphan or absentee); and so likewise of an executor appointed by the mother or uncle; for as the mother and uncle are permitted to interfere in the management of the property so far as relates to its preservation, so also is the executor who represents them.—Hidáyah, vol. iv, p. 554.

DCCCLXXXVIII. If a father die without appointing an executor, the grandfather represents† the father. *Principle.*

Because a grandfather is most nearly related to the children of his son, and most interested in their welfare; whence it is that the grandfather is empowered to contract the infant wards in marriage, in preference to the father's executor, notwithstanding the latter have precedence of him in point of managing and acting with the property, for the reasons already assigned.—Hidáyah, vol. iv, p. 555. **Reason.**

Responsibility and Non-responsibility of a Testator.

DCCCLXXXIX. If an executor, without proof, satisfies the claim of a person against his testator's estate, he is responsible for the same. But when he has satisfied a claim upon the same being proved against the estate, he incurs no responsibility.* *Principle.*

* Fatáwá Alamgírí. vol. vi, pp. 219 & 223.—B. Dig., p. 679.

† Literally "is in the stead of," or "stands in the place of."

A man having appointed two executors, dies, and a claim is made against his estate, which they pay without proof; they are responsible to the creditors of the deceased for what they have paid. But when an executor has paid a debt of the deceased to which there are witnesses, the payment is lawful, and he does not incur any responsibility. Whether he can pay when two just persons testify to a debt in his presence, but do not testify to it before the judge, and the debt is denied by the heirs,—is a point on which "our" shaikhs have differed; some saying that he may pay the debt, and others that he may not.—Fatáwá Alamgírí, vol. vi, pp. 216 & 235.—B. Dig., p. 679.

Principle. DCCCXC. If an executor pays the debt of one creditor without an order of the judge, he is responsible to the other creditors; but not so, if he pays by the judge's order.*

Principle. DCCCXCI. If, after the executor's expending the whole of the testator's estate upon his young children, a claim is made against it, and is established before the judge and decreed by him, the executor is not held responsible if the expenditure was made by order of the judge.*

When an executor has expended the whole of an estate upon young children, and nothing remains, after which a claim is made against the estate, and is established by proof before the judge who decrees it, can this creditor make the executor liable? No mention is made of the case in the book, but it seems that, if the expenditure was made by order of the judge, the executor is not responsible; whereas if it were made without the judge's order, he is liable.*

Principle. DCCCXCII. If, by the decree of a judge, a debt has been made obligatory on a testator's estate, and the executor has paid it by the judge's order, he is not in any way responsible.

Illustration. When a debt has been made obligatory on the estate of the deceased by the decree of a judge, and the executor has paid it, after which another debt arises against the deceased, as, for instance, if he had dug a well in his lifetime, into which a beast has

---

* Fatáwá Alamgírí, vol. vi, pp. 227, 235, 237.—B. Dig. pp. 579—681.

fallen so as to make him liable for the damage, or if he had sold a piece of armour which the purchaser returns to the executor on account of a defect, so as to make its price a debt against the deceased; is the executor in any way responsible? If he paid by order of the judge, he is not liable; nor is the judge.*

DCCCXCIII. But the second creditor may have recourse against the first for a share of what he received, proportionate to the debt, if what he received be still subsisting; and if it has perished in his hands, he is responsible to the second in the same proportion; but the executor is nowise liable. If, on the other hand, the executor had paid without the order of the judge, the second creditor may claim, either from the executor or the first creditor, a due proportion of what was received by the latter.* *Principle.*

DCCCXCIV. When an executor wishes to pay a debt to a creditor, and is apprehensive of other creditors appearing against the deceased, he may sell something belonging to the estate to the creditor in exchange for the debt, and will not then be responsible should another creditor appear as apprehended.* *Principle.*

DCCCXCV. An executor may give out the property of a minor in *muzárabat,* but he cannot lawfully give a long lease of part of the deceased's estate for the payment of debts; nor lend the property of a minor according to all reports; and if he should do so, he would be responsible.* *Principle.*

When an executor sells the orphan's property to himself, or his own to the orphan, the sale is lawful according to Abú Hanífah and Abú Yusuf also, by one report, when the sale is obviously for the benefit of the orphan, though unlawful when not obviously for his benefit. According to Muhummad and Abú Yusuf by another, and more probable report, such a sale is unlawful under any circumstances.*

---

* Fatáwá Alamgírí, vol. vi, pp. 227, 235, 237.—B. Dig., pp. 679—681.

Principle.

DCCCXCVI. When an executor of two orphans sells the property of one of them to the other, the sale is unlawful. So also, when he authorizes them to enter into such a transaction with each other, and one accordingly sells his property to the other, the sale is unlawful.*

* Fatáwá Alamgírí, vol. vi, pp. 227, 235, & 237.—B. Dig., pp. 679—681.

LECTURE IV.

ON WAKF, OR APPROPRIATION.

WAKF, in its primitive sense, means *detention.* In the language of the law (according to *Abú Hanífah),* it signifies the appropriatinn of a specific thing in such a way that the appropriator's right in it shall still continue, and the advantage thereof will be applied to charitable purposes nr other good objects.* The appropriator is held to be at liberty to resume it, and the sale or gift is consequently lawful. But the appropriator's right to all this is extinguished as soon as the judge has pronounced a decree.† — *Vide* Hidáyah, vol. ii, pp. 334, 335, 337 & 338.

According to the two disciples, however, *wakf* is the detention of a thing in the implied ownership of Almighty God, in such a manner that its profits may revert to, or be applied for, the benefit of mankind, and the appropriation is obligatory, so that the thing appropriated can neither be sold, nor given, nor inherited‡ In the *Ayún* and *Yatámá* it is stated that *the fatwá,* or decision, is in conformity with the

---

* Mr. Hamilton has unnecessarily restricted the legal meaning to appropriations of a "pious or charitable nature" (Hidáyah, vol. ii, note, p. 334) ; and he has been followed by Sir William Macnaghten, who renders the word *(wakf)* by "endowments." But it will be seen hereafter that the term is more comprehensive, and includes settlements on a person's *self* and children.—Note by Mr. Baillie, p. 549.

† There are two ways, however, in which it may be made obligatory : one is by the order of the judge making it so, and the other by the use of words of bequest in its constitution, as by saying "I have bequeathed the produce of my mansion," in which case also the appropriation becomes obligatory.—Fatáwá Alamgírí, vol ii, p. 454.—B. Dig., p. 550.

‡ According to the two disciples, *wakf* signifies the appropriation of a particular article in such a manner as subjects it to the rules of divine property, whence the appropriator's right in it is extinguished, and it becomes a property of God, by the advantage of it resulting to his creatures. The two disciples, therefore, hold the appropriation to be absolute ; and, consequently, that it cannot be resumed, or disposed of by gift or sale ; and that inheritance also does not obtain with respect to it.—Hidáyah, vol. ii, p. 335.

opinion of the two disciples.* The Hidáyah, as usual, gives the signification of *wakf* both by Abú Hanífah and his two disciples, Abú Yusuf and Muhammad, and then the arguments on both sides by saying, "Thus the term '*wakf*,' in its literal sense, comprehends all that is mentioned both by *Hanífah* and by the two disciples. Now, such being the case, no preference can be given to the tenets of one party over those of the other, as drawn from *the measuring of the term;* this preference, therefore, must be given as drawn from arguments."—*Vide* Hidáyah, vol. ii, pp. 335—339.

But it is clear from the following passage that the author of the Hidáyah gives preference to the doctrine of Abú Hanífah:—"With respect to what is reported from Hanífah,† that 'the appropriator's right of property is extinguished by a decree of the magistrate,'—our author remarks that this is approved doctrine, as such a decree removes all difference of opinion."—Hidáyah, vol. ii, pp. 337 & 338. His giving preference to the doctrine of Abú Hanífah can also be concluded from his citing the arguments of this lawyer *after* those of his two disciples (Abú Yusuf and Muhammad).‡

So, according to Abú Hanífah, the right of the appropriator abates as soon as the judge has pronounced his decree. The way to obtain which, say the compilers of Fatáwá Alamgírí, is for the proprietor to deliver the subject of the *wakf* to the *mutawallí*, or superintendent, and then to require it back

---

* *Vide* Fatáwá Alamgírí, vol. ii, p. 454.—B. Dig., p. 550.

The right of the appropriator ceases, in the opinion of Abú Yusuf and Muhammad (without the order of a judge); it, however, does so, according to the former, on his merely speaking the word; but, according to the latter, it does not cease till the appointment of a *walí*, or governor, and the delivery of the property to him. The opinions of the learned seem to be nearly balanced between them, two authorities declaring that the *fatwá* is with Abú Yusuf, while two more allege that it is with Muhammad.—Fatáwá Alamgírí, vol. ii, p. 455.—B. Dig., p. 551.

† It is reported by *Kadúrí* from Hanífah, that the appropriator's right of property is not extinguished, except where the magistrate so decrees, or where the appropriator himself suspends it upon his decease, by declaring "When I die, this house is appropriated to such a purpose," (and so forth). Abú Yusuf alleges that his right of property is extinguished upon the instant of his saying "I have appropriated,"—(and such also is the opinion of *Sháfií*), because that is a dereliction of property in the same manner as *manumission*. *Muhammad* says that it is not extinguished until he appoint a procurator, and deliver it over to him: and decrees are passed upon this principle.—Hidáyah, vol. ii, p. 337.

‡ *Vide* p. 42, Lecture I, delivered in 1873.

from him on the ground of the appropriation not being obligatory; whereupon the judge may pronounce his decree that it shall be obligatory, and it becomes so accordingly.—*Vide* Fatáwá Alamgírí, vol. ii, p. 484.—B. Dig., p. 550.

Thus the appropriation becomes valid, that is absolute, according to the various opinions of the three great lawyers,—according to Abú Hanífah, in consequence of the appropriator's declaration, and the magistrate's subsequent decree,—according to Abú Yusuf, by his simple declaration,—and according to Muhammad, by his declaration and delivery to a procurator. It passes out of the possession of the appropriator; but yet it does not become the property of any other person;* because, if this were the case, it would follow that it is not in a state of *detention*, but may be sold in the same manner as other property; and also, because if the person or persons to whom it is assigned were to become the *proprietor* of it, it would follow that it could not afterwards pass out of his possession in consequence of any condition stipulated by the former proprietor,—whereas it is *not* so, for if a person were to appropriate a *dwelling-house* (for instance) to the *poor* of a particular tribe, and the poverty of any one of those were afterwards removed, the right in it passes to the others, which it could not do if this person were a *proprietor.*—*Vide* Hidáyah, vol. ii, p. 339. Conclusion.

Decisions appear to be in both ways. Preference, however, seems to be given to the opinion of Muhammad. See the Foot note at page 114, and Hidáyah, vol. ii, p. 337.

DCCCXCVII. The pillars or essentials of *wakf* are special words declaratory of the appropriation† by the owner (*a*). Principle.

(*a*.) Such as "I have given this my land," or "bequeathed it as an appropriated or perpetual *sadakah* (charity)."†

DCCCXCVIII. The legal effect of *wakf*, according to the two disciples, is "an abatement of the propriator's right of Principle.

---

* When the property has passed out of the appropriator whether by decree of the judge, according to Abú Hanífah, or by the mere appropriation, according to Abú Yusuf, or by the appropriation and delivery, according to Muhammad, it does not enter into the property of the persons for whose benefit the appropriation is made.—Fatáwá Alamgírí, vol. ii, p. 455.—B. Dig., p. 551.

† Fatáwá Alamgírí, vol. ii, pp. 454 & 455.—B. Dig., pp. 451 & 452.

property in the thing appropriated in favor of Almighty God," and, according to Abú Hanífah, "a detaining of it in the ownership of the appropriator, but without the power of alienation,"* and "bestowing of its produce in charity."†

Conditions.

Principle. DCCCXCIX. Among the conditions of *wakf* are—"understanding and puberty on the part of the appropriator;"—as an appropriation by a boy or insane person is not valid. Freedom is also a condition, but not so *Islám.*†

Principle. DCCCC. It is also a condition that there be a nearness, that is, relation between the appropriator and the objects of the appropriation.†

So, appropriation by a Muslim or a Zimmí for a *temple,* or *church,* or for the poor of the enemy, is not valid.†

Principle. DCCCCI. It is further a condition that the thing appropriated be the appropriator's property at the time of the appropriation (*b*) †

Illustration. (*b.*) So that, if one were to usurp a piece of land, appropriate, and then purchase it from the owner, and pay the price, or compound with him for other property, which is actually delivered up, it would not be a *wakf.* When a man makes an appropriation for certain good purposes of land belonging to another, and then becomes the proprietor of it, the *wakf* is not lawful, though it would become so if allowed by the proprietor. And if a bequest were made of land of which the legatee immediately makes a *wakf,* after which the testator dies, the land is not *wakf;* or if a donee of land should make an appropriation of it before taking possession, and should then take possession, the *wakf* would not be valid. Yet, if possession were taken of land, given under an invalid gift, and it were then made a *wakf,* it would be lawful, the donee being responsible for its value; and if one should purchase by an invalid sale, take possession, and then make an appropriation of the subject of sale in favor of the poor, the *wakf* would be lawful, subject to the like responsibility for its value to the seller; but if the appropriation were made before taking posses-

---

* This, however, is till no decree is pronounced by the *Kází.*

† Fatáwá Alamgírí, vol. ii. pp. 454. 455, 457.—B. Dig.. pp. 451. 452, 554.

sion, it would not be lawful. When a man buys land by a lawful sale, and makes an appropriation of it before taking possession and paying the price, the matter is in suspense until he pays the price and takes possession, when the *wakf* is lawful; but if he die without leaving any property, the land is to be sold, and the *wakf* is void. And if a right is established in the property, or it is claimed by a *shafí*, under his right of pre-emption, after the purchase has been made, the *wakf* is void.*

DCCCCII. It is not necessary that there should be an entire freedom from the rights of other parties, as, for instance, in cases of pledge and lease (*c*).* *Principle.*

(*c*.) So that if one were to give a lease of his land, and then to make a *wakf* of it before the expiration of the term, the *wakf* would be binding according to its conditions, but the lease would not be void; and, on the expiration of the term, the land would revert to the purposes to which it was appropriated. In like manner, if a man should pledge his land, and then appropriate it before redeeming it from the pledge, the land would not be withdrawn from the pledge; and if it should remain for two years in the hands of the pledgee, and then be redeemed, it would revert to the uses for which it was appropriated. Even though the pledgor should die before the redemption, yet if he leave enough to redeem the land, it is to be redeemed, and the *wakf* is obligatory. But if he should not leave enough for that purpose, the land may be sold, and the *wakf* is void. In the case of a lease, when either of the contracting parties dies, it is void, and the land immediately becomes *wakf*.* *Illustration.*

DCCCCIII. Even though the pledgor should die before the redemption, yet if he leave enough to redeem the land, it is to be redeemed, and the *wakf* is obligatory. But if he should not leave enough for that purpose, the land may be sold, and the *wakf* is void. In the case of a lease, when either of the contracting parties dies, it is void, and the land immediately becomes *wakf*.* *Principle.*

DCCCCIV. It is also a condition that the party making the appropriation is not under inhibition at the time, either for facility of disposition, or debt.* *Principle.*

DCCCCV. The absence of uncertainty is also required; and if a person were to appropriate anything out of his land, without naming it, the appropriation would be void, *Principle.*

* Fatáwá Alamgírí, vol. ii, pp. 457 & 458.—B. Dig., pp. 554 & 555.

though if it were the whole of his share, without naming the portion, it would be lawful on a favorable construction (*d*).*

Illustration. (*d.*) A man makes *wakf* of his land, on which there are trees, excepting trees,—it is not lawful; because the trees, being excepted, with their sites, what enters within the *wakf* is unknown.

Principle. DCCCCVI. An appropriation is not complete according to Hanífah and Muhammad, unless the appropriator destine its ultimate application to objects not liable to become extinct (*e*).—Hidáyah, vol. ii, p. 341.

Example. (*e.*) As where, for instance, a man destines its application ultimately to the *poor* (as by saying—" I appropriate this to such a person, and after him to the *poor* "), because these never become extinct.—*Ibid.*

Principle. DCCCCVII. If a person appropriate land, and it should afterwards appear that an indefinite portion of the land was the property of another person, the appropriation is void with respect to the remainder also, according to Muhammad (*f*). If, however, it should appear that another is entitled to a portion of the land, of a *specific,* and not of an *undefined* nature, in this case, the appropriation is not void with respect to the remainder (*g*).—Hidáyah, vol. ii, p. 340.

(*f.*) Because, in this instance, the separation into *indefinite divisions* is associated with the appropriation, which is consequently invalid, in the same manner as a gift.†—*Ibid.*

(*g.*) Because of no indefinite division existing in this instance: and gifts and charitable donations are also subjects to the same analogy.—*Ibid.*

Principle. DCCCCVIII. It is also a condition that the appropriation be at once complete and not suspended on anything (*h*).*

---

* Fatáwá Alamgírí, vol. ii, p. 458.—B. Dig., pp. 555 & 556.

† It is otherwise where a donor resumes a part of his gift, or where the *heirs* of a donor, who had made the gift upon his death-bed, resume *two-thirds* of his gift after his decease, for if a person, upon his death-bed, make a gift or appropriation of the whole of his property, and the heirs resume two-thirds, still the gift or appropriation is not rendered void, because, in this instance, the separation into indefinite divisions is *supervenient*, and not *associated;* that is, at the time of the gift or appropriation the article was not divided into undefined portions, but became so afterwards.—Hidáyah, vol. ii. pp. 340 & 341.

(*h.*) As, if one should say "If my son arrives, my mansion is a charity appropriated to the poor," and the son should arrive, the mansion does not become *wakf*. And if one were to say "This my land is charity if such an one please," and the person referred to should indicate his pleasure, still the *wakf* would be void. But when one has said "If this mansion be my property, it is appropriated as charity," the appropriation is valid if the mansion actually be his property at the time of speaking; for the suspension is here on a condition that is actually fulfilled, and there is no contingency. A man loses his property, and says "If I find it, by God, I will make a *wakf* of my land," and he finds the property, it is incumbent on him to make a *wakf* of his land, for the benefit of those to whom it is lawful for him to pay *zakát*, or poor's-rate; and if he should make it for those to whom it is not lawful for him to pay *zakát*, the *wakf* would not be valid, nor he be released from his vow. If he should say "When such an one arrives," or "If I speak to such an one, this my land is charity," it is obligatory, being in the nature of an oath and a vow; and if the condition happen, it is obligatory on him to bestow his land in charity, but this is not an appropriation. When a man says "If I die of this my disease, I have made this my land *wakf*," it is not valid, whether he die or recover; but if he should say "If I die of this my disease, make this my land *wakf*," it is lawful. The difference is, that the latter expression amounts to a conditional appointment of an agent, which is lawful.* Illustration.

DCCCCIX. It is further a condition that there be no stipulation in the *wakf* for a sale of the property and expenditure of the price on the appropriator's necessities; and if there be so, the *wakf* is not valid.* *Principle.*

DCCCCX. Perpetuity is also among the conditions of *wakf* according to all opinions,—though, according to Abú Yusuf, the mention of it is not a condition, and this is correct (*i*).* *Principle.*

(*i.*) A man appropriates his mansion for a day, a month, or any specified time, without further addition,—the *wakf* is valid and perpetual. But if he should say "This my land is a *sadakah* appropriated for a month, and when the month has expired, the *wakf* is void," the *wakf* would be void immediately according to Hallál; because perpetuity being a condition, limitation to a par- Illustration.

* Fatáwá Alamgírí, vol. ii, pp. 457 & 458.—B. Dig., p. 556.

ticular time, is not lawful. If one should say "This my land is a *sadakah,* appropriated after my death for a year" without further addition, the appropriation would be lawful in perpetuity for the benefit of the poor, for the words have the meaning of a bequest. And if one should say "This my laud is a *sadakah,* appropriated to such an one after my death for a year, and when the year has expired the appropriation is void," it would be a bequest after his death to the person referred to for a year, and then it would become a legacy to the poor, and its produce would be distributed among them. But if he should say "My land is appropriated to such an one for a year after my death," without further addition, the produce would be to him for a year, and then it would revert to the heirs.*

According to Abû Hanífah and Muhammad,—

Principle. **DCCCCXI. It is further a condition, that the ultimate destination to which the rent or produce is to be applied is one that can never be cut off or fail, and, unless such be mentioned in the *wakf,* it is not valid.***

But, according to Abú Yusuf, the mention of it is not a condition. Nay, the *wakf is valid,* in his opinion, though a purpose is mentioned which is actually cut off or fails ; for, in that case, the rent or produce would revert to the poor, which must be supposed to be the appropriator's design, though he should fail to mention it.*

Principle. **DCCCCXII. Further, it is required that the subject of the *wakf* be either *akár,*† or a mansion. So that the *wakf* of anything that is movable, except beasts of burden, and arms, is not valid (unless accessory, or customary).*** ***Vide post,* pp. 123, 124.**

As to an option being annexed to a *wakf,* Muhammad is of opinion that no option should be annexed to it, and in case the condition of option is annexed to a *wakf,* the *wakf* would not be valid, though the condition itself is cancelled.‡ But Abú Yusuf,

---

* Fatáwá Alamgírí, vol. ii, pp. 457, 458 & 460.—B. Dig., pp. 557 & 558.

† The strict meaning of the word is "a space covered with buildings," so that properly speaking the term is not applicable to *zayat.* Fatáwá Alamgírí, vol. iii, p. 605. But according to the *Kifáyah* (vol. iv, p. 940) and the *Ináyah* (vol. iv, p. 263), *akár,* in the sense in which it is liable to pre-emption, includes a *Zayat.*

‡ The opinion of Muhammad being cited in the Hidáyah *after* that of Abú Yusuf, seems to have been approved by that authority.

maintains that a condition of option in favor of the appropriator for three days is valid. They both, however, were agreed with regard to the *wakf* of a *masjid* made on the condition of the appropriator's having an option, that the *wakf* would be lawful and the option void.*

If the appropriator reserve to himself a right of changing the lands he appropriates for any other lands, at pleasure, it is lawful according to Abú Yusuf. Muhammad maintains that the appropriation itself is valid, but that the condition reserved is void, because the condition does not prevent an extinction of right of property; and the appropriation is consequently complete, because of the extinction of this right; but the *condition*, as being invalid, is void, in the same manner as the reserve of a right of change, in the foundation of a mosque, is void.—Hidáyah, vol. ii, p. 351.

The words by which wakf is, and is not, effected.

DCCCCXIII. *Wakf*, or appropriation, is effected by the expression of the word *wakf* (detention or appropriation), combined with that of *sadakah*, or charity (*f*); or the expression of the word *wakf* alone is sufficient for the purpose (*g*). *Principle.*

(*f*.) When a person has said "This my land is a *sadakah*, or charity, freed and perpetual, during my life and after my death," or "This my land is a *sadakah*, appropriated, detained, and perpetual, during my life and after my death," or "This my land is a *sadakah*, detained and perpetual during my life and after my death," the land becomes a *wakf*, lawful and obligatory for the benefit of the poor according to all opinions. And if he should say "a *sadakah* appropriated and perpetual," it would be lawful according to the generality of "our" learned men; or if he should say "a *sadakah* appropriated," or "a *sadakah* detained," without saying "perpetual," the land would become a *wakf* according to all who consider appropriation lawful, because a perpetual *sadakah* is established which does not admit of cancellation. The words, "This my land is a *sadakah*, appropriated to what is good" or "to good purposes," also amount to a *wakf*.* *Illustrations.*

(*g*.) Though no mention be made of *sadakah*, yet if *wakf* is mentioned, as by a person's saying "This my land is *wakf*," or "I have made this my land *wakf*," or "appropriated," the land would be a *wakf* for the poor according to Abú Yusuf. And Sadar-ush-Shahíd and the Shaikhs of Bulkh have said, "Decrees

---

* Fatáwá Alamgírí, vol. ii, pp. 459 & 460.—B. Dig., pp. 557 & 558.

are given on the opinion of Abú Yusuf, and we decree according to it; also, from regard to custom." And if he should say "it is appropriated to Almighty God for ever," it would be lawful without the word *sadakah*, and would be a *wakf* for the poor. The word "*wakf*" alone, or in combination with *habs*, establishes a *wakf* according to the approved opinion, which is that of Abú Yusuf. If one should say "I have made this my land prohibited," or "it is prohibited," that would be the same in the opinion of Abú Yusuf; according to Abú Jaafar, as if he had said "appropriated." If a person should say "This my land is appropriated for such an one," or "on my son," or "the poor of my kindred, being good persons," or "orphans, and the appropriation of it is not to be reversed," it would be no *wakf* according to Muhammad, because it is for a purpose that may be cut off or fail, and is not perpetual: but it would be a *wakf* according to Abú Yusuf, because the making of it perpetual is not a condition with him. If one should say "My land," or "my mansion is a *sadakah*, appropriated for such an one," or "the children of such an one," they would be entitled to the produce while they lived, and after their decease it would go to the poor. If one should say "My land is *sadakah* for God," or "appropriated to Almighty God," it would become *wakf*. So also, if he were to say "My land is appropriated for a good purpose," it would be as lawful as if he had said "a *sadakah* appropriated."*

Remarks.

There is a distinction between a *wakf* and a vow, and it is as follows:—A man says "This my land is *sadakah*;" this is a *nazr*, or vow, to bestow in charity; and if he bestow the specific thing or its price, it is lawful. And if he say "I have made a *sadakah* of this my land on the poor," there is no *wakf*, but a vow which obliges him to bestow the specific thing or its value; and if he do so, he is absolved from his vow; but if not, the land may be inherited from him, and the judge cannot compel him to apply it in charity, for what he has said is in the place of a vow. Nor if he should say "This my land is *sadakah* for good purposes," would this be a *wakf*? Nay, it would be a vow. And if the words were "I have given the produce of this my mansion to the poor," it would be a vow to give the produce in charity; or if the words were "I have given this my mansion to the poor," it would be a vow to give the mansion itself. And if he should say "*Sadakah* not to be sold," it would be a vow of charity, not a *wakf*. But if he were to add "not to be given, and not to be inherited," it would be a *wakf* for the poor.*

---

* Fatáwá Alamgírí, vol. ii, pp. 460 & 461.—B. Dig., p. 559 & 560.

On the proper subjects of wakf, or appropriation, and of what things appropriation is or is not lawful.

DCCCCXIV. An appropriation of *akár** is lawful,—as of lands, mansions, shops; so also of every movable that may be an accessory to it (*a*).† *Principle.*

(*a*.) As when a man has appropriated his land with its slaves, cattle and implements of husbandry. But when a person appropriates his land with the slaves and cattle at work thereon, he ought to mention them, and specify their number; and should further make it a condition that they are to be maintained out of the produce; though if he fail to do so, they are to be maintained notwithstanding. But when their maintenance is made an express condition, it is to be continued as long as they live, though they should be sick and disabled from working, unless it be added "for working on the land."† Illustration.

DCCCCXV. With regard to movables, when designedly appropriated, if they are beasts of burden or weapons of war, the *wakf* of them is lawful (*h*).† *Principle.*

ANNOTATIONS.

dccccxiv, dccccxv. The appropriation of *land* is lawful; because several of the Prophet's companions appropriated their lands; but the appropriation of *movable* property is altogether unlawful, whether purposely, or as a dependant. This is the opinion of *Hanífah*. *Abú Yusuf* alleges that if a person appropriate lands, together with the cattle and slaves attached to them, it is lawful; and the same of all instruments of husbandry; because those are all dependants of the soil in the fulfilment of the design; the appropriation of these, therefore, as dependants of the land, is lawful; for many things are admissible *dependantly*, which are not so *positively*; thus the sale of *wine* (for instance) *by itself* is unlawful, whereas *along with land* it is lawful;—and in the same manner the appropriation of the beam of a house is unlawful, whereas *along with* the house it is clearly legal. The opinion of *Muhammad*, also, accords with that of *Abú Yusuf* in this point.—Hidáyah, vol. ii, pp. 342 & 343.

* See the foot-note at page 120.

† Fatáwá Alamgírí, vol. ii, p. 462.—B. Dig., pp. 561 & 562.

DCCCCXVI. As to other things than the above, if they are not such things as it is not the custom to appropriate, the *wakf* of them is unlawful. When, again, they are such as it is customary to appropriate (*Kurán*, for instance), the *wakf* of them is lawful according to Muhammad, whose opinion is approved by the great body of the learned, and has been adopted for the *fatwá*.*

Principle.

Illustration.

The appropriation of things which are consumed in using, such as gold and silver, or eatables and drinkables, is not unlawful according to the generality of the lawyers; but by gold and silver are not to be understood *dínárs* and *dirhams*, or what is not ornament. And if one should make an appropriation of *dirhams* or things estimated by measure, or clothes, it would not be lawful. But it is said that in places where this is customary, decrees are given in favor of the legality of the appropriation.*

If it be asked how, that is, how can the money be applied? it is answered that the *dirhams* may be lent to the poor and taken back again,† or given in *muzárabat*, and the profit laid out in charity; and wheat may be lent to the poor to sow and then taken from them, and clothes lent to them to wear when necessary, and then taken back.*

ANNOTATIONS.

dccccxvi. It is not lawful to appropriate movables, the appropriation of which is unusual or uncommon according to our doctors. The argument of our doctors is that appropriation requires *perpetuity* according to what has been already stated; and this cannot exist in *movables*, since these are not of a lasting nature: analogy, therefore, suggests that the appropriation of movables *in general* is unlawful:—it is admitted, however, in some articles, (although contrary to analogy), because of the traditions already recorded,—and in other articles (such as *axes*, *saws*, and so forth), because of *utility*: but the appropriation of furniture, clothes, and slaves is unlawful, as being contrary to the suggestions of analogy, because they have neither tradition nor utility to support the legality, and therefore resemble *dirhams* and *dínárs*.—Hidáyah, vol. ii, p. 344.

* Fatáwá Alamgírí, vol. ii, p. 462.—B. Dig.. pp. 561 & 562.

† Without interest is implied.—If the money were laid out in Government securities, or the like, and the interest or dividends applied to the purposes of the *wakf*, it does not appear to me that the objection would apply, as in the buying and selling of these there is no exchange of things of the same kind; and it is by no means uncommon for Musalmáns in India to take interest in that way.—Note by Mr. Baillie.

DCCCCXVII. Confusion in things (*mushâá*) that do not admit of partition does not prevent the validity of a *wakf;* and on this point there is no difference of opinion.* *Principle.*

For the *wakf* of half a bath is lawful, though it be confused. But the *wakf* of an undivided share in a thing that admits of partition is not lawful according to Muhammad, whose opinion has been adopted by the learned of Bukhara. The moderns, however, decide according to the opinion of Abú Yusuf. who said that it was lawful; and that is approved.† Hence,— Illustration

DCCCCXVIII. The *wakf* of an undivided share in a thing that admits of partition is also lawful.* *Principle.*

However,—

DCCCCXIX. Both doctors agreed in negativing the *wakf* of a *mushâá* (that is, a thing not divided) for a masjid, or a burial ground, whether the property be susceptible of division or not.* *Principle.*

DCCCCXX. They were also agreed that if the whole of a thing be appropriated, and a partition is subsequently decreed, it is not lawful.* But,— *Principle.*

ANNOTATIONS.

dccccxviii. The appropriation of an undivided part or portion is lawful according to Abú Yusuf. Such as the half, or the fourth, of a field, house, &c.—Hidáyah, vol. ii, p. 339.

Abú Yusuf also maintained that the *wakf* of a *mushâá* is valid, while Muhammad was of a contrary opinion.—Fatáwá Alamgírí, vol. ii, p. 454.—B. Dig., p. 551.

dccccxx. When one has appropriated his share in land held in joint ownership, the person with whom a partition is to be made is the partner, and, after his death, his executor. And when a person has appropriated half of his own land, the proper party to make a partition is the judge; or if he sell his remaining share, the purchaser may make the partition, and the seller may then purchase back the share from him.—Fatáwá Alamgírí, vol. ii, p. 466.—B. Dig., p. 564.

* Fatáwá Alamgírí, vol. ii, p. 466.—B. Dig., p. 564.

† According to the law officers of the Sudder Dewanny Adawlut of Calcutta (Reports, vol. i, p. 214) the whole series of *fatwás*, or expositions of the law, coincide with Abú Yusuf on this point.

Principle. DCCCCXXI. When the judge has given his decree for the validity of a *wakf* of *mushaâ*, his decree is operative, as in all other matters on which there is a difference of opinion.*

Illustration. If a person appropriate his share in partnership lands, he must divide it off, and detach it from those of his partner. If, on the other hand, a person appropriate the half (for instance) of his own land, in this case, the *Kází* is to divide it off, and alienate it from the appropriator. For the appropriator is not at liberty himself to divide off the portion of land which he has appropriated, or to separate it from that portion which he has *not* appropriated, because *one* person is incapable of *himself* making a division and thus giving *to himself*, since division can take place only between *two*.—Hidáyah, vol. ii, p. 345.

Principle. DCCCCXXII. Upon an appropriation becoming valid and absolute, the sale or transfer of the thing appropriated is unlawful according to all lawyers.—Hidáyah, vol. ii, p. 344.

On the Purposes for which a Property may be appropriated.

Principle. DCCCCXXIII. An appropriation for the kindred of the Prophet is lawful according to the most approved opinion.†

Principle. DCCCCXXIV. An appropriation for travellers is lawful; but it is to be applied to the poor among them exclusively of the rich.†

And if one should say "to perform the *hajj* every year with the produce," or "to bestow every year in charity instead of my sins of omission," or "to pay my debts," it would be lawful, if the ultimate destination were a perpetuity for the poor. So also if he should say "My land is a *sadakah* appropriated for *jihád*, or religious wars," or "shrouds for the dead," or "digging their graves," it would be lawful.†

Principle. DCCCCXXV. An appropriation for *súfís* is not lawful according to some; but others have said that it is lawful, and that the produce is to be expended on the poor among them. This opinion is correct.†

---

* Fatáwá Alamgírí, vol. ii, p. 466.—B. Dig., p. 564.

† Fatáwá Alamgírí, vol. ii, pp. 467 & 468.—B. Dig., pp. 566 & 567.

What is included in wakf without express mention, and what is not so included.

DCCCCXXVI. When a mansion has been appropriated without mentioning that it is with all its rights, and every thing small and great belonging to it, or *in* or *of* it, every thing that would be included in the sale of it is included in the *wakf.* So also in the *wakf* of *shops*, every thing is included that would be included in the sale thereof.* *Principle.*

DCCCCXXVII. In the *wakf* of a land the buildings and trees standing thereon are included therein, but not the fruit then on the trees: nor the crop if the land has already been sown. Canes and other plants that are cut annually are not included, but such as are cut biennially are included in the *wakf* of the land. *Principle.*

Khassáf has mentioned in his book on *wakf*, that when a man in good health has made an appropriation of his land for specified purposes, and after these for the poor, the buildings and the palm and other trees on the land are included in the *wakf.* He has also mentioned that fruit is not included in an appropriation of trees; and most of "our" Shaikhs are of that opinion, and it is correct. And if one should say "I have appropriated this my land as a *sadakah*, with its rights and all that is *in* it and *of* it," and there happens to be at the time fruit on the trees, he ought to bestow the fruit in charity on the poor, though not by way of *wakf*, but by virtue of his vow, on a favorable construction, and what is subsequently produced is to be applied to the purposes specified in the *wakf.* And if he should say "My land is appropriated as a *sadakah* after my death to the end, that what produce God may cause to come out of it shall be to the servants of God," and then dies leaving fruit actually on the trees, the fruit does not enter into the bequest by virtue of the *wakf.** *Illustrations.*

When land is appropriated which has been sown, the growth is not included, whether it have any value or not. Canes and other plants that are cut annually are not included, but such as are cut biennially are included in a *wakf* of the land.*

* Fatáwá Alamgírí, vol. ii, p. 466.—B. Dig., p. 563.

DCCCCXXVIII. When a man has appropriated his land without mentioning a right of water or way, both are included on a favorable construction.*

Principle.

Because land is not appropriated except on account of what it will produce, and for that purpose both are included.*

Mills in a field (*Zayat*), whether water or landmills, and Persian wheels and buckets used for raising water, are included in the appropriation of it.*

On Disbursements with respect to a wakf property.

Principle. DCCCCXXIX. The income of a *wakf* is to be expended in the first place or necessary repairs, whether the appropriator has made it a condition or not; and next, if nothing else has been specified, on such things as are nearest and most essential to the general purpose of the appropriation (*a*).*

Example. (*a.*) As, for instance, in providing an Imám for a *masjid*, or place of worship, and a professor for a *madrasah*, or college.*

Principle. DCCCCXXX. But if anything else has been specified, the income must be applied to that immediately after the repairs.*

Illustration. If a person should say "I have given the produce to such an one for a year, or for two years, and after that to the poor," and should make it a condition that the repairs are to be made out of the produce, the repairs are to be postponed to the right of the person, unless the postponement of them should be for the manifest injury of the *wakf*, in which case the repairs must first be made.*

ANNOTATIONS.

dccccxxvii. It is incumbent that the income of an appropriation be in the first instance expended in the repairs† of it, whether the appropriator may have stipulated this or not; because his design was that the income should serve as a perpetual fund; and as a perpetual income cannot be drawn from the article appropriated unless it be preserved in continual repair, that is a necessary attendant upon it, and also, because all acquisition must be attended with expense,—in other words, he who enjoys the profit must also bear the loss.—Hidáyah, vol. ii, p. 346.

* Fatáwá Alamgírí, vol. ii, p. 468.—B. Dig., p. 565.

† Arab. *Támír:* meaning, the rendering of a place habitable, by *cultivation*, if it be *land*, or by *rebuilding*, *&c.*, if it be houses.—Note by the Translator of the *Hidáyah*.

DCCCCXXXI. If a person appropriate a *house* with this condition, that his *son* or any other person shall reside therein during life, the repairs are incumbent upon him who has the right to inhabit it. *Principle.*

Because he who enjoys the profit must also bear the loss.—Hidáyah, vol. ii, p. 347.

DCCCCXXXII. If, therefore, the person in question refuse or neglect to repair the house, or be incapable of so doing from poverty, the magistrate must, in this case, let it, and provide for the repairs out of the rent; and must return it to him upon the repairs being completed.—*Ibid.* *Principle.*

Because by this means attention is paid to the rights both of the appropriator and of the person to whose use it is appropriated.—*Ibid.*

DCCCCXXXIII. If any part of the buildings of the *wakf* should fall down, the *hákim* should use the materials for repairs, if any are required, and if not, preserve them for a future occasion; or if there, is any good objection to his doing so, he may sell them, and apply the price in making repairs when required.* *Principle.*

It is proper to observe that—

DCCCCXXXIV. It is not lawful for the *occupant* to let the house, since he is not the *proprietor*. The magistrate, on the contrary, possesses a general power, as being the agent of the community.—Hidáyah, vol. ii, p. 348. *Principle.*

Such buildings or materials of an appropriation as become damaged or useless, must be employed by the magistrate, in the repairs of it, where necessary; and if these be not immediately necessary, he must keep the articles in question until such time *Illustration.*

ANNOTATIONS.

dccccxxxiii, dccccxxxiv. If one should appropriate his mansion for the residence of his child, the repairs are to be made by the person who has the right of residence; and if he refuse, or is poor, the *hákim*, or judge, is to let the mansion, and to make the repairs out of the rent; and when these have been completed, he should restore it to the person entitled to reside in it. But that person cannot be compelled to make the repairs, nor is he at liberty to let the mansion.—Fatáwá Alamgírí, vol. ii, p. 468.—B. Dig., pp. 565 & 566.

* Fatáwá Alamgírí, vol. ii, p. 468.—B. Dig., pp. 565 & 566.

as occasion offers, when he must employ them in making the necessary repairs; as repairs are required from time to time, in order that the appropriation may be continually preserved, and the design of the appropriator answered. If the materials of the decayed place be damaged so much as to render it impracticable to employ them in the repairs (by the *timbers* being *broken*, for instance), it is incumbent on the magistrate to sell them, and expend the price in such repairs: but it is not lawful for him to give them to the occupants, because the timbers, and so forth, are constituent parts of the actual appropriation, in which no person has any right,—their right being merely to the *use*, and not to the thing itself.—Hidáyah, vol. ii, pp. 348 & 349.

On the wakf or settlement by a person on himself, his children and offspring (Nasl).*

Principle.

DCCCCXXXV. A person can lawfully settle his land first on himself, then on another person, and after him upon the poor; or first upon a person and then upon himself.

Illustration.

A man says "My land is a *sadakah* settled on myself." Such an appropriation is lawful according to what is approved. So also if he should say "I have settled* it on myself, and after me on such an one, and then upon the poor," it would be lawful according to Abú Yusuf. And if one should say "My land is settled on such an one, and after him upon me," or should say "upon me and upon such an one," or "upon my slave and upon such an one," the approved opinion is that it would be valid.†

Principle.

DCCCCXXXVI. When a man has made a valid appropriation of his land upon his child (*valad*), and after him upon the poor, the child who may be in existence at the time of the existence of the produce enters into the benefit of the *wakf* whether he were born at the time of the appropriation of the *wakf* or not (*a*). And, in like manner, if the words were "on my child, and what child may happen to me, and when they fail, upon the poor" (*b*).†

(*a*.) Such was the saying of Halláh, and it was adopted by the learned of Balkh, and is approved.†

---

* Though I use the words "settlement" and "settled" in this section as being more appropriate to the subject of the *wakf*, the original words are the same as those generally translated "appropriation" and "appropriated." Note by Mr. Baillie, who made the above translation from the *Fatáwá Alamgírí*.

† Fatáwá Alamgírí, vol. ii, p. 471.—B. Dig., p. 567.

(*b.*) When a man has made use of these words, though he have no child at the time, the appropriation is valid; and the produce, when there is any, is to be divided among the poor. If a child should be born to him after the division, the subsequent produce is to be expended on his child so long as he lives; and when there is no surviving child, it is to be expended on the poor.*

DCCCCXXXVII. If a man should say "I have settled on my children (*oulád*)," males and females are included (*c*).* *Principle.*

(*c.*) But in every case in which a right is established in favor of *children*, it is children of known paternity (*nasab*) that are included. Hence, if there be a child who is not of known paternity, but whose paternity is known on the word of the appropriator, such child is not included.* Illustrations.

For example, when a man has said "I have settled this my land on my child," and his bondmaid is subsequently delivered of a child within six months of there being produce of the land, and he claims the child, though its descent from him is established, it has no share in the produce. But if his wife, or *um-i-walad*, should be delivered of a child within six months from the time of the produce, the child would be entitled to a share in the *wakf*. If, however, the delivery should not take place till six months or more, the child would have no right to participate.*

DCCCCXXXVIII. A right attaches to the produce as soon as it has value. *Principle.*

For determining the day when a right attaches to the produce, Hallâl has said that it is the day when the produce has value: and he has not made it a condition that there shall be anything over and above the actual expenses.* But,—

DCCCCXXXIX. When a right is annexed to a quality, it has reference to the time of the *wakf*, or to the time of the produce, according as the quality is fixed or transient. *Principle.*

If one should say "My land is a *sadakah* settled on my one-eyed and blind children," the *wakf* is theirs to the exclusion of all others; and one-eyedness or blindness is to be regarded as of the day of the settlement, not of the existence of the produce. So also if he should say "On the little ones among my children," the *wakf* is for them specially, and the right is to be reckoned as appertaining to such of them as are little at the time of the settlement, not of the existence of the produce. But if the appropria- Illustrations.

* Fatáwa Alamgírí, vol. ii, p. 471.—B. Dig., pp. 567 & 568.

tion were "for my children who are dwelling in Bussorah," the residence is to be regarded as having reference to the time of the existence of the produce. The result is that when the right is established on a quality that does not cease, or if it ceases, does not return after it has once ceased, it is to be regarded as having reference to the existence of the quality at the time of the settlement; but when the right is established on a quality that ceases and returns again after it has ceased, the right is regarded as having reference to the existence of the quality at the time of the coming of the produce. When a man has settled his land on his male child, males only are included and not females, because he has described the child by a quality that does not cease. And if he should say "My land is settled on the males of my children, and the children of the males of my children," those only are included who are in existence having this quality on the day of making the settlement. But if he should say "I have settled it on those of my children who profess the Muslim faith," or "on those of my children who are married," all those are included who have professed the Muslim faith, or been married since that day, and not those who were *then* Muslims or married. And if he were to say "Among the poor of my children," without further addition, those who are poor at the time of the occurrence of the produce are included. If he should say "Among those who have become poor among my children," though, according to Muhammad, the produce would be for those only who from being rich have become poor; yet, according to others, it would be for all those who are poor at the time of the produce, whether they were previously in better circumstances or not; and this is correct. And if the words were, "all who are in need of my children," every one answering that description at the time of the produce would be included.*

Child means "child of loins" where there is in existence, and if none, "child of a son." Failing whom it includes all of the lower generations in existence.

The child and child of a child include two generations, and child and child of a child and his child include the present and future generations.

A man has said "This my land is a *sadakah* settled on my child" (*walad*); the produce is for the child of his loins, males and females taking equally, and so long as there is in existence one child of his loins, the produce is to him or her only. When there no longer remains one of the first generation (*batn*), the produce is to be expended on the poor, nothing being allowed to the

* Fatáwá Alamgírí, vol. ii, p. 473.—B. Dig., pp. 569–571.

child of a child. But if he had no child of his loins at the time of the settlement, and there was then a child of a son, the produce is to the son's child, none of the generations besides him participating with him; the child of a son in the event of there being no child of the loins, thus coming into his place. The child of a daughter is not included, according to the *Záhir ur-Rawáyet*, which is correct. If, after this, he should have a son of his loins, the future produce is to be expended on him. When there is no child of the first or second generations, but there happens to be a third and fourth generation, and others besides, the third generation, and those below them, participate together, even though there should be many of them. Everything that has been said of the words "my child" is applicable to the words "child of such an one."*

If one should say "This my land is a *sadakah* settled on my child, and child of my child," the child of his loins, and the child of his child in existence on the day of the settlement, and those who are born afterwards are included, and the two generations participate in the produce, but none below them are included, nor the children of daughters, according to the *Záhir ur-Rawáyet*, and the *fatwá* is in accordance with it. And if he should say, "Upon my child, and child of my child, and child of the child of my child," mentioning three generations, the produce is to be expended upon his children for ever, so long as there are any descendants, and is not to be applied to the poor; while one remains the *wakf* is to that one, and the lowest among them; the nearer and more remote being alike, unless the appropriator say in making the *wakf*, "the nearer is nearer," or say "on my child, then afterwards on the child of my child," or say "generation after generation" *(batnan baád batn)*, when a beginning must be made with them with whom the appropriator has begun.*

If he (the appropriator) should say "This my land is a *sadakah* settled on my children" *(oulád)*, all generations are included on account of the general character of the name; but the whole is to the first generation while any remains; and when they are exhausted, to the second; and when they are exhausted, to the third, fourth, and fifth; all these generations participating in the division, and the nearer and more remote being alike.*

If he should say "I have settled it on my children," and he has only one child at the time of the produce, half of it will be for that child and half to the poor. But if the words were "on my child," and he has only one, the whole of the appropriation is

---

* Fatáwá Alamgírí, vol. ii, p. 474.—B. Dig., pp. 571 & 572.

for that child. So also when he has had several children and they have failed, leaving only one remaining.*

A man appropriates an estate by the words "*sadakah* on my two children, and when they fail then upon the children of both, and the children of the children of both for ever so long as there are descendants," and one of the children dies leaving a child, half of the produce is to be expended on the surviving child, and half to the poor; but when the second of the children of the appropriator dies, the whole of the produce is then to be expended on the children of the two, and the children of the children of the two. If he should say "This estate is *sadakah* settled on the needy of my children," and there is only one needy child among them, the half of the produce is to be expended on him and half on the poor.*

Principle. DCCCCXL. If a person should say "This my land is a *sadakah* settled on my sons," and has two or more sons, the produce is to them. If he have but one at the time of the existence of the produce, half of it is to him and the other half to the poor; and if he have sons and daughters the produce is to them equally, according to Hallál, and this is correct, and is as if he had said "My land is settled on my brothers," having brothers and sisters, when they would all participate.*

Principle. DCCCCXLI. And if he should say "Upon my sons," and he has no sons, but only daughters, the produce would be to the poor; and, in like manner, if he should say "Upon my daughters," and he has only sons, the produce would be to the poor.*

Principle. DCCCCXLII. If one should settle his estate "on his son and his children and the children of his children, for ever so long as there are descendants," the produce is to be divided among them, according to the number of heads, males and females being on an equal footing, and the children of daughters being included.*

Principle. DCCCCXLIII. If one should make a settlement on his *nasl* or *zariyat* (both words meaning progeny), the children of his sons and the children of his daughters would be included, whether near or remote. But if the settlement were on one who is related to him (*man yunsibu*), the children of daughters would not be included.*

---

* Fatáwá Alamgírí, vol. ii, pp. 174 & 175.—B. Dig., pp. 571—573.

A man has said "My land is *sadakah* settled on my child and my *nasl*," the settlement is valid, and the males and females of his children and children's children are included; the near and the remote, the children of sons and the children of daughters, the free and slave, being all equal, though the share of the slaves belong to their master. And if he should say "I have settled it on my child and my *nasl*," and he has also a grandchild at the time, but a child of his loins is born to him after the settlement, they both enter into the right. So also if he should say "This my land is *sadakah* settled on my children in being, and on my *nasl*," a child subsequently born would enter by means of the word used, *nasl*. If the words were "on my children in being and their *nasl*," the children in being and their *nasl* would enter, whether the *nasl* were in being or not, but none of his children who are not in being, nor their *nasl*, would be included. So also if he had said "Upon my children in being, and their children," and there should afterwards be born to him a child of his loins, that child would not be included. And if he should say "Upon my children in being, and on the children of their children, and their *nasl*," his children in being and their children, and the children of their children for ever while there are any *nasl* or descendants, are included; but if he should say "Upon my children in being, and the children of their children," and were silent, the child of a child would have nothing.* Illustration.

DCCCCXLIV. Under a settlement on children and their *nasl*, all descendants are equally entitled, unless there are words to indicate that generations are to take successively. *Principle.*

When one in good health says "I have made this my land a *sadakah* appropriated to Almighty God for ever, for my child, and child of my child, and children of their children, and their *nasl* for ever so long as there is *nasl*," every child that he had at the time of the appropriation, and every child born to him thereafter before the existence of the produce, and child of the child for ever, enter into the benefit of the produce of this *sadakah*; and if any of them should die before the existence of produce, the share of the person so dying would fall to the ground; but if the death should not occur till after the existence of the produce, the person dying would have acquired a right to his share, which would pass to his heirs—the higher and lower generations sharing equally, unless it had been said in making the appropriation that a beginning was to be made with the higher generation, and Illustration.

---

* Fatáwá Alamgírí, vol. ii, p. 475.—B. Dig., pp. 573 & 574.

then the generation below it. In that case, if all of the higher generation but one person should die, the whole would go to that person alone to the exclusion of the generation below. And if one should say "For my child and child of my child for ever, so long as there is any *nasl*," adding, "as often as one dies his share of the produce is to his child," the produce would be among the whole of the children and children's children and their *nasl* equally; and if one of them should die leaving a child, the share of the person so dying would go to his child, who would thus have his father's share in addition to that appointed for himself by the appropriator.*

Principle.

DCCCCXLV. A settlement for children is for the benefit of survivors.

Illustration.

A man has settled his land on his children (*aulád*) with an ulterior destination for the poor, and some of the children die: their shares, according to *Hallál*, are to be expended on the survivors, and when they all die, the produce is to be expended on the poor, and not on any child of a child. But if he had settled it on his children, naming them, saying "Upon such an one, and such an one, and such an one," with an ulterior destination for the poor, and one of them should happen to die, his share would go to the poor.*

Principle.

DCCCCXLVI. Under a settlement on the heirs, they all share equally with benefit of survivorship.

Illustrations.

If one should make a settlement on the heirs of Zayid, and Zayid is living, there is nothing for his heirs, and the whole produce passes to the poor. But if Zayid should die, the whole of the produce must then be divided among his existing heirs, according to the number of them, males and females sharing alike; and if some of them should die, their shares would belong to those alive at the time of the coming of the produce; while, if only one survived, half of the produce would be to him, and the other half to the poor. If, instead of the heirs, he should say "The children of Zayid, being such an one and such an one," naming them up to five, none but the five would be entitled, and if a child were born subsequently he would have no share.*

If a man should say "This my land is a *sadakah* settled after my death on my child, and child of my child, and their *nasl*," and should then die, the appropriation as to the child of his loins is not lawful, but as to his child's child it is lawful. So long,

---

* Fatáwá Alamgírí, vol. ii, p. 475.—B. Dig., pp. 573—575.

however, as there is a child of the loins living, the produce is to be divided every year according to the number of heads, and what comes to the child of a child is *wakf*, and what comes to a child of the loins is heritage, to be divided among all the heirs, so that a husband and wife and others participate. If in these circumstances some of the children of the loins should die, the produce is to be divided according to the number of heads of the children's children and surviving children of the loins, and what pertains to the surviving children of the loins is to be divided among all the heirs living and dead of those who were alive at the death of the appropriator.—Fatáwá Alamgírí, vol.ii, p. 478.—B. Dig., p. 575.

Settlement on karábat, or kindred.*

Abú Yusuf and Muhammad have said that by *karábat* is to be understood everyone related to a person through a common ancestor up to the farthest back in *Islám,* either on the father's or the mother's side, and whether within the prohibited degrees or not, and that the near and the remote are alike in this respect, whether the word be in the singular or in the plural.†

But, according to Abú Hanífah, when the settlement is made in the singular, as, for instance, "on my *karábat*—on a person of my *karábat*," it is the nearest of the relatives within the prohibited degrees that enters into the benefit of the *wakf;* while if the settlement be in the plural, as, for instance, "on persons of my *karábat*—on my *akrabah*" (or relatives), the whole of those above-mentioned are included; so that the words are applicable to less or more.†

DCCCCXLVII. In a *wakf* on the *Karíb*,‡ the produce is divided according to heads—the young and the old, the male and female, the poor and rich being alike.† *Principle.*

Because the noun is equally applicable to all. But neither the father of the appropriator nor the children of his loins are included, nor his grandfather, according to the Záhir-ur-Rawáyet.†

---

* *Karábat* means literally propinquity or relationship, but here it is used in the sense of persons related.

† Fatáwá Alamgírí, vol. ii, pp. 477 & 478.—B. Dig., pp. 575—577.

‡ "*Karíb*" is the singular of *Akrabah*, and means near, whence a relative.

DCCCCXLVIII. If a person has made a settlement on the needy of his *karábat*, and then died, the needy child of his child is not entitled to it, he not being of the *karábat*.

Principle.

Illustration.

A man has made a settlement on the needy of his *karábat*, and then died, may the superintendent give of the produce to a son of the appropriator's son when poor? According to Abú Hanífah and Abú Yusuf, he cannot, for the child of a child, according to them, is not of the *karábat*.*

Principle.

DCCCCXLIX. When a person has made a settlement on the nearest of men to him, and after that to the indigent, and has a son or a father, he enters into the benefit of *wakf*; though his words were "on the nearest of men among my *karábat*," they would not enter into it.*

Illustrations.

If he has a son or a daughter, or both parents, the son or daughter alone is entitled, and on their death the produce belongs to the indigent and not to the parents; while, if he have his parents only, the produce is to them in halves, and if either should die, his or her half would pass to the poor. In like manner, if he have ten sons, and one of them should die, his share goes to the indigent.*

And if he has a mother and brothers, or a mother and grandfather, the produce is to her alone to the exclusion of the others, she being the nearer. The same is true of the father also.*

And a father is nearer than a son's son; but a son's son is preferred to a full brother, and a daughter's daughter to a son's descendant in a lower grade. So also a daughter's daughter's daughter is preferred to a full sister.*

Settlement on the poor of one's kindred.

Principle.

DCCCCL. When a man has said "This is my *sadakah* settled on the poor of my kindred, or the poor of my children, and after them on the indigent," the settlement is valid, and the persons entitled are those of them who are poor at the time of coming of the produce (*a*).*

(*a*.) According to Hallál, whose opinion we approve, and the *fatwá* is in accordance with it.*

The answer would be the same if, instead of "the poor," he had said "the indigent and the needy of my kindred."*

---

* Fatáwá Alamgírí, vol. ii, pp. 479 & 483.—B. Dig, pp. 576 & 377.

DCCCCLI. If one, after making a settlement on the needy of his kindred, and then on the poor (*b*) should die leaving a poor son, Abú Yusuf has said that he does not come within the meaning of his kindred; and this is correct.* *Principle.*

(*b.*) When there are poor of an appropriator's kindred in another city than that in which he resides, the produce is not to be sent to them, but is to be divided wholly among those of his own city; though if the superintendent should send any of it away to them he would not be responsible.* **Illustrations.**

In this matter all are held to be poor who are so accounted in the matter of *zakát*, or poor's rate. In both cases a person who has only a dwelling-house, or that and a servant, is held to be poor. So also when with this he has a sufficiency of clothes without anything superfluous, or house furniture that cannot be dispensed with. But if he have an excess of 200 *dirhams* above his clothes and furniture, he is to be accounted rich, and can take neither of the *zakát* nor of a *wakf*. So also if he have two dwelling-houses or two servants, and the superfluous house or servant is of the value of 200 *dirhams*, he is to be accounted rich, so as to render it unlawful for him to participate in *zakát* or *wakf*, but not so as to render him liable to the former. And though the surplus above his dwelling-house, or the surplus above his clothes or his furniture, should not each by itself be of the value of 200 *dirhams*, yet if all taken together are of that value, he is rich, and cannot lawfully participate either in *zakát* or in *wakf*. And if he have land of the value of 200 *dirhams*, though the income from it be insufficient for his maintenance, still he is rich according to what is approved. Though he should have plenty of property not immediately available, or in debts owing to him by other persons, he may be allowed to take of the *zakát* or the *wakf*, for he is in the condition of a traveller: yet if he can borrow, it is better for him to do so than to receive from a charity.*

Settlements on Neighbours.

DCCCCLII. When a man has made a settlement on his neighbours, the produce (of the *wakf*) ought to be expended, according to analogy, on all who are adjacent to him; but on a free construction, it is for those who assemble together with him, *Principle.*

---

* Fatáwá Alamgírí, vol. ii, p. 483.—B. Dig., p. 577.

and come to the *masjid*, or place of worship, of the *mahullah*, or quarter; and this is approved.*

Principle. DCCCCLIII. Residence is the condition, according to the plain doctrine of Abú Hanifah, whether the resident be proprietor or not; and this also is correct.*

Principle. DCCCCLIV. The neighbour, whether *Muslim* or infidel, male or female, free or *mukátab*,† minor or adult, is entitled; and the produce is to be divided among them according to the number of heads, the superintendent being responsible if he give more to some than to others.*

Principle. DCCCCLV. An *um-i walad, mudabbar*,† or absolute slave, has no right to participate; nor a debtor who is imprisoned within the *muhullah* for debt; nor the son, father, grandfather, or wife of the appropriator; nor the child of a child though he be a neighbour, on a liberal construction. But his brothers and paternal and maternal uncles do participate.*

Settlement on the people of one's bayit or *house, and on his ál,* or *jins,*‡ *and akab.*

Principle. DCCCCLVI. When a person has made a settlement on the people of his *bayit* or house, every one is entitled who is connected with him through his fathers to the most remote of them in *Islám;* and the *Muslim* and the infidel, the male and the female, the prohibited and the unprohibited, the near and the remote, are in this all alike.*

The remotest ancestor, however, is not included. But the child and parent of the appropriator are included, though the children of his daughters and sisters are not; nor the children of any other females besides these, except when married to paternal nephews of the appropriator.*

Principle. DCCCCLVII. When a man has made a settlement on the people of his house, those in existence are included, and those who may come after them of their children and children's children.*

---

* Fatáwá Alamgírí, vol. ii, pp. 488—490.—B. Dig., pp. 579—581.

† *Vide* p. 275 of Lectures for 1873.

‡ *Vide ante*, p. 66 note.

A man's saying on my "*ál*," or on my "*jins*" (kind), is like his saying "on people of my house;" and there is no speciality in favor of the poor, unless the *wakf* is made specially for them. His saying "on the poor of them," and "on those who become poor," is the same thing. So that the produce is for him who is poor at the time, though he were rich when the settlement was made; and it is not restricted to those who were rich and have become poor.* Illustrations.

If a woman should make a settlement "on the people of her house," or "on her *jins*," her mother and her child would not be included.*

If a man should say "on the *ahl* of *Abdullah*," it would be for his wife specially, according to Abú Hanífah. Hallál, however, has said, "We think it better to make it include all free persons of his family living together with him in his house;" and this is approved. But slaves are not included, nor Abdoollah himself, nor persons of his family living in another house.*

By "*akab*" is to be understood all those who are connected with a person through his father; and the children of daughters are not included, except females, whose husbands are among these. And if one should make a settlement on Zayid and his *akab*, Zayid himself being alive and having children, these would have nothing, for the child of a man called his *akab*, except after his death.*

Iyál comprehends every one maintained by a person, whether living in his house or not; and *hasham* is instead of *iyál*.*

Cases where after an appropriation for the poor, the appropriator himself, or some of his children, or kindred, are in want.

DCCCCLVIII. The appropriator himself, though he should become poor, cannot participate in the produce of the property appropriated by him. *Principle.*

It is declared in certain *fatáwá*, or decisions, that when a man has made his land a *sadakah* appropriated to the poor and indigent, and has subsequently fallen into want himself, nothing is to be given to him thereout. And if a man should say, being in health at the time, "My land is a *sadakah*, appropriated to the poor after me," or if he should say this in sickness, and die, leaving a little daughter, it would not be lawful to expend the produce on her; and so it has been decided.—Fatáwá Alamgírí, vol. ii, p. 493.—B. Dig., p. 583. Illustration.

---

* Fatáwá Alamgírí, vol. ii, p. 490.—B. Dig., pp. 581—583.

But if some of his kindred, or some of his children, should fall into want, and the *wakf* were made in health, the produce is to be disposed of subject to the following rules :—

DCCCCLIX. It is to be expended, in the first place, on the poor of his kindred, and the surplus only given to strangers. 2.—Poverty on the day of the produce coming into existence is not to be regarded, but rather poverty on the day of distribution. 3.—The nearest in kindred are first to be supplied, and then the more remote, that is, the child of the loins has priority, and after him the child of a child, then the third generation, and then the fourth, and a lower generation. If none of these remain, or there is a surplus after satisfying them, it is to be bestowed on the more remote of poor kindred, beginning here also with the nearest among them. 4.—That to each person to whom a portion is given, something less than 200 *dirhams* be given, that is, when the *wakf* is for the poor generally, and some of the kindred are in need. But if the *wakf* be for the poor of a person's kindred, the whole produce is to be distributed among them, though the share of each should exceed two hundred *dirhams*.*

Principle. DCCCCLX. When an appropriator has appointed the produce for debtors, or travellers, or in the way of God, or for pilgrimage, and some of his children or kindred fall into want, part of it is to be given to them, unless the child or the relative be a debtor, or a traveller, &c., when, also, a beginning is to be made with them.*

What depends upon a condition in the wakf.

Principle. DCCCCLXI. When a man has made an appropriation of land or something else, with a condition that the whole or part of it shall be for himself while he lives, and after him for the poor (*a*), the appropriation is valid according to Abú Yusuf.†

---

* **Fatáwá Alamgírí, vol. ii, pp. 493—495.—B. Dig., pp. 583—585.**

† **Muhammad maintains that the appropriation itself is valid, but that the condition reserved is void; because the condition does not prevent an extinction of right of property; and the appropriation is consequently complete, because of the extinction of this right; but the *condition*, as being invalid, is void, in the same manner as the reserve of a right of change in the foundation of a mosque is void.—Hidáyah, vol. ii, p. 351.**

The Shaikhs of Balkh have adopted this opinion, and the *fatwá* (decision) is in conformity with it, as an inducement to the maker appropriations.*

(*a.*) There are several ways in which this may be done; as, for instance, by a person's saying "On condition that he will pay my debts out of the produce," or "When death happens to me, if I should be in debt, that he will begin with the payment of my debts," or "When death happens to such an one" (meaning the appropriator himself), "take every year one-tenth share of the produce, and apply it to the performance of the *hajj*, or pilgrimage to Mecca, on his account, or in the expiation of his vows, and so and so" (naming something), or "Take every year out of this *sadakah* such and such *dirhams*, and expend them in such a manner, and the remainder so and so." And in all these cases the *wakf* would be lawful. And if he should say "A *sadakah* appropriated to Almighty God—he will pass its produce to me while I live," without adding anything more, it would be lawful, and after his death be for the benefit of the poor. So also if he should say, "This my land is a *sadakah* appropriated,—he will pass the produce to me while I live; then, after me, to my child's child and their *nasl* for ever, while there are any, and when they cease, to the indigent;" this also would be lawful. So also if he should make it a condition, "That he may maintain himself and his child, and pay his debts out of the produce, and that when death happens to him, the produce of this estate is for such an one, the son of such an one, and this child and child's child, and his *nasl*;" or if he should begin by saying "for such an one, and then for himself," it would be lawful as conditioned, the putting himself first or last making no difference.* Illustrations.

A person makes an appropriation for the poor, with a condition "that he may eat and feed others" (out of its produce) "so long as he lives, and that after his death it is to be for his child, and in like manner to his child's child for ever, while there are any descendants:" the *wakf* is lawful with such a condition.*

DCCCCLXII. If a person appropriate land with a reserve of his authority over it, it is lawful according to Abú Yusuf.—Hidáyah, vol. ii, p. 352. *Principle.*

Annotations.

dcccclxii. If the appropriator reserve to himself the right of changing the lands he appropriates for any other lands, at pleasure, it is lawful according to Abú Yusuf.*—Hidáyah, vol. ii, p. 351.

---

* Fatáwá Alamgírí, vol. ii, p. 495.—B. Dig., p. 585.

Our author remarks that *Kadúrí* has expressly declared this. Such also is the doctrine of Hallál, and it is, indeed, the generally received opinion.—Hidáyah, vol. ii, p. 352.

Principle.

DCCCCLXIII. When there is a condition in the *wakf* that he (the proprietor) may exchange the land for other land, as he pleases, and that the land so obtained shall become *wakf* instead of the first, the appropriation and the condition are lawful, according to Abú Yusuf; and so also when there is a condition that he may sell and make an exchange for the price.*

And it has been said that Hallál was of the same opinion, and the *fatwá* is in conformity with it.*

Principle.

DCCCCLXIV. But after the exchange has been once made, it cannot be made a second time, unless there are words indicative of an intention that he may exchange continually.*

Principle.

DCCCCLXV. If, however, the appropriator who makes this condition (namely, a reservation of authority to himself) be a person of infamous character and unworthy of confidence, the magistrate (*kází*) may take the appropriation out of his hands, from a regard to the interest of the poor; in the same manner as he is at liberty to suspend the powers of an *executor*, where he happens to be a person of bad character, from a regard to the interest of the orphans.—Hidáyah, vol. ii, p. 353.

Annotations.

dccccIxiii. A condition on the part of the appropriator, that he shall have the power of exchanging the land for other land, is valid according to Abú Yusuf on a favorable construction of law, and the *fatwá* is in accordance with his opinion.*

*** Fatáwá Alamgírí. vol. ii, pp. 455,495—497.—B. Dig.,pp. 551, 586 & 587.**

DCCCCLXVI. When the words are "that I may exchange for other land," he cannot exchange for a mansion; nor *vice versâ*. But he may purchase *khirájí* land with the price.*

DCCCCLXVII. When the power to exchange is reserved to himself, he may appoint an agent for the purpose, but his executor cannot exercise it. And if the power is reserved to another and himself, the other cannot exercise it singly, but he can when the power to exchange is given to "every one that may preside over this *wakf*," it is lawful, and every president may exercise the power.* *Principle.*

DCCCCLXVIII. Without an express condition in the *wakf*, the land, though saltish and useless, cannot be sold or exchanged.* *Principle.*

In one place the Kází Khán has said that the judge may order its sale, though there should be no condition to that effect, when he thinks it expedient; but in another he denies that the judge has any such power.*

DCCCCLXIX. The most trustworthy opinion, however, is, that the judge may lawfully sell the land if it be quite useless, and there is no increase from it, provided that the sale is not at an inadequate price.* *Principle.*

Appropriation in death-illness.

DCCCCLXX. If the appropriator suspends the appropriation (*wakf*) on his death, it takes effect (like a testamentary disposition), to the extent of a third of his property, the excess, if any, not being allowed, unless consented to by the heirs of the appropriator. *Principle.*

If the appropriator suspends the *wakf* on his death by saying "When I die I have appropriated my mansion to such purposes," it is valid and obligatory to the extent of a third of his property, the excess (if any) being in abeyance till it is seen if there is any other property, or the heirs will allow the appropriation. If there be no other property, and the heirs do not allow the appropriation, the produce must then be divided into three parts, and one-third set apart for the *wakf* and the other two-thirds for the heirs. If the suspension on death be made during death-illness, the effect is the same as if it were made in health.† *Illustrations.*

* Fatáwá Alamgírí, p. 497.—B. Dig., p. 587.
† Fatáwá Alamgírí, vol. ii. p. 455.—B. Dig., p. 550.

If a person make an appropriation upon his death-bed, Taháví reports that, according to *Hanífah*, it stands in the same predicament with a bequest after death (that is to say, is *absolute*), contrary to an appropriation made during *health*, which is held by *Hanífah* not to be of an *absolute* nature. The true statement, however, is that the appropriation in question is *not* absolute according to *Hanífah*; but it is *absolute* according to the *two disciples*, with this distinction, however, that the appropriation here treated of is regarded as from the *third* of the appropriator's estate, whereas an appropriation made during health is regarded as from the *whole* of the appropriator's property.—Hidáyah, vol. ii, p. 338.

When a man who is sick of death-illness makes an appropriation of his mansion, and the mansion is within a third of his property, or the appropriation is allowed by his heirs, it is lawful. But if the mansion exceeds the third of his property, and the appropriation is not allowed by his heirs, it is void as to the excess above the third.*

Principle. DCCCCLXXI. And when a man has made his land "a *sadakah*," appropriated to Almighty God, for his child, and child's child, and his *nasl* for ever, so long as there are any, and after them for the necessitous, and this land is within a third of his property, it becomes settled, so that its produce is divisible among all his heirs, according to their shares in his heritage.*

Principle. DCCCCLXXII. If the land does not come out of the third of the property, but is allowed by the heirs, the appropriation is lawful, and the produce divisible among them equally, without any preference of the male over the female, neither the wife nor the parents taking anything. And if the heirs do not allow it, the appropriation is lawful, from a third of the property, and one-third of the area becomes *wakf* for the poor, the produce being divisible among all the heirs according to the rules of inheritance.*

Principle. DCCCCLXXIII. When a person during illness† has appropriated his land, and also made bequests, the third of his property is to be divided between the *wakf* and the whole of the bequests, in proportion to the value of the land, for

* Fatáwá Alamgírí, vol. ii, pp. 542 & 543.—B. Dig., pp. 601, 603.

† That is death-illness.

the people of the *wakf*, and in proportion to the amount of the legacies for the legatees, and a quantity equal to what may fall to the value of the land is to be taken out of the land, and it becomes *wakf* for the purposes specified.*

DCCCCLXXIV. When a person in sickness has appropriated his land for his child and his child's child, having no other property beside it, one-third of the land is an appropriation for the benefit of the child's child,† whether assented to by the heirs or not; and the other two-thirds are the property of the heirs, if the appropriation is disallowed by them; but if it is allowed by them, the two-thirds are also to be divided between the child and child's child equally.* *Principle.*

---

* Fatáwá Alamgírí, vol. ii, pp. 542 & 543.—B. Dig., pp. 602 & 603.

† The child is excluded from the benefit of the third, because he is an heir, and a legacy to an heir is not lawful.

LECTURE V.

ON THE WAKF, OR APPROPRIATION, OF MASJIDS, CARAVANSERAS, CEMETERIES, INNS, RESERVOIRS, WAYS, AQUEDUCTS, AND THE GOVERNANCE OF A WAKF.

On the wakf of a Masjid or Mosque.

Principle. DCCCCLXXV. When a man has erected a *masjid*, his right therein does not abate till he has separated it with its way from the rest of his property, and permitted prayers to be said in it.*

ANNOTATIONS.

dccccIxxv. If a person build a mosque, his right of property in it is not extinguished so long as he does not separate it from the rest of his property, *or*† give general admission to people to come and worship in it: but as soon as the people in general, or a single person, say their prayers in it, his right of property is extinguished according to Abú Hanífah.—Hidáyah, vol. ii, p. 353.

The utter separation of it from the rest of the appropriator's property is indispensable, for this reason, that the mosque cannot become dedicated solely to God until that be effected: and the performance of *prayer* in it is a condition; because, as a consignment (according to Hanífah and *Muhammad*) is indispensable, it follows that consignment is requisite in this way, since consignment must be carried into execution in whatever way may be proper to the nature of the appropriation, and the mode of consignment proper to a mosque is *public worship*; or, the performance of prayer is a condition, because as it cannot be conceived that God *himself* should take possession of a mosque, it follows that that which is the *design* must stand, as a substitute for the *taking possession* of it. It is proper in this place to observe that if a *single person* say his prayers

---

* Fatáwá Alamgírí, vol. ii, p. 545.—B. Dig., p. 504.

† Mr. Hamilton, in his translation of the Hidáyah (vol. ii, p. [illegible]), has used *or* instead of *and*, as if either separation *or* the permission of prayer were sufficient. Mechanical separation is probably intended; and wherever it already exists, the actual use of the *masjid* for prayer, with the owner's permission, may perhaps be sufficient.

Separation is necessary, because without that the *masjid* is not made special to Almighty God; *and* prayer is necessary, because delivery is requisite, according to Abú Hanífah and Muhammad.*

DCCCCLXXVI. When a *mutawallí* (superintendent) has been appointed for the purposes of a *masjid*, and delivery of it has been made to him, the *masjid* is lawful, though no prayers be said in it: and this is correct. So also when delivery of it is made to the judge or his deputy.* *Principle.*

DCCCCLXXVII. It is also the most correct opinion that a *masjid* may be constituted so as to be obligatory, according to Abú Hanífah, without any reference to the death of the appropriator (*wákif*), or making it the subject of a bequest, contrary to the other cases of *wakf.** *Principle.*

DCCCCLXXVIII. If a person appropriate ground for the purpose of erecting a mosque, he cannot afterwards resume or sell it, neither can it be inherited.—Hidáyah, vol. ii, p. 356. *Principle.*

Because this ground is altogether alienated from the right of the individual, and appertains solely to God.—*Ibid.*

DCCCCLXXIX. When a man has an unoccupied space of ground fit for building upon, and has directed a *kowm*, or body of persons, to assemble in it for prayers, the space becomes a *masjid*, if the permission were given expressly to pray in it for ever, or, in absolute terms, intending that it should be for ever; and the property does not go to his heirs at his death. But if the permission were given for a day, or a month, or a year, the space would not become a *masjid*; and on his death, it would be the property of his heirs.* *Principle.*

ANNOTATIONS.

in the mosque, it suffices (according to one report from *Hanífah* and *Muhammad*), because, as it is impossible that *all* men should perform their prayers in it, the circumstance of a single individual performing his prayers is the condition.—Hidáyah, vol. ii, p. 354.

---

* Fatáwá Alamgírí, vol. ii, pp. 545 & 546.—B. Dig., pp. 504 & 605.

istration. A sick man has made his mansion a *masjid* and died, but it neither falls within a third of his property, nor is allowed by his heirs: the whole of it is heritage, and the making it a *masjid* is void; because the heirs having a right in it, there has been no separation from the rights of mankind, and a confused portion has been made a *masjid*, which is void. In the same way as if he should make his land a *masjid*, and another person should establish a right in it confusedly; in which case the remainder would revert to the property of the appropriator; contrary to the case of a person making a bequest that a third of his mansion shall be made a *masjid*, which would be valid; for in such a case there is a separation, as the mansion may be divided, and a third of it converted into a *masjid*.*

inciple. DCCCCLXXX. When a man has made his land a *masjid*, and stipulated for something out of it to himself, it is not valid according to all.*

inciple. DCCCCLXXXI. It is also generally agreed that if a man make a *masjid* on condition that he shall have an option, the *wakf* is lawful and the condition is void.*

inciple. DCCCCLXXXII. When a man has built a *masjid*, and called persons to witness that he shall have the power to cancel and sell it, the condition is void, and the *masjid* is as if he had erected a *masjid* for the people of the *muhallah*, saying "it is for this *muhallah* especially," when it would, notwithstanding, be for others as well as for them to worship in.*

inciple. DCCCCLXXXIII. When a *masjid* has fallen into decay and is no longer used for prayer, nor required by the people, it does not revert to the appropriator or his heirs, and cannot be sold, according to the most correct opinions.*

inciple. DCCCCLXXXIV. When of two *masjids*, one is old and gone to decay, the people cannot use its materials to repair the more recent one, according to either Muhammad or Abú Yusuf. Because, though the former thought that the materials may be so applied, he held that it is the original appropriator

---

* Fatáwá Alamgírí, vol. ii. pp. 546—548.—B. Dig., pp. 606 & 607.

or his heirs, to whom the property reverts, that can so apply them, and because Abú Yusuf was of opinion that the property in a *masjid* never reverts to the original appropriator, though it should fall to ruin and be no longer used by the people. The *fatwá* is in accordance with the opinion of Abú Yusuf.*

DCCCCLXXXV. If a man appropriate his land for the benefit of a *masjid*, and to provide for its repairs and necessaries, such as oil, &c., and when nothing more is required for the *masjid*, to apply what remains to poor Muslims, the appropriation is lawful.* *Principle.*

DCCCCLXXXVI. A man has appropriated his land for the benefit of a *masjid*, without any ultimate destination for the poor: our* Shaikhs have said, and it is approved, that the appropriation is nevertheless lawful according to all opinions.* *Principle.*

DCCCCLXXXVII. If a man gives money for the repairs of a *masjid*, also for its maintenance and for its benefit, it is valid.* *Principle.*

For if it cannot operate as a *wakf*, it operates as a transfer by way of gift to the *masjid*, and the establishing of property in this manner to a *masjid* is valid, being completed by taking possession.*

If a person should say "I have bequeathed a third of my property to the *masjid*," it would not be lawful unless he say "to expend on the *masjid*." So if he were to say "I have bequeathed a third of my property to the lamps of the *masjid*," it would not be lawful unless he say "to give light with it in the *masjid*." If he say "I have given my mansion to the *masjid*," it is valid as a transfer, requiring delivery.* Illustration.

DCCCCLXXXVIII. If a man, having a house in *Mecca*, appropriate it to the accommodation of pilgrims, or, if a person, having a house in any other place, appropriate it to the accommodation of the poor, or mendicants, or, having a house upon the frontiers, dedicate it to the accommodation of the *Musalmán* warriors and their cattle, or dedicate the revenue from his lands to the support of the warriors in the *Principle.*

---

* *Vide* Fatáwá Alamgírí vol. ii, pp. 516—518 & 550.—B. Dig., pp. 606 & 607.

way of God, and make over or consign those houses or lands to the prince (who is empowered to act in those particulars), such consignment is lawful. If, therefore, the person in question be afterwards desirous of revoking his appropriation, he cannot lawfully do so for the reasons before alleged.—Hidáyah, vol. ii, p. 358.

Principle. **DCCCCLXXXIX. The revenue arising from the lands, however, is lawful to the *poor only*, and not to the *rich;* but the use of any of the other articles (such as residing in the *caravansera*, or drinking water from the well, fountain, or reservoir,) is lawful to *rich* and *poor* alike.—*Ibid.***

The reasons for this distinction are twofold. First, people in general, in the appropriation of a revenue, intend only the relief of the needy, whereas, in that of the other articles, the accommodation of rich and poor is equally intended. Secondly, the articles of drink and lodging are requisite equally to the rich and to the poor; but in the article of pecuniary assistance the rich are not necessitous on account of their wealth, whereas the poor are necessitous.—*Ibid.*

On Caravanseras, Cemeteries, Inns, Reservoirs, Ways and Aqueducts.

Principle. **DCCCCXC. If a person erects an aqueduct for Musalmáns or an inn, or a caravansera for travellers, or has made his land a cemetery for Musalmáns, his proprietary right therein abates by his declaration to that effect, or after such declaration upon the same being used by people, or upon being delivered to the superintendent (*mutawallí*).**

Illustration. When a person has erected an aqueduct for Musalmáns, or an inn for the occupation of travellers, or a caravansera, or has made his land a cemetery, his property does not abate according to Abú Hanífah without an order of the *hákim*, or judge, or referring the matter till after death, when it would become obligatory after his death, but revocable in the meantime, as has been already explained in the case of appropriations for the poor. According to Abú Yusuf, the appropriator's property abates by speech, and according to Muhammad, it abates when people have used the aqueduct, or have occupied the inns and caravanseras, or buried in the cemetery; and it is sufficient if one person do so. The rule is the same as to a well and cistern ; and if they are delivered to a superintendent the appropriation is valid in like manner. It is stated in the *Mabsút* that the *fatwá* is with the two ; and so it is generally agreed.*

DCCCCXCI. In the use of all such things as above-mentioned, there is no difference between the rich and poor. So that it is lawful for all alike to put up at inns and caravanseras, and to irrigate from acqueducts, and bury in a cemetery. *Principle.*

DCCCCXCII. If, in the cases last recited, the founder consign the article to a *mutawallí*, or procurator, such consignment is approved.—Hidáyah, vol. ii, p. 358. *Principle.*

Because the procurator is in the character of a deputy, and the act of the deputy is the act of the principal.—*Ibid.*

DCCCCXCIII. When a person has bought a place and made it a way for Musalmáns, and called witnesses to the fact, it is valid.*

ANNOTATIONS.

dccccxc—dccccxciii. If a person construct a reservoir for public use, or a *caravansera* for travellers, or erect a house upon the infidel frontiers for the accommodation of the Musalmán warriors in their excursions, (which is termed a *Ribât*), or dedicate ground as a burying-place, his right of property therein is not extinguished until the magistrate issue a decree to that effect; because no termination of the proprietor's right takes place in this instance, insomuch that he may still lawfully continue to use those things (by residing in the house or *Ribât*, or drinking water out of the reservoir, or interring in the burial-place). It is, therefore, requisite either that the magistrate issue a decree, in order to complete the alienation, or that the founder himself refer the appropriation to his decease, in order that it may stand as a *bequest*, and become absolute upon that event,—in the same manner as in the case of an appropriation made to the use of the *poor*. It is otherwise in the case of a mosque, because in that instance no right of usufruct remains to the founder, as the mosque appertains solely to God independent of any magisterial decree. All that is here advanced is according to *Hanífah*. *Abú Yusuf* is of opinion that the person's right of property ceases on the instant of his saying "I have made this *wakf* for such and such purposes" (of residence, interment, or so forth), because with him it is a rule that appropriation is absolute, and that consignment is not a condition of it.

---

* Fatáwá Alamgírí, vol. ii, pp. 554—556.—B. Dig., pp. 609 & 610.

But it is a condition of the completeness of the thing that one Musalmán should pass over it, according to those who think delivery necessary.*

Hallál has said that the rule is the same as to a bridge which a man has built for Musalmáns, and they have made use of it as a way. The building in consequence does not pass as inheritance to hi heirs, but becomes a *wakf*, being especially set apart by the cancellation of their rights.*

The Appointment of Superintendent of a Wakf, and the Wiláyat† or Governance of the Wakf.

The proper person for the superintendence of a *wakf* is one who does not seek for the office, and in whom there is no known or apparent wickedness.‡

Principle. DCCCCXCIV. None but a trustworthy and qualified person, whether male or female,§ should be appointed *mutawallí*, or superintendent of a *wakf*.

ANNOTATIONS.

Muhammad maintains that as soon as people drink water out of the reservoir, or enter the *caravansera*, or warriors take up their residence in the *Ribât*, or interment takes place in the burying-ground, the proprietor's right is extinguished; because consignment (which he holds to be a condition) is established by such acts as the consignment of anything must be made in the mode proper to that thing. It is sufficient also, (according to him), if these acts be performed by, or with respect to, only a *single individual;* because as the *whole community* cannot engage in those acts, regard must necessarily be had to them as performed in any single instance. Wells and fountains are also subject to the same rule.—Hidáyah, vol. ii, p. 357.

---

* Fatáwá Alamgírí, vol. ii, pp. 555 & 556.—B. Dig., pp. 609 & 610.

† "*Wiláyat* or *Waláyat*," governance, superintendence, or management.

‡ Fatáwá Alamgírí, vol. ii, p. 504.—B. Dig., p. 591.

§ As to the competence of females to be *Mutawallís*, *vide* Calcutta Sudder Dewanny Adawlut Reports, vol. i, p. 217.

When the management of a *wakf* was combined with its *Sajjádah-nishíní*, or superintendence of a religious establishment—a function which a female cannot exercise—it was decided on the opinion of the law officer, that the former office could not be held by a female.—Calcutta Sudder Dewanny Adawlut Reports. vol. i, p. 107. *Sajjádah-nishíní* is the sitting on the carpet used by Musalmáns for prayer.

No one should be appointed but an *amín*, or trustee, who is able to act by himself or by deputy; and in this males and females are alike;* and so also the blind and those who are possessed of sight, and even one who has undergone the *hadd*, or specific punishment for slander, if he have repented.†

DCCCCXCV. A person may appoint *himself* or his children a *mutawallí* or *mutawallís* of the *wakf* made by him. Principle.

Muhammad, the son of Alfazl, being asked respecting one who had made it a condition in constituting a *wakf* that the governance of it should be for himself and children, answered, "It is lawful, according to all." A man makes a *wakf* without mentioning any one for its governance,—it has been said that the governance is for the appropriator himself; and this is agreeable to the opinion of Abú Yusuf, for with him delivery was not a necessary condition, but according to Muhammad, the *wakf* is not valid; and so it is decided.† Illustration.

DCCCCXCVI. If the appropriator (*wákif*) appointed two men to be *mutawallís* after his death, then if one of those two men died after making his companion executor in respect of the matter of *wakf*, the management by the survivor (of those two) over the whole of the *wakf* is valid. It is so (laid down) in the *Fatáwá Kází Khán*.‡ Principle.

DCCCCXCVII. If a person appointed two men his executors, and one of them accepted, and the other refused, then the judge (*kází*) is to appoint in his place another man until the two men are agreed (in accepting) as was intended by the appropriator. And if the *kází* entrusted the entire (management of the) *wakf* to the man who accepted, the same is valid, without conflict of opinions (as is laid down in the *Zahíriyah*). And if he (the appropriator) appointed an adult and a minor to be his executors, the *kází* should appoint a man in the stead of the minor.‡ Principle.

---

* See, however, the last note of the preceding page.

† Fatáwá Alamgírí, vol. ii, p. 504.—B. Dig., p. 591.

‡ Fatáwá Alamgírí, vol. ii, p. 506.

Principle.

DCCCCXCVIII. If the appropriator should make it a condition—that "such an one shall appoint, I shall not have the power to discharge," the appointment shall be lawful, but the prohibition to remove would be void.*

Principle.

DCCCCXCIX. If he (the appropriator) should give the governance during his life and after his death, it would be lawful, and the person appointed be his agent during his life and his executor after his death. The effect would be the same if he should say "I have appointed thee my agent in this *sadakah* during my life and after my death." But if he should say "I have invested thee with the governance of this *wakf*," he would have it only during his life, and not after his death.*

Principle.

M. If he should make no appointment of a *Kayyim*, or administrator, till the approach of death, and then appoint an executor, the person appointed would be the executor with regard to his property, and administrator of his *wakf*. But if he should make a new appointment of executor, he would only be executor for the property, and not administrator of the *wakf*.*

Principle.

MI. If, however, he should say "I have revoked every appointment of executor made by me," the governance would be to the new executor, and the former *mutawallí*, or superintendent, would be discharged.*

Principle.

MII. When one appoints a person as the executor of his *wakf*, and makes it a condition that he shall not have the power to appoint another, the condition is lawful.*

Principle.

MIII. When the superintendent has died, and the appropriator is still alive, the appointment of another belongs to him and not to the judge;

---

* Fatáwá Alamgírí, vol. ii, pp. 504 & 505.—B. Dig., pp. 592 & 593.

and if the appropriator be dead, his executor is preferred to the judge. But if he had died without naming an executor, the appointment of an administrator is with the judge.*

MIV. So long as a person fit to be a *mutawallí* is (found) among the relatives of the appropriator (*wákif*), a stranger cannot be appointed as a *mutawallí*, as the former will take a greater interest.—Durr-ul-Mukhtár, p 422. *Principle.*

MV. In the *Asal* it is stated that the judge (*hákim*) cannot appoint a stranger to the office of administrator so long as there is any of the house of the appropriator fit for the office; and if he should not find a fit person among them, and should nominate a stranger, still if he should subsequently find among them one who is qualified, he ought to transfer the appointment to him.* *Principle.*

When a person fit to be a *mutawallí* is found among the offspring or in the family of the appropriator, a stranger must not be appointed as a *mutawallí*; but when a fit person cannot be found, (among the above), a stranger may be appointed, still, if a fit person can afterwards be found in the family, he shall have the office. —Radd-ul-Muhtár, vol. iii, p. 636.

MVI. If the *wákif*, or appropriator, has made it a condition that a *mutawallí* shall be appointed from *Principle.*

ANNOTATIONS.

mvi. It is stated in the *Jámi ul-Fasúlain*, that if the appropriator has made it a condition that there must be a *mutawallí* from amongst his children and children's children, then is the judge (*kází*) competent to appoint a stranger without malversation (on part of the former); and if he does (appoint a stranger), shall such person be the *mutawallí?* Shaikh ul-Islám Burhán ud-dín† has declared in his Fawáyid that he *shall not*. Nahr-ul-Faïk quoted in the Fatáwá Alamgírí, vol. ii, p. 508.—*Vide* B. Dig., p. 594, and Radd-ul-Muhtár, vol. iii, p. 636.

* Fatáwá Alamgírí, vol. ii, pp. 507 & 508.—B. Dig., pp. 593 & 594.

† The author of the *Hidáyah*.

amongst his children and children's children, the judge (*kází*) is not competent to appoint a stranger without malversation (on the part of the former), and if the *kází* should still appoint (a stranger), he shall not become the *mutawallí*.

Principle. MVII. If the persons of a neighbourhood be unanimous in favor of a person and make him *mutawallí* without the order or sanction of the *kází* (judge), the man would, nevertheless, be *mutawallí*.—Ináyah, cited from Bahr and Nahr in the Radd-ul-Muhtár, vol. i, *p*. 686.

Principle. MVIII. If a man having appropriated his estate and delivered up possession of it to the administrator, desire to take it from his hands, he cannot do so unless the appointment was with such condition.

Illustration. A man having appropriated his estate, and delivered up possession of it to the administrator, desires to take it out of his hands. If he made it a condition in the *wakf* that he should have the power to discharge the administrator, and withdraw the *wakf* from his hands, he may lawfully do so; otherwise he cannot according to Muhammad; but according to Abú Yusuf, he can; the *Shaikhs* of Balkh deciding with the latter, and those of Bakhárá with the former, with whom also is the *fatwá*.*

On the Duties and Powers of a Mutawallí.

Principle. MIX. A superintendent may on the point of death commit his office to another, in the same way as an executor may commit his to another.*

ANNOTATIONS.

mvii. If the persons who say their prayers in a mosque agree to appoint a man as *mutawallí* for the welfare of a mosque, it is valid according to the ancient lawyers; it would, however, be better to do so with the permission of the *kází*. But, subsequently, the modern lawyers agreed unanimously and said—"in our time it would be valid if it is done without the knowledge of the *kází*, it being a well known fact that the *kázís* covet *wakf* properties."—Radd-ul-Muhtár, vol. iii, p. 633.

* Fatáwá Alamgírí, vol. ii, pp. 504 & 507.—B. Dig., pp. 591 & 592.

MX. But when the appropriator has assigned some particular property for this superintendent, it does not belong to the person whom he (the latter) has appointed to the office; and the matter must be submitted to the judge, in order that he may assign for him the hire, or salary of similar work, unless the appropriator had assigned the allowance for every superintendent.* *Principle.*

MXI. A superintendent, while alive and in good health, cannot lawfully appoint another to act for him, unless the appointment of himself were in the nature of a general trust.* *Principle.*

MXII. If an administrator should die after he has given a lease, the lease is not made void. Nor is a lease granted by the appropriator himself dissolved by his death, on a liberal construction, though it ought to be so† by analogy.* *Principle*

MXIII. When a judge who has granted a lease is dismissed from his office, the lease is not made void.* *Principle.*

MXIV. And if the lease has been granted by a superintendent who is himself the party entitled to the benefit of the *wakf*, it is not dissolved by his death, though the produce is his.* *Principle.*

MXV. When the superintendent of a *wakf* has let a mansion appropriated for the poor, for more than a year, the lease is unlawful.* *Principle.*

MXVI. In the absence of any condition, the approved doctrine is that the lease of estates in land may be decreed to be lawful for three years, unless it be for the benefit of the *wakf* to annul them; and that with regard to leases of other property, they should be decreed to be unlawful when they exceed one year, unless it be for the benefit of the *wakf* to sustain them. But this varies with the change of places and times. This is approved for *Principle.*

---

* Fatáwá Alamgírí, vol. ii, pp. 508, 543, 514.—B. Dig., pp. 594—596.

† As in the case of an ordinary lease, which according to Muhammadan law is cancelled by the death of the lessor.

the *fatwá;* the same being also applicable to contracts of *muzárat* and *muámalat.**

Principle. MXVII. If an appropriator had made it a condition that leases shall not be granted for more than a year, and people are unwilling to take them for so short a period, still the administrator has no power to grant a longer lease, but should lay the matter before the judge, that he may lease it for more than a year.*

Principle. MXVIII. When the appropriator himself has granted a long lease, and there is ground to apprehend that the substance of the *wakf* is to be injured, the judge (*hákim*) may cancel the lease.*

Principle. MXIX. It is not lawful to let a *wakf* except for the rent of similar property. But when a *wakf* has been let for three years at a known rent, equal to that of similar property, so that the lease is lawful, it is not to be cancelled, though rents should fall or rise during the period.*

Principle. MXX. When the superintendent has let the property of a *wakf* at an inadequate rent, so that the lease is unlawful, and the tenant has occupied it, he is liable for the rent of similar property, whatever it may amount to, according to what is approved by the moderns. So, also, if he occupy under an invalid lease.*

MXXI. If the superintendent of a *wakf* should give a lease of it to his adult son, or to his father, it would not be lawful according to Abú Ḥanífah, except at a rent above that of similar property. But the administrator of a *wakf* may cultivate the lands himself, and hire labourers, and pay them wages out of the income of the *wakf*. He may also hire labourers about its business, and in digging reservoirs of water, and in every other thing beneficial to it, when required.*

---

* Fatáwá Alamgírí. vol. ii. pp. 513—515.—B. Dig., pp. 596 & 597.

MXXII. When the *kharáj*, or land-tax, and *jabáyát*, or tribute, are demanded of a superintendent, and he has no means of paying them out of the *wakf*, he may borrow for the purpose, if that be allowed by the appropriator, and if not, he should lay the matter before the judge, who may direct that debt be incurred on this account, to be afterwards repaid out of the produce.* *Principle.*

MXXIII. For repairs, debts may be incurred under the directions of the judge. But as to other purposes, it cannot be incurred, even with his permission to expend on persons who are entitled to the benefit of the *wakf*.* *Principle.*

For the price of seed it may certainly be incurred, with his permission; but whether it can be so without his permission, authorities vary.*

MXXIV. When the appropriator has given to the person whom he has set over the business of the *wakf* a certain known property every year for the administration of its affairs, this is lawful; and the administrator must take the same trouble as is done in similar cases, and as is customary in regard to repairs and the receiving and distributing of the produce. It is not proper that he should fall short of this. But as to what is required of agents and hirelings that is not required of him.* *Principle.*

MXXV. If the governance were given to a woman and a known hire were assigned for her, she is not to be troubled except for the like of what is customary for women† to perform.* *Principle.*

MXXVI. When a *wakf* building is in a ruinous state and the *mutawallí* is unable to repair the same, the judge should let it out, and rebuild or repair it with the income; and return it to the *mutawallí* when rebuilt or repaired.* *Principle.*

---

* Fatáwá Alamgírí, vol. ii, pp. 515—519.—B. Dig., pp. 597 & 598.

† See the foot-note attached to principle dccccxciv.

MXXVII. If the people of the *wakf* should complain of the administrator, and say to the judge (*hákim*) that "the appropriator gave this in exchange for work which he does not perform," the judge is not to trouble him on account of work which is not usually done by governors.*

Principle.

MXXVIII. Though a calamity, such as blindness or deafness, should befall the superintendent, still, if he is able to do his work, the salary is to be continued to him; but if disabled, he is to have no part of it.*

Principle.

MXXIX. If a complaint is made against a governor (*mutawallí*), the judge is not to remove him from the governance of the *wakf*, except for manifest malversation.*

Principle.

MXXX. If he remove him, he is to deprive him of the hire appointed by the appropriator for administering the affairs of the *wakf*.*

Principle.

MXXXI. If the person whom the judge has removed should again become good and competent, the governance of the *wakf* is to be restored to him; and if he think fit, he may appoint another to act with him, who will be entitled to part of the salary. Or if the allowance is too small for two, and the judge is of opinion that some further provision should be made for the person appointed with him out of the income of the *wakf*, there is no objection to this.*

Principle.

MXXXII. If it is established to the judge that the administrator is unfit for the affairs of the *wakf*, and he has accordingly dismissed him and put another in his place; and then another judge (*hákim*) comes, whereupon the displaced administrator complains to him, his complaint and assertion are not to be received; but if this judge is satisfied that he is competent for the administration, he should restore him to it, and assign him the allowance out of the produce. So, also, if he were removed for wickedness and malversation, yet after a time repents towards God, and produces proof that he has become competent, he is to be restored.*

Principle.

---

* **Fatáwá Alamgírí, vol. ii, pp. 519 & 520.—B. Dig., pp. 598 & 599.**

MXXXIII. If the appropriator, who reserves the governance of the *wakf to* himself be himself, a bad character unworthy of confidence, and neglect the performance of his duty, the judge may take the *wakf,* or appropriation, out of his hands. *Principle.*

If the appropriator who makes this condition (namely, a reservation of authority to himself*) be a person of infamous character and unworthy of confidence, the judge may take the appropriation out of his hands, from a regard to the interest of the poor; in the same manner as he is at liberty to suspend the powers of an *executor,* where he happens to be a person of bad character, from a regard to the interest of the orphans.—Hidáyah, vol. ii, p. 353.

MXXXIV. Should he (the appropriator) neglect to make repairs, having (some) of the produce in his hands, the judge may compel him to do so, and if he fail to make them, take the *wakf* out of his hands. And though he should have made it a condition that neither the Sultán nor the judge shall have the power to remove him, yet if he cannot be trusted with the *wakf,* the condition is void, and the judge may remove him and appoint another. The judge may also remove one appointed by the appropriator when it is for the advantage of the *wakf.* † *Principle.*

MXXXV. If, also, the proprietor constitute another the *mutawallí,* declaring that "the sovereign or magistrate shall not take the appropriation out of *his* charge," yet these are at liberty to take it from him, where he happens to be a person of bad character; because, as such a declaration is repugnant *Principle.*

ANNOTATIONS.

maxxxiii. Though the appropriator should make it a condition that the governance is to be for himself, † the judge may, nevertheless, take it out of his hands, if he is not trustworthy.—Fatáwá Alamgírí, vol. ii, p. 505.—B. Dig. p. 592.

* *Vide* Principle dccccxcv.

† Fatáwá, Alamgírí, vol. ii, p. 505.—B. Dig., p. 592.

to the precepts of law, it is consequently void.—Hidáyah, vol. ii, p. 353.

Principle. MXXXVI. When the superintendent of the *wakf* has sold or pledged anything belonging to it, this is malversation for which he may be dismissed,* or another trustworthy person conjoined with him in the management.†

Illustration. When the land of a *wakf* is bad and uncultivated, and the administrator desires to sell part of it, in order to improve the rest with the price of what he has sold, this is not within his competence; and if an administrator should sell any part of the building that has fallen down, with a view to its removal, or palm-trees of a garden that they may be cut down, the sale is void; and if the purchaser shall pull down the buildings, or cut the trees, it is the duty of the judge to dismiss the superintendent from his office, because this is malversation; and he may make either the seller or the purchaser responsible for the value; but if he make the seller responsible, operation is given to the sale, while if the purchaser is made responsible, the sale is void.†

Principle. MXXXVII. When a *wakf* is made in favor of several persons, then upon the death of any of them, his share goes to the poor, and the remainder is for the survivors.

Illustration. If a person should make his land a *sadakah,* appropriated for Abdullah and Zayid, the produce is for both. When both die, the whole is for the poor; and when one of them dies, his half is for the poor. In like manner, when a class of persons (*kowm*) is named, the produce is to be divided according to the number of heads; and if one dies, his share goes to the poor, and the remainder to the survivors.‡

Principle. MXXXVIII. When the appropriation is for a class of persons (*kowm*), and they all reject, the produce is for the poor; while, if only some reject, then, if the name of the class be applicable to the remainder, the whole of the produce is to be divided among them, but if the name is inapplicable to the remainder, the share of those who reject passes to the poor.‡

---

* The alienation for which he is dismissed must be unlawful.—*Vide* B. Dig., pp. 550, 552, and Moore's Indian Appeals, vol. ii, p. 390.

† Fatáwá A'lamgírí, vol. ii. p. 509.—B. Dig., pp. 594 & 595.

‡ Fatáwá Alamgírí, vol. ii, pp. 521 & 523.—B. Dig., pp. 599 & 600.

LECTURE VI.

INTRODUCTORY DISCOURSE ON THE MUHAMMADAN LAW OF THE IMÂMIYAH SCHOOL.

THE word *Shíah* or *Shíat*, which signifies an adherent or sectary in general, has become a distinctive appellation of those Muhammadans who assert and maintain that *Alí*,* the cousin-german and son-in-law of Muhammad, was the only lawful successor of the said Prophet, and that both the *Imámat* and *Khiláfat*, that is, the supreme, spiritual, and temporal authority, devolved of right upon him and his posterity by his wife Fátimah, the daughter of the Prophet, though unjustly ousted by the *Khalífahs* of *Baní Umayyah* and *Baní Abbás*.† The Shíah Sect.

Thus *Alí* was, according to them, the first *Imám;* his eldest son *Hasan*, the second; his second son *Husain*, the third; and *Alí*, surnamed *Zain-ul-Abidín*, the son of *Husain*, the fourth. On the death of the last named *Alí*, a schism took place in the sect, a part of whom adhered to one of his sons, called *Zayid;* thence taking the name of the *Zaydiah* sect,‡ while the greater part of them acknowledged another of his sons, named *Muhammad Bákir*, as the fifth *Imám*. *Muhammad Bákir* was succeeded by his son *Jaafar Saádik*, as the sixth *Imám:* these two are the great heads of the *Imámiyah* sects. Jaáfar Sádik appointed his eldest son *Ismáíl* to succeed him in the *Imámat*, and on his premature death, he nominated his second son *Músá Kásim*, sometimes called Músí Razá, to be his successor. This second appointment gave rise to another and greater division among the Shíahs,

---

* *Alí* was the son of Abú Tálib, paternal uncle of Muhammad, and was the first convert to Islám, and one of the ablest and bravest of the Arabian chieftains.

† See the Annotations at pp. 5—8 of Lecture I, delivered in 1873.

‡ See the last foot-note at p. 12 of Lecture I, delivered in 1873.

for part of them denying Jaafar Saádik's right to make it, declared in favor of the son of Ismáíl, thence taking the name of the *Ismáílí sect;* while the greater number of them adhered to Músá Kásim, whom they acknowledged as the seventh *Imám.* From him the dignity descended lineally for five more generations, till it ended in Mahadí, the twelfth and last Imám, who is supposed by the sect to be still alive, though he has withdrawn for a time from human observation, since his last appearance on earth. Hence the great body of the Shíahs, who acknowledge Músá Kásim and his descendants as the true Imáms are called "*Isná ashariahs*" (Twelve-eans),—that is, followers of the twelve Imáms,—and also Imámiyahs.* In the absence of the Imám, the spiritual and temporal government of the whole Musalmán community is supposed by them to have devolved on the *Mujtahids,*† who are considered as the representatives of Imám Mahadí.

The Shíahs constitute one of the two general Muhammadan sects,‡ and though they are in themselves divided into some sub-sects,§ which differ from each other in several religious points, yet they collectively differ from the *Sunnís,* in the interpretation of the *Kurán,* in admitting and

---

* "They assert," says the learned translator of the *Kurán,* "that religion consists solely in the knowledge of the true Imám."—*Vide* p. 238 of the Preliminary Discourse to Sale's Translation of the *Kurán.*

The Shíahs, therefore, arrogate to themselves the title "*Muminín,*" or the true believers.

† In its common acceptation, "*Mujtahid*" signifies one who strives to accomplish a thing or to make a great effort; but in speaking of the law-doctors, "*Mujtahid*" denotes one who brings into operation the whole capacity of forming a private judgment relative to a legal position.

In Persia, where the sect has prevailed since the accession of the *Súfí* dynasty, it was not till a late period in its history that the actual obedience of the sovereign to these devout teachers of the law was in any degree dispensed with. An officer with the title of *Mujtahid* was found in Oudh at the time of its annexation. The Lecturer has heard personally from the present *Mujatahid* of Oudh that the first *Mujtahid* was appointed soon after the assumption of the royal title by the Nawáb Vizier, and that he himself is the fifth *Mujtahid.* The duty of a *Mujtahid* is confined to the superintendence and care of endowments for pious and charitable purposes, though they seem occasionally to be called upon by the Courts of Justice for their opinions on the *Shíah* law.

‡ The other sect being formed by the *Sunnís.*—*Vide* pp. 11—13 of Lecture I, delivered in 1873.

§ *Vide* p. 12 of Lecture I, delivered in 1873.

rejecting various *ahádís,* and in many other respects in point of faith and religious doctrines.*

The *Kurán* is the origin and fountain-head of the *Shíah* as well as of the *Sunní* school of the Muhammadan law. The *Sunnat* or *Hadîs* constituting the other basis of the former. The origin of Muhammadan law.

In addition to the *Kurân, Sunnat,* or *Hadís,* the *Ijmaa** (concurrence of the Learned) is another source to which the Shíahs had recourse wherever the former were not applicable to any particular case: they had also recourse to *Kiyás* † (ratiocination), and that only to draw inferences directly or by implication.‡ The basis of Muhammadan law.

The works on *Hadís,* or traditions, compiled by the *Shíahs,* are very numerous. A glance over any of the Biographical and Bibliographical Dictionaries will be sufficient to bear out this fact (1). Of the principal works on hadís, or tradi- Works on Hadis.

ANNOTATIONS.

(1.) The Biographical and Bibliographical Dictionaries are also numerous. Of these, the work written by Núr-ullah Bin Sharíf al-Husaini A'sh-Shustarí, entitled the "Majális-ul-Muminín," is a mine of valuable information respecting the most notable persons who professed the Shíah faith. The author has devoted the whole of the fifth majlis or section to the lives of the traditionists and lawyers, and he has specified the principal works composed by each of the learned doctors at the end of their respective histories. Núr-ullah does not mention the period when he wrote the Majális-ul-Muminín. The fact, however, of his not having written respecting the life of the celebrated lawyer Bahá ud-dín

* An account of the Shíah tenets will be found in the celebrated work *Hakk-ul- Yakín* by Muhammad Bákir Bin Muhammad Fakíh, who dedicated his work to Sháh Sultán Husain ; and in the Risálat-i or Kitáb-i Hasaníyah which, though a little work composed by Abú ul-Fatúl Rází Makkí, has a great reputation amongst the Shíahs, particularly in Persia. The latter work was translated from the Arabic into Persian by Ibráhím Istarábádí in A. H. 958 (A. C. 1551). Both of these works have been printed in Persia. Some accounts of the Shíah tenets will also be found in Sale's *Kurán,* Preliminary Discourse, Sect. 8; in Malcolm's History of Persia; in the *Tabsarat ul-Awám,* and in the *Milal-wa-nahal,* which last gives the particulars of the tenets of all the different sects of Muhammadans as well as of the sects themselves.

† *Vide* pp. 23 & 24 of Lecture I, delivered in 1873.

‡ For instance, where the *Kurán* enjoined "speak kind words to your parents," they infer therefrom that "parents must not also be insulted."

tions, one is compiled by Abdullah Bin Alí Bin Abú Shuabah al-Halabí, whose grandfather is said to have collected traditions in the time of the Imáms Hasan and Husain. Abdullah appears to have collected traditions and presented his work, when completed, to Imám Jaafar us-Saádik,* by whom it is said to have been verified and corrected.

ANNOTATIONS.

al-Ámilí, who died in A. H. 1031 (A. C. 1621), whilst the latest lawyer named in his collection is stated to have died in A. H. 996 (A. C. 1587), fixes the composition of the work in the early part of the eleventh century of the Hijrí era.—*Vide* Morl. Dig., vol. i, Introd., p. 244.

In addition to the Majális-ul-Muminín of Núr-ullah, there are several biographies of eminent Shiáhs. The most celebrated works of this nature, and which have been constantly quoted by Núr-ullah, are the writings of Muhammad Bin Amar at-Tamímí, the great Biographical Dictionary of Abú ul-Hunain Ahmad Bin Alí an-Najáshí† on the lives of the traditionists, which is generally quoted by the name of Kitáb-i Rijál; and the Khulásat ul-Akwál by the famous Shaikh Allámah Jamál-ud-dín Hasan Bin Yusuf al-Mutahhir Hillí, commonly known by the appellation of Shaikh Allámah Hillí.† An author of equal reputation, Shaikh Jaafar Muhammad Bin al-Hasan At-Túsí,‡ who was one of the Chief Mujtahids of the Imamiyah sect, and died in A. H. 460 (A. C. 1167), wrote a work which is frequently referred to in the Majális-ul-Muminín; it is a Biographical Dictionary of Shíah works, together with the names of the authors, and is entitled "Fihrist-i-Kutab-i Shíah wa Asmá-ul-Musannifín." He also wrote a voluminous commentary on the *Kurán* and many other works. Abú Yahiyah Ahmad Bin Dáúd al-Farází al-Jurjání, who was originally a Sunní, but became a convert to the Imámiyah faith, was also the author of a biographical work called "Kitáb fí Muárafati ur-Rijál."

---

* Abú Hanífah received his first instructions from Imám Jaafar Sádik, though he afterwards separated from him, and established a school of his own. He remained, however, during his life a devoted partisan of the family of *Ali*. But his adherence to it seems only to have been political; for, on questions of law, he diverged considerably from the opinions of his instructor. The differences between the leaders, whatever they may have been, were probably aggravated by the religious rancour of their followers; and there are now many important points on which the schools differ.—Baillie's Digest of Muhammadan Law, part ii, Introd., p. xiv. *Vide Tabsarat ul-Awám.*

† An-Najáshí died A. H. 405 (A. C. 1015), and Shaikh Allámah in A. H. 726 (A. C. 1325).

‡ The greater part of Abú Jaafar Túsí's works was publicly burnt in Baghdad in the tumult that arose between the Sunnís and Shíahs in A. H. 448 (A. C. 1056).

This author was one of the earliest writers both on Hadís and law of the Imamiyah sect. The book on traditions, written by Abú Muhammad* Hishám Bin al-Hákim al-Kindí ash-Shaibání, is also a work of great reputation.

The Ilál-ul-Hadís and the Ikhtiláfát-ul-Hadís were written by Yanas Bin Abd-ur-Rahman al-Yuktainí, who was celebrated as a Shíah traditionist.†

These are the earliest collections and compilations of the Shíah Hadís. The Shíahs in India consider four later works as the most authentic: these are called the "*Kutab-i Arbaa*," and are, as it seems, held by them in the same estimation as the six *Sahíhs*‡ are amongst the *Sunnís*.

The two first in order of these four books are the "*Tahzíb ul-Ahkám*" and the "*Istibsár*." They were composed by Shaikh Abú Jaafar at-Túsí, already mentioned as the author of the Fihrist, and of a voluminous commentary on the *Kurán*.

The third (in order) of the *Kutab-i-Arbaa* is the Jámi ul-Káfí by Muhammad Bin Yákúb al-Kalíní ar-Rází, who is called the Raís ul-Muhaddisín, or chief of the traditionists. This work is of the highest authority both in India and Persia; it is of vast extent, comprising no less than thirty books; and its author is said to have employed twenty years in its composition.§

The fourth of the four authentic books on the Shíah traditions is, the 'Man-lá-Yahzur ul-Fakíh,' by the celebrated Abú Jaafar Muhammad Bin Alí Bin Bábavaih al-Kumí, the author of two Tafsírs or commentaries on the *Kurán*. This collection is of great note in Persia, as well as in India. Ibnu Bábavaih wrote many other works on tradition, the principal of which, according to Núrullah, was the Kitáb ul-

---

* Abú Muhammad lived in the time of Hárún ur-Rashíd, and died in A. H. 179 (A. C. 795): he is famed also as being one of the first compilers of Shíah traditions.—Morl. Dig., vol. i, Introd., p. 259.

† This author is said to have performed forty-five pilgrimages and forty-four umrats to Mecca, and to have written the surprising number of one thousand volumes, controverting the opponents of the Shíah doctrines. He died at Madínah in A. H. 208 (A. C. 823).—Morl. Dig., vol. i, Introd., p. 259.

‡ *Vide* pp. 18 & 19 of Lecture I, delivered in 1873.

§ Al-Kalíní also wrote several other works of less note, and died at Bagdád in A. H. 328 (A. C. 939).

Masábíh. The large number of one hundred and seventy-two works on law and Hadís are mentioned, on the authority of An-Najáshí, to have been composed by this voluminous writer.

A vast number of traditions was collected by Abú al-Abbás Ahmad Bin Muhammad, commonly called Ibnu Ukdah, who was one of the greatest masters of the science of traditions, and was renowned for his diligence in collecting them, and the long and frequent journies which he undertook for the purpose of obtaining information on the subject.*

A compilation of the Shíah traditions was also made by Alí Bin al-Husain al-Masnúdí al-Hudailí, the far-famed author of the Murowaj az-Zahab.†

Another collection of traditions was by Abú al-Faraj 'Alí Bin al-Hosain al-Isfahání, who is scarcely less celebrated amongst the writers on the same subject.‡

The chief works on traditions by the great Shíah Lawyer Shaikh Allámah al-Hillí, who is the author of the Khulásat ul-Akwál, and a very high authority on traditions, are the "Istiká al-Istibár, the Masábíh ul-Anwár," and the "Durar wa al-Murján."

The work on traditions entitled the "Bahar ul-Anwár," composed by Muhammad Bákir Bin Muhammad Takí, the author of the Hakk ul-Yakín already noticed, may be placed as the last of the principal works exclusively on traditions.

Books on civil and criminal laws

One of the earliest works on civil and criminal laws was written by Abdullah Bin Alí al-Halabí. But it does not appear that any of his legal compositions are extant.

---

* Ad-Dárakutní, the Sunní traditionist, was reported to have said that Ibnu Ukdáh knew three hundred thousand traditions of Ahl-i Bayit and the Baní Háshim. Ibnu Ukdah died in A. H. 333 (A. C. 954).—Morl. Dig., vol. i, Introd., p. 260.

† This author, with some justice, has been termed the Herodotus of the East. He died in A. H. 346 (A. C. 957).—*Ibid.*

‡ Abú al-Faraj Alí is said to have devoted fifty years to the composition of the well known Kitáb ul-Afghání. It is stated that Ad-Dárakutní, and others of the Sunní traditionists, drew largely for their materials from the writings of the last named author who died in A. H. 356 (A. C. 966).

A number of law-treatises of the present class was composed by Yunas Bin Abd ur-Rahmán (already spoken of as a writer on traditions). The most famous of these treatises is entitled the Jámi-ul Kabír.

Several works on law were written by Abú al-Hasan Alí Bin al-Hasan al-Kumí, commonly called Ibnu Bábavaih, one of which works is entitled the "Kitábu ash-Sharáyah."*

The Maknaa fí al-Fikah is the best known of the law books of the present class composed by Abú Jaafar.†

Abú Abdullah Muhammad an-Nuamání, surnamed the Shaikh Mufíd and Ibnu Muallim, a renowned Shíah lawyer, is stated to have written two hundred works,‡ amongst which one called "the Irshád" is well known. When Shaikh Mufíd is quoted in conjunction with Abú Jaafar at-Túsí, they also are spoken of as "the two *Shaikhs* (*Shaikhain*)."

The chief works on law, written by Abú Jaafar Muhammad at-Túsí, who has been already noticed as a writer on biography, a commentator on the *Kurán,* and one of the most distinguished compilers of traditions, are "the Mabsút, the Khiláf, the Niháyah, and the Muhít." These works are held in great estimation, and he is considered one of the highest authorities in law. The Risálat-i Jaafariyah is likewise a legal treatise by at-Túsí, which is frequently quoted.

The Sharáya ul-Islám, written by Shaikh Najm ud-dín Abú ul-Kásim Jaafar Bin Muayyid al-Hillí, commonly called Shaikh Muayyid, is a work of the highest authority, at least in India, and is more universally referred to than any

---

* This writer is looked upon as a considerable authority, although his fame has been almost eclipsed by his more celebrated son, Abú Jaafar Muhammad, already mentioned as a traditionist. When these two writers are quoted together, they are called "the two Sadúks." Ibnu Bábavaih died in A. H. 329 (A. C. 940).—Morl. Dig., vol. i, Introd., p. 276.

† Abú Jaafar is said to have written in all one hundred and seventy-two works, and to have been especially skilled in *Ijtihád.—Ibid.*

‡ These are enumerated in the Majális ul-Muminín, on the authority of Shaikh Najáshí. Abú Jaafar at-Túsí describes him in the Fihrist as the greatest orator and lawyer of his time, the most eminent *Mujtahid,* the most subtle reasoner, and the chief of all those who delivered *Fatwás.* He died in A. H. 413, or, as some say, in A. H. 416 (A. C. 1022 or 1025).—Morl. Dig., vol. i, Introd., pp. 276 & 277.

other Shíah law book, and is the chief authority for the law of the Shíahs in India.*

A copious and valuable commentary upon the Sharáya ul-Islám, entitled the Masálik ul-Afhám, was written by Zayin-ud-dín Alí as-Sáïlí, commonly called the "Shahíd-i Sání (second martyr)." There are two other commentaries on the Sharáya ul-Islám, respectively entitled the "Madár-ul-Ahkám" and "Jawáhir ul-Kalám," the latter of which was written by Shaikh Muhammad Hasan an-Najafí.

Of the works on jurisprudence, written by Yahiyah Bin Ahmad al-Hillí,† who was celebrated for his knowledge of traditions, and is well known amongst the Imámiyah sects for his works, the Jámi ash-Sharáya and the Mudkhal dar Usúl-i Fikah are held in the greatest repute.

Of the numerous law books written by Shaikh Allámah Jamál-ud-dín Hasan Bin Yusuf Bin al-Mutahhir al-Hillí, who is called the chief of the lawyers of Hilliah, and who has been already mentioned as the author of the Khulásat ul-Akwál, and whose works are frequently referred to as authorities of undisputed merit, the most famous are the Talkhís ul-Marám, the Gháyit ul-Ahkám, and the Tahrír ul-Ahkám, which last is a justly celebrated work. The Mukhtalaf-ush-Shíah is also a well known composition of this great lawyer, and his Irshád ul-Azhán is constantly quoted as an authority under the name of the Irshád-i Allámah.

The Jámi-ul-Abbásí is a concise and comprehensive treatise on Shíáh law, in twenty books or chapters. It is generally considered as the work of Bahá-ud-dín Muhammad Áámilí, who died in A. H. 1031 (A. C. 1621).‡

---

* The original text of this valuable work was edited by Maulaví Sayyid Oulád Husain of Lucknow, late Head Professor of Muhammadan Law, according to the Shíah doctrines in the College of Hájí Muhummad Muhsin at Hooghly, and Maulaví Zahúr Alí of Bareilly, and published by the Asiatic Society of Calcutta, at the suggestion and with the aid of Nawáb Sayyid Muhammad Husain Khán Bahádur Tahowar Jung in the year 1839. The above work has also been printed in Persia and Lucknow.

† This great lawyer died in A. H. 679 (A. C. 1280).

‡ "But," says Mr. Morley, "that lawyer only lived to complete the first five books dedicating his work to Sháh Abbás II. The remaining fifteen books, as I have ascertained from a manuscript preserved in the Radcliffe Library at Oxford, and forming part of the collections procured in the East by Mr. James Fraser, were subsequently added by Nizám Ibnu Husain as-Sávaí. This fact is not mentioned in the only manuscript of

The Mafátíh by Muhammad Bin Murtazá surnamed Muhsan, and the commentary on the book by his nephew, who was of the same name, but surnamed Hádí, are modern works deserving of notice.

The Rouzat ul-Ahkám, written in Persian by the third *Mujtahid* of Oudh, consists of four chapters. The first of those is on Inheritance, which is treated of therein most fully and perspicuously. This work was lithographed at Lucknow first in 1257, and again in 1264 Hijrí.

A general Digest of the Imámiyah law in temporal matters was compiled under the superintendence of Sir William Jones. This book is composed of extracts from the work called the Káfí, which is a commentary on the Mafátíh, as well as from the Sharáya ul-Islám. The manuscript of this Digest still remains in the possession of the High Court of Judicature at Calcutta.

Books on Succession to Inheritance.

The earliest treatises on the Faráïz, or Inheritance, of the Shíahs appear to have been written by Abdul Azíz Bin Ahmad al-Azádí and Abú Muhammad al-Kindí, the latter of whom is said to have lived in the reign of Hárún ur-Rashíd.

A work on the Law of Inheritance, entitled the al-Ijáz fí al-Faráïz, has been left by Abú Jáafar Muhammad at-Tusí in addition to his general works on the *Kurán*, the Hadís and Jurisprudence.

The best known and most esteemed works on the Law of Inheritance are the Ihtijáj ush-Shíah by Saád Bin Abd ullah al-Asharí,* the Kitáb ul-Mawáris by Abú al-Hasan Alí Bábavaih, the Hamal ul-Faráïz, and the Faráïz ush-Shariyah by Shaikh Mufíd.

---

the entire work which I have met with ; but in the Fraser manuscript, which comprises two volumes, the first containing the first five books, there is a distinct preface to the sixth book, where it is expressly stated ; and it is corroborated by the existence of a manuscript in the Library of the East India Company, which contains the first five books only of the Jámi-ul-Abbásí, illustrated with notes, forming a perpetual commentary taken from the Principal Shíah Law Authorities, by Izz ud-dín Muhammad Bin Mír Abú al-Husainí al-Musaví, who entitled his work 'the Majmúa-i Izdiyád.' "—Morl. Dig., vol. i, Introd., pp. 278 & 279.

* This author died in A. H. 301 (A. C. 913).

The Sharáya ul-Islám which, as already stated, is one of the highest authorities on the Shíah Law, contains also a chapter on Inheritance, which is generally referred to in this country.

Of all the above-mentioned books on Civil and Criminal laws, those that are commonly referred to in India are the following: — The Sharáya ul-Islám, Rouzat-ul-Ahkám, Sharah-i Lumá, Mafátíh, Tahrír, and Irshád ul-Azhán.*

Of the books on this branch of Muhammadan Law, only that part of the Sharáya ul-Islám which treats of the forensic law has been translated, though not fully, by Mr. Neil Baillie.†

A considerable part of the Digest compiled under the superintendence of Sir William Jones (as already noticed) was translated by Colonel Baillie, out of which the chapter on Inheritance has been printed by Mr. Neil Baillie at the end of the second part of his Digest of Muhammadan Law. Although the chapter above alluded to is copious, yet it must be remarked that it is not so clear and useful as the Sharáya-ul-Islám and Rouzat ul-Ahkám.

Sir William Macnaghten has, in his work on Muhammadan Law, devoted only a chapter on the Inheritance of the Shíah school, which, I cannot help remarking, is deficient and erroneous in several parts. It is a mere summary containing only thirty-three short paragraphs; so that one can easily imagine what knowledge of the Shíah Law can be derived therefrom. Had not Mr. Neil Baillie translated important portions of the Sharáya ul-Islám, the forensic part of the Imámiyah Law would have continued very imperfectly known to the English reader.

The Shíah branch of the Muhammadan Law is applicable to all the Muhammadans who profess the Shíah doctrine. In India, the Nawábs and their relatives (with a very few exceptions) are Shíahs; there are also many other Musalmáns who profess the Shíah religion. By far the greater part of the Musalmáns in the province of Oudh held

* The last four have been printed in Persia.

† This translation constitutes almost the whole of that volume of his work on Muhammadan Law called "Baillie's Digest. part ii."—See the Preface.

the Shíah faith together with their kings.* In Moorsheda-bad, too, the greater part of the Musalmáns profess the religion of the Nawáb Názim, who is and always has been a Shíah.* In Calcutta and its suburbs, besides the Mughals, who are hereditary Shíahs, the members of that sect are not much less than that of the *Sunnís*. Add to this, the Shíahs abound almost in all other parts of India. According to the British Regulations, in whatever suits the Muhammadan Law is applicable, the Shíah branch thereof is adhered to, not only in the suits wherein both parties are Shíahs, but also wherein the defendants belong to that sect.

---

* This may be said according to the Arabian adage, "All the people follow the religion of their kings." "This saying," says Mr. Niel Baillie, "was exemplified to the fullest extent in Persia, where the whole of the people have become Shíahs since the accession of the *Súfi* dynasty in A. D. 1499. The process of assimilation was less rapid in India, where, though several of the Nawábs or local Governors' were Shíahs, they yet acknowledged at least a nominal dependence on Delhí, and never ventured to make any ostensible change in the law of their provinces. This was eminently the case in Oudh, the Nawábs of which were hereditary Viziers of the empire, and though long virtually independent, did not throw off their allegiance to it till the year 1818, when the *Nawáb Vizier Ghází ud-dín Hyder*, with the consent, and, indeed, at the suggestion, of the British Government, assumed the title of Pádshah, or King. It was not, however, till the accession of *Umjad Ali Sháh* that any formal alteration was made in the law. Until that time, the only *Mufti*, or public expounder of the law, was a *Sunní*, and all cases that came before the King's tribunals were decided by the Sunní law. The last-mentioned sovereign appointed a *Shiah Muftí*, and thenceforth the *Shiah* tenets became the general law of the province. Still, however, in suits where both the parties were *Sunnis*, or one of them was a *Sunní*, and the other a Hindoo, the *Sunní* law continued to be the rule of decision. In all other suits judgment was given according to the *Shíah* code. This system seems to have continued till the province was annexed to the British dominions, by which time the *Shíahs* had acquired so great an ascendancy that they were found numerically to preponderate very much over the other sect of Musalmáns. After the annexation the more equitable rule of the British Regulations was introduced, and *Shiah* law is now administered only in suits regarding marriage and inheritance, and other collateral matters, where the parties are *Shíahs*. There is no doubt, however, that its general importance is much increased by the larger number of persons who have been brought within the sphere of its operation."—Baillie's Digest of Muhammadan Law, Part ii, Introd.. pp. xi & xii.

LECTURE VII.

ON THE CAUSES OF HERITABLE RIGHT, AND ON SUCCESSION, IN GENERAL, TO INHERITANCE.

I. The heritable right is founded either upon consanguinity (*nasab*), or upon special cause (*sabab*),* that is connection.

II. Under consanguinity are comprehended three classes (*tabkah* or *martabah*).† *First*,—Immediate parents and children how low soever; *Second*,—Grand-parents how high soever, and brethren‡ and the children, how low soever, of the latter; and *Third*,—Maternal and paternal uncles and aunts* how high soever.

Annotations.

i, ii. The causes of heritable right are of two kinds :—*First*, consanguinity ;—and persons related by consanguinity are, in law, of three classes in consecutive order.—Rouzat ul-Ahkám, p. 3.

In the law of religion, the causes of heritable right are necessarily three :—1, Consanguinity; 2, Conjugality, and 3, *Valá* (dominion or patronage).—*Mafátíh*.

i, ii. According to the tenets of this sect, the right of inheritance proceeds from three different causes. *First*, it accrues by virtue of consanguinity; *Secondly*, by virtue of marriage; *Thirdly*, by virtue of *valá*.—Macn. M. L., chap. ii, princ. 1 & 2.

---

* *Sharáya ul-Islám*, p. 440.

† "*Tabkah*" is used in the *Mafátíh*, and other works, and "*Martabah*" in the *Sharáya ul-Islám*, *Irshád* and other works. Here both these terms would be better rendered by "*class*," than by "*degree*." The latter, however, is adopted by Sir William Macnaghten, and the former, by Mr. Niel Baillie as well as by Colonel Baillie. I, however, adopt the former term not only because it suits better, but also because the word "*degree*" is used in the present work especially to indicate each grade of grand-parents and children or descendants, as will subsequently appear.

‡ The term "*brethren*" comprehends both brothers and sisters of the whole and half blood, as will hereafter be seen.

III. Special cause or connection is of two kinds: 1, *Zoujíyat*, or conjugality, and 2, *Valá** (dominion or patronage). *Principle.*

IV. The *valá*, again, is of three descriptions:— 1, the *valá* of emancipation; 2, the *valá* of responsibility for offences; and 3, the *valá* of *Imámat** or leadership in religious matters.† *Principle.*

Annotations.

iii. The cause (of heritable right) of the second kind is special cause or connection (*sabab*); and this is of two descriptions,—the one is conjugality, that is relation between the married couple; and the other, *valá*, that is dominion or patronage.—Rouzat ul-Ahkám, p. 4.

iv. The *valá*, again, is of three kinds,—*first*, the *valá* of emancipation; *second*, the *valá* of responsibility for offences; and *third*, the *valá* of *Imámat* or leadership in religion.—*Ibid.*

In default of the *valá* of emancipation, that is failing the emancipator, comes the *valá* of responsibility for offences; and in default of the person responsible for offences *(jámin-i jarírah)*, the inheritance goes, according to the correct doctrine, to the *Imám*.—Extract from *Mafátíh.*

---

* *Sharáya ul-Islám*, p. 440.

† Sir William Macnaghten says,—"In a note to his translation of the *Hidáyah* Mr. Hamilton observes that 'there is no single word in *our* language fully expressive of this term *(valá)*. The shortest definition of it is the relation between the master (or patron) and his freed man.'" And he (Sir William) adds: "But even this does not express the whole meaning. Had he proceeded to state that 'the relation between two persons who had made the reciprocal testamentary contract, the definition might have been more complete.'" But even what Sir William has added, considering Mr. Hamilton's definition incomplete, is not sufficient to express the *whole* meaning of *valá*. Had he proceeded to add to the additional meaning given by him,—"and the *Imám's* right by virtue of patronage," the definition would then have been a complete one according to the Imámiyah code, in which Sir William has given the above. In truth, the meaning of *valá* as given by Mr. Hamilton is correct according to the *Sunní* code in which it is inserted, the *Sunnis* not recognising any *valá* except that of emancipation. But the meaning of that term as given by Sir William in the Imámiyah code, is as defective as the principle itself to which it is attached. *Vide* Macn. M. L., chap. ii, princ. 2, and the note attached thereto. This will be manifest by comparing the same with Principles Nos. iii & iv, and their annotations, all of which are translations from the most authentic Arabic works.

Principle. V. Heirs are of four kinds:—The first comprises those who inherit only as *sharers*, and such are they for whom special shares have been appointed in the *Kurán;**—the second comprises those who take only by *karábat* (relationship), and they are those who inherit according to the holy text of the *Kurán* (*a*);—the third comprises those who inherit sometimes as *sharers* and sometimes *by relationship* (*b*) ; and the fourth comprises those who inherit *by relationship* as well as *by being sharers*, and they are those for whom shares have been appointed, and besides that, something goes to them by way of return (*c*).—Rouzat ul-Ahkám, p. 5.

(*a.*) As maternal and paternal uncles.—*Ibid.*

(*b.*) These are : a father, a daughter or daughters, and a paternal† sister or sisters : because a father with a child (of the deceased) inherits as a sharer, and without such child, he takes by relationship alone (that is by residuary title) : daughters with sons (of the deceased) inherit by relationship, while without them they (as sharers) take their appointed shares ; the paternal sisters with brothers (of the same description) inherit by relationship, but when alone (that is, without such a brother or brothers), they take as sharers.—*Ibid.*

ANNOTATIONS.

V. Know that every heir whom Almighty God hath named in the *Kurán*, and for whom He hath allotted a specific portion of the inheritance, is by us denominated "*Zú-farz*,"‡ or a sharer ; in the same manner as we term that portion of inheritance assigned, "*farz*," or a share ; and, further, that every heir to whom a specific share has not been allotted in the Book of God is called "*Zú-Karábat*,"§ or a *residuary*.—Col. B., Trans., p. 377.

---

* *Vide* p. 73 of Lecture II, delivered in 1873 ; and *post*, pp. 181—183.

† Here by "paternal" is meant "related by both parents as well as by the same father only."

‡ Literally, "master of a share."

§ Literally, "master of relationship."

(c.) As (in the case of there being) the mother and a daughter, a moiety goes to the daughter and a sixth to the mother as their appointed shares, and the remainder returns or reverts to them in fourths.—Rouzat ul-Ahkám, p. 5.

In the *Sharáya-ul-Islám*, however, the heirs are arranged under three heads, the third of which comprehends the second and fourth kind of heirs mentioned in the *Rouzat-ul-Ahkám*. The above is as follows:—"The heirs again, are (thus) subdivided:—1, those who have no heritable right except by *farz*, or appointment of shares (d.); 2, those who inherit sometimes by *farz*, and sometimes by mere *karábat* or relationship (e); and 3, those who are exclusive of the above, and who do not inherit except by virtue of relationship.—Sharáya ul-Islám, p. 440.

(d.) Of these, the mother is one, she being among the persons who inherit (their appointed shares) by virtue of consanguinity, besides by return;* and the husband or widow (is another), he or she being amongst those heirs who, except in rare cases,† inherit (only) for special cause or connection.—Sharáya ul-Islám, p. 440.

(e.) These are the father, a daughter or daughters, a sister or sisters and the persons related by the same mother only.—*Ibid.*

VI. The heirs who are entitled to appointed shares, and thence are called "*sharers*," are: 1, a daughter or daughters when without a grandfather, a brother or brothers; 2, a sister or sisters of the whole blood, or of the half blood on the father's side, when without a brother or brothers of the same description, or without a grandfather;‡ 3, a father with a child or children of the deceased; 4, a mother; 5, a husband; 6, a wife; and 7, the person or persons related by the same mother only.§ *Principle.*

---

* The mother, gets by return the whole of the residue in one case, and participates therein in two cases.—*Vide* Principles 78, 89, & 90.

† *Vide* Principles 11, 12, 72 & 73.

‡ Because a grandfather with a sister or sisters of the deceased is considered as a brother.—*Vide* Principles 129 *et seq.*

§ All heirs of whatever class or description, besides the above-mentioned, are denominated *simple residuaries.*—Col. B., Trans., p. 378.

Principle. VII. In particular cases, however, almost all the sharers become only residuaries, or residuaries in addition to their being sharers. Thus,—

Principle. VIII. A daughter or daughters with a brother or brothers become only residuaries; but with a parent, parents, husband or wife of the deceased, they take shares as *sharers*, and the residue as *residuaries*;* a sister or sisters of the whole blood or of the half blood on the father's side become residuaries with a brotheror brothers of the same description, or with a grandfather;† a father becomes a residuary when the deceased has left no issue how low soever, or when there exists with him (*i.e.*, the father) a daughter or daughters, a husband or wife of the deceased.‡ In certain instances, the mother, as a residuary, participates in, or takes, the whole of the residue in addition to her appointed share,‡ the husband becomes a residuary (*f*) when there exists with him no heir other than the *Imám;* the widow, however, does not become a residuary, even on failure of all other heirs (except the *Imám,* whose failure does not occur,)§ and the person or persons related by the mother alone become residuaries (*f*) only upon failure of all other heirs capable of being associated with them.‖

ANNOTATIONS.

vii. Now it often happens that the same heir is in one case a sharer, and in another, a residuary.—Col. B., Trans., p. 378.

viii. The sharers mentioned in the Book of God are nine persons; a single daughter if there be no son of the deceased; two or more daughters also on failure of a son; a single sister by the same father and mother, or by the same father only, if there be no brother or grandfather; two or more sisters also on failure of a brother and grandfather; a father, if there be issue of the deceased; a mother in all situations; a husband and a widow in every situation; and lastly, a relation who is connected with the deceased by the mother's side only. Of

---

* *Vide* Principles 84, 88 *et seq.*
† *Vide* Principles 118, 121, 129 *et seq.*
‡ *Vide* Principles 78, 88 *et seq.*
§ *Vide* Principles 72 & 73.
‖ *Vide* Principles 123, 124 & 131.

(*f.*) By the expression "becomes a residuary" or "become residuaries," is meant that the person or persons becoming so are entitled to the residue remaining after allotment of the appointed share or shares of the other heir or heirs happening to be in the case. For instance, in the case of (there being) a daughter, and a widow, the residue, remaining after allotment of the appointed share of the widow, goes to the daughter, or, in other words, after all otment of the specific shares of the daughter and widow which are respectively "a moiety, and an eighth," the remainder reverts to the daughter

On Shares, their Proportions, and the Persons entitled thereto.

IX. There are six shares:—a half, fourth, and an eighth; two-thirds, one-third, and a sixth.* *Principle.*

The shares and sharers according to the Muhammadan law of the *Imámiyah* school are the same as according to that of the *Sunní* school; such shares and sharers having been ordained in the *Kurán*† from which the Muhammadan law in general has originated.

ANNOTATIONS.

these, the five first are often residuaries also, as where, with a daughter or with two daughters, there is a son; where, with a sister, or two or more sisters, there is a brother, or grandfather; and where, with a father, there is no issue of the deceased. The remaining four, again, can never, in any situation, be residuaries, except upon entire failure of every heir that is capable of being associated with them, in which case of necessity they take the whole inheritance, first as sharers and then the *residuum* by return.—Col. B., Trans., p. 378. This, however, is not entirely accurate, as will appear on comparison with the above.

The father of the deceased, upon failure of issue, is not a specific sharer in the estate, but has by law merely a residuary title to all that remains after distribution of the other shares. Thus, if a person deceased should leave, for example, a father, a mother, and a husband, the mother, in this case, takes a third, if not partially excluded by brothers or sisters; the husband also enjoys his appointed share, *viz.*, a half, and the remaining sixth is all that would go to the father.—Col. B., Trans., p. 383.

---

* *Sharáya ul-Islám*, p. 445.

† *Vide* p. 78 of Lecture II, delivered in 1873.

Principle. X. Half is the share of a husband when there is no issue how low soever; of an only daughter; and of a full sister, or half sister on the father's side (*g*).*

(*g.*) Know that six shares have been distinctly ordained in the holy *Kurán.* The first share is half, which is ordained for three parties, (of whom,) the first is a husband,—that is, when a woman dies leaving no issue of her womb how low soever, the share of her husband in the property left by her is a moiety thereof; the second an only daughter, on whom devolves half of the property of her father or mother, when he or she dies; and the third an only sister by the same father and mother, or by the same father only, who gets half of the deceased's property when there is no nearer heir than herself.—Rouzat ul-Ahkám, p. 4.

Principle. XI. A fourth is the share of a husband when the deceased has left no issue how low soever (*h*); or of a widow (or widows†) without any issue (*i*)* of the deceased.

(*h.*) By the term "child or issue," is meant the deceased's son or daughter, and by "children or issue," his son *and* daughter, sons *or* daughters, a son *and* daughters, a daughter *and* sons as well as sons *and* daughters; and the expression "how low soever" indicates the deceased's child's child or children, or children's children in any stage of descent in the female as well as in the male line.

(*i.*) The second share is a fourth, which is ordained for a widow,—that is when a man dies leaving a wife married permanently, or by a temporary contract but with a condition to inherit, and leaves no issue, how low soever, born even of the womb of a wife other than herself, then a fourth part of the deceased's property, excepting land and the like,‡ goes to the wife or widow;—also for a husband when his wife dies leaving issue of her own how low soever, even though begotten by a former husband.—Rouzat ul-Ahkám, p. 4.

Principle. XII. An eighth is the share of a widow (or widows†) where the deceased has left a child or children (*h*) how low soever in descent (*j*).*

(*j.*) The third share is an eighth, which is the portion of a wife in case of the existence of her husband's issue how low soever.—Rouzat ul-Ahkám, p. 5.

---

* *Sharáya ul-Islám*, p. 445.

† Where there is more than one widow, the fourth or eighth, as the case may be, is divisible among them *equally*.—Note by Mr. Neil Baillie.—*Vide* Principle 123.

‡ This will be stated *in extenso* in the Succession of Spouses in Lecture IX.

XIII. Two-thirds are the portion of two or more (brotherless) daughters, or of two or more (brotherless) sisters by the same father and mother, or by the same father only* (*k*). *Principle.*

(*k.*) The fourth share is two-thirds, which is ordained for two or more (brotherless) daughters, as well as for two or more (brotherless) sisters of the whole blood, or of the half blood on the father's side.—Rouzat ul-Ahkám, p. 5.

XIV. A third is the share of a mother when the deceased has left no issue how low soever, nor brethren (*l*) to exclude her (that is, to reduce her share from a third to a sixth), or of two or more children (*m*) by the same mother only*(*n*). *Principle.*

(*l.*) Here by "*brethren*" is meant two or more brothers, or at least one brother and two sisters,† or only four sisters by both parents or by the same father only, as no less than this number of such brethren can exclude the mother, that is deprive her of a third, and reduce it to a sixth.—*Vide* Exclusion from Inheritance.

(*m.*) By "two or more children by the same mother only" is meant a brother *and* sister, brothers *or* sisters, two or more brothers *and* sisters, a brother *and* sisters, or a sister *and* brothers of the half blood on the mother's side.

(*n.*) The fifth share is one-third, and this is ordained for the mother, if the deceased has left no issue how low soever, and there do not exist brethren who exclude her (partially); and also for two or more brethren by the same mother only.—Rouzat ul-Ahkám, p. 5.

XV. A sixth is the share of each of the parents if the deceased has left issue how low soever,—or of the mother if there are with her (the deceased's) brethren by both parents or by the same father only, the father himself being in existence. It is also the share of a single child by the same mother only, whether such child be male or female (*o*).* *Principle.*

(*o.*) The sixth share is a sixth, which is the portion of a father or mother in the case of the existence of the deceased's (child or) children how low soever; it is also ordained for the mother in

* *Sharáya ul-Islám*, p. 445.

† Two sisters are considered in law as equal to one brother.

the case of her being (partially) excluded by (the deceased's) brethren, and also for a single brother or sister by the same mother only.—Rouzat ul-Ahkám, p. 5.

The conclusion of the foregoing is as follows :—

Principle. XVI. The large or full share of a husband is "a moiety," that of a widow, "a fourth," and that of a mother, "a third," and their small or reduced shares are respectively "a fourth, an eighth, and a sixth."

Principle. XVII. An only daughter without a brother or brothers gets, as her appointed share, a half of her late father's, as well as mother's, estate; and two or more daughters without a brother or brothers collectively get, as their appointed share, two-thirds of such estate.*

Principle. XVIII. On failure of a nearer heir, an only whole sister without a grandfather,† or without a brother or brothers of her own, gets, as her appointed share, a moiety of her deceased brother's or sister's estate, while two or more such sisters, under the above circumstance, collectively get, as their share, two-thirds of the said estate.* Failing the whole sister, the half sister on the father's side takes her place in succession,‡ and, accordingly, gets a moiety, and two or more of such sisters get two-thirds, when without a grandfather,† a brother or brothers of her or their own.

Principle. XIX. An only brother *or* sister by the mother alone gets a sixth, while two or more of them collectively get one-third,* which is divided *equally* among them, the general rule "to each male goes the portion of two females" not being applicable to the persons related by the same mother only.

---

* *Vide* Principles 83, 119, & 120.

† Because a grandfather with a sister or sisters of the deceased is considered as a brother.—*Vide* Principles 129 & 130.

‡ *Vide* Principles 121, 122.

XX. A father gets a sixth as his specific share in the case of there being a child or children how low soever, while in default of such issue of the deceased, he gets the whole of the residue remaining after allotment of the appointed share or shares.* *Principle.*

XXI. The mother too gets a sixth in the case of there being a child or children how low soever, or brethren, of the deceased; in other cases she is entitled to one-third, and to no residuary portion except in rare instances.† *Principle.*

XXII. A husband is entitled to a moiety of his deceased wife's property if she has left no issue, how low soever, of her own, but to a fourth only, if there is any such issue. *Principle.*

XXIII. The widow or widows permanently married are entitled to a fourth of their deceased husband's property, excepting land or the like, if the deceased has left no child or children how low soever; and to an eighth of his property if he has left any child or children; but even *then* a widow is not entitled to an eighth of land or the like, if such child or children were born not of her, but of another wife of the deceased. A woman married under a temporary contract is entitled to inherit if the contract contained a stipulation to that effect; and when entitled to inherit, she gets a fourth or an eighth under the same circumstance as a permanently married widow does.‡ *Principle.*

ANNOTATIONS.

xxiii. If there are several widows, all of them equally share the fourth or eighth (as the case may be).—Irshád.

---

* *Vide ante*, p. 181, and Principles 78, 79, 84 *et seq.*

† *Vide* Principles 78, 79, 84, 88 *et seq.*

‡ For further particulars of, and necessities in, the widow's succession. *vide* Succession of Spouses.

On Combination and Non-combination of Shares.

Principle. **XXIV.** Of the shares above mentioned, some are combined, or are susceptible of combination, with others, and some are not.* Thus,—

Principle. XXV. A half is combined, or may occur together, with the other half (*p*), with a fourth (*q*), an eighth (*r*), a third (*s*), and a sixth (*t*).†—Rouzat ul-Ahkám, p. 6.

(*p*.) As (in the case of there being) a husband and a brotherless paternal sister.‡—*Ibid.*

(*q*.) As a widow and paternal sister; or a husband and an only daughter.—*Ibid.*

(*r*.) As a widow and an only daughter.—*Ibid.*

(*s*.) As a husband and a mother; or a husband and two or more children by the same mother only.—*Ibid.*

(*t*.) As a husband with a single brother or sister by the same mother only; or a daughter with one of the parents.—*Ibid.*

Principle. XXVI. A fourth is combined with two-thirds (*u*), a third (*v*), and a sixth (*w*).†—Rouzat ul-Ahkám, p. 6.

(*u*.) As (in the case of there being) a husband and two (or more) daughters.—*Ibid.*

Annotations.

xxv. A half is combined with its like, with a fourth, and with an eighth; but it does not combine with two-thirds, on account of the nullity of the doctrine of *Oul* or Increase, the deficiency (in case of such occurrence) falling on the two or more sisters, and not on the husband. A half is also combined with a third, and with a sixth.—Sharáya ul-Islám, p. 445.

xxvi, xxvii. A fourth and an eighth do not combine together; but a fourth may be combined with two-thirds, one-third, and a sixth.—Sharáya ul-Islám, p. 446.

---

* *Sharáya ul-Islám*, p. 445.

† And *vice versâ*.

‡ Here by "a paternal sister" is meant a sister by both parents as well as one by the same father only.

(*v.*) As a widow and a mother.—Rouzat ul-Ahkám, p. 6.

(*w.*) As a widow and a brother or sister by the same mother only.—*Ibid.*

XXVII. An eighth occurs together with two-thirds (*x*), and a sixth* (*y*).—*Ibid.* *Principle.*

(*x.*) As (in the case of there being) a widow and two or more daughters.—*Ibid.*

(*y.*) As a widow and one of the parents with a child or children of the deceased.—*Ibid.*

XXVIII. Two-thirds occur with a third (*z*) and a sixth*(*a*).—*Ibid.* *Principle.*

(*z.*) As (in the case of there being) two paternal sisters and two sisters by the same mother only.—*Ibid.*

(*a.*) As two daughters and one of the parents.—*Ibid.*

XXIX. A sixth occurs with a sixth*(*b*).—*Ibid.* *Principle.*

(*b.*) As (in the case of) a father and mother with a child or children (of the deceased).—*Ibid.*

There are some other combinations of the shares, which in a manner are repetitions of the above, for if one share is combined with another, the latter must be held to combine with the former;—as when an eighth is combined with a sixth, a sixth is of course combined with an eighth. These, therefore, have been intimated in foot notes by the expression "and *vice versá*," it being considered unnecessary to state them separately.

ANNOTATIONS.

xxvii. An eighth combines with two-thirds and a sixth; but not with a third. And a third does not combine with a sixth by name.—Sharáya ul-Islám, p. 446.

xxviii. Two-thirds combine with one-third, also with a sixth, likewise with a fourth, as two sisters with a widow; and with an eighth,—as in the case of two daughters with a widow of the deceased.—Col. B., Trans., p. 382.

xxix. A sixth admits of combination with two-thirds, with a half, and with a fourth, as formerly exhibited, also with a sixth, as in the case of both parents, should there be issue of the deceased; and lastly with an eighth, as in the case of a child with the widow and both parents, or any one of them.—Col. B., Trans., p. 383.

---

* And *vice versâ.*

The shares which cannot combine with each other are the following:—

Two-thirds cannot combine with two-thirds or with a half; one-third cannot combine with a third, nor with a sixth, nor with an eighth; one-eighth can never be allotted with an eighth, nor with a fourth; and, lastly, two-fourths can never be assigned from the same estate. This incapacity of combination in some of the foregoing cases, and the various grounds thereof, will be evident from a retrospect of the shares and persons entitled to them with the established conditions on which they are allotted; but a further cause of incapacity in some will hereafter be made manifest when we come to describe the nullity, according to our law, of the doctrine of *Oul*, a prevailing system amongst all doctors of the opposite sect.*—Col. B., Trans., p. 383.

Those shares of the inheritance which do not admit of combination can never be allotted from one and the same estate, partly because the parties entitled to such shares do not occur together (*c*), and partly because, if such parties do occur in one and the same case, still one of them cannot have his or her full share by reason of this (share), coupled with the other, exceeding the whole, and the system of Increase not being recognised in the Imámiyah Law (*d*).

(*c*.) As a fourth and an eighth do not admit of combination, because the parties entitled to them are a husband and a widow, and they can never occur together in one and the same case.

(*d*.) In the case of there being a husband and two paternal sisters, the husband is entitled to a half, and the sisters are entitled to two-thirds, but a half and two-thirds cannot combine by reason of their exceeding the whole, though the parties entitled thereto can occur in one and the same case, the share of the two sisters is, therefore, reduced to a half, since the whole could not be increased in the proportion of two-thirds and a half, as done according to the law of the *Sunní* school.*

General Rules of the Order of Succession by Consanguinity (nasab).

The consanguinous heirs are (as already mentioned) divided into three classes.

* *Vide* pp. 228–232 of Lecture VI, delivered in 1873.

XXX. The consanguinous heirs of the first class consist of the deceased's immediate parents and children how low soever; of the second class consist the deceased's paternal and maternal grand-parents how high soever, also brothers and sisters, and their (the two latter's) children how low soever; and of the third class are the children, how low soever, of the deceased's paternal and maternal grand-parents how high soever.—*Vide* Sharáya ul-Islám, p. 440. *Principle.*

XXXI. The heirs of the first class are subdivided into two sections, of which the first consists of the *Principle.*

ANNOTATIONS.

xxx—xxxv. Persons related by consanguinity are of three classes in consecutive order. Each of these classes is divided into two sections; of the first class the (deceased's) father and mother constitute one section, and children how low soever constitute the other section, the nearest being preferred to the more distant. The second class comprises grand-parents and brethren, and, therefore, has two sections, the first comprising the grand-parents, by which is meant the father's father and mother, and mother's father and mother how high soever, and the second comprising collaterals, by which is meant brothers and sisters, how low soever, whether they be by both parents or by the same mother only, or by the same father only, (and this last set succeeds) in the event of there being none by both parents. The third class comprises paternal and maternal uncles and aunts, that is brothers and sisters of fathers and mothers. In this class also, there are two sections in lieu of one.—Rouzat ul-Ahkám, p. 4.

xxx—xxxvi, lxi. In the first class are included by law the father and mother, or the immediate parents of the deceased, without extending to more remote ancestors, and his children, extending to the lowest, as grandchildren, great-grandchildren, and so on, however remote in descent, with this proviso, that, of these, the nearer always excludes from succession one more remote in degree. The second class of consanguinous heirs comprehends grandfathers and grandmothers of the deceased, how high soever in degree of ancestry, and brothers and sisters and their children however remote in descent, the nearest always excluding one more removed. Under the third class of consanguinous heirs are comprehended brothers of the deceased's father, brothers of

immediate parents, and the second, of children how low soever. The heirs of the second class are likewise subdivided into two sections, the first of them comprising the deceased's paternal and maternal grandparents how high soever, and the second comprising the deceased's brothers and sisters of the half

---

ANNOTATIONS.

the mother, and the sisters of both; commonly known by the characteristic appellation of paternal and maternal uncles and aunts; and upon faillure of these, their children and children's children, and so on, the nearest in descent always excluding one more remote.—Col. B., Trans., pp. 324, 326 & 328.

xxx, xxxvi. Persons related by consanguinity are of several classes (*tabkát*), the nearest of which comprises the deceased's immediate parents, and children how low soever in consecutive order: the nearest (first), then the nearest (after him or her). *Next*, the grandfather and grandmother how high soever, in consecutive order, brothers and sisters, and on failure of these (*i.e.*, the two latter), their children how low soever, in consecutive order. *Next*, paternal uncles and aunts, maternal uncles and aunts; and in default of them, their children how low soever, in the same manner or order. *Next*, the father's and mother's paternal uncles and aunts, maternal uncles and aunts, and failing them, their children how low soever, in the same manner or order. *Next*, grandfather's and grandmother's paternal uncles and aunts and maternal uncles and aunts, failing them, their children how low soever—the nearest (first), then the nearest (after him or her); and so in all the classes. Thus in the two first classes there are two sections *(sanaf)*, and in each of the other classes there is but one section, inasmuch as they are (composed of) brethren of the fathers and mothers.—Mafátíh.

xxx, xxxvi, xli. There are three degrees* of heirs, who succeed by virtue of consanguinity. The first degree comprises the parents and children, and grandchildren, how low in descent soever, the nearer of whom exclude the more distant. The second degree comprises the grandfather, grandmother, and other ancestors, brothers and sisters, and their children how low soever, the nearer of whom excludes the more distant. The third degree comprises the paternal and maternal uncles and aunts, and their descendants, the nearer of whom excludes the more distant.—Macn. M. L., chap. ii, princ. 3, 4, 8 & 10.

---

* "*Degrees*," that is classes, *vide* foot-note at p. 176.

as well as of the whole blood, and the children, how low soever, of the two latter. The heirs of the third class, though not so subdivided, are arranged under two heads—paternal and maternal. Again,— *Principle.*

XXXII. The second section of the first class comprises heirs of different series or degrees in consecutive order, *viz.:* — 1, Immediate children; 2, Grandchildren; 3, Great grandchildren, and so on the other generations of progeny lower and lower and step by step. *Principle.*

XXXIII. The first section of the second class too comprises different degrees of heirs, *viz.:*— 1, Grand-parents; 2, Great grand-parents; 3, Great great grand-parents and so on in the ascending line. *Principle.*

XXXIV. The second section of the above class likewise comprises different degrees of heirs, *viz.:*— 1, Brothers and sisters; 2, Their children; 3, The children of the latter, and so on successively in the descending line. *Principle.*

ANNOTATIONS.

xxxi, xxxii. The first class, as may have been observed, comprehends two descriptions, *viz.:* first, the *root* of the deceased, which is limited in number, as including only the immediate parents, whose place in succession with children cannot be supplied by ancestors more remote; and second, the *branch* or offspring of the deceased, which is unlimited in number and degree, as comprehending children and children's children however remote in descent, observing always the rule of precedence by proximity in degree, and thus supplying the place of each step in the event of failure, by the next thereto in descent.—Col. B., Trans., p. 324.

xxxiii, xxxiv, xxxvi. The second class likewise involves two separate descriptions of heirs: one comprehending all grandfathers and grandmothers of the deceased, how high soever in the line of ancestry, with application of the rule of precedence by proximity, to the nearer first

Principle. XXXV. The two heads of the third class comprise also different degrees of heirs in the ascending as well as in the descending line, *viz.:*—1, Uncle and aunt; 2, Grand-uncle and aunt; 3, Great grand-uncle and aunt, and so on upwards: 1, Uncle's and aunt's children; 2, Grandchildren; 3, Great grandchildren, and so on downwards.

Principle. XXXVI. The heirs of the first class being the nearest to the deceased inherit in preference to those of the second and third classes, and the heirs of the second class being nearer to the deceased than those of the third class inherit in preference to the latter.

Example. As, for example, where there are immediate parents or children, also grand-parents and uncles, there the immediate parents or children, who are of the first class, inherit to the exclusion of the grand-parents and uncles who are not so; and where there is none of

---

ANNOTATIONS.

and then to the more remote; and the other including all brothers and sisters and their children, how low soever, always observing the same rule. To each of these descriptions there being unlimited degrees of ascent and descent.—Col. B., Trans., p. 326.

xxxv. This (third) class, it may be observed, involves only one general description of heirs, because their title to succession is derived from one general relation to the deceased, *viz.*, that of brotherhood or sisterhood to their parents, for brothers and sisters, we have already seen, to be included in one description of the second series; and, consequently, all persons connected by this tie must also be considered in one and the same description, which, however, like the former, unlimited, possesses numberless degrees of proximity and distance that are necessarily referred to in settling the succession.—Col. B., Trans., p. 329.

xxxii, xxxvi, xli. Under the first title are comprehended several series (degrees), each of which, in the order here described, enjoys a preference in succession over that which follows it, to the utter exclusion of the latter; and thus, whilst of the first class, a single member, whether male or female, exists, there is no title of inheritance in the second; and the same of the second with respect to the third.—Col. B., Trans., p. 323.

the first class, but only the grand-parents and uncles exist, there the grand-parents who are of the second class inherit to the exclusion of the uncles who are of the third class.

A grandfather of the deceased cannot inherit with any one of the immediate parents, nor of the children how low soever; and, in like manner, a brother of the deceased is completely excluded by the existence of any member of this series (*i.e.*, class); as are also all uncles both paternal and maternal.—Col. B., Trans., p. 324. Example.

Consequently,—

XXXVII. So long as there exists a single person, male or female, of any of the two sections of the first class, no person belonging to any of the sections of the second class can inherit and so long as there exists a single person, male or female, of any of the two sections of the second class, none of the third class can inherit. *Principle.*

Accordingly,—

XXXVIII. Where there is but a single person of the first class, the whole property goes to him or to her, to the exclusion of the relative or relatives, if any, of the second or third class; and where there is no heir of the first class, but only one of the second class, the whole property devolves on him or her to the exclusion of the relative or relatives, if any, of the third class. *Principle.*

As, if there be an immediate parent or an only daughter, and a single brother, and also uncles and aunts, then the immediate parent or the only daughter being of the first class will take Example.

ANNOTATIONS.

xxxvii—xli. So long as there exists an heir of the first class, the heirs of the two other classes do not take the inheritance; in like manner, so long as there exists an heir of the second class, none of the third class takes the inheritance.—Rouzat ul Akhám, p. 3.

So long as there is any one of the first degree (*i.e.*, class),* even though a female, none of the second degree can inherit; and so long as there is any one of the second degree, none of the third can inherit.—Macn. M. L., chap. ii, princ. 3.

---

* *Vide* foot-note at p. 176.

the whole of the inheritance to the exclusion of all the rest: if, on the other hand, there be none of the first class, but only a brother or sister in the second, and uncles and aunts in the third class, then the only brother or sister will take the whole inheritance to the entire exclusion of the uncles and aunts.

Principle. XXXIX. Among the members of the *same class*, an individual or individuals of one section inherit with an individual or individuals (as the case may be) of the other section, with this difference, however, that the individual or individuals of one section, who are the nearest or the *then* nearest to the deceased, inherit with such individual or individuals of the other section of the class, and *vice versâ*.

That is to say,—

Principle. XL. The nearest or the *then* nearest individuals of both the sections inherit together, but such individual or individuals of one of the sections do not inherit with the remoter relative or relatives of the other section so long as the nearest or the then nearest relative or relatives of *that* section are in *esse*. Again, the individuals of the different degrees of one

ANNOTATIONS.

xxxix—xli. The nearest of each section does not exclude the distant of another section of the same class, but the nearest excludes the distant when the latter is in the same section of a class; even though the nearest be a female she would exclude others of other degrees; except in a single case by general assent, which is, that—'the son of a paternal uncle by the same father and mother, excludes a paternal uncle by the same father only, and takes his share. This rule, however, does not extend to other cases.'—Mafátíh.

xxxix—xli. An individual of one class* does not exclude an individual of the other, though his relation to the deceased be more proximate, but the individuals of either class* exclude each other in proportion to their proximity.—Macn. M. L., chap. ii, princ. 5.

xxxix—xli. No member of one description, even the nearest in degreee (*i. e.*, section), can exclude even the most remote of the other from inheritance, because exclusion by proximity can only take effect amongst heirs that are of one and the same description, in the same manner as a child of the deceased, even the most remote in descent, is not excluded by the existence of both father and mother, or any one of them.—Col. B., Trans., pp. 326 & 327.

* "*Class*," that is "*section*," *vide* foot-note in p. 176.

and the same section do not inherit together, but the first, or the *then* foremost, of them being the nearest or comparatively nearer to the deceased takes the inheritance in preference to the remoter degrees of the same section. And if there be individuals of different degrees of both sections of a class, then those of the first or *the then* foremost degree of one section inherit together with the individual or individuals of the like degree of the other section, and not with those of a remoter degree, so long as a person or persons of the nearest or the then nearest degree be in *esse*. Hence,—

XLI. The members of the second and third classes are excluded by a member or members of the first class,* but a member or members of one section of a class are not excluded by a member or members of the other section thereof, even though the latter be more proximate to the deceased, while, on the other hand, members of remoter degrees of a section are excluded by a member or members of the first or the then foremost or nearest degree of the same section, though not by such of the other section. *Principle.*

Both parents or one of them inherit together with a child, a grandchild, or a great grandchild; but a grandchild does not inherit together with a child, nor a great grandchild together with a grandchild.—Macn. M. L., chap. ii, princ. 4. **Example.**

ANNOTATIONS.

xxxix—xli. No member, even the nearest one, as a father, for example, of the deceased, can exclude from succession the most remote of the other as a great grandchild; but, on the contrary, this exclusion by proximity of degree takes effect only where the heirs are of one and the same description, like a son, for instance, or a daughter of the deceased, who necessarily excludes a grandchild from inheritance.—Col. B., Trans., pp. 322 & 325.

xxxix—xli. A grandfather of the deceased, however near, inherits with the immediate offspring of a brother or sister, and their children's children how low soever; but does by no means exclude them from succession; and, in like manner, a brother or sister of the deceased may be associated with a great grandfather or grandmother however remote in ascent.—Col. B., Trans., p. 327.

* See *ante*, pp. 192—194.

For example, if there be a grandfather and a great grandfather who belong to one section of the second class, and a brother and brother's children who belong to the other section of that class, then the grandfather, who is nearer than the great grandfather, and the brother who is nearer than the brother's children, and both of whom are the then nearest to the deceased, inherit together, and *not* also the great grandfather and brother's children. Thus the great grandfather is excluded by the grandfather, because the former is in the *second* degree and the latter in the *first* degree of one section, and, in like manner, brother's children are excluded by the brother, because the former are in the second degree and the latter is in the first degree of the other section of the second class. But the grandfather could not exclude the brother's children by reason of his not being in the same section of the class as they are: likewise, the brother could not exclude the great grandfather by reason of his (the brother's) not being in the same section of the class as that ancestor is. On the contrary, the grandfather would have inherited together with the brother's children if the brother had not been in existence, and, in like manner, the brother would have inherited with the great grandfather if the grandfather had not been in existence. If, instead of heirs belonging to both the sections of a class, there were heirs belonging to one section only but in the different degrees thereof, for instance, if there were only the grandfather, great grandfather and great great grandfather who belong to one and the same section of the second class, then the grandfather alone would have inherited to the exclusion of the other ancestors; or if there were not a brother, but a brother's immediate children, their children, children of the latter, and so on, all of whom belong to the other section of the second class, but are in the different and successive degrees thereof, then only the brother's immediate children would have inherited to the exclusion of the rest for the reasons stated.

The great grandfather cannot inherit together with a grandfather or a grandmother; and the son of a brother cannot inherit with a brother or a sister; and the grandson of a brother cannot inherit with the son of a brother, or with the son of a sister.—*Ibid*, princ. 8.

A paternal uncle or aunt is obviously nearer in degree to the deceased than the son of a paternal or maternal uncle, and an uncle or aunt by the mother's side nearer than the son of a paternal or maternal uncle or aunt. It follows, therefore, that with a maternal uncle only of the deceased, or with a single maternal aunt, not one of their children, nor the children of a paternal uncle or aunt, can have any title to inheritance; and by the same rule, if a paternal uncle or aunt of the deceased exist, no part of the succession can go to their children, or to those of a maternal uncle or aunt.—Col. B., Trans., p. 329.

A grandfather's father cannot inherit with a grandfather or grandmother, and even a brother's son has no title with a brother or sister of the deceased; a brother's grandson is excluded by a brother's or by a sister's son; and, in short, the arrangement respecting children and children's children of the deceased, formerly explained, has a similar influence exactly over members of this class; of which, further, no individual can possibly inherit whilst any member, even a female of the first series, exists. The degree of grandfathers and grandmothers is nearer to the deceased, and necessarily excludes that of their parents, and the degree, in like manner, of brothers and sisters is nearer than that of their children.—*Ibid*, p. 326.

The son of a paternal uncle does not inherit with a paternal uncle or aunt; and, in like manner, the son of a maternal uncle is excluded by a maternal uncle or aunt.—*Ibid*, pp. 328 and 329.

A grandfather, though he be a distant one, inherits with brethren, though the latter be nearer to the deceased, and *vice versâ*, that is to say, the children of brethren, how low soever in descent, become, like their fathers and mothers, co-heirs of the grand-parents, though the latter be nearer to the deceased; for this reason that the two sections are unalterable. But if there be relatives of the nearer and remoter degrees and of one and the same section (of a class), the nearer exclude the remoter. So the deceased's immediate grandfather excludes his own father, in like manner a brother and sister exclude their children.—Rouzat ul-Ahkám, p.45.

XLII. Thus the general rule, or order, of succession is, that the relative or relatives nearest to the deceased succeed first, failing them, the next in the order of proximity, and so on to the remotest degree of relationship. *Principle.*

The only exception to the above rule and order of succession is, that—

XLIII. When there is a son of a paternal full uncle with a paternal half uncle or aunt, or of both, *Principle.*

ANNOTATIONS.

xliii. Generally, a nephew or niece, whose father was of the whole blood, does not exclude his or her uncle or aunt of the half blood; except in the case of there being a son of a paternal uncle of the whole

on the father's side, and with none else, then the former excludes the latter.

Thus the *Rouzat ul-Ahkám*:—" Although the nearest (relative) in one section excludes the more distant (relative) in the same section, yet there is an anomaly in one case by general assent, which is, that the son of a paternal full uncle excludes a paternal half uncle on the father's side."—P. 4.

So the *Irshád*:—" There is one case by general assent, and that is, when a person dies leaving an uncle by the same father only, and the son of a paternal uncle of the whole blood, then the whole inheritance devolves on the son of the paternal full uncle, and nothing goes to the paternal uncle of the half blood on the father's side."

ANNOTATIONS.

blood, and a paternal uncle of the half blood by the same father only, the latter of whom is excluded by the former.—Macn. M. L., princ. 14.

With respect to the particular exception above described, in addition to the unanimous assent of all our doctors, it is established by an express tradition of the *Imám Jaafar Saádik*, on whom be peace, recorded by *Husain Ibnu Amaru* in these words: "The *Imám*, on whom be peace, put this question to me: 'Who is preferred in succession to a person deceased, the son of a paternal full uncle, or his paternal uncle by the same father only?' I replied that I had heard a tradition from the Commander of the Faithful to this effect: 'The sons of paternal full uncles are preferred to kinsmen by the father's side only.' He observed, 'you have explained it in a clear and obvious manner. Verily, *Abdullah*, father to the Prophet of God, was full brother of *Abú Tálib* by the same father and mother, whence the Commander of the Faithful, as son of *Abú Tálib*, had no issue of the Prophet remained, would have excluded *Abbás* his uncle by the same father only, from inheritance.' "—Col. B., Trans., p. 331.

And hereupon a question has arisen whether the exception is by law restricted to the particular instance before us without application to any other, or may be also legally extended to all similar cases. The most common and prevalent doctrine has restricted its influence to this particular case alone, and the author of the *Sharáya* has expressly declared that if with these two persons, *viz*., the son of a paternal full uncle and a paternal uncle of the half blood, any other heir, even a maternal uncle, should exist, the decision of law would be completely altered, and the title of the uncle's son entirely cut off.—*Ibid.*

So also the *Mafátíh* :—"The son of a paternal uncle by the same father and mother excludes a paternal uncle by the same father only, and takes his portion. This rule does not, however, extend to other cases."

So also the *Sharáya ul-Islám* :—"The son of a paternal uncle does not inherit with a paternal uncle, nor does any one who is remoter from the deceased inherit with one who is nearer to him, except in one case, which is that of the son of a paternal *full* uncle with a half paternal uncle on the father's side, when the paternal full uncle's son is preferred while the case remains exactly so; but if it is changed by the addition even of a maternal uncle, the son of the paternal uncle is excluded."

On the mode of Succession to the whole or a particular portion of the Inheritance.

The consanguinous heirs inherit, as already stated,* in virtue of their being sharers or relations.

XLIV. If there is only one heir without an equal, or a superior, whether he or she be entitled—1, only as a sharer (*zú-farz*), or 2, as a mere relative (*zú-karábat*), or 3, only for special cause,—such heir takes the whole property; in the first case, partly as his or her appointed share, and partly by return (*e*); in the second, the whole at once (*f*); and in the third, partly as the appointed share and partly by return or the whole at once (*g*). *Vide* Principles 78, 80, 83, 117, 119, 126, 131 146, & 152. *Principle.*

ANNOTATIONS.

xliv. If the heir is a sharer (*zú-farz*), he or she takes, as such, the appointed share, and if there is no equal (that is, if there is no co-heir of such heir), he or she takes the surplus also by *radd* or return.—Sharáya ul-Islám, p. 440.

If there should be only one heir of the person deceased, such individual takes the whole property to himself, whatever the nature of his title

* See *ante*, p. 176 *et seq.*

(e.) As in the case of there being an only daughter, and no co-heir of hers, the daughter first takes her appointed share, which is a moiety, and then the other moiety returns or reverts to her.*

Examples. (f.) As in the case of there being an only son and no co-heir of his, the son at once takes the whole by relationship (*karâbat*), he not being a specific sharer like the daughter.*

As when there is a daughter with a brother, or a sister with a paternal uncle (of the deceased), the daughter or sister takes first her appointed share, and *then* the remainder reverts to her by return, because she is nearer to the deceased.—Sharáya ul-Islám, pp. 440 & 446.

(g.) As in the case of there being a husband and no other heir (except the Imám), he first takes his full share, which is a half, and then the remainder by return, or the whole at once.

ANNOTATIONS.

may be, consanguinous, emancipatory, or of patronage, in whatsoever class or description he may be placed, and if even the lowest or most remote member of that class, without any distinction whatsoever, and this by unanimous assent. The only distinction that can occur is this: that where such individual or sole heir happens to be of the class of *sharers*, he inherits under two separate titles ; first, his own appointed share and then the *return*, as a *residuary*. Where, on the other hand, he is not a sharer, his simple residuary title alone embraces the whole property at once, whether founded upon emancipation, patronage, or any other ground whatsoever. Thus, if we suppose a sister by the mother's side to be the sole heiress of a person deceased, she receives first her appointed share, *viz.*, a sixth part of the estate, and then the remainder as a residuary. If, again, a brother by the father should be sole heir, he inherits the whole property at once as a residuary, having no specific share allotted to him ; and upon these two examples all other classes and degrees may be conceived without repetition.—Col. B., Trans., p. 392.

xliv, xlvi. When an heir is a person for whom no share has been appointed, and there is none to participate with him, the property (*mál*) is his, whether his right be by consanguinity (*nasab*), or for special cause (*sabab*); but if he has a co-heir for whom (also) no share has been appointed, then the property is for them both.—Sharáya ul-Islám, p. 440.

---

* *Vide* Principles 80 & 83.

If a person dies leaving only a father surviving him, the whole property goes to him by virtue of relationship (*karábat*). So also to the mother (in the above circumstance), though a third goes as her specific share, and the remainder by return.—Rouzat ul-Ahkám, p. 32.

When the deceased has left no heir except her husband, then the whole inheritance goes to him,—half as his appointed share, and the other half by return.—Irshád.

As establishing the general principle, in addition to unanimous assent, we have the following traditional documents:—First, a report of *Salmá Ibnu Muhraz* from the *Imám Jaafer Sádik,* on whom be peace, to this effect: "I reported the death of a man who had bequeathed to me all his property by will, having at the same time a daughter. The *Imám* inquired if there were any witnesses to the will, and upon my answering in the negative, directed me to surrender all the property to the daughter as hers of right." Secondly, by a report of *Abdullah Ibnu Sinán* from the same *Imám* in these words: "I enquired concerning a person deceased who had left a brother by his mother and no other heir besides. He replied, 'The property goes all to that brother.'" Further, in the commentary of *Alí Ibnu Ibráhím,* a tradition is quoted from *Bukhyr Ibnu Ayún* of the *Imám Muhammad Bákir,* on whom be peace, to this effect: "If a man die leaving an only sister, she takes first her appointed share,—*viz.*, one-half of his inheritance, agreeably to the sacred text, in the same manner as a daughter would have done if in existence, and the remaining half also reverts to her should there be no other nearer heir, in virtue of a residuary title." If instead of this sister there be a brother of the deceased, he inherits the whole property under one general title, agreeably to the saying of Almighty God,—"And he is sole heir if there be no issue."—Col. B., Trans., pp. 392 & 393.

Exception to the above rule,—

XLV. The widow, though there be no other heir (except the Imám, whose failure never takes place), gets only her

---

ANNOTATIONS.

xliv. If there be only one heir of any class or degree, he will take a portion of the property as his specific share, if he is a sharer, and the remainder by relationship (*Karábat*), or he will take the whole by mere relationship, or by *Valá*, in consecutive order, as already mentioned.—*Mafátih.*

xlv. In the case of a husband, the principle is exactly the same according to the most prevalent doctrine, but with regard to a widow, her residuary title in any case is most generally denied.—Col. B., Trans., p. 392.

appointed share, which is a fourth, and nothing of the remainder.—*Vide* Principles 11, 12, 23, 73 & 74.

Principle. XLVI. With a sharer if there is another heir (or heirs) equal in rank as well as a sharer (or sharers), and the property left by the deceased is proportionate to their shares, (that is, it does not exceed their proportionate shares), then it is divided in the proportion of their shares (1), but if it exceeds their shares, then the excess or surplus reverts to them *proportionately* to their respective shares (2), unless any of them is excluded (therefrom) by an excluder (*hájib*), or is alone entitled to the surplus by virtue of his connection (3). If, on the other hand, the property falls short, then the deficiency falls upon the portion of the daughter or daughters (happening to be in the case), or upon the person related through the father, and *not* upon the person related through the mother alone.—Sharáya ul-Islám, p. 441.

Example of the first case—(is the existence of) both parents and two or more daughters;—or two children by the same mother

---

ANNOTATIONS.

xlvi. Should there be two sisters, these receive first two-thirds of the estate as their share appointed in the Book of God, and the remaining third reverts to them as residuaries. To the same effect are various other documents.—Col. B., Trans., p. 393.

xlvi. If all the heirs of a person deceased should be specific sharers in the estate, without an individual amongst them who claims under a simple residuary title, this admits of three different suppositions,—*first* that the estate is capable of embracing and discharging all the appointed shares without surplus or deficiency of any fraction whatever; *second*, that it falls short of all the shares; and third, that after payment of them all, a surplus of some fraction remains.—Col. B., Trans., p. 395.

Under the second supposition, again, *viz.*, when the property falls short in distribution of all the appointed shares, and which can only happen when a husband or widow interferes, all our doctors are agreed that the loss or deficiency must invariably fall upon daughters or sisters of the deceased by both parents, or by the father's side.—Col. B., Trans., p. 395.

only with two full sisters or with two sisters by the same father only;—or, a husband with a (full or) half sister on the father's side.—Sharáya ul-Islám, p. 441.

Example of the second case,—An only daughter with both parents.—In this case, the daughter first takes a moiety, and each parent, a sixth, as their appointed shares, and then the surplus or residue, which is a sixth, is divided among them in fifths.—*Vide* Principle 90.

Example of the third case,—Both parents, a daughter, and brethren (excluded).*—Here the daughter takes a moiety, the father, a sixth, and the mother also, a sixth, as their specific shares, and then the surplus returns or reverts in fourths to the daughter and father, and not to the mother, by reason of her being excluded by brethren from participating therein.

XLVII. If of several heirs, one is, or some are, entitled as sharers, and the rest are entitled by virtue of relationship (*karábat*), then after allotment of the shares of the former, the remainder goes to the latter (*g*). *Principle.*

ANNOTATIONS.

xlvii. If, again, amongst these heirs, neither of whom excludes any other, some sharers and some residuaries are observed, the former are preferred to their appointed shares in the first place, and the remainder of the estate goes to the residuaries;—as where, for example, a woman leaves both her parents, her husband, and children, both male and female, in which case the parents take a third part of her estate betwixt them, her husband takes a fourth, and the remaining five-twelfths go to her children, of whom a male has the portion of two females; and when, also, a woman leaves her husband, a paternal and a maternal uncle, in which case the husband takes the half, his appointed share, her maternal uncle, being also a sharer, receives his third, and the residue, or one-sixth only, goes to the paternal uncle. Again, the case is exactly the same where, with her husband, a woman leaves children of her paternal and maternal uncles, for here also the husband takes his half, the maternal uncle's children, in right of their father, a third, and the remaining sixth part goes to the children of the paternal uncle. Upon these three examples all similar cases may be conceived, without the trouble of repetition.—Col. B., Trans., p. 394.

* It is the second case in the Sharáya ul-Islám.—*Vide ibid*, p. 441.

(*g.*) As in the case of there being a father, mother, widow, and two sons, a sixth is allotted to the father, another sixth to the mother, an eighth to the widow, and the remainder goes to the sons.

"There is no room with us," says the author of the *Sharáya ul-Islám*, "for succession by *tásib*, or lineal right,* so long as there exist any right by *farízat*, or appointment of shares;—so that where there is an equal in the case, but he has no share appointed for him, the residue remaining (after allotment of the appointed share or shares,) goes to him by virtue of *karábat*, or relationship.† As (in the case of there being) both parents or one of them, and a son;—or a father with husband or wife; or a brother with a husband or wife.†

Principle.

XLVIII. If there are two or more heirs who inherit, not as sharers, but by relationship or residuary title, they take the estate in the proportion of their respective rights,—as in the case of there being two sons (1), or a son and a daughter (2).

In the first case, the two sons *equally* divide the estate among themselves, and in the second, the son takes two-thirds, and the daughter one-third‡ of the estate.

ANNOTATIONS.

xlvii, xlviii. If there be more than one heir of a person deceased, some of whom do not exclude the others from inheritance, then attention must be paid to their titles and lines of descent, and if amongst them no specific sharer should appear, the property must be divided according to their own respective portions;—as where, for example, a person leaves children, male and female, in which case each of the former has double the portion of one of the latter; and where also he leaves brothers and sisters all by the same father and mother, or by the same father only, in which case the same rule is observed, and so on.—Col. B., Trans., p. 393.

---

* That is, for the succession of *Asabat*, or residuaries, as according to the Hanifites.

† *Sharáya ul-Islám*, p. 446.

‡ Because a daughter with a brother of her own is no longer a specific sharer, but becomes a residuary in conjunction with her brother, who in this case takes double the portion of his sister.—*Vide ante*, p. 180.

XLIX. The father of the deceased upon failure of issue is not a specific sharer in the estate, but has by law merely a residuary title to all that remains after distribution of the shares,* if any (*h*);—with a son, he is mere sharer (*i*); while with a daughter, he is not only a sharer but also a residuary, as he participates with her in the residue remaining after they have taken their appointed shares (*j*).—*Vide* Principles 78, 84 *et seq.* *Principle.*

(*h.*) Thus, if a person deceased should leave, for example, a father, a mother, and a husband, the mother in this case takes a third, if not partially excluded by brothers and sisters; the husband also enjoys his appointed share, *viz.*, a half, the remaining sixth is all that would go to the father.*

(*i.*) If a man should leave a son and a father, the latter will get a sixth as his appointed share and no more, and the whole of the remaining estate will go to the son.

(*j.*) If a man should leave his father and an only daughter, the daughter takes a moiety, and the father, a sixth, as their specific shares, and then they divide the remainder between them in fourths.

L. Grand-parents, paternal and maternal, upon failure of heirs as far as brothers and sisters and their children, are considered in the situation of immediate parents, or of a father and mother respectively.*—*Vide* Principle 126 *et seq.* *Principle.*

LI. When the associates in succession differ in the channels through which they are connected (to the *Principle.*

ANNOTATIONS.

l. Should these ancestors stand single in succession, that is, upon failure of brothers and sisters and their children, then they are considered in the situation of immediate parents, or of a father and mother respectively.—Col. B., Trans., p. 391.

li, lii. The most known or approved doctrine is that a third goes to a maternal uncle or aunt when with a paternal uncle or aunt, because

* Col. B., Trans., p. 383.—*Vide* Annotation at p. 181.

deceased), then to each party goes the portion of the person through whom that party is connected (*a*).*

(*a*.) As when there is a maternal uncle or uncles, with a paternal uncle or uncles (of the deceased), then the mother's share, which is a third, goes to the maternal (uncle) or uncles and the father's share, which is two-thirds, goes to the paternal (uncle or) uncles.*

Example.

If a man leave a paternal uncle of the half blood and a maternal aunt of the whole blood, the former will take two-thirds in virtue of his claims through the father, and the latter one-third in virtue of her claim through the mother, as the property would have been divided between the parents in that proportion, had they been the claimants instead of the uncle and aunt.†

Principle.

LII. If there be both paternal and maternal relatives, then one-third goes to the maternal kindred even if there be only one, male or female, and two-thirds go to the paternal kindred, even though there be only one, male or female.—Sharáya ul-Islám, p. 451. Again,—

ANNOTATIONS.

that is the portion of the mother. And such is the case with a grandfather or grandmother of the mother with a father's grandfather or grandmother according to the doctrine which is most generally received.—Mufátíh.

li, lii. If there be paternal and maternal uncles and aunts, two-sixths go to the maternal uncle (or kindred), whether one or more in number, and whether of the male or female sex, and the remainder goes to the paternal uncle or kindred, even if there be one, and that one—a male or female.—Irshád.

The proportion of every person related to the deceased through one of his parents (whether related also through the other or not), provided such person himself be not a specific sharer, is exactly the portion of that parent, or, in other words, is the portion of that person from whom the title or relation to the deceased, by however many intermediate steps is derived, whether such means of consanguinity was a specific sharer or not.—Col. B., Trans., p. 385.

---

* *Sharáya ul-Islám*, p. 440.

† Macn. M. L., chap. ii, princ. 16.

Only the succession of brothers and sisters of the different descriptions is not regulated in strict accordance with the above general principle, but according to special rules, as will be observed upon a comparison of the mode of succession of those relatives with that of their parents.*

LIII. If the individuals related through one channel are in themselves of different descriptions then the share primarily and collectively received by them is divided among them in reference to the sources of variation or the sub-channels of relationship.—*Vide* Principles 128, 137, 139—143, 150, 153 *et seq.* *Principle.*

LIV. The children of consanguinous heirs, if not in any way excluded, supply the place in succes- *Principle.*

ANNOTATIONS.

li, lii. The share of a maternal grandfather is exactly that of a mother, as is also that of a maternal grandmother, a paternal grandfather's that of a father, and likewise of a paternal grandmother's. A paternal uncle also receives the portion of a father through whom he is related, as does also a paternal aunt; and a maternal uncle has that of a mother through whom his title is derived, and likewise a maternal aunt. —Col. B., Trans., pp. 386 & 387.

liii. If there are paternal uncles with maternal uncles, then a third goes to the maternal uncle (*i.e.*, kindred), even though there be one, male or female, of any description, and if they (the maternal kindred) be of different descriptions, they divide the one-third portion among them in the manner stated.—Rouzat ul-Ahkâm, p. 46.

liv. Children of sons take the portion of sons, and the children of daughters take the portion of daughters, how low soever in descent.—Macn. M. L., chap. ii, princ. 7.

The children of a daughter or of two daughters supply the place in succession of their mother, taking either a half or two-thirds of their grandfather's estate, and also the surplus or return, should there be any, in the same manner as their mothers, if existing, would have done. Again, the children of a son supply the place of their father from whom their title is derived, and enjoy his portion of the inheritance.—Col. B., Trans., p. 385.

---

* *Vide* Principles 117—125.

sion of their deceased or disqualified (*k*) parents, and proportionately (*l*) take those shares of the inheritance which would have devolved on them had they been alive.—*Vide* Principles 103, 107, 109, 139—143, 159, 160 & 164.

(*k.*) "*Disqualified*,"—that is, become a slave, an apostate, or the like.—*Vide* Exclusion from Inheritance.

(*l.*) "*Proportionately*,"—that is, each male related through an heir of the whole blood or of the half blood on the father's side, taking double the portion of each female of the same description; and males and females related through the same mother only taking share and share alike.—*Vide* Principles 117—125.

Illustration. If we suppose an assemblage of the children of sons and daughters, each class takes the portion of inheritance which their own root or immediate ancestor would have enjoyed if in existence. For example, if a person deceased should leave a son's son and

---

ANNOTATIONS.

liv. The children also of a brother or sister, whether by the father's or mother's side, receive exactly that portion of the inheritance, which their parent—such brother or sister—would have enjoyed, upon the same principle and by the same rule with grandchildren and great-grandchildren, whether their ancestor was a sharer or a residuary.—Col. B., Trans., p. 386.

The children, again, of uncles, whether paternal and maternal, inherit the portions of their parents; and in general every branch as representing its root in succession receives by law the portion of inheritance assigned to that root, without any distinction whatsoever except this, that in the secondary distribution betwixt relations by both parents or by the father's side, attention must be always paid to sex, the male having a portion adequate to two females, whereas amongst relations by the mother's side only, in the distribution of their ancestor's portion males and females are alike, there being no preference to one over the other. This rule is universally prevalent amongst our doctors, and has by some been further extended in its application to the children or descendants of daughters, amongst whom, in their opinion, as equally in the female line, no distinction of sex can be observed. This opinion is, however, now generally abandoned, and we may, therefore, lay it down as a fixed maxim, that amongst the children of daughters as of sons, the distribution is to a male, double the portion of a female, notwithstanding their relation through the mother, considering them as in the place of immediate offspring, to whom the application of the sacred text is therefore indispensable.—Col. B., Trans., p. 387.

children of a daughter, the former would receive two-thirds, and one-third only would go to the daughter's children. Upon the same principle, should there be children of a son's son, and a daughter's daughter, the former would have two-thirds of the estate, and one-third goes to the daughter; and if we substitute in the room of children a single daughter of the son's son, the case is exactly the same, as such daughter being a descendant in the male line would still receive two-thirds or the portion of her root. Further, if we suppose the deceased to leave children of his daughter's son, and a daughter of his son's daughter, the former as descended from a female would inherit amongst them only one-third of his estate, whilst the daughter would receive two-thirds thereof.*

Further Illustrations.

The children of brothers or sisters by the same father and mother, or by the same father only, paternal grandfathers and grandmothers, paternal full uncles and aunts, if by the father's side, and their children divide the portions of their inheritance enjoyed by them, to a male as much as the share of two females; whereas the children of brothers and sisters by the mother's side, maternal grandfathers and grandmothers, paternal half uncles and aunts if by the mother's side only, maternal uncles and aunts of every description, and their children divide their portions of inheritance as derived through the female line *equally* without distinction or preference of sex whatsoever.*

If we suppose the children of a brother by the mother's side only, with the son of a sister of the same father, the former would receive only a sixth part of the estate as the appointed share of their father, to be divided equally amongst them, and the remaining five-sixths would go all to the sister's son.*

Lastly, we shall suppose an assemblage of the children of paternal uncles of different descriptions with the children of maternal uncles also varying in description, and here the primary distribution would be one-third of the estate to the latter class, and the *residuum*, or two-thirds, to the former; secondly, the third assigned to the children of maternal uncles would be thus distributed:—to those whose ancestor was related only by the mother's side, a sixth part thereof, if one, or a third, in case of plurality, and the residuum to the full maternal uncle's descendants, or to those of one related by the father's side; but the final distribution as to both these classes would be without distinction of sex, to a male the same portion with a female. With respect again to the two-thirds first allotted to the paternal uncle's descendants,

* Col. B., Trans., pp. 385—389.

the secondary distribution would be to those of a half uncle by the mother's side, a sixth, or a third, in case of plurality, divisible equally amongst them without distinction of sex; and to those of full uncles, or of half uncles by the father's side, all the remainder divisible amongst them, to a male double the portion of a female.—Col. B., pp. 389, 390.

Principle.

LV. Whenever an assemblage occurs of relations by both parents or by the father's side, with relations by the same mother only, the latter, if one, takes a sixth part of the estate, and a third in the event of plurality (to be divided among them *equally* without distinction between male and female), and all the *residuum* goes to the relations by both parents (divisible to a male double the portion of a female), to the utter exclusion of the relatives by the same father only.* However,—

Principle.

LVI. In default of the relatives of the whole blood those by the same father only supply their place in succession.

ANNOTATIONS.

lvi. In default of the brethren or relatives by the same father and mother, those by the same father only stand in their place. And the rule for them, when single or several, is the same† as is applicable to those of the whole blood.—*Sharáya ul-Islám*, pp. 448 & 449.

lvi. A person related by the father's side only supplies the place of a full kinsman upon failure of the latter.—Col. B., Trans., p. 336.

Every person related to the deceased by both sides,—*viz.*, the father's and mother's—in any degree of consanguinity, excludes from inheritance a person in the same degree by the father's side only, and this whether a male or female, the latter being deprived of every title to succession.—Col. B., Trans., p. 332.

The principle of exclusion by double tie or full blood relationship is established by the following tradition of *Imám Jaafer Sáadik*, recorded by *Yazíd Kanási*, in these words:—"Your full brother by the same father and mother is preferred to your half brother by the same father only;

---

* *Vide* Col. B., Trans., p. 388.

† Except, however, with espect to Return. *Vide*, pp. 222 & 223.

Thus, a brother, for example, or a sister of the deceased by the same father and mother, excludes a brother or sister being in the same degree by the same father only. The same principle likewise applies to paternal uncles and aunts of the deceased, and also to maternal uncles and aunts, provided they are in one and the same degree of propinquity. A paternal uncle, again, related by both sides, meaning thereby a brother of the deceased's father, by the same father and mother, does not exclude a brother of the deceased by the same father only, nor even the son of such brother; but certainly excludes an uncle by the same father only.*

If, for example, therefore, a person dying should leave a brother by the same father only, and a sister by the same father and mother, the brother could in this case take no part of the inheritance, which would descend entirely to the sister; and this rule universally applies not only to all brothers and sisters with regard to each other, and to their children in like manner, but also to all paternal uncles and aunts with respect to each other, and to their descendants; and likewise to all maternal uncles and aunts, and to their children, how low soever.*

LVII. The husband or widow is not excluded by any of the deceased's heirs, but happening to be with any of them takes his or her full or reduced share, as the case may be.† *Principle.*

Annotations.

and also the son of your full brother is preferred to the son of your half brother only; your paternal uncle, the full brother of your father, to your paternal uncle, his brother by the same father only; and the son of such paternal full uncle to the children of a paternal half uncle only." Likewise, by a tradition of the Commander of the Faithful, quoted by *Hárias* in these words:—"Surely kinsmen by the same father and mother shall inherit in preference to kinsmen by the same father only."—Col. B., Trans., p. 334.

lvii. The husband and wife are (as any of them happen to be) associated with any of the classes (of heirs), and none of these two is excluded by any one on account of a general text of the *Kurán*. They take their appointed shares, and no more, unless there is no (other) heir by consanguinity or patronage (except the *Imám*, whose non-existence never happens), when the surplus returns to the husband, though not to the widow.—Mufátih.

* Col. B., Trans., pp. 332 & 333.

† *Vide* Principles 11, 12, 15, 86, 89, 96, 124, 163 & 164.

Principle.

LVIII. Where there are male and female heirs of the same degree of a class and of the same side, there each male has double the portion of each female (*e*).—*Vide* Principles, 84, 85, 118, 149 & 153.

Illustrations.

(*e*.) If there be a daughter and a son, the latter would take double the portion of the former. Such also is the case between the daughter of a daughter and son of a son, as well as brother and sister of the whole blood, or of those of the half blood on the father's side.

The children of brothers or sisters by the same father and mother only, or by the same father only, paternal grandfathers and grandmothers, paternal full uncles and aunts, paternal half uncles and aunts if by the father's side, and their children divide the portions of inheritance enjoyed by them, to a male as much as the share of two females.*

ANNOTATIONS.

lvii. No claimant has a title to inherit with children but the parents and the husband and wife.—Macn. M. L., chap. ii, princ. 6.

Those who succeed by virtue of marriage are the husband and wife, who can never be excluded in any possible case; and their shares are half for the husband, and a fourth for the wife where there are no children, and a fourth for the husband, and an eighth for the wife, where there are children.—*Ibid.*

These principles of law are established as well by the unanimous assent of most of our doctors, as by the express traditions of the two holy *Imáms*,† on whom be peace, reported by Zarárah in these words:—"Not one of the creation of God can inherit with a child of the deceased, except the immediate parents and the husband, or wife; should there be no immediate children, grandchildren, whether male or female, supply their place in succession; those from a son inheriting the share of a son, and those of a daughter taking her portion of the inheritance; and be these ever so remote in descent, whether two or three generations, or more, still they inherit the portion of the immediate offspring, and exclude from succession every description of heirs that a child begotten by the deceased would have excluded if in existence.—Col. B., Trans., p. 325.

---

* Col. B., Trans., p. 387.

† Muhammad Bákir the fifth Imám, and his son Jaafir Saádik, or the just.—Col. B., p. 325.

LIX. The only exceptions to the above rule are the individuals related by the same mother only, since males and females so related inherit in *equal* shares (*f*).—*Vide* Principles 124, 125 150, 152, 153 *et seq.*

Illustrations.

(*f.*) Thus, if there be a brother or sister by the same mother alone, he or she gets only a sixth, but if there be a brother *and* sister, a brother and sisters, a sister and brothers, brothers *or* sisters, or brothers *and* sisters of this description, they collectively get a third, and divide it among themselves in *equal* shares without any preference being given to the male sex.

The children of brothers and sisters by the mother's side, maternal grandfathers and grandmothers, paternal half uncles and aunts if by the mother's side only, maternal uncles and aunts of every description and their children, divide their portions of inheritance, as derived through the female line, *equally* without distinction or preference of sex whatsoever.*

Principle.

LX. The right of primogeniture is partially recognized in this branch of Muhammadan law though not at all in the Sunní branch.†

On Increase and Return.

The doctrine of Increase is not recognized in the law of the *Immiyah* school. Consequently,—

Principle.

LXI. If the shares of the heirs happening to be in a case cannot be given *in full*, by reason of those

ANNOTATIONS.

lix. Amongst the relations by the mother's side only, in the distribution of their ancestor's portion, males and females are perfectly alike, there being no preference of one over the other.—Col. B., Trans., p. 387.

lxi. When a property falls short in distribution of all the appointed shares, and which can only happen when a husband or widow interferes, all our doctors are agreed that the loss or deficiency must invariably fall upon daughters or sisters of the deceased by both parents or by the father's side: in other words, there are only four of the appointed shares of inheritance which can be affected by deficiency arising in the distribu-

* Col. B., Trans., p. 387.
† *Vide* Principles 81 & 82.

shares or parts exceeding the integral, then recourse is not had to the process of Increase,* but the shares of the heirs other than those related by both parents or by the same father only, are given in full, and the remainder is given to the latter. So the deficiency falls on a relative or relatives of the whole blood, or of the half blood on the father's side according as may happen to be in a case.

Thus the *Sharáya ul-Islám*:—"The *oul* or Increase is null (*bátil*) with us." "The occasion for it arises in consequence of a conflict between the claim of a husband or wife, with the claims of other heirs, and in cases of that kind the loss falls on the

ANNOTATIONS.

tion, *viz.*, the share of one daughter and two or more daughters, the share of one sister and of two or more sisters by both parents or by the father only.—Col. B., Trans., p. 395.

The legal nnmber of shares into which it is necessary to make the property, cannot be increased if found insufficient to satisfy all the heirs without a fraction. In such a case a proportionate deduction will be made from the portion of such heir, as may, under certain circumstances, be deprived of a legal share, or from any heir whose share admits of diminution. For instance, in the case of a husband, a daughter, and parents. Here the property must be divided into twelve, of which the husband is entitled to three or a fourth, the parents to two-sixths or four, and the daughter to half; but there only remain five shares for her instead of six, or the moiety to which she is entitled. In this case, according to the orthodox (*i.e.*, sunní) doctrine, the property would have been made into thirteen shares; but according to the Imámiyah tenets, the daughter must be content with five shares that remain, because in certain cases her right as a legal sharer is liable to extinction; for instance, had there been a son, the daughter would not have been entitled to any specific share, and she would have become a residuary; whereas the husband or parents can never be deprived of a legal share under any circumstance.†—Macn. M. L., chap. ii, princ. 31.

* As it is the case according to the law of the *sunni* school. *Vide* pp. 228—231 of Lecture VI, delivered in 1873.

† The above, specially the argumentative parts thereof, are not quite correct, as will be known by comparing the same with the *dicta* of the paramount authorities cited in the body hereof.

father,* on a daughter or daughters, or on the persons (as a sister or sisters) related by both parents or by the same father alone, and not on those related only by the mother's side. As, when a deceased (person) has left a husband, both parents, and a daughter; or a husband, a parent, and two or more daughters, or a widow, both parents and two daughters; or a husband with relatives by the same mother only, and a sister or sisters by both parents or by the same father only.—P. 446.

Remarks. Although the author of the *Sharáya ul-Islám* has, in the above passage, included the father among the persons on whom the deficiency should fall, and although he has mentioned the father in the first, second, and third of the above examples given by him, yet it does not appear that, even in those examples, the deficiency falls on him. It is clear from the subjoined passage of the *Irshád*, in which though the father is, in like manner, included among the heirs on whom the deficiency falls, yet, in the examples given, a *full* share is allotted to the father without any deficiency or deduction.

"A defective divisor is that which does not suffice to pay the portions of (all) the sharers on account of the intervention of a husband or wife. The deficiency falls on daughters, father, and relatives by both parents or by the father alone. As when a person dies leaving a father, mother, husband and two daughters, the divisor of their share is twelve—of which, the shares of the father and mother are four (two or one-sixth of each), the share of the husband is three, and the remainder, which is five, becomes (therefore) the portion of the daughters, though their (*full*) share amounts to eight; thus a deficiency of three falls on them."—Irshád.

In fact it appears to have been decided by the generality of the Learned that the deficiency should fall on the persons related by both parents or by the father alone, but *not* on the father himself, not also on any other relative.

Thus the *Rouzat ul-Ahkám*:—"When the root of the case or the divisor falls short of the shares happening to be in a case, the rule is that the deficiency should fall on those persons on whom return is conferred, except on the husband or widow. Thus when it is supposed that a woman died leaving no heirs excepting her husband and two sisters, then the root of the case, that is the divisor, must be *six*, of which half must be given to the husband without any deduction, the same being his share, and the deficiency

---

* In other parts of the *Sharáya ul-Islám* it is laid down that the deficiency falls on the daughters, or on the sisters of the whole blood, or of half blood on the father's side without any mention of the father.—Note by Mr. Neil Baillie. See *ante*, p. 202.

must fall on the sisters, because the deficiency is to fall on the person who (in other cases) gains an advantage (by return). The deficiency falls on *no other* (heir) except a daughter or daughters, a sister or sisters by both parents, or by the same father only. The *Muhakkik* has, in the *Sharáya ul-Islám* and *Nafiyah,* included the father as being one of those on whom the deficiency falls, but that is erroneous, as has been decided by the generality of the Learned."—Rouzat ul-Ahkám, p. 24.

"When a deficiency occurs in the root of the case or the divisor, the same falls on the paternal relatives,* and not on the maternal relatives; in the same manner, as when there remains any portion of the divisor, the same goes (by return) exclusively to the paternal relatives,* the maternal kindred having no title to participate therein. The difference of opinion existing upon this point has been stated in the section treating of the mother's relatives."—*Ibid,* p. 45.

So also the *Mafátíh;*—"If all the heirs are sharers, the share of each will be given to him or to her; but if the property fall short of their shares, then the deficiency will fall on a daughter, or daughters, or on a sister or sisters by both parents or by the same father only, and *not on any other,*—as there is no *Oul* or Increase with us."—P. 476.

In another part of the *Irshád* it is clearly laid down that the deficiency *does not fall on the father,* nor on the mother, nor on the husband, nor on the wife. The passage laying down the above is as follows :—"If the residue remaining after allotment of the share of one of the spouses, and one of the parents, or of both parents, be less than the share to which a daughter is entitled, then the deficiency falls on the share of the daughter and *not on the shares of the others.*—Irshad.

On Return.

When a sharer or sharers and a residuary or residuaries happen to be in a case, then what remains after allotting the appointed share or shares goes to the residuary or residuaries;—as in the case of there being a parent or parents, and a son or sons, a sixth is allotted to the parent or to each of the parents, and the remainder goes to the son or sons as the case may be. And when there are only residuaries, or only a single residuary and no sharer, then

---

* Here by "paternal relatives" is meant "persons related by both parents, as well as those related by the same father only."

the whole property goes to the residuary or residuaries as the case may be;—as in the case of there being an only brother, or two or more brothers by both parents or by the same father only, the whole property at once devolves on the brother or brothers. But,—

LXII. When there is only one sharer and no residuary (*p*), or no other heir *equal* to that sharer (*q*), then the sharer first takes the appointed share and the remainder reverts to him or to her by return. *Principle.*

(*p.*) If a person dies leaving only a father surviving him, the whole property goes to him in virtue of his relationship. So also to the mother (in the above circumstance), though (first) a third as her appointed share, and then the remainder by return.—Rouzat ul-Ahkám, p. 32.

As, when there is only a brotherless daughter, or a brotherless full sister, she first takes her appointed share which is a moiety, and then the remainder reverts to her by return.

(*q.*) When there is a daughter with a brother (of the deceased), or sister with a paternal uncle, the daughtor or sister takes first her appointed portion, and then the remainder reverts to her, because she is nearer to the deceased.—Sharáya ul-Islám, pp. 440 & 441.

LXIII. When there happen to be in a case *only* sharers, and the property exceeds their shares, then the excess returns or reverts to *all* of them in the proportion of their respective shares, if *all* of them are *Principle.*

ANNOTATIONS.

lxii. When the heir is a sharer (*zú-farz*), he takes his appointed portion as such; and if he has no *equal*,—that is, if there is no other heir in the same degree,—he takes the surplus also by return or reversionary title.—Sharáya ul-Islám, pp. 440 & 441.

lxiii. If, after arrangement, the root of the case or the divisor exceeds the shares of the sharers, and there be no (other) person to whom the excess should go, then, in that case, it must return or revert. Return is conferred on a daughter or daughters, sister or sisters by the same father only or by both parents. With respect to return being conferred on the brethren by the same mother only, there is a difference of opinion, which will be presently stated. Return is also conferred on the parents, and on the husband.—Rouzat ul-Ahkám, p. 30.—*Vide* post, pp. 222 & 223.

entitled to the return (*r*), otherwise, only to *those* of them who are entitled thereto (*s*).

Illustration. (*r*.) When a person dies leaving a daughter and a father as heirs, the daughter's share, in this case, being a moiety, and the father's, a sixth, the root of the case, or the divisor, must be six, of which half or three-sixths being given to the daughter, and one-sixth to the father, there remain two-sixths, which, in fourths, revert to both of them in the proportion of their respective shares.—Rouzat ul-Ahkám, p. 30.

ANNOTATIONS.

lxiii. Under the third and last supposition regarding an estate to be distributed, *viz*., that a surplus thereof shall remain after payment of all the shares, we observe that this surplus reverts by our law to the consanguinous sharers in proportion to their respective shares, and is divisible amongst them either by fourths or by fifths; for the *return*, or reversion, admits of no other distribution. Thus, if there be one daughter and the mother of a person deceased, the latter takes first the appointed share, or a sixth part of the property, the regular divisor being six: the daughter has her moiety, or three parts produced by this division; and the remaining two-sixths are divided betwixt them by fourths in the return, one-fourth to the mother and three to the daughter, corresponding, this latter division, obviously to their original shares of the inheritance. If, again, with a daughter there be both father and mother of the deceased, each of the latter taking first a sixth part of the property, and the daughter her half or three-sixths thereof, the surplus in this case of one-sixth returns to all proportionately, and is, therefore, divided into five parts, one-fifth thereof to each of the parents, and the remaining three to the daughter. But a more simple and easy method of distribution, in examples of this nature, occurs by a primary arrangement of their shares, in cases where return is by fourth parts into four, and where by fifteenths into five; and thus in the first example the mother would at once receive a fourth part of the estate, and three-fourths go to the daughter. Hence, in every case where the surplus or return is divisible by fourths, a primary arrangement of the whole estate into four parts must obviously answer all the purposes of distribution; and, in like manner, where by fifths, an arrangement into five will produce the true shares without any fraction.—Col. B., Trans., pp. 398 & 399.

lxiii–lxxiii. Where the assets exceed the number of heirs, the surplus reverts to the heirs. The husband is entitled to share in the return; but not the wife. The mother also is not entitled to share in the return, if there are brethren; and where there is any individual possessing a double relation, the surplus reverts exclusively to such individual.—Macn. M. L., chap. ii, princ. 32.

(*s.*) If, in the above case, there had been the mother instead of the father, then she would have got the same one-sixth as her appointed share, and one-fourth of the remainder or surplus as the father got; but, had there been also brethren in the case, then the mother would have been deprived of the share in the surplus, because brethren, though themselves excluded, not only reduce the mother's share from a third into a sixth, but also deprive her of the surplus.*

Special Rules.—

LXIV. The *whole* of the surplus goes to a brotherless daughter in the case of her being alone or with one of the spouses, or with both parents and the husband or wife (of the deceased); but it goes *partly* to her and partly to the parents if the husband did not happen to exist; as also *partly* to her and partly to one of the parents if the other parent did not happen to be in *esse.** *Principle.*

LXV. The surplus returns to two or more brotherless daughters, *wholly* if they be alone or with one of the spouses, but *partly* to them (*i.e.*, such daughters) and partly to a single parent, if the other parent and the husband of the deceased did not happen to exist.† *Principle.*

LXVI. The surplus goes to a single parent, *wholly* if alone or with one of the spouses, but *partly*, if there be in the case a brotherless single daughter with or without a husband or wife of the deceased, or two or more brotherless daughters without the husband of the deceased; in either of which cases, the surplus goes partly to the parent and partly to the daughter or daughters.‡ *Principle.*

LXVII. The surplus returns to both parents, *wholly* if they be alone or with one of the spouses, but *partly*, if there is in the case no husband, but a single daughter, who would take the other part.§ *Principle.*

LXVIII. The mother with her husband is entitled to a portion (a fifth) of the surplus *only* when there is with them a daughter of the deceased,‖ and *not otherwise* (*t*); *Principle.*

---

* *Vide* Principles 72, 73, 83, 88, 89 & 90.

† *Vide* Principles 72, 73, 83, 96 & 97.

‡ *Vide* Principles 72, 73, 78, 88 & 97.

§ *Vide* Principles 72, 73, 90 & 93.

‖ *Vide* Principles 90 & 93.

but if brethren* of the deceased intervene in the case, then, even in the event of there being a daughter the mother is not entitled to the above, but the father gets one-fourth of the surplus.†

(*t.*) As where a person leaves her father and mother him surviving, but no daughter, then the mother gets only her full share, one-third, and the remainder goes to the father.—*Vide* Principle 89.

rinciple. LXIX. Where, in the second or third class, there are several sharers of the same degree or rank, the surplus returns or reverts to those related by both parents, to the exclusion of those related by the same mother only, as well as to the exclusion of those who are related by the same father only. The latter are deprived by the whole blood relations not only of the surlpus but also of the inheritance in general (*u*).

lustration. (*u.*) Thus, if a person leave a brother or sister by the same father and mother, with a brother or sister by the same mother only, the latter receives but a sixth part of the estate, and the remainder goes to the relation by both parents, whether a specific sharer or not, by reason of his uniting two causes of relationship to the deceased, *viz.*, the paternal and maternal sides, in consequence of which he enjoys a natural preference in succession over the relation by the one side only; and, further, because the loss or deficiency, should there be any,—as where a husband or widow of the deceased interferes,—must invariably fall on the relation by both sides, as already explained, whence obvious justice would necessarily dictate his superior title to the surplus or return, when these do not interfere, to make up for his loss in the other

ANNOTATIONS.

lxviii. If a person leave both parents and no children, then a sixth goes to the mother, if there be brethren to exclude her, while a third (goes to her) if there be no such excluders, and the remainder goes to the father.—Rouzat ul-Ahkám, p. 32.

* Here by "brethren" is meant two or more brothers by both parents or by the same father only, or at least one brother and two sisters, or four sisters of that description.—*Vide* Exclusion from Inheritance.

† *Vide* Principles 91. 94.

event; and this doctrine is particularly supported by a tradition of the *Imám Muhammad Bákir*, on whom be peace, recorded by *Muhammad Ibnu Muslim*, in these words :—"I inquired concerning the son of a sister by the father's side with the son of a sister by the same mother only. He replied, 'To the latter a sixth part of the estate, and all that remains to the former.'" Now it is evident that, if the relation by the father's side were not expressly preferred, the surplus or residue in this example, after distribution of a half and a sixth, would necessarily have been divided betwixt the sons of both sisters by fourths, in proportion to their specific shares; whereas this decision clearly demonstrates the exclusive preference to one. And if this preference is expressly conferred on the relation by the father's side, it must belong to one by both parents *a fortiori*.*—Col. B., Trans., p. 403.

However,—

LXX. In default of their excluders, the relatives by the same father only supply their place in succession to the inheritance.* *Principle.*

Annotations.

Where there is any individual possessing a double relation, the surplus reverts exclusively to such individual. — Macn. M. L., chap. ii, princ. 32.

lxx. The person related by both parents excludes the person who is related by the same father only. The former excludes also the person or persons related by the mother alone from participation in the surplus, but *not* from the appointed share, provided they be equal in the proximity of degree.—Mafátíh.

Where there are brethren by the same mother only, with those related by both parents, or by the same father only, then such maternal kindreds if one, gets a sixth of the inheritance, and a third, if two or more in number, and the remainder goes to the brethren related by both parents, or (in their default) to those related by the same father only, according to the doctrine most generally received.—Rouzat ul-Ahkám, p. 46.

The second general rule regarding inheritance to be described is that,—"Every person related to the deceased by both sides, *viz.*, the father's and mother's, in any degree of consanguinity, excludes a person having the same relation by the mother's side only, from all title to the residue or surplus of an estate after distribution of shares, but not from

---

* *Vide*, however, Principle 171.

But though they do so by general assent, yet there is a difference of opinion with respect to their taking the whole of the surplus like the whole blood relatives, for some of the doctors are of opinion that they take the whole, excluding the maternal kindred from the same, but allowing them to take only their appointed share, while the rest of the doctors maintain that where there are relatives by the same father only, and those by the same mother only, the latter take their appointed share, and also participate with the former in the surplus, if any, proportionately to their original share.

Remarks.

Thus the *Rouzat ul-Ahkám*:—"Some of the learned, however, have asserted that the surplus should be divided between these (that is, between the brethren or relatives by the same mother only, and those by the same father only). The most approved doctrine, however, is that there should be a *compromise* (between them).

The *Sharáya ul-Islám* is more explicit on the point. It is as follows:—"If there is a surplus, as in the case of there being only one (sister) on the mother's side and a sister by both parents, the surplus goes to the (latter) sister exclusively. But if (instead of a sister by both parents) there were a sister by the same father only, would she also have this special right to the surplus remaining after satisfying the sharers? This question has been answered in the affirmative, because the deficiency, if any, by reason of the contending claim of a husband or wife, falls upon her."—Sharáya ul-Islám, p. 449.

Annotations.

his appointed share of inheritance, provided they are *both in the same degree;* for a paternal uncle having this full relation does not exclude a sister of the deceased by the mother only, either from her residuary title or her appointed share, by reason of their disparity in the degree.—Col. B., Trans., p. 335.

lxx. "It is further to be remarked that a person related by the father's side only supplies the place of a *full* kinsman upon failure of the latter in all cases, and therefore excludes those related by the mother's side, from all residuary title, in like manner as the former."—Col. B., Trans., p. 336. This passage, being contrary to the approved doctrine as inculcated in the passages contained in the body of this and the following page, must be held to be incorrect.

It has been maintained (on the other hand) that the surplus would revert to those connected by the same mother only, as well as to the sister or sisters connected by the same father only, (in fourths or in fifths as there may be one or more of them), on account of the *equality* of the degree; and *this opinion is preferred.*—Sharáya ul-Islám, p. 445. Thus,—

LXXI. According to the preferable doctrine, where there are relatives on the father's side only, and those on the mother's side only, and both equal in degree and rank, the latter not only take their appointed share, but also participate with the former in the surplus, if any, in the proportion of their original share (*v*). *Principle.*

(*v.*) As in the case of there being a sister by the same father only, and a sister by the same mother only, first the former takes a half, and the latter a sixth, as their appointed shares, and then the surplus, which is a third, is divided between them in fourths, of which the former gets three parts, and the latter one part, as being proportionate to their original shares.

LXXII. The husband is entitled to the surplus when there is no other heir, except the *Imám*. But,— *Principle.*

ANNOTATIONS.

lxxii, lxxiii. A husband and wife have each their appointed shares of inheritance in every possible situation, and the remainder of the estate, only after payment of these, descends to the other heirs, whether by consanguinity or patronage, if such exist; if otherwise,—as where a wife may die leaving no heir of any description, save her husband, and the succession is thus limited to him, and the *Imám*, or public treasury,—the husband, in this event, takes not onlyh is appointed share, *viz.*, a half, but has also a residuary title to the remainder. Such at least, is the most common and prevalent doctrine, which, further, the two *Shaikhs* as well as *Sayyid Murtazá* have declared to be incontestable, by reason of an authentic tradition related by *Abú Basír* in these words: "I was present with the *Imám Jaafar Saadik* when he assembled the people to prayer, and was informed of a woman's decease, who had left her husband, and no other heir. He replied, 'The property goes all to her husband.'" And another decision of the same *Imám*, in the case of a woman who left her husband, and no other relations known, *viz.*, "The succession is for the husband entirely;" as well as several other authentic documents to a similar effect.—Col. B., Trans., pp. 338 & 339.

Principle. **LXXIII. The surplus never returns to a widow: when there is no other heir, the *Imám* (whose failure never happens) takes the same excluding her therefrom.**

Remarks. With respect to the widow's being or not being entitled to the surplus, there are different opinions; but the right doctrine is that the surplus does not return or revert to her.

Thus the *Irshád*:—"If the deceased has left no heir except her husband, then the whole inheritance goes to him, —half as his appointed share, and half by return. If the deceased has left no heir except a widow, then a fourth of the inheritance goes to her, while with respect to the remaining three-fourths there are three different opinions. Some of the Doctors say, that the same belongs to the *Imám*; some assert that the same must revert to the widow; while others affirm that the above should go to the *Imám* if he is visible or present, otherwise to the widow."

So also the *Mafátíh*:—"They (the husband and wife) take their appointed shares, and no more, unless when there is no (other) heir, either by consanguinity or for special cause, save and except the *Imám*, in which case, the surplus remaining after allotment of the husband's share returns or reverts to him according to the opinion most generally received. The surplus never returns to the widow according to the most approved opinion.

So also the *Rouzat ul-Ahkám*:—"Know that if something remains after allotment of the share of the husband or wife, the same goes to the other heir, if any (in the case), whether such heir be by consanguinity, or for special cause, and whether he be a sharer, or no sharer. If there be no such person except the *Imám*, then the remainder is to return to the husband. With respect to return being conferred on

---

ANNOTATIONS.

lxxiii. It is otherwise in the case of a husband's decease leaving no heirs of any description save his widow, for she receives only her appointed share, *viz.*, a fourth part of his property, and the remaining three-fourths go to the *Imám*, or public treasury, as a widow has no residuary title in any situation whatsoever.—Col. B., Trans., p. 339.

the wife, there are different opinions. The first of which is, that the residue returns to the *Imám,* and not at all to the widow,—and this opinion is the most generally received and approved one.—P. 39.

The *Sharáya ul-Islám* is decisive on the point. The above is as follows:—"There may be neither an heir by blood nor any by special connexion other than a husband, in that event the husband has his half, and the remainder by virtue of the return or the reversionary right, while the *widow is restricted to her fourth.* Upon this point, however, there are three different opinions. According to one of these she takes the remainder by virtue of the reversionary right; and according to another, it never reverts to her; while according to the third opinion it reverts to her in the absence of the *Imám,* but not if he is present."—P. 445.

"The surplus never returns or reverts to a wife; not also to a husband except in the single case of there being no other heir than the *Imám.*"—Sharáya ul-Islám, p. 441.

The conclusion therefore is, that—

LXXIV. The surplus remaining after allotment *Principle.* of the husband's share reverts to him if there is no other heir except the *Imám;* but if there is any other heir,—be he even the deceased's manumitor or surety for offences,—the surplus goes to him to the exclusion of the husband. As respects the widow, the surplus *never* reverts to her, but goes to any other heir that may happen to exist at the time, even to the *Imám,* who is the last of all heirs, and whose existence is always recognised.

LECTURE VIII.

GENERAL AND SPECIAL RULES OF SUCCESSION OF ALL THE THREE CLASSES OF CONSANGUINOUS HEIRS.

On the Succession of the First Class.

THE first class comprises, as already stated,* the deceased's parents and children how low soever. Consequently,—

Principle. **LXXV.** The co-heirs of the parents of the deceased are, in general, his or her husband or widow,† and children of the first degree, in default of whom, those of the second degree, failing them, those of the third degree, and so on; and *vice versá.*—*Vide ante*, pp. 190—194.

ANNOTATIONS.

lxxv—lxxvii. The father and mother of a person deceased inherit with his children, his children's children, and his children's children's children, and so on; whereas grandchildren do not inherit with the immediate offspring of the deceased, nor do great grandchildren with the latter; but, on the contrary, each degree of posterity totally excludes that more remote from any title to succession. Further, no member of the two following classes can inherit, whilst any individual, even a female of this series (*i.e.*, class) exists, and however remote in descent such female may be. Thus, a grandfather of the deceased cannot inherit with any one of the immediate parents, nor of the children how low soever; and, in like manner, a brother of the deceased is completely excluded by the existence of any member of this series; as are also all uncles, both paternal and maternal, whom we shall hereafter describe as being placed in the third series of consanguinous heirs.—Col. B., Trans., p. 324.

No claimant has a title to inherit with children, but the parents, or the husband and wife.—Macn. M. L., chap. ii, princ. 6.

---

* See *ante*, p. 176 *et seq.*

† *Vide ante*, pp. 111 & 112.

LXXVI. At the same time, one parent of the deceased is the co-heir of the other, and the children of the first degree, that is the immediate children, are co-heirs with each other as also with the parent or parents (as the case may be), and so are the children of each succeeding degree. Hence,— *Principle.*

LXXVII. The deceased's parents inherit with their own co-heirs as above, and these with them, to the exclusion of all other relatives. As regards the deceased's children in particular, the nearer, whether male or female, excludes the more remote of them as well as the members of any other class, and inherits alone or with his or her own co-heir or co-heirs (if any), since a co-heir is never excluded by a co-heir.—*Vide ante*, pp. 190—197. *Principle.*

Annotations.

It is further to be observed of these descriptions, that no member, even the nearest one, as a father, for example, of the deceased, can exclude from succession the most remote of the other, as a great grandchild; but, on the contrary, this exclusion by proximity of degree takes effect only where the heirs are of one and the same description, like a son, for instance, or a daughter of the deceased, who necessarily excludes a grandchild from inheritance.—Col. B., Trans., pp. 324 & 325.

lxxvii. Not one of the creation of God can inherit with a child of the deceased, except the immediate parents and the husband, or wife; should there be no immediate children, grandchildren, whether male or female, supply their place in succession: those from a son inheriting the share of a son, and those of a daughter taking her portion of the inheritance; and be these ever so remote in descent, whether two or three generations, or more, still they inherit the portion of the immediate offspring, and exclude from succession every description of heirs that a child begotten by the deceased would have excluded if in existence.—Col. B., Trans., p. 325.

Both parents or one of them inherit together with a child, a grandchild, or a great grandchild; but a grandchild does not inherit together with a child, nor a great grandchild together with a grandchild.—Macn. M. L., chap. ii, princ. 4.

Principle. LXXVIII. If the father be alone, the (whole*) property goes to him; and if the mother be alone, a third of the property goes to her (as her appointed share), and the remainder returns or reverts to her.†

Principle. LXXIX. If there be both parents (and no child, nor the husband, nor the widow of the deceased), then a third goes to the mother, and the remainder to the father. But if there be also brethren (*a*) of the deceased, the share of the mother is (reduced to) a sixth, and the father has the remainder, while the brethren have nothing.†

(*a.*) Here by "brethren" is meant two or more brothers by both parents or by the same father only, or at least one brother and two sisters, or only four sisters of the above description.—*Vide* Partial exclusion from Inheritance in Lecture X.

Principle. LXXX. If there is only a son (and no other heir of equal degree), the whole property goes to him: if there are two or more sons, they inherit the property in equal shares.†

Principle. LXXXI. The eldest child, if male, and not prodigal and deficient in understanding, is to have the wearing apparel, ring, sword and *Kurán*,‡ of his father, and is liable for the fulfilment or performance of what was due by the deceased, *viz.*, prayers and fasts. The eldest son's right to those articles accrues, however, upon the father's having left property *other* than the same, but not otherwise.§

ANNOTATIONS.

lxxix. The father of the deceased, upon failure of issue, is not a specific sharer in the estate, but has a residuary title to all that remains after allotment of the specific shares, if any; if not, he at once takes the whole.—*Vide* Col. B., Trans., p. 383.

lxxxi. On a distribution of the estate, the elder son, if he be worthy, is entitled to his father's sword, his *Kurán*, his wearing apparel, and his ring.—Macn. M. L., chap. ii, princ. 33.

---

* *Irshád.*

† *Sharáya ul-Islám*, p. 446.

‡ According to the *Irshád*, not only the above articles, but also the father's *ship* and *boat*, if any.

§ *Sharáya ul-Islám*, p. 448.

LXXXII. If the eldest child be a female, she is not entitled to those articles, but they are to be given to the eldest of the male children.* *Principle.*

LXXXIII. If there is only a daughter, half goes to her (as her appointed share,†) and the remainder reverts to her by return: if there are two or more daughters, they have two-thirds (as their appointed shares,†) and the remainder by return.‡ *Principle.*

LXXXIV. If there are (children of) both sexes, then the property is inherited by them according to the rule—"to each male goes the portion of two females."‡ *Principle.*

LXXXV. When there are both parents, or one of them, combined with children (of the deceased), then a sixth goes to each of the parents, and the remainder to the children, *equally* if they are *all* males; but if there is a female or females among them, then each male has the portion of two females.‡ *Principle.*

LXXXVI. If (in the above case) there be a husband, or wife, then the husband or wife gets his or her small (that is the reduced) share, so do the parents,§ and the remainder goes to the children.‡ *Principle.*

LXXXVII. A son with a single parent or both parents of the deceased takes the whole of what remains after allotment of the appointed share of the parent or parents. But,— *Principle.*

LXXXVIII. If there be a daughter with a single parent (of the deceased), then the property goes to them in fourths (*b*).‡ *Principle.*

(*b.*) Of which the parent gets one-fourth, and the daughter, the remaining three-fourths.

Annotations.

lxxxvi, lxxxix. No claimant has a title to inherit with children, but the parents and the husband and wife.—Macn. M. L., chap. ii, princ. 6.

Not one of the creation of God can inherit with a child of the deceased, except the immediate parents and the husband or wife.—Col. B., Trans., p. 325.

---

* *Sharáya ul-Islám*, p. 448.

† See *ante*, pp. 182—184

‡ *Sharáya ul-Islám*, pp. 446 & 447.

§ See *ante*, pp. 182—184.

Principle. LXXXIX. If (in the above case) there be a husband or wife, then the surplus (remaining after allotment of the appointed shares) reverts to the daughter and the parent, and not to the husband or wife (*c*).*

Illustration. (*c.*) That is, in the first place, a sixth goes to the parent, a fourth to the husband, or an eighth to the widow, and a moiety to the daughter (as their appropriate shares), and then the surplus returns or reverts to the parent and daughter in the proportion of one-fourth and three-fourths as above.

Principle. XC. If there is only a daughter with both parents (of the deceased), then two-sixths go to the parents (one to each), a half to the daughter, and the residue reverts to them in fifths (*d*).*

(*d.*) That is one-fifth thereof goes to each of the parents, and the remaining three-fifths go to the daughter.

Principle. XCI. If (in the above case) there be also brethren (of the deceased) on the father's side,† then the remainder reverts to the father and daughter in fourths (*e*).*

Illustration. (*e.*) That is, after allotment of the appropriate shares of the parents and daughter, the surplus is divided between the father and daughter in the proportion of their original shares, *viz.*, one-fourth to the father, and three-fourths to the daughter, the brethren being excluded.

Principle. XCII. If there be with them (*i.e.*, with the daughter and parents) a husband, then the latter takes his small or reduced share, so does each of the parents, and the remainder goes to the daughter (*f*).*

(*f.*) There is, in this case, a deficiency of one-twelfth, which falls on the daughter.‡

Principle. XCIII. But if there be with them (*i.e.*, the daughter and parents) a *wife* (instead of a husband), then each sharer takes his or her fixed share, and the remainder reverts to the daughter and parents, but not to the wife.*

---

* *Sharáya ul-Islám*. p. 417.

† Or by both parents. *Vide* Principles 91, 101 & 102.

‡ See *ante*, pp. 213—216.

XCIV. But if (instead of a husband or wife) there be with them brethren (*g*), then the surplus would revert to the daughter and father in fourths.* *Principle.*

(*g*.) Here by brethren is meant at least two brothers, or one brother and two sisters, or only four sisters by both parents or by the same mother only, as no less than such number of such brethren can deprive the mother of the surplus, and also reduce her share (from a third) to a sixth.—*Vide* Partial exclusion from Inheritance in Lecture X.

XCV. When there are two or more daughters (with the parents of the deceased), then two-sixths go to the parents, and two-thirds to the daughters in *equal* shares.* *Principle.*

XCVI. If with them (*i.e.*, the parents and daughters) there is a husband or wife, then he or she gets his or her small share, the parents get two-sixths, and the remainder goes to the two or more daughters.* *Principle.*

XCVII. If (with two or more daughters) there is only one parent, then he or she gets a sixth, the two or more daughters get two-thirds (as their appointed shares), and the remainder reverts to them in fifths* *Principle.*

XCVIII. If (in the above case) there was also a husband, then the deficiency† would fall on the two or more daughters.* *Principle.*

XCIX. But if there was a wife (instead of a husband in the above case), then her (small or reduced) share, that is, an eighth, would go to her, and the remainder would be divided among the single parent and the daughters, in fifths.* *Principle.*

C. If there be a husband with both parents (of the deceased) then half goes to him, a third of the original estate to the mother, and the remainder to the father.* *Principle.*

CI. But if there be brethren with the parents (of the deceased, instead of her husband), then a sixth goes to the mother, and the remainder to the father.* *Principle.*

---

* *Sharáya ul-Islám*, p. 447.

† *Vide ante*, pp. 213—216.

CII. If there is a widow with both parents (of the deceased), then a fourth goes to her, and a third of the original estate to the mother if there are no brethren, and the remainder to the father; but if there are brethren, then a sixth only goes to the mother, and the remainder to the father.*

Principle. **CIII. On failure of (the immediate) children, the children of children take the places of their respective parents (that is, they represent them) in the division of property with the parents (of the deceased).***

Principle. **CIV. Children prevent the succession of every one connected with the deceased through them, and also of every one connected with him through his parents *(h)*.***

(*h.*) As his (the deceased's) brethren and their children, his grand-parents and their ancestors, and his paternal and maternal uncles and aunts and their children.*

They (the children) are so arranged that the nearest (in relationship) is the nearest* (in succession). Hence,—

Principle. **CV.** One. generation is excluded by another more proximate to the deceased (*i*).* And,—

(i.) For example, if a person left at his death a son or daughter and a pre-deceased son's son, this grandson would not inherit together with the son or daughter of the deceased.

ANNOTATIONS.

civ. Ibnu Bábavai made a condition in the succession of the children's children that there should be a failure of both parents (of the deceased), but this has been exploded and abandoned.*

Both parents or one of them inherit together with a child, a grand-child or a great grandchild ; but a grandchild does not inherit together with a child, nor a great grandchild together with a grandchild.—Macn. M. L., chap, ii, princ. 4.

* *Sharáya ul-Islám*, p. 447

CVI. Each descendant inherits the portion of the person through whom he or she is related to the deceased (*j*).* *Principle.*

(*j*.) Thus the child, male or female, of a daughter inherits his or her mother's portion, which is a half, if she was alone, or in conjunction with both parents, and the remainder reverts to the child in the same manner as it would have reverted to his or her mother if she were in existence. A son's child, male or female, inherits that which was inheritable by his or her father—the whole estate if he (the son) was alone, or the surplus after allotment of the shares of other heirs, if there were any in conjunction with him (the son), as parents, or one of them, a husband or wife.*

CVII. If there are only children of a son and children of a daughter, two-thirds go to the former; and one-third goes to the latter,—according to the best founded authority.† *Principle.*

CVIII. If (in the above case) there is also a husband or wife, he or she gets his or her small (that is reduced) share, and the remainder is divided between the daughter's and son's children, the former getting one-third, and the latter, two-thirds.† *Principle.*

CIX. The daughter's children divide their portion (that is their mother's portion) in the proportion of two shares to a male and one share to a female (*k*), in the same manner as the son's children divide† (the portion of their father). *Principle.*

(*k.*) It has been said that a daughter's children divide (and take) her portion in *equal* shares: This opinion is, however, abandoned.†

CX. The grandfather or grandmother, when with one of the parents (of the deceased), does not inherit anything; but it is proper and becoming that a sixth of the original estate be bestowed on them as maintenance, in case the parent's portion exceed that amount (*l*).† *Principle.*

(*l.*) As, for instance, when the deceased has left both his parents, with a paternal or maternal grandfather and grandmother, then his mother having a third of the estate, should bestow a half of her portion on his grandfather and grandmother in

---

* *Sharáya ul-Islám*, p. 447.

† *Ibid*, p. 448.

equal proportions, or, if there is only one (of them), the whole sixth is his or hers. And the father having two-thirds should bestow a sixth of the original property on the grandfather and grandmother *equally*, or if there is only one of them, the whole sixth belongs to *that* one.*

Principle. CXI. If one of the parents obtains a sixth and no more, while the other gets more than that, then the latter ought to maintain (the grand-parents), and not the former who gets only a sixth.*

Principle. CXII. If the deceased has left both parents and brethren, then the maintenance of the grand-parents ought to be supplied or provided by the father, and not by the mother; while if the deceased is survived by both parents and a husband (instead of brethren), then not the father, but the mother, ought to maintain the grand-parents.*

However,—

Principle. CXIII. The paternal grandfather and paternal grandmother have a claim to maintenance from the deceased's estate, *only* in the case of the deceased being survived by his or her father, and the maternal grandfather and grandmother have a similar claim in the case of the deceased being survived by his or her mother.

The foregoing rules which prescribe a sixth part of the deceased's property to the grand-parents out of the immediate parent's share are for providing maintenance to the former, and so they are regarded as precepts *moral* rather than obligatory.

On the Second Class.

This class, as already stated,† comprises brethren and their children how low soever, and also grand-parents, how high soever.

ANNOTATIONS.

cxiii. The paternal grandfather and grandmother have no claim to maintenance except in the case of the deceased being survived by his or her father, and the maternal grandfather and grandmother have no (such) claim except in the case of the deceased being survived by his or her mother.*

---

* *Sharáya ul-Islám*, p. 448.

† See *ante*, pp. 76, 89 *et seq.*

CXIV. The co-heirs, in general, of the grand-parents, how high soever, of the deceased, may be his or her husband or widow, and the children, how low soever, of his or her both parents or of either of them, and *vice versâ*. But,— *Principle.*

CXV. As among the different degrees of the children of the deceased's parent or parents, the nearer excludes the more remote, and such also is the case with the grand-parents how high soever, consequently, the then nearest grand-parent or parents of the deceased, and the then nearest degree of the children of his or her parent or parents, as also the husband or widow (happening to be in the case), inherit together as co-heirs (*m*).* *Principle.*

(*m.*) That is to say,—the then nearest or the lowest of the grandparents are co-heirs with each other, as well as with the then nearest degrees of the children of the deceased's parent or parents, and these among themselves are co-heirs with each other as well as with the grand-parent or parents of the deceased, and the husband or wife of the deceased is a co-heir with all or any of the above mentioned relatives then in existence. Whence, the then nearest of the grand-parents of the deceased inherit together with the then nearest of the children of his or her parent or parents as well as with a husband or widow as the case may be.

ANNOTATIONS.

CXV. This second class likewise involves two separate descriptions of heirs: one comprehending all grandfathers and grandmothers of the deceased, how high soever in the line of ancestry, with application of the rule of precedence by proximity, to the nearer first and then to the more remote; and the other including all brothers and sisters and their children, how low soever, always observing the same rule.—Col. B., Trans., p. 326.

The second class of consanguinous heirs comprehends grandfathers and grandmothers of the deceased, how high soever in degree of ancestry, and brothers and sisters and their children however remote in descent, the nearest always excluding one more removed. Thus, a grandfather's

* See *ante*, pp. 189, 190 *et seq.*

Principle. CXVI. If there exist a co-heir, of the then nearest grand-parent or parents, or of the then nearest child or children of the deceased, they inherit together in proportion to their respective rights; but should any of them happen to be without a co-heir, *he* or *she* takes the whole property.—See the following Principles and also 44 & 46.

Principle. CXVII. When there is only a brother by the same father and mother, the (whole) property goes to him; and where there is with him another full brother or brothers, the property is shared by them *equally*.*

Principle. CXVIII. Where there is a female or females (that is a sister or sisters) with a brother or brothers of the *same* description, then two shares go to each male and one share goes to each female.*

Principle. CXIX. If there is only one sister (without a co-heir), then half goes to her (as her fixed share), and the remainder reverts to her by return.*

Principle. CXX. If there are two or more (such) sisters, then two-thirds go to them (as their fixed shares), and the residue reverts to them by return.*

ANNOTATIONS.

father cannot inherit with a grandfather or grandmother, and even a brother's son has no title with a brother or sister of the deceased; a brother's grandson is excluded by a brother's or by a sister's son; and in short, the arrangement, respecting children and children's children of the deceased, formerly explained, has a similar influence exactly over members of this class; of which, further, no individual can possibly inherit whilst any member even a female of the first series, exists.—Col. B., Trans., p. 326.

The second degree (*i.e.*, class†) comprises the grandfather and grandmother and other ancestors, and brothers and sisters and their descendants, however low in descent, the nearer of whom exclude the more distant. The great grandfather cannot inherit together with a grandfather or a grandmother; and the son of a brother cannot inherit with a brother or a sister; and the grandson of a brother cannot inherit with the son of a brother, or with the son of a sister.—Macn. M. L., chap. ii, princ. 8.

---

* *Sharáya ul-Islám*, p. 448.
† See *ante*, p. 176 note.

CXXI. The brother and sister by the same father only do not inherit with a brother or sister by the same father and mother, on account of the latter bearing two relations.* But,— *Principle.*

CXXII. In default of full brothers and sisters, the brothers and sisters by the same father only take their place (in the succession of inheritance), and the rule for them, whether single or several, is the same† as for the full brothers and sisters* (in like circumstances). *Principle.*

ANNOTATIONS.

cxxi. The principle of exclusion by double tie or full blood relationship is established by the following tradition of the *Imám Jaafar Saádik*, recorded by *Yazíd Kunásí* in these words:—"Your full brother by the same father and mother is preferred to your half-brother by the same father only; and also the son of your full brother is preferred to the son of your half-brother only; your paternal uncle, the full brother of your father, to your paternal uncle his brother by the same father only; and the son of such paternal full uncle to the children of a paternal half uncle only." Likewise, by a tradition of the Commander of the Faithful, quoted by *Háras* in these words: "Surely kinsmen by the same father and mother shall inherit in preference to kinsmen by the same father only."—Col. B., Trans., pp. 334 & 335.

cxxi. Every person related to the deceased by both sides, *viz.*, the father's and mother's, in any degree of consanguinity, excludes from inheritance a person in the same degree by the father's side only, and this whether a male or female, the latter being deprived of every title to succession. Thus, a brother, for example, or a sister of the deceased by the same father and mother, excludes a brother or sister being in the same degree by the same father only.—Col. B., Trans., p. 332.

cxxii. It is further to be remarked that a person related by the father's side only supplies the place of a *full* kinsman upon failure of the latter in all cases, and therefore excludes those related by the mother's side from all residuary title,† in like manner as the former. This is agreeable to the doctrine of *Sadúk* and most of our lawyers, because the full kinsman and he by the father's side only, on failure of the former, suffering alike the loss or deficiency, they ought in justice to have a similar exclusive title to the *residuum* or surplus.—Col. B., Trans., p. 336.

---

* *Sharáya ul-Islám*, p. 448.

† *Vide*, however, *ante*, pp. 222 & 223, also the mode of distribution in Lecture XI.

Principle. CXXIII. When a child by the same mother only (that is, a half brother or sister on her side) stands alone (*i.e.*, without a co-heir), such child, whether male or female, gets a sixth (as his or her fixed share), and also the remainder by return.*

Principle. CXXIV. If there are two or more (of such children), one-third of the estate is shared by them *equally*, whether they are (only) males *or* females, or males *and* females,* and if there is no other equal in degree, the remainder reverts to them.†

Principle. CXXV. When the brethren are of different kinds,—then the single brother or sister by the same mother only gets a sixth, while two more such relatives (male *or* female, or male *and* female) get a third, to be *equally* divided among them, and two-thirds go to such relative or relatives of the whole blood: if there be only one such female relative, then a half goes to her as her fixed share, and the remainder by return; while if there are only two or more such female relatives, then two-thirds go to them (as their fixed shares), and the surplus also reverts to them; but if they be only males, then what remains after satisfying the portion of the individual or individuals related by the same

ANNOTATIONS.

cxxiii, cxxiv. Brothers and sisters by the mother can never inherit more than a third, nor can their share be less than a sixth.*—Col. B, Trans., p. 336.

cxxv. If there are brethren of different kinds, those connected only by the mother take a sixth, if there is only one such, or a third, if there are more, the same being *equally* divided among them; and two-thirds go to those connected by the father and mother, whether they be one or more; but if there is only one, and *that* one a *female*, she has a half of the two-thirds by appointment, and the remainder by return; while if there are two (or more), and they are females, they take two-thirds by appointment, and the surplus, if any, by return. Again, if those connected by the father be *males*, the remainder, after satisfying the portions of those connected by the mother only, belongs to them equally; while if there are both males and females, the remainder goes to them in the proportion of two shares to each male, and one share to each female.—Sharáya ul-Islám, p. 449.

* *Sharáya ul-Islám*, p. 449.

† *Vide* Principles 44, 46 & 73.

mother only, is divided among them *equally*, while if there be both male and female relatives of the whole blood, the remainder (as above) is divided among them in the proportion of two shares to each male, and one share to each female. If, in the above case, there be also a child or children of the same father alone, such child or children are excluded by the child or children of both parents, these, as above shown, taking the whole of what remains after satisfying the share of the child or children by the same mother only. The excluded child or children of the father alone, do, however, in default of their excluders, take their place in succession, and get what they would have got had they been in *esse*.*

CXXVI. The grandfather—whether he be on the father's or on the mother's side—if alone (that is without a co-heir), gets the (whole) property: so also the grandmother.† *Principle.*

CXXVII. When there are (only) a paternal grandfather and a paternal grandmother, two shares (*i.e.*, two-thirds) go to the grandfather, and one share (*i.e.*, one-third,) goes to the grandmother; but if both of them are on the mother's side, then they take the property in *equal* shares.—Rouzat ul-Ahkám, pp. 32 & 33. *Principle.*

CXXVIII. If a grandfather or grandmother, or both, on the mother's side, be combined with a grandfather or grand- *Principle.*

Annotations.

cxxvi. The grandfather, paternal or maternal, when alone, is entitled to the whole property by relationship (*karábat*). But, as in the case of such ancestor being on the mother's side, he takes the mother's portion, it may be said that one-third goes to him as the appointed share, and the remainder by return. Such also is the case with the grandmother.—Rouzat ul-Ahkám, p. 32.

cxxviii. When there is an assemblage of paternal and maternal grand-parents, then, according to the approved doctrine, two-thirds are the portion of the paternal grand-parent and one-third goes to the maternal grand-parent, whether such ancestor be one or more in number.—*Ibid*, p. 33.

* *Vide* Principle 122.

† *Sharáya ul-Islám* p. 449.

mother, or both, on the father's side, then those related through the mother take a third in *equal* portions, while those related through the father take two-thirds in the proportion of two shares to the male and one share to the female.*

The most generally received doctrine is, that when there are grand-parents, how high soever, on both sides, then those related through the father divide two-thirds among themselves, with distinction (between male and female), while those related through the mother take a third in equal shares,—no regard being had to the relation with the deceased himself. Consequently, a third of a third goes equally to the parents of the maternal grandmother and two-thirds thereof go equally to the parents of the maternal grandfather, one-third of the (remaining) two-thirds goes to the parents of the paternal grandmother in *equal shares;* and two-thirds of the said two-thirds go to the parents of the paternal grandfather in thirds, regard being had to both sides. —*Mafátíh.*

When the two sections† of this (second class) are combined, then,—

Principle. CXXIX. In conjunction with whole brothers and sisters or *any* of them, or the child or children

ANNOTATIONS.

cxxix & cxxx. Whenever grandfathers and grandmothers, both paternal and maternal, are assembled with half-brothers and sisters by the father's and by the mother's side, or with their children, a maternal grandfather and grandmother are by law on equal footing in succession with a brother and sister by the same mother only, and a paternal grandfather and grandmother equal to a full brother and sister, or to those by the father's side, but should these ancestors stand single in succession, that is upon failure of brothers, and their children, then they are considered in the situation of immediate parents, or of a father and mother respectively.—Col. B., Trans., p. 391.

This principle is established by a tradition of the Imám Jaáfar Saádik on whom be peace, quoted by *Fuzayil* Ibnu Isár, in these words: "Verily a grandfather is associated in succession with brothers, his portion is equal to one of theirs, and neither more nor less. Further, by an

* *Sharáya ul-Islám*, p. 449.

† *Vide* ante. pp. 189—191.

of any of them, the paternal grandfather is as a whole brother, and the paternal grandmother is, as a whole sister; and in conjunction with half brothers and sisters on the father's side, or any of them, the paternal grandfather is like such a brother, and the paternal grandmother is like such a sister, and in both the cases the grandparents and brethren take two-thirds of the estate and divide it among themselves in the proportion of two shares to each male and one share to each female.

The author of the *Sharáya ul-Islám,* however, says :— "When a paternal grandfather or grandmother, or both of them, are conbined with an only *sister* or with two or more *sisters* by the same father and mother, or by the same father only, the grandfather is as a brother on the father's side, and the grandmother, as a sister ; and the property remaining after satisfying the relations connected by the mother is divided among them in the proportion of two parts to the male and one part to the female (p. 449)."* It appears from the above that this author considers the paternal grandfather and grandmother respectively as a brother and sister *only* in conjunction with a *sister* or *sisters,* and *not* in conjunction with a brother or brothers, a brother and sister, or brothers *and* sisters; but the decision founded upon the opinion and decision of the majority of the Doctors seems to be *that* which is inculcated by or in the above principle. See the Annotations.

ANNOTATIONS.

authentic report of *Abú Basír* from the same *Imám* in these words : "I stated the case of a person who died leaving six brothers and a grandfather ; he replied, 'The grandfather is as one of the brothers.' " By another decision in the case of a brother's son and a grandfather, to this effect: "The property is to be divided equally betwixt them." And by another in the instance of a sister's daughters with a grandfather, to this effect: "To the sister's daughters one-third, and the remainder to the grandfather,"—which last decision obviously proceeds on the supposition that both sister and grandfather were related by the same side, whence the distinction of male and female would have bestowed a double portion on the latter.—Col. B., Trans., pp. 391 & 392.

* *Vide,* however, Principle 145.

Thus the *Rouzat ul-Ahkám*:—"On the assemblage of two sections (of the second class),* know that the paternal grandfather is like a whole brother or half brother on the father's side, and the paternal grandmother is like such a sister. So the paternal grandparents and paternal *brethren* divide among themselves two-thirds of the property in the proportion of two shares to each male and one share to each female. And the maternal grandparents and maternal *brethren* take one-third and divide it among themselves in equal shares."—P. 35.

So the *Mafátíh*:—"The grandfather and grandmother of any side are like a brother and sister of the same side."

So also the *Irshád*:—"When grandfathers and grandmothers and *brothers* and *sisters* are combined, the paternal grandfather is like a paternal and maternal brother, and the paternal grandmother is like a paternal and maternal sister. In like manner, a maternal grandfather and grandmother are like a maternal brother and sister."

Principle. CXXX. When the maternal grandfather and grandmother are, or one of them is, combined with half brethren on the mother's side, the grandfather is as a brother, and the grandmother is as a sister, and one-third (of the estate) is divided among them *equally*.†

Principle. CXXXI. An only maternal brother (or sister) takes a sixth of the inheritance, and when there are two or more of such relatives, a third of the property goes to them, while the maternal grand-parent, though alone, takes one-third (of the inheritance).—Rouzat ul-Ahkám, p. 35.

Principle. CXXXII. The grandfather, though remote, inherits with brethren though these be nearer, and *vice-versâ*, that is the children of brethren how low soever in descent, do, like their fathers and mothers, inherit with the grand-parents, though the latter be more proximate.—Rouzat ul-Ahkám, p. 35.

ANNOTATIONS.

cxxxii. A grandfather, though remote, participates with brethren when there is no ancestor lower than he, or nearer to the deceased.†

---

* See *ante*, p. 189 *et seq.*

† *Sharáya ul-Islám*. p. 449.

CXXXIII. If there are several grandfathers (in different degrees of ascent) in combination with brethren, then the lowest of them participates, with the brethren (of the deceased), and the others are excluded.* *Vide* Exclusion. *Principle.*

CXXXIV. The husband and wife get their large or full shares appointed for them respectively, when combined with brethren of the same side or of different sides;—the brethren on the mother's side take their appointed portion from the original estate, and the remainder goes to the person or persons related by both parents; failing them, to those related by the same father only. The deficiency (in such case) falls on the portions of the full brethren, or those connected by the same father only.* *Principle.*

As in the case of there being a husband with a half-brother or sister on the mother's side, and a sister by both parents.* *Example.*

CXXXV. And if there is a surplus,—as in the case of there being only one relative on the mother's side, and a sister by both parents,—that surplus goes to the sister exclusively.* *Vide ante*, p. 220. *Principle.*

ANNOTATIONS.

cxxxiii. The great grandfather cannot inherit together with a grandfather or a grandmother, and the son of a brother cannot inherit with a brother or sister, and the grandson of a brother cannot inherit with the son of a brother or with the son of a sister.—Macn. M. L., chap. ii, princ. 8.

cxxxiv. When a husband or wife participates with them (the brethren), the former (*i.e.*, the husband or wife) takes his or her large or full share;† and if the divisor fall short, the deficiency falls on the paternal, and *not* on the maternal, relatives; in the same manner as when something remains of the divisor, the same goes exclusively to the paternal relatives, the maternal relatives having no title to participate therein. The difference of opinion which is stated in the section on Return with respect to the maternal relatives† is applicable also to the present case.—Rouzat ul-Ahkám.

---

* *Sharáya ul-Islám*, pp. 449 & 450.

† *Vide ante*, p. 222.

But if (instead of a sister by both parents), there were a sister by the same father only, would she have this special right to the surplus remaining after satisfying the shares? This question has been answered in the affirmative, because the deficiency (if there is any, by reason of the contending claims of a husband or wife,) falls upon her.* However,—

Principle. CXXXVI. It has been maintained that the surplus reverts to the persons connected by the same mother only as well as to the sister or sisters by the same father only (as there may be one or more of them,) in fourths, or in fifths, on account of the equality of degree, and *this opinion is preferred.*†—Sharáya ul-Islám, p. 450.

Principle. CXXXVII. When the deceased has left a paternal grandfather and grandmother, also a maternal grandfather and grandmother of his father, and also the like relatives of his mother, *her* grand-parents have a third (of the estate) in fourths, and the grand-parents of the father have two-thirds, two-thirds of which (two-thirds) go to his grand-parents on the father's side, in the proportion of two parts to a male and one to a female, and the other (third) goes to his grand-parents on the mother's side in thirds; according to what has been reported by the *Shaikh*, on whom may God have mercy!‡

So that the original number of the shares is three which do not quadrate with the two classes, consequently four must be multiplied by nine, and the product (thirty-six) must again be multiplied by three, which will give one hundred and eight,‡ as the number of the parts into which the estate must be divided in order to give the several parties their respective portions without a fraction (*n*).

(*n.*) That is to say, the root of the case is three,—the relatives on the father's side being entitled to double the portion of the mother's relatives. But as there are four relatives on the father's side (*viz.*, his paternal grandfather and grandmother, and maternal grandfather and grandmother), and the paternal grandfather is entitled to *double* the portion of the maternal grandfather, as well as to that of the paternal grandmother, and the maternal grandmother is entitled to half the portion of her husband, so, *two*, which

---

* *Sharáya ul-Islám*, p. 449.

† *Vide* Mode of distribution in Lecture XI.

‡ *Sharáya ul-Islám*, p. 450.

is their portion from the root of the case, cannot be divided among them in integral parts or numbers, for, if the maternal grandmother's portion, which is the smallest of all the shares, be taken to be one (the lowest of all integral numbers), the share of the maternal grandfather must be two, and that of the paternal grandfather, four,—whence the share of his wife (the paternal grandmother of the deceased) must be two: thus assuming the lowest numbers, the shares of the paternal relatives amount to nine (*viz.*, $1+2+4+2=9$); in like manner, as *one*, the portion of the mother's relatives (from *three*, the root of the case), cannot be divided among them without a fraction, and there is no difference between the males and females of such relatives—they all being entitled to *equal* shares, so, for the sake of working out the problem, the share of every one of them is assumed to be one (the lowest of all the integral numbers), and accordingly their shares amount to four (*viz.*, $1+1+1+1=4$). Now four multiplied by nine gives thirty-six, which being multiplied by three, the root of the case, the product amounts to one hundred and eight, which settles the case. The relatives on the mother's side had one each, so now they will get thirty-six collectively, or nine each, (one multiplied by nine amounting to nine), and the remaining seventy-two of one hundred and eight will be divided among the relatives on the father's side in the proportion of their original shares. So, eight, the one-ninth of seventy-two, will go to the maternal grandmother (of the father), since, originally, she had one out of nine; two-ninths of $72 = 16$ will go to his maternal grandfather, and the same amount to the paternal grandmother, each of them having had originally two out of nine; and four-ninths of 72, that is 32, will go to the paternal grandfather, he having had four out of nine.

CXXXVIII. When there is a half-brother by the same mother only, and the son of a full brother, the whole of the inheritance goes to the former, because he is nearer to the deceased.* *Principle.*

Ibnu Sházan maintains that he (the said half brother) ought to have only a sixth, and the son of the full-brother, the remainder, by reason of the junction of the two causes of inheritance in his case. The reason, however, is weak; for the rule with regard to the junction of several causes has effect only when accompanied with equality of degree, and does not operate when the degrees differ.*

---

* *Sharáya ul-Islám*, p. 450.

Principle. CXXXIX. The children of brothers and sisters represent their respective parents on their failure, and each one of them inherits the portion of the person through whom he or she is connected to the deceased.*

Principle. CXL. If there be only one (child), he or she takes the whole of the (above) portion, or if there be several, and they are all males or all females, they take the portion *equally* between them; but if they are partly male and partly female, the division between them is in the proportion of two shares to a male and one share to a female, unless there are children of half-brethren on the mother's side, when the division among (the male and female of) them is equal.*

Principle. CXLI. The children of a brother take the remainder like their father, the children of a full sister take a half, the share of their mother, besides what may revert by return; and the children of two or more sisters have two-thirds, except when there is a deficiency in the property by reason of the intervention of a husband or wife, when they have the remainder, as happens to those who are connected with the deceased through his father.* *Vide ante*, pp. 213 & 214.

Principle. CXLII. If there are no children of full brethren, the children of half brethren (on the father's side) take their place, and the children of a half brother or sister on the mother's side have a sixth, while if there are children of both, they have a third, each set taking the share of the person through whom the same is related to the deceased, and (the individuals) dividing it among themselves equally.*

Principle. CXLIII. If the brethren were of different kinds, the children of half brethren on the mother's side take a third, and the children of full brethren take two-thirds,—while the children of the half brethren by the same father only are excluded.*

Principle. CXLIV. If in combination with them there is a husband or wife, he or she takes the large or full share appointed for him or her, and the children by the same mother only take a third of the original estate, if they are more than

* *Sharáya ul-Islám*, pp. 450 & 451.

one; or a sixth, if only one; and the remainder, whether more or less (than the appropriate portion) goes to the children of full brethren, or failing them, to the children connected through the father alone.*

CXLV. If grand-parents are combined with the above (children of brethren), these divide the estate with them, like brethren as has been already stated.* *Principle.*

On the third class of Consanguinous Heirs.

This class comprises (as already stated,†) paternal and maternal uncles and aunts, how high soever, of the deceased.‡

CXLVI. A paternal uncle, when alone (that is without a co-heir), inherits the whole property.‡ *Principle.*

CXLVII. So do also two or more such uncles inherit, and divide the property *equally*‡ (if they are of the same kind). *Principle.*

CXLVIII. The same also is the case with one, two or more paternal aunts.‡ *Principle.*

CXLIX. When there are both paternal uncles and aunts, then to each male goes the portion of two females.‡ *Principle.*

CL. When they are of different kinds, then a sixth goes to the half paternal uncle or aunt on the mother's side, and a third goes to more than one (of such relatives), males and females taking *equally,*—and the remainder goes to the full paternal uncle or uncles (and aunt or aunts) in the proportion of two shares to a male and one share to a female: half paternal uncles (and aunts) on the father's side are excluded by full paternal uncles (and aunts); but in default of the latter the former take their place‡ (in succession). *Principle.*

ANNOTATIONS.

cl. & cli. Uncles and aunts all share together; except some be of the half and others of the whole blood. A paternal uncle by the same father only is excluded by a paternal uncle by the same father and mother; and the son of a paternal uncle by the whole blood excludes a paternal uncle of the half blood.—Macn. M. L., chap. ii, princ. 11.

---

* *Sharáya ul-Islám*, pp. 450 & 451.

† *Vide ante*, pp. 190—192.

‡ *Sharáya ul-Islám*, p. 451.

Principle. CLI. The son of a paternal uncle does not inherit with a paternal uncle, nor does any one who is more remote from the deceased inherit with one who is nearer to him, except in one case, which is that of the son of a full paternal uncle with a half paternal uncle on the father's side, when the full paternal uncle's son is preferred while the case remains exactly so; but if it is changed by addition even of a maternal uncle, the son of the paternal uncle is excluded.*

Sir William Macnaghten says:—"The son of a paternal uncle by the whole blood excludes a paternal uncle of the half blood."† To the above should be added "on the father's side," inasmuch as a paternal uncle of the half blood on the mother's side is not excluded by the son of a paternal uncle of the whole blood; but, on the contrary, the latter is excluded by the former.—*Vide* Principle cxxxviii.

Principle. CLII. If there is but a single maternal uncle, the (whole) property goes to him. So also to the two or more maternal uncles (when without a co-heir). Such also is the case with a single maternal aunt as well as with two or more maternal aunts.‡ If they (the maternal uncles and aunts) occur together, then the males and females share *equally*, (there being no distinction among them in favor of the male sex).

Principle. CLIII. But if they are of different kinds, then a sixth goes to one and a third to several persons related by the same mother only,—males and females sharing alike; and the remainder goes to the full maternal uncles and aunts in the proportion of two shares to a male and one share to a female: the half maternal uncles and aunts on the father's side are excluded (that is, they do not inherit), except on failure of the full maternal uncles and aunts.‡

Principle. CLIV. If there are both paternal and maternal uncles (and aunts), a third goes to the maternal kindred even though there is only one male or female, and two-thirds go to the paternal kindred even though there is only one such male or female.‡

---

* *Sharáya ul-Islám*, p. 451.—See *ante*, pp. 197 & 198.

† Macn. M. L., chap. ii. princ., 11.

‡ *Sharáya ul-Islám*, p. 451.

For example, if a person dying should leave a paternal half-uncle and a maternal full aunt, no exclusion here taking place, the former would inherit two-thirds of the property, and one-third thereof would descend to the latter. Again, if he should leave a maternal half-uncle and a paternal full aunt, the division of inheritance would be guided by the same rule,—*viz.*, to the former one-third, as deriving his title from the mother, and two-thirds to the latter; for it is reported by *Abú Ayúb*, from the *Imám Jaáfar Saádik*, on whom be peace, to be written in the book of *Alí*, on whom be blessing and peace, "that a paternal aunt is by law in the exact situation of a father; a maternal aunt in that of a mother; and, in general, every distant kinsman in the situation of that relation more near through whom his title is derived."—Col. B., Trans., p. 334. Example.

CLV. If there are several maternal uncles and aunts (of one kind), the property goes to them in the proportion of two shares to a male and one share to a female.* *Principle.*

CLVI. When they (the maternal uncles and aunts) are of different kinds, then if there is only one related through the mother alone, he or she gets a sixth of a third (of the estate); but if there are several so related, they get a third of it in *equal* shares; and the remainder (of the third) goes to the person or persons connected by both parents, and the remaining two-thirds go to the paternal uncles and aunts, who, if all of them are of one side, get the same in the proportion of two shares to a male and one share to a female; but if they are of different sides, then the single person connected by the same mother only gets a sixth, while two or more such relatives get a third between them in *equal* shares; and the remainder (of the two-thirds) goes to the full paternal uncles and aunts in the proportion of two shares to a male and one share to a female; while those related by the same father only do not inherit except on failure of the individuals connected by both parents.* *Principle.*

CLVII. When paternal and maternal uncles and aunts of the father and paternal and maternal uncles and aunts of the mother are combined, it is said in the *Niháyah*, that those of them who are related through the mother alone get a third *equally* among them; while those related through the father get two-thirds—one third of which (two-thirds) goes to (his) maternal uncle and aunt in *equal* shares, and two-thirds *Principle.*

---

* *Sharáya ul-Islám*, pp. 451 & 452.

go to (his) paternal uncle and aunt in the proportion of two parts to a male and one part to a female (*o*).*

Illustration. (*o*.) So that the original number of shares is three, which do not quadrate with the two classes, four must, therefore, be mutilplied by nine, and the product, thirty-six, must again be multiplied by three, which will give one hundred and eight* (as the number of the parts, into which the estate must be divided to give the several parties their respective portions without a fraction).†

Principle. CLVIII. The deceased's own paternal and maternal uncles and *their* children how low soever have a better right to inherit (from him) than the paternal uncles and aunts of his father and the paternal uncles and aunts of his mother.*

Reason. Because his *own* paternal and maternal uncles and aunts are nearer (to him) in degree, and their children stand in their place.*

Principle. CLIX. On failure of the deceased's paternal and maternal uncles and aunts, and their children how low soever, the paternal and maternal uncles of his father, and the paternal and maternal uncles of his mother, and their children how low soever, take their places; such also is the case with other ascending generations, the lower (of them) being always preferred to the higher.*

Principle. CLX. The children of uncles and aunts on different sides, take the shares of their (respective) parents (*p*).*

(*p*.) So that the son of a half paternal uncle on the mother's side gets a sixth, and if there are sons of two such uncles, they get a third, while the sons of a full paternal uncle and aunt or uncles or aunts get the remainder. The same rule is applicable to the sons of maternal aunts.*

Principle. CLXI. When two causes of inheritance combine in the same heir, he inherits by virtue of both, if one of them does not counteract or impede the operation of the other (*q*).*

Annotations.

clxi. A more simple and obvious example occurs in supposing any person whom we shall name *Zayid* to have a half-brother by the father's side, and half-sister by the mother's, and these two to intermarry, in

* *Sharáya ul-Islám*, p. 452.

† *See ante*, pp. 244 & 245, where this is fully explained.

(*q.*) As in the case of (there being) a son of a half paternal uncle on the father's side, who also is the son of a half maternal uncle on the mother's side;—or as (in the case of) a son of a paternal uncle, who is also the husband;—or a daughter of a paternal uncle, who is also the wife;—or as (in the case of) a half paternal aunt on the father's side, who is also the half paternal aunt on the mother's side.* Example.

CLXII. But if one of the causes is an impediment to the operation of the other, the person (in whom they combine) inherits by virtue of the impending cause(*r*).* *Principle.*

(*r.*) As (in the case of there being) the son of a paternal uncle who is also a brother, he inherits by virtue of brotherhood alone.* Example.

CLXIII. When there is a husband (or wife) with maternal uncles and aunts, or paternal uncles and aunts, the husband or wife takes the large or full share appointed for him or her,† the relatives connected by the mother alone have their original share of the entire estate left by the deceased, while the remainder goes to those connected by both parents; or failing them, to those connected through the same father only.* *Principle.*

ANNOTATIONS.

which event *Zayid* is manifestly both paternal and maternal uncle to all the offspring of that marriage.—Col. B., Trans., p. 337.

Every person having two different relations to the deceased of a nature whereof one impedes not the other, does not exclude a person having only one relation, provided it be in the same degree; but the former receives two portions of inheritance in virtue of his double title, and the latter has only one portion in virtue of his single relation. This principle is ratified by unanimous assent without any difference of opinion, because exclusion from inheritance is founded by law on the disparity of degrees in propinquity and distance, and by no means on the unity or plurality of relationship.—Col. B., Trans., pp. 336 & 337.

* *Sharáya ul-Islám*, p. 452.

† *Vide ante*, pp. 182 & 185.

Principle.

CLXIV. The rule for the children of maternal uncles and aunts combining with the husband or wife is the same as that for the uncles and aunts themselves in that combination (*s*).*

Illustration.

(*s*.) Thus if there is a husband or wife with sons of maternal uncles and also with sons of paternal uncles, the husband or wife takes his or her appointed (full) share, and the sons of maternal uncles have a third of the original estate, while the remainder passes to the sons of the paternal uncles.*

ANNOTATIONS.

clx—clxiv. In short, the rule of preference in succession by proximity of degree has a uniform influence over this description of heirs, their children and children's children *ad infinitum*, with one only exception, which the general assent of all our doctors has ratified and confirmed, *viz*., that the son of a paternal full uncle excludes a paternal half uncle only of the deceased, and takes the whole inheritance preferably to the latter, although nearer in degree, it the succession should be limited to these two; and it is in virtue of this exception that, had the Prophet of God, on whom and his posterity be blessing and peace, left no issue at the period of his dissolution, his whole succession must by law have devolved on the Commander of the Faithful, *Alí*, on whom be the blessing of God, in preference to, and complete exclusion of, *Abbás*; for *Abú Tálib* was the full brother of *Abdullah*, both by the father's and mother's side, and consequently his son, the Commander of the Faithful, although more remote in degree; must have excluded *Abbás*, half uncle of the Prophet, as being brother to *Abdullah* by the father's side only.—Col. B., Trans., pp. 329 & 330.

---

* *Sharáya ul-Islám*, pp. 452 & 453.

LECTURE IX.

ON THE SUCCESSION OF SPOUSES TO EACH OTHER, AND OF THE IMÂM,—ON ACKNOWLEDGMENT OF RELATIONSHIP,—ESTABLISHMENT OF DESCENT OR CONSANGUINITY,—AND ON ILLEGITIMATE CHILDREN.

On the Succession of Spouses to each other.

ONE of the causes which operate in law as a title to succession is marriage, by virtue of which a surviving husband or wife enjoys a definite and fixed share of the deceased spouse's inheritance; nor can either of them be excluded from that share by any heir whatsoever; but, on the contrary, he or she inherits with every class and description of heirs, whether by consanguinity or patronage.* Thus a husband or wife (as the case may be) has his or her appointed share of inheritance in every possible situation, and after allotment of his or her share, the remainder of the estate descends to the other heir or heirs, if any, whether by consanguinity or patronage.

CLXV. The reciprocal right of inheritance of the married couple is grounded upon their marriage being a permanent one. Hence, in a temporary marriage none of them inherits from the other, unless there was a condition (to inherit). This is *Principle.*

ANNOTATIONS.

clxv. The husband and wife inherit from each other though their marriage may not have been consummated, unless the marriage was contracted during illness.—Irshád.

---

* This is by unanimous assent agreeably to the word of Almighty God: "And for you is the half of what your wives shall leave if they have no issue; but if they have issue, then ye shall have a fourth part of what they leave after the legacies they may bequeath and payment of their debts. They also shall inherit the fourth of what ye shall leave in case ye have no issue; but if ye have issue, then they shall receive an eighth part of your inheritance, after the legacies ye may bequeath and payment of your debts."—*Kurán.* *Vide* p. 78 of Lecture II, delivered in 1873.

the approved opinion.—Rouzat ul-Ahkám, p. 38.—*Vide* Temporary Marriage and Sharáya ul-Islám, p. 282.

Principle. CLXVI. A wife inherits (from her husband) if she was under his control, though he did not consummate marriage with her.*

Consummation of marriage is not a condition (of inheritability), unless the husband was sick at the time of the contract, and died of that sickness.—Rouzat ul-Ahkám, p. 38. Hence,—

Principle. CLXVII. The marriage contracted by a sick man is dependent upon consummation. So that if he died of that illness without having consummated (the marriage), the contract is void, and the woman has no right to dower, nor to inheritance.*

ANNOTATIONS.

clxvii. It is a prevalent opinion amongst all our doctors that marriage contracted in sickness or upon death-bed does not found a title to inheritance in the widow; that death-bed divorce, on the other hand, does not operate to her exclusion; and, further, that temporary marriages, or contracts of *Mutaâ*, by no means establish a title to succession in either of the parties.—Col. B., Trans., p. 339. *Vide*, however, Temporary Marriage.

If a sick man contract marriage with a woman, whether his distemper be dangerous or otherwise, and die of that distemper, without intervenient recovery or convalescence, previous also to consummation of his nuptials, such contract of marriage is thereby null; or, in other words, is not considered to be established in law, until consummation, or recovery of the husband from that disease with which he was afflicted at the time. It follows that in this case there can be no title of inheritance between the parties, no dower even incumbent on the husband, and that the woman is not bound to observe an *iddat*, or term of probation. This law of annulment of contracts entered into by parties legally qualified to contract, without divorce or voluntary dissolution, may certainly at first sight appear irreconcilable, but all objection and doubt are removed necessarily by a reference to those authentic proofs of their nullity, already detailed in the Book of Marriage.—Col. B., Trans., p. 340.

---

* *Sharáya ul-Islám*, p. 453.

On the other hand,—

CLXVIII. If a sick man (who married in that state) died *after* consummation, or if he recovered of that illness, and died of another, then the marriage contract would, doubtless, be valid and effective, and the results thereof,—(*viz.*) dower, inheritability, and *iddat*—will ensue.—Rouzat ul-Ahkám, p. 38. *Principle.*

CLXIX. If the married woman died before her sick husband as well as before consummation of marriage, then the approved opinion is that inheritability will ensue, though some of the doctors have doubted it.—Rouzat ul-Ahkám, p. 38. Further,— *Principle.*

CLXX. If a woman on her death-bed, or whilst afflicted with any distemper, should contract herself in marriage to a man in health at the time, but who dies without consummation, and she thus survives him, the contract is perfectly valid according to the best authority, and the right of inheritance fully established.—Col. B., Trans., p. 341. *Principle.*

ANNOTATIONS.

clxviii. If, on the other hand, the contracting party should die of any other complaint, or of that same distemper after intervenient recovery, or after consummation of his marriage, the contract is, in this case, valid and binding; consequently the right of succession is fully established beyond the possibility of doubt by reason of the absolute and comprehensive sense of the sacred text already quoted, and the particular traditions establishing, in this case, the validity of contract which were formerly referred to in treating of marriage.—Col. B., Trans., p. 340.

clxix. If, again, the woman should die previous to consummation of the marriage with a man who was sick at the period of contract, and notwithstanding survives her, his right of inheritance is liable to difficulty and doubt, arising, on the one hand, from the validity of contract, which, if allowed, gives room for the application of the sacred text; and, on the other, from a consideration that its validity is suspended upon recovery, or consummation of the husband, neither of which is in this case established. The first suggestion, however, appears the stronger, as, from the husband's survival, in whose prior death alone, without consummation or recovery, the objection to validity of contract could in such cases occur, there appears full ground for the application of the sacred text regarding inheritance by marriage.—Col. B., Trans., p. 340.

This (*i.e.*, the above) doctrine, both the Allámah and Martyr have approved.—*Ibid.*

Principle. CLXXI. If a woman was irrevocably divorced by her husband during his illness, she will nevertheless continue to be his heiress, till one year, provided the husband did not get well in the meantime, and the woman did not marry another husband. This rule, however, is applicable to the inheritability of the woman alone; consequently, if the woman died within one year, her husband will not inherit from her.—Rouzat ul-Ahkám, p. 38.

ANNOTATIONS.

clxxi. If a husband divorce his wife upon death-bed, or whilst afflicted by any distemper, of which, without intervenient recovery, he afterwards dies, such divorce has no operation in law to deprive the widow of her right of succession, unless a full year shall have elapsed from the date thereof until his death, or that she herself in the meantime have married another. If, on the contrary, the husband survive a full year from the date of divorce, or recover of that distemper, and afterwards die within a year, or the widow herself has during his illness taken another husband: in each and all of these cases, she has no title whatever to inherit any part of his property.—Col. B., Trans., p. 341.

clxxi. "If a man divorce his wife whilst in sickness, she is still considered as having a right to inherit whilst he continues in that sickness, even after her *iddat* has elapsed, should he not recover therefrom." The reporter thus proceeds: "I inquired what if his distemper should be prolonged? He replied, 'She inherits although it should last for a year;'" or, as this answer has been conveyed by another reporter, "She inherits if he should die of that distemper during the influence of which he divorced her without intervenient convalescence." A further judgment of the same *Imám* is recorded by *Abdul Rahmán Ibnu Hajjáj* upon the question of death-bed divorce to the following effect: "Should the husband die of that disease, and the woman have continued single, she enjoys her share of his succession; but should she marry another person, as this clearly demonstrates her satisfaction at what he has done, she can have no claim to inheritance." This decision is reported by *Samâa* in a manner somewhat differing from the above, *viz.*, "She inherits as long as she continues in her *iddat* (*i.e.*, does not marry any other); and if he has divorced her with an intention to injure her by depriving her of this title, she inherits although he should survive a full year; but if beyond

CLXXII. **In the inheritability of the husband and wife, it is a condition that the marriage should subsist really or constructively.—Rouzat ul-Ahkám, p. 39. Hence,—** *Principle.*

CLXXIII. When a woman is irrevocably divorced or separated (*a*), she does not inherit (from her husband), nor does the husband inherit* (from her), though she be in her *iddat.*† *Principle.*

(*a*.) As a woman who is divorced thrice or before consummation, or when passed child-bearing, or not in the age of menstruation, or who is released by *Khulá, Mubárat,* or is in her *iddat* after connection under a semblance of right, or after cancellation.*

CLXXIV. A husband inherits from (his) wife though she should have been revocably divorced, and their mutual right of inheritance subsists, if one of them died during *iddat*, the woman still being within the meaning of "a wife."* *Principle.*

ANNOTATIONS.

this time even a single day, she has no longer, in any event, a claim to inheritance." In another report it is expressed that the following question was particularly put to the *Imám*: "What is the longest term of sickness during which the right of a divorced wife to inherit may be preserved?" And this answer is recorded: "That the husband shall continue ill thereof until he dies, and *that* within a year."—Col. B., Trans., p. 342.

clxxii, clxxiii. The woman divorced irrevocably cannot inherit (from her husband), though she be in her *iddat*, nor can the man so divorcing inherit from her. Consequently, the woman who was divorced by her husband before consummation, or who was past child-bearing, or who was thrice divorced, does not inherit (from her husband).—Rouzat ul-Ahkám, p. 39.

clxxiii, clxxiv. In like manner, they inherit from each other even if there was a revocable divorce, provided one of them died within the *iddat*. But there is no right of inheritance in the absolute or irrevocable divorce.—Irshád.

---

* *Sharáya ul-Islám*, p. 453.
† *Rouzat ul-Ahkám*, p. 39.

According to the ordinance of the *Kurán*,—

Principle. CLXXV. The share of the husband (in the property left by his deceased wife) is of two kinds: *viz.*, large and small; the large share is a moiety; and the small, a fourth. He gets a moiety in the case of the deceased having left no child (how low soever) of her own, and a fourth in the case of her leaving a child, male or female, begotten by him, or by another husband.—Rouzat ul-Ahkám, pp. 39, 40.

In like manner,—

Principle. CLXXVI. The wife's or widow's share is also of two kinds (large and small). Her large share is a fourth, and her small share is an eighth. She gets the large share when there is no child, how low soever, of her deceased husband; and the small share when such exists.—*Ibid.*

Principle. CLXXVII. If there be several widows, they collectively take the wife's portion—a fourth or an eighth (as the case may be), and divide the same *equally* amongst themselves. —*Ibid.*

Principle. CLXXVIII. When a man has divorced one out of four wives, and married another, then a doubt applies in general

---

ANNOTATIONS.

The woman revocably divorced is constructively the wife of the divorcer so long as she has not completed the *iddat.*—Rouzat ul-Ahkám, p. 38.

clxxv, clxxvi. When a deceased person has left no child or child's child how low soever, the husband (of the deceased) gets a half, and (in the case of the deceased's being a male) the wife gets a fourth; but if the deceased has left no child (or child's child), a fourth goes to the husband, and an eighth to the wife.—Irshád.

clxxvi, clxxvii. If the deceased left no child, a fourth goes to his widow; and if there be more than one widow, they, in that case, share it *equally.*—Sharáya ul-Islám, p. 453.

But if the deceased has left a child, then an eighth goes to his widow. If there is more than one widow, the same (eighth) devolves equally among them, nothing being added thereto (*i.e.*, to the eighth).—*Ibid.*

If there are several wives or widows, all of them share *equally* the fourth or eighth (as the case may be).—Irshád.

clxxviii. If a man having four wives divorces one of them, and marries a fifth wife, after expiration of the (term of) *iddat* in a revocable to those previously married, and a fourth of an eighth goes to the last married (wife) in the case of there being a child (of the deceased), and the remainder of the eighth is equally divided among the four.* And in the case of no child being left by the man, a fourth of a fourth goes to the wife last married, and the remainder of the fourth goes equally to the four wives previously married.*

CLXXIX. When a girl under puberty is given in marriage by her father or paternal grandfather, her husband inherits from her, and she inherits from him.* *Principle.*

CLXXX. So also, if two minors are married (to each other) by their fathers or paternal grandfathers, they inherit from each other.* *Principle.*

CLXXXI. But if they (the minors) were contracted in marriage by persons *other* than their fathers and paternal grandfathers, the contract remains in suspense till assented to by the spouses themselves upon arrival at puberty and discretion; and if one of them should die before such assent (should have been given), the contract would be void and there would be no right of inheritance.* *Principle.*

ANNOTATIONS.

divorce, or during the *iddat* in an irrevocable divorce, and afterwards dies, and there arises a doubt as to which of the four wives was divorced, then the wife married last will get a fourth of an eighth of the property in the case of there being a child, or a fourth of a fourth in the case of there being no child of the deceased; and what remains of the wife's portion will be divided equally among the four wives to all of whom a doubt was attached though one of them was divorced. So it is in the *Nass* or *Hadis.*—Rouzat ul-Ahkám, p. 43.

If such doubt attaches to one of *two* wives, then it is a *vexata quaestio,* as the *Nass*† respects four wives, consequently, it would be better if a compromise were effected.—*Ibid.*

---

* *Sharáya ul-Islám*, p. 453.

† The *Kurán* or *Hadis.*

Principle. CLXXXII. The same would be the result if one of them attained puberty and then assented (to the marriage), and the other died before attaining puberty.*

Principle. CLXXXIII. But if the one who assented should die, the share of the other ought to be separated from the rest of the deceased's estate, and kept with the survivor; and if on attaining puberty, he or she should reject the marriage, the contract would be void, and the party would have no right to inherit.*

Principle. CLXXXIV. If, on the other hand, the marriage is assented to, the same would be valid; the party, however, must be sworn to state that the assent has not been from greed to inherit.*

Principle. CLXXXV. The husband inherits all (kinds of) the property of his wife; so does the wife or widow if she has a child by the deceased, or child's child.—Irshád.

Principle. When a wife or widow has had a child (born of her own womb) by the deceased, she inherits out of all that he has left.* But,—

Principle. CLXXXVI. If there is no (such) child, she takes nothing out of the (deceased's) *land* (*arz*), but her

ANNOTATIONS.

clxxxvi. If the widow has no such child, she does not inherit *land*, but gets the value of buildings, trees, and also of household effects.—Irshád.

According to most of our doctors, the wife or widow does not inherit land and *akár*,—neither the property itself, nor the value thereof; but she gets the value of the edifices and household effects (such as are not fixtures), though she is not entitled to get the things themselves.—Mafátíh.

Most of the modern lawyers apply the above rule to the wife or widow who has no child (by her deceased husband). It would, therefore, be better to take it in this sense, (more especially) as it accords with the opinion of the Allámah.—*Ibid.*

* *Sharáya ul-Islám*, p. 453.

share of the *household* effects (*álát*), and buildings is to be given to her (*a*).*

(*a.*) It has been said, however, that she is to be excluded from nothing except the mansions and dwellings; while Murtazá, may God be gracious to him! has expressed a third opinion to the effect that the land should be valued, and her share of the value assigned to her. But the first opinion is best founded on (traditional) authority.*

CLXXXVII. If a woman dies leaving her husband, and no other heir except the *Imám*, then the husband takes his appointed share, which is a half, and the other half also reverts to him,—he having in this case a residuary title to the remainder. It is otherwise in the case of a husband dying or leaving no heir except his wife and the *Imám*, as she then receives only her appointed share, *viz.*, a fourth, and the remaining three-fourths go to the *Imám*,—a widow having no residuary title in any situation whatever.† And,— *Principle.*

ANNOTATIONS.

clxxxvii. Such, at least, is the most common and prevalent doctrine, which, further, the two *Shaiks*,‡ as well as *Sayyid Murtazá*, have declared to be incontestable, by reason of an authentic tradition related by *Abú Basír* in these words: "I was present with the *Imám Jaáfar Saádik* when he assembled the people to prayer, and was informed of a woman's decease, who had left her husband, and no other heir. He replied, 'The property goes all to her husband.'" And another decision of the same *Imám*, in the case of a woman who left her husband, and no other relations known, *viz.*, "The succession is for the husband entirely;" as well as several other authentic documents to a similar effect.—Col. B., Trans., p. 339.

According to the most prevalent opinion, and to a positive judgment of the *Imám Muhammad Bákir*, on whom be peace, quoted by *Muhammad Ibnu Muslim*, in the instance of a man who died leaving only his widow, to this effect: "She receives only a fourth part, and the residue

* *Sharáya ul-Islám*, p. 453. B. Dig., Part II, p. 295.

† See *ante*, pp. 224 & 225.

‡ That is, Shaikh Abú Jaafar Túsí and Shaikh Mufíd.

CLXXXVIII. If there be an heir between the husband or widow and the *Imám*, then the property remaining after allotment of the appointed share of the husband or widow, goes to such heir alone.*

Principle.

On the Valá† *of Imámat, or Succession of the Imám.*

Principle.

CLXXXIX. The whole property of the person who leaves no other heir of any description whatever, goes to his *Imám*; but if the deceased has left a widow, then the property remaining after she has received her specific share (which is a quarter) goes to the *Imám*.‡

ANNOTATIONS.

goes to the *Imám*." To the same purport are several other authentic documents.—Col. B., Trans., p. 339.

When a person leaves no consanguinous heir, nor an heir for special cause, except a wife, a part of the inheritance goes to the *Imám*.—Irshád.

clxxxviii, clxxxix. When there is no surety for offences, the *Imám* is the heir of the person who has no (other) heir, and this is the third kind of *valá*.—Sharáya ul-Islám, p. 456.

clxxxix. The *Imám* is an heir when there is no (other) heir by consanguinity or for special cause, except a widow, who participates with him in the inheritance and takes her large share.—Rouzat ul-Ahkám, p. 50.

The last species of *valá*, or legal title to inheritance thereby, is that enjoyed by the *Imám*, in virtue whereof, if a person die leaving no heirs by consanguinity, no husband or widow, with the provisions and restrictions already quoted respecting the latter, no emancipator and no surety

---

* *See ante*, pp. 224 & 225.

† *Valá* is a term of various applications, but signifies, in this place, the connection of one of two persons with the other, produced, *first*, by emancipation from slavery; *second*, by responsibility of crimes,—observing, however, the order of succession; and, *thirdly*, upon failure of these descriptions, bestowing a title of succession upon the *Imám*, or public treasury at his disposal, who is by law the heir of every person deceased having no heir besides, and this may be considered in the third class or degree of succession by *valá*.—Col. B., Trans., pp. 345 & 346. See *ante*, p. 177.

‡ See *ante*. pp. 176 & 177.

CXC. If then the *Imám* be present, the property (left by the deceased) goes to him to do with it as he pleases (*a*).* *Principle.*

(*a.*) *Alí,* on whom be peace, used to give the property to the poor and indigent (of the deceased's) city or village,† and to the weak and infirm among his (the deceased's) neighbours.*

There are, however, different opinions as to how the property, which thus devolves on the *Imám,* in his absence, should be dealt with.

The author of the *Sharáya ul-Islám* says,—"If the *Imám* is absent, the property is to be distributed among the poor and indigent, and not to be given up or surrendered to any but to a righteous Sultán or ruler, except under fear or actual compulsion."*

ANNOTATIONS.

for fines, the property, or inheritance, of such person is by law entirely vested in the *Imám,* who is, in other words, the sole heir of every person deceased leaving no individual member of any of the foregoing classes. This principle is established, according to the *Shaikh,* as well by universal assent as by an authentic tradition of the *Imám Muhammad Bákir,* on whom be peace, quoted by *Buríd Ajálí* in these words:—"If a person should not have engaged in a contract of clientage with any believer previous to his death, the inheritance of such person is vested in the high priest of the Faithful," that is, the *Imám*; to which effect there are many other traditions generally known.—Col. B., Trans., p. 362.

cxc, cxci. If the *Imám* be visible or present, the property may be applied to any purpose that he pleases. The Commander of the Faithful (*i.e., Alí*) used to distribute it by way of alms among the poor of the town and the weak and infirm neighbours (of the deceased).—Irshád.

With respect to the application of this fund, during the absence of the *Imám,* the doctrine of *Muhakkik* in his *Sharáya,* as well as of most other lawyers, prescribes its partition amongst the poor and indigent of our sect, by reason of the impossibility to deliver it to him, upon whom be blessing and peace, and consequently the preferable title of his indigent posterity and followers to enjoy it, in the same manner as they enjoy his *fifth* of spoils taken in battle, of wines, and various other subjects with which this right is connected.—Col. B., Trans., p. 363.

---

* *Sharáya ul-Islám,* p. 456.

† Arab "*Balad.*"

The author of the *Irshád* is of the same opinion. He says,—"If the *Imám* be absent, the property should be distributed among the poor and beggars, and it should not be given to a tyrant, except under fear."—Irshád.

Principle. **CXCI.** The most approved opinion, however, is, that the property thus vested in the *Imám* should, while he is absent, be distributed among the *Sayyids*, who are his descendants,—preference, nevertheless, being given to such of them as are poor and indigent.*

On the acknowledgment of Relationship establishing Heritable Right.

Principle. **CXCII.** The acknowledgment of a young child's descent is not established unless its childship be possible, the child acknowledged be unknown, and there be none to dispute it.†

With respect to this (acknowledgment) there are three conditions (*viz.*):—

Principle. CXCIII. If it be impossible (for the acknowledger) to be the child's parent, the acknowledgment is null (1).†

Example. As when the person acknowledged is older than the acknowledger, or his equal in age, or only so much younger than he, that the difference between their ages is less than is usual in the birth of such child; or where one should acknowledge the child of a woman to be his, when there has been between them (that is the acknowledger and woman) such distance as to preclude his having access to her during the age of such child.†

ANNOTATIONS.

cxciii. With respect, again, to the case of parents and their infant children, reciprocal acknowledgment is not required by law to establish the right of succession, but, on the contrary, the simple declaration of the parent, or adoption of the child as his own, is perfectly sufficient to establish inheritance betwixt them, as has already been fully explained in treating of the acknowledgment of parentage, and there is no distinction upon this point betwixt a father and mother, as a majority of our doctors have decided.—Col. B., Trans., p. 377.

* *Vide Rouzat ul-Ahkám*, pp. 50 & 51.

† *Sharáya ul-Islám* p. 376.

CXCIV. In like manner, if the child be of known parentage, the acknowledgment cannot be accepted (2). So also if any one should dispute (with the acknowledger) *Principle.*

ANNOTATIONS.

cxciii, cxciv. If, however, the acknowledging parties should be generally known as not related to each other by the tie, whether of blood or affinity, which they allege, such acknowledgment cannot in law be received, as, obviously in this case, tending to affect the rights of third parties; for the title of succession is established by law in the known heirs of the acknowledger, and his simple confession in favor of another, as tending to exclude these, or at least to introduce a sharer in their rights, cannot be received without proof, although verified by the person in whose favor it is made.—Col. B., Trans., p. 376.

And here, as an appendage to the legal causes of succession by birth and affinity, we observe the mutual acknowledgment of two persons with respect to each other of a relationship establishing the right of inheritance, provided both these persons be of unknown parentage and connections. Thus, if two persons mutually recognize each other by the titles, for example, of father and son, or any other founding a claim to succession, who are not known to the contrary, they are by law acknowledged as the heirs of each other, nor can either be called upon to prove the truth of his confession, because the right is confined to themselves, and there is no person to oppose it, as well as by the saying of him, on whom be peace, " Acknowledgments of sane people are valid and binding as to themselves." Further, it is related by *Abdur-Rahmán Ibnu Hijjáj Bijily* that he asked the *Imám Jaáfar Saádik*, upon whom be peace, respecting a woman brought prisoner from her own country, and with her an infant child whom she called her son; and a man also a prisoner, who, meeting by accident with his brother, recognized him by that title, and they both knew each other, but neither could adduce any proof of their relationship except this mutual acknowledgment. The reporter thus proceeds,—" The *Imám* inquired of me my own opinion of these cases; I observed that the parties could not inherit from each other as having no proof of their relationship from being born in a foreign country. He exclaimed, 'Almighty God! if a mother has brought with her into captivity a son or a daughter, whom she constantly acknowledges as such, or when a man recognizes his brother, and they both being of sane mind continue to acknowledge the relations, surely they must be considered the lawful heirs of each other.'—Col. B., Trans., pp. 375 & 376.

in respect of the childship of the child, the acknowledgment cannot be accepted without proof (3).*

Principle. CXCV. No regard is to be paid to the assent of a young child.*

But should not some regard be had to the assent of the acknowledged person when adult in age? Apparently not, as is in the *Niháyah.* It is otherwise in the *Mabsút,* which is most agreeable to the general principles of the law.* So,—

Principle. CXCVI. If the adult should deny the parentage (*nasab*), it is not established.*

Principle. CXCVII. The descent of any other than a child cannot be established without the assent or concurrence of the person acknowledged.*

Principle. CXCVIII. When the acknowledgment is in favor of any other than a child of the loins, and the acknowledger has no other heirs, and the person acknowledged has assented to the truth of the

ANNOTATIONS.

cxcviii. This right of inheritance by mutual acknowledgment, except in the instance of parent and child, is invariably restricted to the acknowledging parties themselves, and does by no means, according to the most prevalent opinion, descend to their heirs, unless the latter should also verify and avow the connection. Thus, if a person declare another to be her brother, who on his part also avows the relationship, and they are not known to the contrary, the right of inheritance is thereby established betwixt them as to each other, but does not extend to the others, brothers, for example, of either, nor to any relations besides. It is otherwise with respect to parents and children. If one person acknowledges himself the father of another, who verifies and avows the filial tie, these are not only by law the heirs of each other, but this right also extends to all the heirs or descendants of both. This distinction betwixt the two cases, however, is founded upon a principle whereof the grounds are by no means obvious; and the various objections thereto may be seen at large with their answers in their proper place.—Col. B., Trans., p. 377.

* *Sharáya ul-Islám,* p. 376.

acknowledgment, they inherit from each other; this, however, is not to affect the rights of others than themselves.*

CXCIX. If the acknowledger has any known heirs, his acknowledgment of *nasab* is not to be accepted.* *Principle.*

CC. When a person has acknowledged a young child (as his offspring), and the *nasab* is established, but is subsequently denied by the child on his attaining puberty, no regard can be had to his denial, because the *nasab* had already been established previous thereto.* *Principle.*

CCI. When the child of a deceased person has acknowledged another to be his child, and the two then concur in acknowledging a third, the *nasab* of the third is established, provided that the two first are just and righteous persons; but if the third should deny the second, the *nasab* of the second would not be established, and the third would take half the estate, the first, a third, and the second a sixth, being the complement of the share of the first.* *Principle.*

CCII. If, again, the two (first) were of known *nasab*, and should both acknowledge the third, his *nasab* would be established, provided the two were just and righteous persons; and though the third should deny (the *nasab* of), either of the other two, no regard should be had to his denial, and the estate of the deceased must be divided among them (all) in thirds.* *Principle.*

CCIII. If a deceased person has left brothers and a widow, and the widow acknowledges a child to be his, her share of the estate is only an eighth; and if the brothers should verify her acknowledgment, (the whole of) the remainder would go to the child, and not to the brothers.* *Principle.*

CCIV. In like manner, every one who is in appearance an heir, and acknowledges another person to be nearer (to *Principle.*

---

* *Sharáya ul-Islám*, p. 376.

the deceased) than himself, must surrender to such person the whole of whatever may be in his hands (that belonged to the deceased). But if the person acknowledged be equal in degree to himself, he has only to surrender out of his own share a due proportion for the share of the person so acknowledged. But if the brothers (in the supposed case) should deny the person (acknowledged by the wife), three-fourths of the property would go to them, one-eighth to the wife, and the remainder of her share to the child.*

Principle. CCV. When a youth (*sabí*) of unknown descent (*nasab*) has died, and a person acknowledges *him* to have been his son, the *nasab* is established, whether he were of tender age or more advanced (*kabír*), and whether he has left any property or not. Accordingly his inheritance belongs to the acknowledger; and the case is not affected by any suspicion that may attach to his motives in such a circumstance as it would be if the person were alive and had property.*

Principle. CCVI. In the case of a deceased person the absence of assent is of no importance, even though he were adult; for (being dead) he comes within the meaning of the case of a little child.*

So also,—

Principle. CCVII. If a person should acknowledge an insane person to be his son, the absence of his assent is of no consequence, as no regard can be had to the words uttered by a person in such a state.*

Principle. CCVIII. When a female slave has borne a child, and her master acknowledges the child to be his, it is attached (affiliated) to him, and adjudged to be free, provided that the woman has no husband.*

Principle. CCIX. And if a man should acknowledge as his son the child of one of his slaves, particularizing the child, he is (in like manner) to be affiliated to him* (the acknowledger).

---

* *Sharáya ul-Islám*, p. 376.

And if another of his slaves should allege that it was her child which he acknowledged, the question is to be determined by the word and oath of the acknowledger.*

If, however, the man should die without particularizing the child, the *Shaikh* has said that the heir should specify some one in particular, and that, if he should refuse to do so, the question must be determined by lots. But it were better to say that recourse should be had to lots (absolutely without any such distinction) when the acknowledger himself has died without particularizing the child.*

CCX. If a person having three children by a slave girl should acknowledge one of them to be his son, then whichever of them he may particularize as the one intended would be free, and the others would remain slaves; and if there should be any doubt as to the individual particularized, or the acknowledger should die without particularizing him, the individual must be determined by casting lots.* *Principle.*

CCXI. The *nasab* or descent cannot be established except by the testimony of two just or righteous men. It is not also established by the testimony of one man and two women according to the most approved opinion. Nor can it be established by the testimony of one man on oath, nor by the testimony of two profligates, even though they should be heirs* (to the deceased). *Principle.*

CCXII. If two brothers, being just persons, should testify to another being a son of the deceased, his descent and right to inheritance would be established; but there would be no reciprocity herein.* *Principle.*

CCXIII. But if the brothers are profligates, the descent would not be established, though he would still have a right to inheritance in preference to them.* *Principle.*

CCXIV. If a person should acknowledge two heirs (of a deceased person) preferable to himself, and each of them assent for himself, their descent would not be established, the right to inherit would, however, be established (in their *Principle.*

---

* *Sharáya ul-Islám*, p. 377.

favor), and he must surrender to them whatever may have been in his hands; and though they should mutually deny as between themselves (that is, though each deny the right of another), no regard is to be had to their denial.*

Principle. CCXV. If a person should acknowledge an heir preferable to himself, and then acknowledge another preferable to them both, then if the person first acknowledged should assent to, or confirm, the same (*i.e.*, the latter acknowledgment), the property (left by the deceased) must be surrendered to the person acknowledged in the second instance.* But if he (the person first acknowledged) should negative the second acknowledgment, the property must be surrendered to the person first acknowledged; and the acknowledger would become a debtor to the person acknowledged in the second instance.*

Principle. CCXVI. Where the person acknowledged in the second instance is equal in degree to the person first acknowledged, and the latter does not verify the second acknowledgment, the acknowledger must make over to the person acknowledged in the second instance a similar half of that which was obtained by the first.*

If a person should acknowledge another as the husband of a deceased woman who has left a child, he must give up a fourth of his own share, or must give a half, if there be no child, to the person so acknowledged; and if he should then acknowledge another husband, the acknowledgment could not be accepted.*

If a person should acknowledge a woman to be the widow of one deceased, who has left a child, he should give up to her one-eighth of whatever may have remained in his hands, or a fourth, in the case of there being no child, but if he should then acknowledge another (to be so), he becomes a debtor to the latter for a similar half of the portion of the first, in case the second acknowledgment be negatived by the first (woman). And if he should acknowledge a third, he must give her a third of the (wife's) share; in like manner, if he should acknowledge a fourth, he must give her a fourth of the wife's share; and even if he acknowledge a fifth, and one of the first (four)

---

* *Sharáya ul-Islám*, pp. 376 & 377.

should deny it, no regard is to be had to the denial (so far as the acknowledger is concerned), but he must be made a debtor to the acknowledged for a portion similar to that which one of them receives.*

On Mutual Acknowledgment of Relationship.

CCXVII. If two persons mutually acknowledge each other (as relatives), they inherit from each other; and they are not obliged to prove their relationship. But if they are generally known to be of a *nasab* or descent other than that, (implied in the acknowledgment), their words alone cannot be accepted.—Sharáya ul-Islám, p. 460. *Principle.*

On Establishment of Nasab.†

Nasab (descent or consanguinity) is established by a valid marriage, or the semblance of it. It is not established by illicit intercourse (*ziná*).‡—Sharáya ul-Islám, p. 366. Hence,—

CCXVIII. All children born under a contract of permanent marriage§ appertain to the husband upon three conditions: 1—Coition; 2—Lapse of not less than six months; and 3—Lapse of not more than the longest period (*a*) of gestation (from the time of the coition).‡ *Principle.*

ANNOTATIONS.

ccxvii. When two persons acknowledge each other as being mutual relatives, they inherit reciprocally without being required to prove (their relationship). This is inculcated in the *Hadís*, and herein there appears to be no difference of opinion.—Rouzat ul-Ahkám, p. 62.

---

* *Sharáya ul-Islám*, p. 377.

† Lineage, race, family name, whence consanguinity, descent.

‡ *Sharáya ul-Islám*, pp. 266, 300.

§ It would seem from what has been said at pp. 14, 43, that children born under a temporary contract also belong to the husband.—Note by Mr. Neil Bailey, *vide* B. Dig., Part II, p. 90.

Although here only the permanent marriage is mentioned, yet a child born under a temporary contract of marriage seems also to belong to the husband,* inasmuch as *that* also is a valid marriage, and consanguinity (as above stated) is established by a valid marriage, whether permanent or temporary.†

(*a.*) That period is nine months according to the opinion most generally received; but some of the doctors have extended it to ten months, and this is (considered to be) good and correct. Others, again, have gone so far as to extend it to the period of a year; but their opinion is now exploded and abandoned.†

The conditions above mentioned are indispensable.

So that if there has been no coition with the woman, there can be no affiliation of the child (to her husband); and though such has taken place, yet if the woman be delivered, at less than six months from its occurrence, of a perfect and living child; or if both the parties should concur (in declaring) that its birth has happened at more than nine or ten months from the time of coition; or if this fact can be established by the husband's absence from his wife longer than the longest period of gestation, the child (of which she has been delivered) is not affiliated to her husband, nor can he lawfully claim it as his own. But (in the case of all these conditions being found) though an adulterer should have done wickedly with the wife, yet her child belongs to her husband, and cannot be repudiated by him otherwise than by *lián* or imprecation; for an adulterer cannot be legally the father of a child; and if married parties differ as to the fact of coition or the birth of the child, a preference must be given to the word of the husband when confirmed by his oath. With coition and expiration of the shortest period of pregnancy (or delivery just at six months from the act), it is unlawful for the husband to deny his parentage on suspicion of the mother's misconduct, or even though he should know her with certainty to have committed adultery; and if he should deny her offspring to be his child, its parentage as from him cannot be rescinded

* See the Lecture on temporary marriage, where it will be found that the same author has declared the child born under a temporary contract of marriage to belong to the temporary husband.

† *Sharáya ul-Islám*, p. 300.

in any other way than by going through the process of *lián.**

CCXIX. If a man has divorced his wife, who, after having observed the *iddat*, has married again; or, if a man has sold his female slave who is subsequently enjoyed by the purchaser, and the woman (in either case) gives birth to a child at less than six full months (from the divorce or sale), the child belongs to the first man (that is, the husband, or seller); whereas if it is born *at six* months or more (from these respective dates), it belongs to the second man (that is, to the second husband, or the purchaser).* *Principle.*

CCXX. If a man has divorced his wife, and she is subsequently enjoyed by another under a semblance of right, becomes pregnant, and is delivered of a child at *less* than six months from the time of the second intercourse, and at full six months from her last connection with the repudiator, the child is to be ascribed to the latter.* *Principle.*

But if, when there is less than six months from the intercourse with the second husband, and more than the longest period of gestation from the last intercourse with the repudiator, the child is not to be ascribed to either.—Sharáya ul-Islám, p. 267.

But if there is a possibility of the child's being the fruit of either intercourse, the case is to be resolved by casting lots, subject, however, to some doubt whether it be not more agreeable to general principles of law to affiliate the child to the second of the two parties.*—Sharáya ul-Islám, p. 267.

CCXXI. But if a man should have carnal connection with a woman, get her with child, and then marry her; or if the woman being a slave, he should subsequently marry her, the child is not lawfully affiliated to him.* *Principle.*

ANNOTATIONS.

ccxix. If a man should divorce his wife, who thereupon observes an *iddat*, or period of probation, and gives birth to a child within the longest period of pregnancy from the date of the separation or divorce, such child belongs to him, if its mother has not been intermediately enjoyed by another man under contract of marriage, or a semblance of right.—Sharáya ul-Islám, p. 266.

---

* *Sharáya ul-Islám*, p. 300.

Principle. CCXXII. It is incumbent on a husband to acknowledge the child of his wife, when he admits that he had cohabited (with her) and that the child has been born by her; but if he should deny the child, his denial is of no avail to the rescinding (of its parentage), unless he goes through the process of *lián.**

Principle. CCXXIII. When a man denies the child of his wife and takes the *lián* or imprecation, the *nasab* is cut off from the master of the bed, or husband of its mother. But if he should afterwards acknowledge the child, its *nasab* is restored, though he can have no title to share in the child's inheritance.—Sharáya ul-Islám, p. 266.

As regards the children begotten under a semblance of right,—

Principle. CCXXIV. If a man should erroneously cohabit (with a woman who is a stranger), supposing the woman to be his wife or his slave, and she should produce a child, its parentage is established in him.*

Principle. CCXXV. If a Muhammadan should marry a woman who is forbidden to him, or with whom marriage is unlawful, either radically, that is, from their birth, or by some recent occurrence,—such as fosterage, former marriage, or any other cause,—there is no right of inheritance betwixt them in virtue of such marriage, whether it proceeded upon an

ANNOTATIONS.

ccxxv. It is otherwise with respect to children produced by erroneous connection of their parents, for these have an undoubted title to inheritance by unanimous assent, although the cause of their birth is certainly illegal as unsupported by valid marriage; and thus if he should have carnal connection with a woman through error, supposing her to be his wife, which proves not to have been the case, the offspring of such connection is held in law to be the child of both parents, if both were alike in error, or of that one alone who was influenced by the mistake, because the laws of descent or establishment of parentage expressly include the case of erroneous connection, and consequently the right of inheritance founded upon descent must equally be established.—Col. B., Trans., p. 373.

* *Sharáya ul-Islám*, p. 301.

error or otherwise, and of the same nature is the birth or descent of children begotten under such unlawful contract of marriage (except in the case of error), for they cannot inherit from their parents.*—Col. B., Trans., p. 373.

On Illegitimate Children.

Nasab, or descent, is established by a *valid* marriage, or by the semblance thereof: it is not established by illicit intercourse (*ziná*).—Sharáya ul-Islám, p. 266.

If a man should have such intercourse with a woman, and a child be generated of his seed, it is not related to him in law. Still, according to the most approved doctrine, the child is prohibited both to him and to the woman; as, however, it is the product of the man's seed, it is, in common parlance, termed his child.—*Ibid.* Consequently,—

CCXXVI. An illegitimate child (*wolad-uz-ziná**) has no parentage (*nasab*), so neither the man who has unlawfully begotten, nor the woman who has unlawfully borne (*a*), the child, nor any of their relatives, can inherit from such child; nor has the child any title to inherit from them.* *Principle.*

(*a.*) According to one report, however, the mother and her relatives can inherit the property of an illegitimate child in the same way as that of the child of a woman separated from her husband by *lián* or imprecation; but this report is rejected.*

CCXXVII. If an illegitimate child has a wife or husband, and legitimate children, then all of them (including the illegitimate child itself) inherit reciprocally; but where an illegitimate child has no such relative or relatives, there the inheritance (of *Principle.*

ANNOTATIONS.

ccxxvi. An illegitimate child neither inherits from, nor is inherited by, its parents and their relations.—Rouzat ul-Ahkám, p. 60.

ccxxvi, ccxxvii. An illegitimate child does not take the inheritance of his or her parents, nor *vice versâ;* but it is established that an illegitimate child, and the husband or wife, and children (of such child) inherit

* *Sharáya ul-Islám*, p. 457.

such child) devolves on the *Imám.*—Rouzat ul-Ahkám, p. 60.

ANNOTATIONS.

reciprocally; that is to say, the former inherits from them and the latter from him or her. And when an illegitimate child leaves no issue, nor a husband or wife, the inheritance (of such illegitimate child) goes to the *Imám*; peace be to him!—Irshád.

ccxxvii. The correct opinion is, that an illegitimate child is not inherited from, except by his or her children, husband or wife (as the case may be).—Mafátíh.

ccxxvii. The inheritance of such child is only for his or her own (legitimate) children; in whose default it goes to the *Imám.*—The husband or wife, however, gets his or her reduced share with a child or children, and a full share without a child or children, of the deceased.—Sharáya ul-Islám, p. 457.

According to the general assent of the learned, *nasab* is established by valid marriage, or by a semblance of right, and not by illicit intercourse (*ziná*).—Mafátíh.

LECTURE X.

ON IMPEDIMENTS TO SUCCESSION,—APPENDAGES THERETO,—AND EXCLUSION FROM INHERITANCE.

Impediments to Succession.

CCXXVIII. Impediments to succession are three:—Infidelity (*a*), Homicide, and Slavery.* *Principle.*

(*a.*) "*Infidelity*"—which operates to impede succession—is that which excludes the believers therein from the title of *Islám.** Consequently,—

ANNOTATIONS.

ccxxviii. Impediments to succession are generally known to be three: First,—infidelity; Second,—murdering the ancestor; and Third,—slavery.—Rouzat ul-Ahkám, p. 64.

By infidelity, as impeding succession, is here to be understood every belief or persuasion which excludes its votaries from the title of *Islám*, for no alien, whether hostile or tributary, and no apostate from the Muhammadan faith, can inherit the property of a believer: whereas the latter may be heir either to an original infidel or to an apostate.—Col. B., Trans., p. 366.

Infidelity cannot be an impediment to succession unless it be on the part of the heir, that is, an infidel cannot inherit from a Muslim, and not that an infidel cannot be inherited from by another infidel, or by a Muslim. There is no difference of opinion in this—that an infidel does not inherit from a Muslim whether the infidel be an alien enemy (*harbí*), or an apostate by birth or by conversion.—Rouzat ul-Ahkám, p. 64.

* *Sharáya ul-Islám*, p. 441.

Principle. CCXXIX. A Musalmán heir excludes all infidel heirs, though the latter be nearer to the deceased.*

Example. If a Musalmán dies leaving an infidel son, and a paternal uncle's son, who is a Musalmán, the inheritance (of the deceased) goes to the latter, and not to the son.—Irshád.

This is according to the general agreement of our doctors as well as to the several traditions generally accepted and followed in practice.—Mafátíh. So,—

Principle. CCXXX. Neither an alien tributary (*zimmí*), nor an alien enemy (*harbí*), nor an apostate from the Muhammadan faith, can inherit from a *Musalmán*, though a Musalmán would inherit from a person originally an infidel, as well as from an apostate.*

Principle. CCXXXI. If an infidel dies leaving several infidel heirs, and a single Musalmán heir, the whole of the inheritance goes to the latter, (though he be only an emancipator, or a patron by responsibility,†) to the total exclusion of the infidels however *more* proximate they might be to the deceased.*

Example. If a deceased Musalmán's son is an infidel, and son's son, a Musalmán, the inheritance will devolve *not* on the son, who is an infidel, *but* on the grandson, who is a believer.—Irshád.

ANNOTATIONS.

ccxxix. According to the *Hadís* and the general agreement of the Learned, infidelity bars succession to the inheritance of a *Musalmán.* And, although a Musalmán inherits from a Musalmán, yet an infidel cannot inherit from him.—Mafátíh.

ccxxx. If an infidel should die leaving several heirs, unbelievers, with one who has embraced the faith, the whole inheritance would go by law exclusively to the latter, however remote, even an emancipator or patron by contract, although the former were the nearest relations by blood.—Col. B., Trans., p. 366.

ccxxxi, ccxxxii. If a Muslim, has (at his death) left only infidel heirs, his inheritance will go the *Imám.*—Mafátíh.

---

* *Sharáya ul-Islám*, p. 441.

† *Vide ante*, p. 177.

CCXXXII. If a Musalmán has left *only* infidel heirs, they do not inherit from him, but his inheritance goes to the *Imám* upon failure of Musalmán heirs.* But,— *Principle.*

CCXXXIII. If an infidel should leave no Musalmán heir, another infidel may, in tnat case, inherit from him, provided, however, that the deceased was originally an infidel; but if he was an apostate, the inheritance would devolve on the *Imám* in default of (any other) Musalmán heir.* *Principle.*

According to one report, the infidel heir would, in that case also, be entitled to take the inheritance.*

CCXXXIV. If, however, an infidel should embrace the faith (after the late owner's death, but) *Principle.*

ANNOTATIONS.

ccxxxii. If a believer leave infidel heirs, they do not inherit his property, which, on the contrary, goes to the *Imám*, upon failure of heirs who are believers.—Col. B., Trans., p. 366.

ccxxxiii. If, however, the deceased infidel should leave no heir whatsoever a believer, an infidel would, in this case, succeed, whereas of an apostate the inheritance devolves on the *Imám* upon failure of Muhammadan claimants; and this decision is applied in one report to the case of an original infidel, but the report is considered unauthentic.—Col. B., Trans., p. 366.

ccxxxiv. When amongst the heirs (of a deceased person) there is one infidel and several *Musalmáns*, and the infidel embraces the faith while yet the property left by the deceased was not divided among them (*i.e.*, the Musalmáns), then the infidel will be entitled to take the (whole) inheritance if he is nearer to the deceased than the rest, or he will participate (with them) in the inheritance if he is equal with them in the degree of relationship. This rule applies to both cases (*viz.*)—to the ancestor's being a Musalmán as well as an infidel. Herein there is no difference of opinion.—Rouzat ul-Ahkám, p. 65.

If any of the heirs is an infidel, and the other heirs are Musalmáns, yet if the former before distribution of the inheritance becomes a Musalmán, he participates therein with the Musalmán heirs if he is equal with them in degree of relationship, and if nearer (than they,) he takes the whole inheritance, whether the deceased was a Muslim or an infidel.—Irshád.

* *Sharáya ul-Islám*. p. 441.

previous to the partition of the property, he would be entitled to participate with those that are equal (to him) in degree of relationship, or would alone take the inheritance if he is nearer to the deceased* (than the other heirs). But,—

Principle. CCXXXV. If he becomes a Musalmán *after* the partition of the estate, or if there is only one other heir (when of course no partition would be required), then he has no share in the inheritance.*

Principle. CCXXXVI. But if that single heir is the Imám, then, in the case of the late owner being a Musalmán, the generally approved opinion is that the infidel who embraced the faith will be preferred to the inheritance. This is supported by a correct tradition.—Rouzat ul-Ahkám, p. 65.

Annotations.

ccxxxiv, ccxxxv. If, however, an infidel should embrace the faith after his ancestor's death, previous to division of the inheritance, this impediment is thereby removed, and the proselyte is associated with all other heirs who are equal in degree, or preferred to the whole succession if nearer; but after distribution of the estate, or total appropriation thereof to a single heir, his conversion has no effect to remove the impediment except in cases of competition with the *Imám*, to whom, even after the transfer is made, his conversion bestows a preference, according to a tradition reported by *Abú Basír*.—Col. B., Trans., pp. 366 & 367.

ccxxxv, ccxxxvi. If, however, there is only one Musalmán heir except the *Imám*, then the infidel, though he embraces the faith, cannot lay a claim against that heir, because in the case of there being a single heir, the property (not requiring to be partitioned) goes to him immediately upon the death of the late owner, and consequently its transfer to another requires an authority (which is wanting). But if that single heir is the *Imám*, and if the late owner was a Musalmán, then the infidel, who embraced the faith, will inherit according to the approved doctrine.—Rouzat ul-Ahkám, p. 65.

ccxxxvi. But in the case of there being no heir (of the deceased) save and except the *Imám*, if the infidel heir embraces the faith, he is to be preferred to the *Imám*, according to a report of *Abú Basír*.*

* *Sharáya ul-Islám*, p. 441.

CCXXXVII. If, on the other hand, the late owner was an infidel, and succession to his inheritance is pending between the infidel (heir) and the *Imám*, then the former, as already stated, must be preferred in taking the inheritance; and if he has embraced the faith, he will laudably have precedence over the *Imám* and take the inheritance.—*Ibid.* *Principle.*

CCXXXVIII. If the (muslim) heir is a husband or wife, and there is another heir who was an infidel, but embraced the faith of Islám, the latter is entitled to the surplus remaining after the allotment of the appointed share of the husband or wife.* *Principle.*

CCXXXIX. In the matter of succession to his deceased wife, the husband is preferred to her infidel relatives, no matter whether the wife herself was an infidel or a *muslimah,* for he takes a half, as husband, if she left *no* child, or left an infidel child who by reason of being excluded is accounted as non-existent, and the remainder by return, or he will take a fourth, if we consider the existence of the infidel child to be sufficient for the purpose of reducing his specific share, and the remainder will revert to him. Rouzat ul-Ahkám, p. 65. *Principle.*

ANNOTATIONS.

ccxxxviii, ccxxxix. If the husband or widow of a person deceased is a believer, and there be also some other heir who is an infidel, but embraces the faith after the ancestor's death, such proselyte becomes thereby entitled to the residue of the estate, after payment of the appointed share to the former. Such, at least, is the prevalent opinion, liable, however, manifestly, to difficulty and doubt, which arises from the impossibility of distribution in the case of a husband; and if, therefore, we pronounce that the proselyte is associated with a widow only, and not with a husband, it would appear the most just decision; because with the former the *Imám's* title being likewise invalid, distribution is obviously possible,—whereas a husband, in virtue of his reversionary title becoming alone sole proprietor of the estate, there is no room for division, and consequently no claim through subsequent conversion. The case is, in fact, therefore, like that of a daughter professing the faith and the deceased's father an infidel, or a sister believing with an infidel brother, in neither of which, evidently, subsequent conversion could have any effect.—Col. B., Trans., p. 367.

* *Sharáya ul-Islám*, p. 441.

Principle. CCXL. If one of the parents of an infant child be a *Musalmán*, the construction of the law is in favor of the child being a musalmán; and if one of its parents (both of whom were infidels at the time of the child's birth) should embrace the faith during its infancy, the rule of law is the same. But if on attaining puberty the child should reject the Muhammadan faith, he is to be treated rigorously, and if he still persists in his rejection of it, he is (to be accounted) an apostate.*

Principle. CCXLI. Musalmáns inherit from each other though they be of different sects differing in religious

---

ANNOTATIONS.

ccxl. If one of the parents of a child become a Musalmán, the child will be attached to such parent, though that parent, that is father or mother, should have embraced the faith after the child's conception and before its attaining majority. But if the child should renounce the faith, he shall be compelled to profess Islámism, and if he still renounces he will be held to be an apostate by birth. Herein there is no difference of opinion; and not also in this that if both parents are infidels the child also will be considered an infidel.—Rouzat ul-Ahkám, p. 66.

If any one of the parents of an infant child be a believer, the construction of the law is in favor also of the infant, and if further any one of the parents, both infidel at its birth, should embrace the faith during its infancy, the rule is exactly the same; but should such Infant, when arrived at maturity, reject the profession of faith and persist in denial, apostasy is thereby established.—Col. B., Trans., pp. 367 & 368.

ccxli. The Musalmáns, though differing in the religious doctrines and tenets, inherit from each other; still, however, the difference must not be so as to cause the parties to be considered infidels, such as *Khárijís*, *Násibís*, and *Ghálís*.†—Rouzat ul-Ahkám, p. 67.

Infidels, though differing in their religious persuasions, inherit from each other, and in this there appears to be no difference of opinion.—*Ibid.*

ccxli. Difference of sect or persuasion in *Muhammadanism* is no impediment to succession, and thus it is to be observed that all professors of our faith inherit from one another promiscuously without regard to their particular *tenets*, as, on the other hand, do also all infidels in general, although of even different religions.—Col. B., Trans, p. 368.

---

* *Sharáya ul-Islám*, p. 442.

doctrines and tenets: infidels also inherit from each other though they be of different persuasions.*

CCXLII. The property of an apostate (*a*), who was a Musalmán by birth or parentage, is to be divided (among his heirs) at the date of his apostasy.* *Principle.*

(*a.*) An apostate is he who becomes an infidel after he was a muslim. Apostates are therefore of two kinds. Of one kind is he who was a muslim by parentage, that is if at the time of his conception one of his parents was a muslim, such an apostate is called an apostate by birth. The rule respecting him is, that if there be no doubt regarding his apostasy, he is to be put to death immediately upon being apostatized; but, whether he is put to death or not, his wife is separated from him, and she must observe the *iddat* even though the marriage was not consummated; and his property is divided among his heirs. There appears to be no difference of opinion with respect to this rule.—Rouzat ul-Ahkám, p. 68

The second kind of apostate is he, who having been originally (that is by birth or parentage,) an apostate, became a muslim, and afterwards he returned to his infidelity. Such an apostate is an apostate by conversion. The rule respecting him is, that at first he is not put to death, but is called upon to repent, and if he does so, his repentance is to be accepted; but if he declines or refuses, he is to be put to death. After that his wife is called upon to observe *iddat;* the iddat is to be observed by her even if he continues to live; and if he dies it will be observed after his

---

ANNOTATIONS.

ccxlii. If a man becomes an apostate from the (Muhammadan) faith, his property is divided (among his heirs), at the time of his being apostatized, whether he is put to death or not. This is in accordance with the *Nasús*† on the subject.—Mafátíh.

The correct opinion is that if a person who was a *Musalmán* turns away from the faith, and disavows or renounces what came down from God to Muhammad, there is no repentance for him; he deserves to be put to death, his wife is separated from him, and his assets are divided among his children (*i.e.*, heirs).—*Ibid.*

---

* *Sharáya ul-Islám*, p. 442.

† The *Kurán* or *Hadís*.

death. With respect to this rule also there appears to be no difference of opinion.—Rouzat ul-Ahkám, p. 68.

ciple. CCXLIII. His (the apostate's) wife becomes separated from him, and she must observe the *iddat** as in the case of her husband's death, whether he is immediately put to death or continues to live; but he is not to be called upon to repent.†

ciple. CCXLIV. As regards a male apostate who was not a muslim by birth or parentage, he is to be (first) called upon to repent, and if he repents, it is well and good, otherwise he is to be put to death; but his property is not to be divided until he dies naturally, or is put to death (by the hand of justice).†

ANNOTATIONS.

ccxlii, ccxliii. The property of an apostate, who was by birth or parentage a believer, comes under the law of inheritance, and is divisible amongst his heirs at the date of his apostasy, which period fixes also the date of divorce from his wife, and commencement of her *iddat*, which is exactly that appointed for a widow, whether he is immediately put to death or survives in apostasy.—Col. B., Trans., p. 368.

ccxliv. With regard to a male apostate, not by birth or parentage a believer, but who had himself first embraced the faith, and afterwards apostatized, he also is not subject to immediate death, but must be called to repent, and only on persistence is liable to capital punishment; consequently, his property does not become divisible until his actual decease, either natural, or by the hand of *Justice*, but his wife nevertheless commences her *iddat* from the date of his apostasy. Should he, therefore, return to the faith previous to expiration of this *iddat*, he is entitled to take her back, but if the *iddat* has once expired, the divorce is thereby irreversible, and he has no future claim whatsoever.—Col. B., Trans., p. 369.

---

* The *iddat* of a wife commences, however, from the date at which the difference of religion occurred between the husband and wife, and if he the (apostate) turns to the faith *before* the expiration of her *iddat*, he has still a preferable right to her; but if the *iddat* has once expired, and he has not returned, he has lost all means of retaining her.—*Sharáya ul-Islám*, p. 444.

† *Sharáya ul-Islám*, p. 442.

CCXLV. If an apostate by birth or parentage dies, his inheritance will go to his muslim heir, though he be more distant and an infidel (heir) nearer.—Rouzat ul-Ahkám, p. 69. *Principle.*

CCXLVI. But if he left only infidel heirs then the *Imám* will inherit from him. Herein there appears to be no difference of opinion.—*Ibid.* *Principle.*

Such also is the case with an apostate by conversion.—But in the case of his leaving only infidel heirs, there is a difference of opinion with respect to the inheritabilty of the infidel heirs, and the *Imám*. The most approved opinion is, that the *Imám* inherits from him, and not the infidels.—*Ibid.* *Principle.*

CCXLVII. A woman, however, is not slain (for apostasy), but is to be imprisoned and scourged at times of prayer, and her property is not to be divided until her actual death.—Sharáya ul-Islám, p. 442. *Principle.*

On Homicide.

CCXLVIII. Homicide, if perpetrated wilfully and unjustly, is an impediment to (the perpetrator's) succession (to the inheritance of the person slain); but if done rightfully, it is no (such) impediment.—*Ibid.* *Principle.*

ANNOTATIONS.

ccxlviii. If a woman renounces the Muhammadan religion, they do not put her to death whether she be an apostate by birth or by conversion, but they imprison her, and scourge her at times of prayer in order that she may repent and return to the faith. If she repents and surrenders herself to God, she has done all that was required of her; or else, she will remain imprisoned for ever.—Rouzat ul-Ahkám, p. 68.

It is otherwise with respect to a female apostate, because she is not liable to immediate death, but must be imprisoned and scourged at the appointed times of prayer; consequently her property cannot be divisible as inheritance until her actual death.—Col. B., Trans., pp. 368 & 369.

ccxlviii. According to the general agreement of the Learned, as well as traditions,—homicide perpetrated wilfully and oppressively, that is unjustly, is an impediment to succession.—Mafátíh.

Principle.

CCXLIX. If homicide was committed by mistake, the slayer can inherit (from the slain), according to the most prevalent doctrine.*

ANNOTATIONS.

According to the Nasús,† as well as the general agreement of the Learned, homicide is an impediment to the perpetrator's inheriting from the person slain wilfully, oppressively, that is unjustly and violently, though in the event of acquital from the charge of murder the slayer takes the inheritance of the person slain.—Rouzat ul-Ahkám, p. 69.

The inheritance of the person slain devolves on the heir other than the slayer, even though such heir be a more distant relative. A slayer, though (in relationship) nearer to the deceased, does not impede the succession of another heir, though more remote than himself.—*Ibid.*

ccxlviii, ccxlix. By murder as an impediment to succession, it is here to be understood, that a person who slays another wilfully and unjustly is not permitted by law to inherit from the slain, but that a person put to death for a just cause, as by retaliation, may be inherited from by his slayer. Accidental or unintentional homicide also is no legal bar to succession according to the most prevalent doctrine, although *Shaikh Mufíd* has expressed an apparently very proper limitation of this rule, *viz.*, that the slayer can inherit no part of the fine he has paid in expiation. This impediment applies equally to parents and children and to all relations, whether by blood, affinity, or otherwise, and if therefore a person thus wilfully murdered should have no other heir than his murderer, his inheritance must go to the public treasury.—Col. B., Trans., p. 369.

ccxlix. But if accidental, homicide does not impede succession according to the Nass.†—Mafátíh.

If a person slays his ancestor, he is excluded from his inheritance, if the perpetration of the act was done wilfully and unjustly, but if it was by mistake, he inherits property other than the *díyat* or quest of blood.—Mafátíh.

Homicide by mistake is not an impediment to succession. Nevertheless, the proprietor does not inherit the *díyat* or expiatory fine.—Rouzat ul-Ahkám, p. 71.

---

* *Sharáya ul-Islám*, p. 442.

† The *Kurán* or *Hadís*.

It is stated in the *Sahíh* that a man killed his mother, and it was held that he would inherit from her if the killing was by mistake, and not, if it was wilfully.—Mafátíh.

Example.

The general opinion in respect of homicide is that the slayer is not entitled to inherit from the slain, if the crime was committed wilfully, and this accords with the correct *Nass* or *Hadís.—Ibid.*

If a person died in consequence of legal punishment being inflicted upon him, or in consequence of retaliation, such homicide does not impede the succession (of the heir who inflicted the punishment). This is without difference of opinion.—Rouzat ul-Ahkám, p. 70. Example.

CCL. If there is no heir other than the slayer, the inheritance goes to the public treasury (*bayit ul-mál*).* *Principle.*

CCLI. If the person slain left no heir other than the *Imám*, the latter may demand the *díyat* (expiatory mulct for murder) with the consent of the slayer, but cannot forgive* (the crime). *Principle.*

CCLII. This impediment applies equally to a father and child, as well as to all others connected with the deceased whether by consanguinity or for special cause.* *Principle.*

ANNOTATIONS.

ccl. If there is no heir save and except the slayer, the inheritanee goes to the *Imám*.—Mafátíh.

If a murdered person leave no heir but the *Imâm*, he may either demand retaliation or may accept the expiatory fine, should the murderer tender it, but is not at liberty to forgive altogether.—Col. B., Trans., pp. 369 & 370.

ccli. When there is no heir to the person wilfully murdered save and except the *Imám*, the latter is to have the *díyat* or expiatory mulct for murder, and place it in the public treasury (bayit-ul-mál) of the muslims; but he cannot remit any of the two.—Rouzat ul-Ahkám, p. 71.

---

* *Sharáya ul-Islám*, pp. 442 & 443.

CCLIII. If a person should slay his father, and the parricide has a child, this child may inherit from his grandfather, should he leave no issue of his loins.*

Principle.

For the crime of a father is no bar to the succession of his children.* But,—

Principle.

CCLIV. If the heir of a murderer be an infidel, both of them are excluded together, and inheritance goes to the *Imám*, unless the infidel should embrace the Muhammadan faith, when he would be entitled to the inheritance and the quest of blood.*

On Slavery.

Principle.

CCLV. According to traditions as well as the general agreement of the Learned, slavery bars succession to inheritance. Nor do slaves inherit from each other, it having been determined that a slave can have no property.—There is no distinction between a *kinn*, *madabbar*, *mukátab* and *Um-i-walad.*†—Mafátíh. Therefore,—

ANNOTATIONS.

ccliii. If a person should murder his own father, and the parricide has a child, this child may inherit from the grandfather, should he leave no issue of his loins, for the crime of a father is no bar to the succession of his children.—Col. B., Trans., p. 369.

ccliv. If the heirs of the murderer be infidels, they are all excluded together, and the inheritance goes to the *Imám*, unless they should embrace the faith, in which case both the right of inheritance and retaliation is established.—Col. B., Trans., p. 369.

cclv. The third impediment to succession, or slavery, has by law an equal operation both as to the heir and ancestor. If, therefore, a person should die leaving one heir who is free and another in servitude, the inheritance goes all to the former, however remote, in preference and exclusion of the latter, however near in degree.—Col. B., Trans., p. 370

A slave does not inherit from any one, nor does any person inherit from a slave.—Irshád.

---

* *Sharáya ul-Islám*, p. 442.

† *Vide* p. 275 of Lecture VIII, delivered in 1873.

CCLVI. If a person should die leaving one heir free, and another, a slave, the (whole) inheritance goes to the free, though he be more remote, to the exclusion of the slave, though nearer* (to the deceased). *Principle.*

If a person dies, and one of his heirs is a slave, and the other a free man, inheritance devolves exclusively on the heir who is free, though he be more remote, and the slave nearer (to the deceased);—as in the case of there being a son and a son's son, the son's son who is free shall be the heir, and the son, who is a slave, excluded.—Rouzat ul-Ahkám, p. 72. Illustration.

CCLVII. But if the slave should leave a child who is free, the latter is not debarred from inheriting by the slavery of his parent.* *Principle.*

CCLVIII. If there are three or more heirs, one of whom (having been a slave) is emancipated before *Principle.*

ANNOTATIONS.

cclvii, cclviii. But should such slave have a child who is free, the latter is not debarred from succession by the parent's bondage; and further, in the case of two or more heirs who are free with one a slave at the ancestor's death, but emancipated previous to distribution of the property, he becomes thereby entitled to his portion if equal in degree, or takes the whole succession if nearer than the others.—Col. B., Trans., p. 370.

cclviii. In the case of two or more heirs who are free with one a slave at the ancestor's death, but emancipated previous to distribution of the property, he becomes thereby entitled to his portion if equal in degree, or takes the whole successsion if nearer than the others.—Col. B., Trans., p. 370.

When a slave is emancipated before division of property, he will inherit as is laid down in the Muatabarah.—Mafátih.

cclviii, cclix. If a slave (heir) is emancipated before division of the (deceased's) property among the free heirs, then if he is equal to them in degree and rank, he will participate with them, but if superior, that is nearer, he will take the whole property; while, on the other hand, he will be entirely excluded if he was emancipated *after* the division. But where there is only one free heir, the slave emancipated will not at all inherit, even though he be more proximate to the deceased than the heir who is free.—Rouzat ul-Ahkám, p. 72.

* *Sharáya ul-Islám*, p. 443.

partition of the estate, the latter, if equal in degree with the others, participates in the succession, but if superior, that is nearer (than they,) takes the whole estate.*

Principle. CCLIX. But if his emancipation took place *after* partition, that would confer no title to any part of the inheritance. Also when there is only one person entitled to inheritance, the slave gets nothing by emancipation* (there being no partition in the case).

Principle. CCLX. When the deceased has left no heir except a slave, the slave is to be purchased out of the (deceased's) property, his master being compelled to sell him: after this, the slave will be emancipated, and will take the residue of the property.*

This is on the supposition that the deceased's property is adequate to the purchase, but,—

ANNOTATIONS.

cclix. Emancipation, however, *subsequent* to distribution, confers obviously no title to a share of the inheritance, and consequently, upon the same principle formerly described regarding conversion to the faith, should there be only one heir of the deceased besides a slave, so as to obviate the necessity of division; manumission after the ancestor's death is also ineffectual to found a claim of succession.—Col. B., Trans., p. 370.

cclx. If, save and except the *Imam*, the deceased's only (other) heir is a slave, then his master will be compelled to receive his price, and the slave purchased of him though it be by compulsion. After this the slave will be emancipated in order that he may take the remainder of the inheritance. Herein there is no difference of opinion, it being according to the *Nass* as well as the decision of the Learned.—Rouzat ul-Ahkám, p. 73.

It is, however, to be observed, that if a person deceased should have no heir except a slave, his property must be applied to the purchase and emancipation of such slave, who, upon being set free, inherits the residue, and the proprietor may be legally compelled to dispose of him.—Col. B., Trans., pp. 370 & 371.

---

* *Sharáya ul-Islám*, p. 443.

CCLXI. Should the deceased's property fall short of the price, the most prevalent opinion is that the inheritance goes to the *Imám.*

Thus the *Sharáya ul-Islám*:—"Should the deceased's property fall short of the price, some doctors have said that the slave must be ransomed to the extent of the property, and left to work out the remainder (of his price by emancipatory labour), while others have maintained that he is not to be ransomed, but that the whole property goes to the *Imám,* and this opinion is the most prevalent one."* So also,— *Principle.*

CCLXII. If the deceased has two or more heirs who are slaves, and the share of every one of them, or of one of them, falls short of his value, none is to be ransomed, but the whole estate goes to the *Imám.** *Principle.*

CCLXIII. If, however, a slave is partially emancipated, he is to receive out of his share a part proportioned to the extent of his freedom, and to be deprived of the part proportioned to the extent of his slavery.* *Principle.*

CCLXIV. The same rule is applicable to the person from whom an inheritance is derived; and the female slaves are (considered by law, to be) in the same predicament* (as males). *Principle.*

ANNOTATIONS.

cclxi, cclxii. This on the supposition that the deceased's property is adequate to the purchase; should it fall short, some doctors are still of opinion that the heir must be released from bondage to the extent thereof; and perform emancipatory labour for the balance of his price. Others have rejected this doctrine, and adjudged the succession to the *Imám,* which latter decision appears better supported by traditional authority. In like manner, if the deceased shall have left two or more heirs who are slaves, and the shares of all or of any one should fall short of their price, not one is in this case entitled to manumission, but the property must all descend to the *Imám.*—Col. B., Trans., p. 371.

cclxiii. If an heir is partly emancipated and partly a slave, he receives a part of his appointed portion of inheritance proportioned to the extent of his freedom, and is debarred or excluded in proportion to his bondage.—Col. B., Trans., p. 371.

cclxiv. The same is exactly the rule in every situation with respect to ancestors; and female slaves are considered by law in the same predicament with males.—Col. B., Trans., p. 371.

* *Sharáya ul-Islám.* p. 443.

Principle. CCLXV. If the deceased has left a son half slave and half free, and a brother entirely free, the inheritance will be divided between them in halves. But if the brother also be a half slave, then a fourth will go to him, and the remaining fourth to a paternal or maternal uncle or to any other relative (as the case may be) in consecutive order, and so on.—Rouzat ul-Ahkám, p. 72.

Appendages to Impediments.

These are: *First, Lián,* or imprecation;‡ *second,* Absence from one's house or country at so great a distance as not to be known or heard of; *third,* The existence of a fœtus or embryo in the womb at the time of the ancestor's death; and *fourth,* A person's dying while involved in debt to the amount of what he leaves behind him.

On Lián, or Imprecation.

Principle. CCLXVI. When a husband charges his wife with adultery, and denies her child to be his, and the woman brings the matter before the judge (*Hákim*), he thereupon compels both to undergo the *lián* or imprecation (as laid down in the book of Imprecation). After the taking place of the *lián*, or imprecation, a perpetual separation and prohibition between them take place.—*Vide* Rouzat ul-Ahkám, p. 62.

The proposition whether a child of imprecation would inherit from the relatives of his or her mother, is by some answered in the affirmative, by reason of his or her descent (*nasab*) from the mother being established; while others have said that such child does not inherit unless (subsequently) acknowledged by his or her father. This (latter opinion) is, however, abandoned.* So,—

Principle. CCLXVII. A child of imprecation inherits from his or her mother's relatives as well as from the mother herself.

ANNOTATIONS.

cclxvii. The child's relation to the father is cut off, so its heritable right is established exclusively on the mother's side.—Col. B., Trans., p. 371.

---

* *Sharáya ul-Islám,* p. 460.

CCLXVIII. The father and those related through him do not inherit from a child of imprecation, even though such child were acknowledged (by the father) after the *lián*. But in that case the child would inherit from the father.* *Principle.*

CCLXIX. It does not follow, however, that such child should, after the acknowledgment, be entitled to inherit from the relatives of his or her father, and according to the more prevalent opinion, neither such child inherits from them, nor do they inherit from him or her.* *Principle.*

Because the (paternal) descent is entirely cut off by the *lián*, or imprecation; and because the effect of an acknowledgment is confined to the person who makes it.* *Principle.*

CCLXX. If a husband disavows the parentage of a fœtus or embryo (in the womb of his wife), and the *lián* or mutual imprecation takes place, after which she produces twins, they are heirs to each other as brothers by the mother's side, but not by the father's.* *Principle.*

CCLXXI. The child of imprecation is inherited by his or her children and mother,—the mother taking a sixth, and the children the remainder in the *Principle.*

ANNOTATIONS.

cclxvii. The child of imprecation, without difference of opinion, can inherit from his or her mother as well as from the maternal brethren and other maternal relations.—Rouzat ul-Ahkám, p. 62.

cclxviii. *Lián*, or accusation of adultery, upon oath by a husband as disproving the descent of his nominal offspring, necessarily cuts off their right of succession to his estate. If, however, subsequent thereto, he should acknowledge their parentage, such confession removes the impediment as to them, and they inherit their father's property; but he is for ever debarred by a personal objection from claiming any part of their inheritance, should he survive them.—Col. B., Trans., p. 372.

When the father acknowledges the child to be his, and falsifies his imprecation, then there is no doubt that the child imprecated shall inherit from his or her father, but the father shall not inherit from the child.—*Ibid.*

* *Sharáya ul-Islám*, pp. 457 & 460.

proportion of two shares for a male, and one share for a female.*

Principle. CCLXXII. If there is no child, the (whole) property goes to the mother,—a third as her appointed share, and the remainder by return.*

But, according to one report, she inherits (only) a third, and the remainder goes to the *Imám*, who is responsible for the fines of the child of imprecation. The first, however, is the more prevalent doctrine* (on the subject).

CCLXXIII. On failure of the mother and children (of a child of imprecation), his or her brothers and sisters on the mother's side, and their children in due order, inherit from a child of imprecation, and his or her maternal grandfathers how high soever inherit in the order of proximity; in default of these, the maternal uncles and aunts and their children inherit in the usual order of succession. In all these degrees, males and females inherit alike.*

Thus the mother with children of such child gets a sixth, and the remainder goes to the children, whether they be only sons *or* sons and daughters. If there is an only daughter, or there are only several daughters, then to the former goes a moiety, and to the latter two-thirds as appointed shares, and the remainder returns to the mother and daughter or daughters. If the imprecated person should have left no children, then a third goes to the mother, and if there be also a husband or wife, then the smaller share goes to him or to her in the first case, and the larger in the second. If the mother be the sole heiress, then the *whole* property goes to her—a third as her appointed share, and the remainder by return. If there is only a child he or she takes the (whole) property, but if there are several children they take (the whole) property either by relationship or as appointed shares as well as by return, as already shown. If the imprecated person left neither children nor mother, then the inheritance will go to the other relatives (*viz.,*) the maternal brothers and grand-parents. In default of these, the inheritance goes to the *Imám,* peace be to him!—Rouzat ul-Ahkám, pp. 62 & 63.

Principle. CCLXXIV. When all the relatives, though remote, on the mother's side have completely failed so as not to leave a single one of them to succeed as an heir, the inheritance passes to the *Imám.**

---

* *Sharáya ul-Islám*, pp. 456 & 457.

CCLXXV. With all the degrees (of heirs), however, the husband or wife (as the case may be) takes the share (respectively) appointed for him or her—(that is,) a half and a fourth when there is no child, and a fourth and an eighth when there is one.* *Principle.*

In distributing the inheritance of persons of the description as above, the paternal relation is not taken into account at all.* So,—

CCLXXVI. Should the deceased have left two brothers— one of them by both parents and the other by the same mother only—the inheritance goes to them in *equal* shares.* *Principle.*

CCLXXVII. The same would be the result, if there had been two sisters, or a brother and sister, one of them by the same father and mother, (and the other by the same mother only). The same also, if the deceased had left the son of a sister by both parents, and the son of a sister by the same mother only;—or if he had left a brother and sister by both parents, with a grandfather or grandmother, the property would be divided between them in thirds, the paternal relation being entirely disregarded.* *Principle.*

CCLXXVIII. If the mother of the child of imprecation died, leaving no heir except that (child), then (the whole of) her inheritance goes to him or to her; but if with such child there exist both the parents (of the deceased) or one of them, then two-sixths go to them both, or one-sixth goes to one (of them), and the remainder goes to the child if a male, but if it be a female, then half goes to her, and the surplus reverts in proportion to the respective shares (of the heirs).* *Principle.*

On a Fœtus, or Embryo.

CCLXXIX. A fœtus or embryo in the womb inherits if brought forth alive. So also if still born

ANNOTATIONS.

cclxxvi. And as in the case of imprecation no regard is paid to the paternal relation,—so when the child of imprecation dies, leaving brethren by the same father and mother as well as those by the same mother only, the shares of all of them shall be *equal*, by reason of the paternal relation being cut off.—Rouzat ul-Ahkám, pp. 62 & 63.

* *Sharáya ul-Islám*, p. 457.

in consequence of violence to its mother, or without such violence, if it has shown any signs of life at its birth.*

Principle. CCLXXX. But if it has come out in the state of half of its body alive and the remainder dead, (that is, if when half-born, those signs of life should appear and totally cease before complete separation from the womb), it does not inherit. In like manner, if it exhibits motions that are not indicative of its being alive, as those of an animal just slaughtered,* (it has no claim to inheritance).

ANNOTATIONS.

cclxxix, cclxxx. A fœtus inherits in the event of its being born alive.—Mafátíh.

The child in the womb inherits upon its coming out alive.—Irshád.

A fœtus inherits if born alive.—Rouzat ul-Ahkám, p. 60.

If at the time of its birth, and after that a sound of its crying is heard, it is, doubtless, a proof of its vitality; and if it displays evident motions indicative of its vitality, that also is sufficient.—*Ibid.*

But if it comes out dead from the womb, or half alive and half dead, the other heirs, holding it to be still born, will take the inheritance.—Irshád.

There are two different opinions with respect to the determination of its vitality. The correct doctrine, however, is, that if it moves, it inherits, inasmuch as it often happens to be dumb.—Mafátíh.

cclxxix, cclxxx. A fœtus or embryo in the womb at the ancestor's death is by law considered an heir upon condition of being brought forth alive, but if produced dead, no portion of the inheritance can be claimed in its name. Whereas immediate death, if once seen in existence separate from the womb, does not impede the right of succession. In cases, again, of miscarriage by violence, the criterion of law is that there be observed in the child that species of motion by which life is proved, or which cannot proceed from a dead body, but not merely shaking or contraction of limbs, which is often observed to take place after death involuntarily.—Col. B., Trans., p. 372.

---

* *Sharáya ul-Islám*, pp. 459 & 460.

On the other hand, it is reported by *Rubayí,* from Abú Jaafar, on whom be peace, that when an infant displays at its birth evident motion (as if it were alive), it both inherits and is inherited from. And there is a report to the same effect by Abú Basír, from Abú Abdullah, on whom be peace.*

CCLXXXI. It is by no means a (necessary) condition that the child should be alive at the death of the ancestor; insomuch that, if born at six months from the death of its begetter, the right of inheritance is established; or even if born at nine months, if its mother has not married again.* *Principle.*

CCLXXXII. If the other heirs divide the inheritance while the fœtus is in the womb of its mother, they must consider it to consist of two sons or two males, and reserve for it, as a precautionary measure, the portion of two males.—Irshád. *Principle.*

ANNOTATIONS.

cclxxxi. It is not the condition that he should be alive at the time of the late owner's death. The knowledge of its *existence* at that time is, nevertheless, a condition for its inheriting.—Mafátíh.

It is not necessary that at the time of the ancestor's death the fœtus in the womb should have vitality, as it is quite sufficient if its mere existence at that time be known, and that is in the case of its being begotten within six months from the late proprietor's death; as also in the case of its being extended to one year, the extreme period of pregnancy,—provided in the meantime the woman has not had carnal connection with another man by which also she might be pregnant.—Rouzat ul-Ahkám, p. 60.

cclxxxii. Evidently, there must be reserved for the fœtus the portion of two males, and the surplus, (or the property) remaining after the reservation of its share, is to go to the other heirs.—Mafátíh.

Abú Jaafar Túsí as well as several other doctors have expressly declared without intimating anything to the contrary, that for the fœtus should be set apart or reserved, as a precautionary measure, the portion of two sons or two brothers of the same description; and they paid no regard to the probability of more being born by reason of the same being of rare occurrence.—Rouzat ul-Ahkám, p. 61.

* *Sharáya ul-Islám,* p. 460.

Illustration. When a deceased has left both his parents, or one of them, or a husband or wife, and also a fœtus in the womb, then to all the sharers are given their reduced shares, and the residue is secured (till the birth of the child) : if it is born dead, the shares of all of them are then to be completed in full.*

Principle. CCLXXXIII. If a person deceased should leave an existing son, and a fœtus in the womb, then only one-third is to be given to the existing son, and two-thirds must be reserved for the event of the birth.*

Because it is probable that there may be twins born; but more (than two) is extremely rare.*

Principle. CCLXXXIV. If, on the other hand, the existing child be a female only, a fifth part (of the estate) is to be given to her, and the remaining four-fifths are to be reserved till the birth of the fœtus. This doctrine is good, or approved.*

The fine or penalty for (occasioning the death of) an embryo is inherited by both its parents, or by the persons related through them jointly, or through the father only, whether by descent or special cause* (as emancipation or otherwise).

Principle. CCLXXXV. If then it is born dead, all that was kept in deposit will be given to the living son or daughter. If, on the other hand, the fœtus is born alive, and proved to be as guessed, then two-thirds or four fifths (as the case may be) will be given (to the children so born); but if it prove other than what was guessed, then a share proportionate to its right being given, the residue will be divided among the heirs including the new born.—Rouzat ul-Ahkám, p. 61.

Annotations.

cclxxxiii. If there be a fœtus in the womb and a son already born, then one-third will be given to the son and two-thirds reserved and preserved (for the fœtus).—Rouzat ul-Ahkám, p. 61.

cclxxxiv. If instead of a son there exist a daughter (already born) and the fœtus in the womb, then one out of five shares will be given to the daughter, and the remaining four will be kept in deposit until the birth of the fœtus.—*Ibid.*

---

* *Sharáya ul-Islám*, p. 460.

CCLXXXVI. But if what was reserved prove to be less or insufficient, then the deficiency will be supplied from what was received by the former heir.—Rouzat ul-Ahkám, p. 61. *Principle.*

CCLXXXVII. If with the fœtus there be an heir whose share could not be decreased or affected by the existence or non-existence of the fœtus, then the share of such heir must be given in full (*a*).—*Ibid.* *Principle.*

(*a*.) As when a person dies leaving a father, a son, and a fœtus, then a sixth of the property will be given to the father—for there could be no difference in the father's portion by the existence or non-existence of the fœtus.—*Ibid.* Example.

CCLXXXVIII. If, on the other hand, there be such an heir or heirs, whose share could be affected by the existence or non-existence of the fœtus, then the portions to devolve on such heir in either of the cases must be determined, and the smaller of the two portions must be allotted to him, the surplus being kept in deposit until the final determination of the matter (*b*).—*Ibid*, p. 62. *Principle.*

(*b*.) As, where a person died leaving a father, a widow, and a fœtus.—In this case, upon the fœtus being born alive, a sixth goes to the father and something by way of return, and an eighth goes to the widow; but upon its being born dead, a fourth goes to the wife, and the remainder to the father. Consequently, an eighth and a sixth, which are the smaller of the shares determined, will be given to them, and the remainder will be kept in deposit until the birth of the fœtus.—*Ibid.* Illustration.

CCLXXXIX. If, however, there should exist such an heir as would be excluded by the child if born alive, and inherit on its being born dead, then nothing will be given to that heir from the assets (of the deceased) until the matter is finally determined by the birth of the fœtus.—*Ibid.* *Principle.*

On a lost or missing Person.

A lost or missing person is he who is absent, and it is not known whether he is living or dead. The Learned have unanimously agreed that it is necessary to wait (for a period), and then to divide his property. There is, however, a difference of opinion with respect to the period of waiting. Many of the Doctors have declared that he must be waited for, or his reappearance must be expected, till the expiration of such a time from his birth-day as no one like him would be expected to outlive it. This opinion is the most approved, and followed in practice.—Rouzat ul-Ahkám, p. 59.

Consequently,—

Principle. CCXC. The property of a lost or missing person is to be reserved (for him), or not to be distributed among his heirs, until his death is established, or such a time has elapsed from his birth as none like him would usually be still alive.*

ANNOTATIONS.

ccxc. According to the opinion of the generality of the Learned the property of a missing person must not be divided until his death is established, or until such a period shall have elapsed as none like him would most probably be alive.—Mafátíh.

If a person is absent and no intelligence is received of him, they (the heirs) must wait for him till such period as none like him would outlive it. After that, his inheritance is to be divided among the persons who survive that time.—Irshád.

In reference to the duration of life, one body of the Learned has declared the period of waiting to be one hundred and twenty years, another to be one hundred years, while a third has asserted it to be ninety years. With us, however, the most approved is that which is the usual term (of life.)—Rouzat ul-Ahkám, p. 59.

If a person absent from his house or country at so great a distance as not to be known or heard of, should be reported dead, his property cannot come under the laws of inheritance until his death is fully established, or until such period shall have elapsed as by the death of all his contemporaries to remove the probability of his existence; after which it may be divided amongst the heirs who are then existing, without retrospect to such as may have died previous to the division. Some doctors have prescribed a period of ten years from his absence, and others have disputed the legality of distribution altogether, directing the surrender of his property in trust to the nearer relation in opulent circumstances, but the first doctrine is obviously best founded on reason and justice.—Col. B., Trans., p. 372.

---

* *Sharáya ul-Islám*, p. 460.

The property of a lost or missing person is to be reserved (for a term): but with respect to the length of the term there are various opinions. Some (doctors) have prescribed five years, and this is (founded on) a report of *Usmán Bin Isá* from *Sawát*, as having been so decided by Abú Abdullah, on whom be peace; but this report is weak or not sufficiently authenticated. Others have alleged that the mansion of such a person may be sold after ten years; and this is approved by *Mufíd* on the ground of a report of *Alí Bin Mahriár*, as having been so decided by *Abú Jaafar*, on whom be peace, with respect to the sale of a part of a mansion; but a *general* inference from a decision of this nature appears to be unreasonable. And the Shaikh, to whom God be merciful, has said that if the property be given up to persons who are present on their becoming responsible for it, it would be lawful. Further, according to a report of *Is-hák Bin Umar* of a decision by Abú Abdullah, on whom be peace, the property of the absent person may be divided among his or her heirs when they are in opulent circumstances, to be restored to him or to her, if he or she should return. But with regard to *Is-hák*, there are some doubts, and though his report is maintained by *Sahal Bin Ziyád*, it is still considered weak or insufficiently authenticated. It is stated in the Khiláf, that the property of a missing person is not to be distributed to his or her heirs until that time has elapsed when not one of his or her equals (in age) would be living. This opinion is the most approved.* Remarks.

On Persons drowned or overwhelmed in ruins.

CCXCI. When persons possessing property, and so connected as to be heirs to each other, met with a sudden death together from the same cause, and it is *doubtful* which of them died first, they inherit from each other. Principle.

Thus the *Sharáya ul-Islám*:—"These inherit from each other when all or any of them left property, and they are so connected as to be heirs to each other, and they died under such circumstances as to render it doubtful which of them died first."*

---

* *Sharáya ul-Islám*, p. 460.

So the *Mafátih*:—"When persons who are heirs to each other perished together, and there is a doubt as to which of them died first, then, under such doubt, no right of inheritance is established, unless they died by being drowned or overwhelmed in ruins. Under the above circumstance, all of them would inherit according to the *Nass* as well as the universal agreement of the Learned."

So also the *Irshád*:—"When a company of persons is drowned, or an edifice fell upon them, and they died, they inherit from each other, under four conditions or circumstances: First,—that it be not known as to who died *first*, and who subsequently, in which case they do not inherit from each other. Second,—that their death was caused by being drowned or overwhelmed in ruins.* Third,—that each of them was the heir of the other, and there was no preferable heir surviving. Fourth,—that all or any of them possessed property, as there could be no inheritance without property." Consequently,—

Principle. CCXCII. If they left no property, or if there were no mutual right of inheritance between them, or if one was heir to another without his companion being heir to him (as in the case of two brothers one of whom has left a child), in none of these cases has this law any effect; nor, further, when their death is not from the same cause,* nor where they are all known to have died at the same instant of time, nor where one is ascertained to have died before another.†

Whether, again, the application should be extended to the case of dying together by any other cause than that of being drowned, or overwhelmed in ruins, where a doubt prevails as to the time of their respective deaths, is a question upon which there is a difference of opinion, though the Shaikh, in his *Niháyah*, has expressly extended it to all cases where there are reasons for this doubt.†

---

* So that if they died of any other cause, such as burning or slaying, the approved opinion is that they do not inherit from each other the property which they died possessed of.—Sharáya ul-Islám.

† *Sharáya ul-Islám*, pp. 460 & 461.

CCXCIII. When the above is proved, then the conditions being established, each party (so dying) inherits from the other (the original property), but not that which is inherited from himself by the other.* *Principle.*

Mufíd has said that the party would inherit what is inherited from himself. The first doctrine, however, is most correct; because the principle of law in this case proceeds upon the supposition of a possibility, whereas making a person the heir of property inherited from himself would require him to be alive after he is supposed to be dead, which is practically impossible. Moreover, there is a tradition to the effect that "where one only of the parties has property, it goes to him who has no property."* **Remarks.**

As to the necessity of presuming that the person having the weakest right of inheritance (that is, the smallest share) should have survived the other, there is considerable doubt. It is said in the *Ijáz* that there is no necessity. But it is observed in the *Mabsút*, that its application does not alter the effect of the law, unless we follow out the doctrine of *Mufíd,* in which case the effect of the preference is obvious; the opinion, however, expressed in *Ijáz,* that there is no necessity in law for observing the arrangement, seems to be by far the best founded, and even if the necessity for the supposition were established, it could be of no advantage to either of the parties.*

Thus, if a husband and wife are drowned together, the death of the husband is first supposed and the widow's share (in the estate), is given, then the death of the wife is supposed and the husband's share is given out of the original estate left by her and not out of what was supposed had been inherited by her from himself.*

In like manner, if a father and son are drowned (together), the father inherits first (from the son), and then the son from the father; but if each should have a better title to the remainder of the other's estate than his other heirs, a mutual transfer or exchange of property takes place, and the succession of each

ANNOTATIONS.

ccxciii. When all those conditions are established, then each one inherits from the other of them the (original) property which he died possessed of, and not what he inherited from another, nor what another inherited from him.—Irshád.

---

* *Sharáya ul-Islám*, p. 461.

devolves upon the heirs of the others.—As where the son leaves brothers on the mother's side only, and the father leaves also brothers, there the property of the son is transferred to the father, and, in like manner, the original property of the father is transferred to the son, and then what has thus become the property of each, devolves upon his own brothers that is his heirs respectively.*

Principle. CCXCIV. If we suppose that every one of the parties has associates with him in his right of inheritance, as, for instance, if the father had other sons than the one drowned with him, and the son leaves also children of his own, then the father (being first supposed to have been the survivor) gets a sixth part of the son's property in common with the (deceased's) children; and then supposing the father to have died, the son inherited his portion of the inheritance, in common with his brethren, which portion, together with the remainder of the original property left by him, descends to his own children.*

Principle. CCXCV. When, again, the heirs (who perished together) have equal rights in the succession of each other,—as, for instance, two brothers, neither of whom is supposed to have preceded the other, and the rights of both are equal,—the estate of each one of them is transferred to the other; and if neither of them leaves any heir, the succession to both devolves on the *Imám;* or if one of them leaves an heir, then what has become his property goes to such heir, and what has become the property of the other goes to the *Imám.**

Principle. CCXCVI. When a person has died involved in debt to the full amount of his property, it is not to be

ANNOTATIONS.

ccxcvi. If a person die who is involved in debt to the full amount of what he leaves behind him, his property cannot be transferred to his heirs, but must continue as if in possession of the deceased, burthened with payment of his debts.—Col. B., Trans., p. 373.

* *Sharáya ul-Islám*, p. 461.

transferred to his heirs, but to remain subject to the same conditions as if it still belonged to the deceased.* But,—

CCXCVII. If the debt should not absorb the whole of his estate, so much of it as is required for the payment of his debt remains subject to the same conditions as if it still belonged to the deceased, and the surplus is transferred to his heirs.* *Principle.*

On Exclusion from inheritance.

CCXCVIII. Exclusion is either from the whole inheritance (1), or from part of, a share (2).—Sharáya ul-Islám, p. 444. *Principle.*

CCXCIX. Exclusion of the more distant heir from the whole is caused by the nearer class (of relatives).†—Rouzat ul-Ahkám, p. 75. *Principle.*

For instance, parents and children, how low soever, entirely exclude brethren and grand-parents; and those entirely exclude paternal and maternal uncles and they entirely exclude the persons who become heirs in v rtue of *valá*.—Rouzat ul-Ahkám, p. 75. Example.

ANNOTATIONS.

ccxcvii. Should these not involve the full amount of his estate, the excess is considered inheritance, and may be immediately transferred to the heirs, leaving a portion adequate to the debt still attachable by his creditors, as if in possession of the deceased.—Col. B., Trans., p. 373.

ccxcix, ccci. With respect to the first, the rule is that regard is to be had to the nearness (of blood or connection). Thus the child of a child cannot inherit with a child, male or female, insomuch that there is no inheritance for a son's son, when there is a daughter.—Sharáya ul-Islám, p. 444.

* *Sharáya ul-Islám*, p. 444.

† *Vide ante*, pp. 192—197.

CCC. In like manner, the nearer degree in each section entirely excludes the more distant (degree) in the same section (of the same class).—Rouzat ul-Ahkám, p. 79.

Principle.

Principle. CCCI. Children of (one's own) loins, that is, the immediate children, though females, entirely exclude children's children, and these exclude children of children's children, and so on. The parents, however, do not exclude (any of) them.—*Ibid.*

Principle. CCCII. A person who is related to the deceased by the same father only is excluded by one who is

ANNOTATIONS.

ccc. When there are several generations together, in different degrees of descent, the nearer of them is preferred to the more remote.—Sharáya ul-Islám, p. 444.

ccci. When there are several children's children, how low soever, combined, the nearer of them excludes the more remote.—*Ibid.*

A child excludes all persons who are related to the deceased through his parents, or through one of them. As brothers and sisters and their children, grandfathers and their parents, paternal and maternal uncles and aunts and their children.—*Ibid.*

Exclusion from inheritance is described by the author of the Sharáya as being of two sorts, either entire, or partial—that , from a part of the share. With respect to the first, the uniform criterion of law is that respect and attention be paid to nearness of blood, upon which principle it follows that a grandchild cannot at all inherit with a child of the deceased, whether male or female, not even a son's son with a daughter, and that whenever an assemblage of children's children occurs, however low in descent, the nearer always exclude those who are more remote. Further, children in whatsoever degree exclude all persons related to the deceased through his parents or one of them, as brothers or sisters and their children, grandfathers and their parents, paternal and maternal uncles and their children; and, in general, no relation can inherit with children of the deceased, except immediate parents and a husband or wife.—Col. B., Trans., pp. 363 & 364.

cccii. Every person related to the deceased by both the father's and mother's side excludes entirely from inheritance a person by the father's side only, provided they are equal in class and degree.—Col. B., Trans., p. 364.

Brethren of the whole blood exclude brethren of the half blood on the father's side.—Rouzat ul-Ahkám, p. 76.

related to him by both parents, provided they are equal in degree.—Sharáya ul-Islám, p. 444.

CCCIII. Brethren in general exclude the children of brethren, and so on in the descending line step by step.—*Ibid.* *Principle.*

CCCIV. Brothers and sisters and their children, how low soever in descent, exclude those who are related through grand-parents,—that is, paternal and maternal uncles (and aunts) and their children,—but they do not exclude the parents of those grandfathers.—Sharáya ul-Islám, p. 444. *Principle.*

For a grandfather, how high soever, is (always) a grandfather, though when there are several generations together, in degrees of ascent, the lowest of them (who is nearest to the deceased) is always preferred to the more distant.—Sharáya ul-Islám, p. 444.

CCCV. The deceased's grand-parents exclude their parents (that is, the ancestors higher than they), and so on in the ascending line, step by step.—Rouzat ul-Ahkám, p. 76. *Principle.*

CCCVI. The paternal uncles and aunts, maternal uncles and aunts, and their children, how low soever, exclude the *Principle.*

ANNOTATIONS.

ccciii. Upon failure of parents and children of the deceased, brothers and grandfathers from the second class; of these, therefore, upon the same principle, a brother, for example, excludes a brother's son, and if we suppose an assemblage of the members of this class in different degrees of descent, the nearest always excludes one more remote.—Col. B., Trans., p. ?64.

ccciv. Brothers and sisters of the deceased, or their descendants in any degree, exclude all those related through grandfathers, as uncles, paternal or maternal, and their children, but do not exclude the parents of those grandfathers, for a grandfather in any degree of ascent, however remote, is still considered a grandfather with respect to the other description of this class.—Col. B., Trans., p. 364.

cccvi. Uncles again, whether paternal or maternal, of the deceased, and their children, how low soever, exclude entirely all uncles of his father, who, in like manner, and their descendants, exclude all uncles of a grandfather.—Col. B., Trans., p. 364.

paternal and maternal uncles (also aunts) of the father, and, in like manner, the children of the father's paternal and maternal uncles exclude the paternal and maternal uncles of the grandfather.—Sharáya ul-Islám, p. 444.

Principle. CCCVII. A consanguinous relation, however remote, excludes an emancipator; and, in like manner, an emancipator or his representative in the inheritance of the freedman, excludes the surety for offences, and the surety for offences excludes the Imám.—Sharáya ul-Islám, p. 444.

Principle. CCCVIII. The husband or wife neither excludes, nor is excluded by, any of the abovementioned relatives, but, happening to be with any of them, takes his or her large or small share as the case may be.—*Vide ante*, pp. 211 & 212.

Partial exclusion, or the diminution of a share, is of two kinds: 1, Exclusion by children, and 2, Exclusion by brothers and sisters.

Principle. CCCIX. A child, how low soever, and whether a male or a female, excludes the parents (of the

ANNOTATIONS.

Such is the case with paternal and maternal uncles, with one exception.—Rouzat ul-Ahkám, p. 76.—*Vide ante*, pp. 179, 198.

cccvii. Lastly, a blood relation, however remote, excludes entirely a manumitor; a manumitor or his representative excludes a patron by contract or surety for offences; and the latter precludes escheat of his client's effects, or, in other words, prevents the title of the Imám.—Col. B., Trans., p. 364.

cccviii. None can participate with children except the husband or wife, and the immediate parents of the deceased.—Sharáya ul-Islám, p. 444.

cccix, cccx. There is partial exclusion in three cases. The one is that children partially exclude the deceased's husband or widow from (his or her) large share, reducing it into the small share; the other is, that children exclude the (deceased's mother from her large share (which is a third), reducing it into her small share, which is a sixth, though in certain cases something more than a sixth goes to her by return;* and the third is, that brethren exclude the mother from anything above a

* *Vide ante*, pp. 229—231.

deceased) from more than two-sixths of the estate (except when they are with one daughter, or one of them is with two or more daughters);* and drives the husband or wife from the large to the small share (appointed for each of them).†—Sharáya ul-Islám, p. 445.

There are three states in which a husband or widow may be (with reference to the inheritance). *First,*—there may be a child how low soever to participate in the inheritance, when the share of the husband is a fourth, and that of the widow, an eighth. *Second,*—there may be neither a child, nor a chid's child how low soever, when the husband's share **Remarks.**

ANNOTATIONS.

sixth. Although they themselves are totally excluded, yet their existence, as already stated, is a cause of the mother's partial exclusion.—Rouzat ul-Ahkám, p. 76.

Partial exclusion or diminution of shares is of two kinds: that by a child, and by brothers or sisters. A child or descendant of the deceased, however remote in degree, restricts the share of his immediate parents to *two-sixths* of the inheritance, except in the case where, with one, two, or more daughters, there is only one of the parents remaining. Further, a child of the deceased, whether male or female, restricts also the husband or widow to their lowest appointed shares of inheritance, agreeable to the words of the sacred text formerly quoted. Husbands and wives therefore may be said to take in three cases: first, with a child in any degree of descent, the husband takes a *fourth*, and the widow an *eighth* of the property; secondly, upon failure of children and children's children how low soever, the husband has in this event a half, and the widow a fourth, of the inheritance; thirdly, upon failure of all other heirs whatsoever, whether by consanguinity or patronage, the husband takes not only his highest appointed share, *viz.*, a half of the wife's estate, but receives also the remaining half by *return* in virtue of the residuary title formerly specified. The widow, also, in this case receives first her appointed share, *viz.*, a *fourth* of her husband's estate; but with respect to her residuary title there are three opinions. The most approved doctrine, however, as formerly expressed, denies any title to the return on the part of a widow.—Col. B., Trans., pp. 364 & 365.

---

* *Vide ante*, pp. 229—231.
† *Vide ante*, pp. 182 & 183.

is a half, and the widow's a fourth. *Third,*—there may be neither an heir by consanguinity nor one by special connection, in which event the husband gets a half as his specific share, and the remaining half by return or reversionary right; while the widow gets no more than a fourth.*—Extract from the Sharáya ul-Islám, p. 445.

Principle CCCX. As to the exclusion by brothers and sisters, these prevent a mother's portion exceeding a sixth of the inheritance upon four conditions. *First,* that there be two or more males, or one male and two females, or only four females. *Second,* that they be neither infidels, nor slaves (*a*). *Third,* that the father of the deceased be in existence. *Fourth,* that the brothers and sisters be either of the full blood, or of the half blood on the father's side; and that, according to the best founded opinion, they exist separate from the mother, and not in her womb.—Sharáya ul-Islám, p. 445.

(*a.*) Whether a muderer would exclude (the mother) is liable to doubt, the most prevalent doctrine, however, is that he would not.—*Ibid.*

The children of brothers and sisters do not exclude the mother or reduce her share (as their parents do).—*Ibid.*

Annotations.

cccx. Brothers and sisters, again, of the deceased restrict the share of the mother to one-sixth of the inheritance, upon these four conditions:—*First*, that they consist of two or more males, or of one male and two females, or of four females without a male. *Second*, that they be neither infidels nor slaves, as will immediately at more length appear in treating of the impediments to succession. Whether on the part of a murderer this exclusion can take place, is a question admitting of doubt, but the most prevalent doctrine has decided in the negative. *Third*, that the father of the deceased shall also be in existence. And, *fourthly*, that the brothers or sisters themselves be either of the full blood, that is, by both parents, or by the father's side, as also agreeable to the best founded opinion, that they exist separate from the mother, not in her womb, for a fœtus does not operate this limitation of her share. Further, the children of brothers or sisters do not in any degree affect the share of a mother, nor of hermaphrodites a less number than four, by reason of the possibility that they may all be females.—Col. B., Trans., p. 365 & 366.

---

* *Vide ante*, pp. 182, 224, 225.

LECTURE XI.

ON THE COMPUTATION OF SHARES—MODE OF DISTRIBUTION—AND VESTED INHERITANCES.

On the Extractors or Divisors of Shares.

By "extractor" or "divisor" of a share we mean the smallest number by which a portion or share can be correctly extracted* (from the mass of the deceased's estate).—Sharáya ul-Islám, pp. 462 & 463.

CCCXI. There are five numbers (for the six appointed shares) :—half is extracted or derived from (the number) two; a fourth, from four; an eighth, from eight; one-third and two-thirds, from three; and a sixth, from six.—*Ibid.* So,— *Principle.*

CCCXII. If there are in a case two halves, or one half and the remainder, it is to be arranged by two,* that is, the division will be by two.—*Ibid.* *Principle.*

CCCXIII. If a fourth and a half, or a fourth and the remainder combine, the division is by four.—*Ibid.* *Principle.*

CCCXIV. If, again, there is an eighth with a half, or an eighth with the remainder, the division is by eight.—*Ibid.* *Principle.*

CCCXV. If one-third and two-thirds, or one-third and the remainder, or two-thirds and the remainder combine, the division is by three.—*Ibid.* *Principle.*

CCCXVI. If there are a sixth and a third, or a sixth and two-thirds, or a sixth and the remainder, the division is by six.—*Ibid.* *Principle.*

CCCXVII. Where there is a half with a third, or two-thirds and a sixth, or with one of these two, the division is by six; but if a fourth is substituted for a half, the division is by twelve, while in the place of a half if there be an eighth, then the division is by twenty-four.—*Ibid.*

Principle.

Principle. CCCXVIII. Thus originally divisions being made by *two*, *four*, *eight*, *three*, *six*, *twelve* and *twenty-four*, these are called extractors or divisors of shares.

Relation between Numbers.

Principle. CCCXIX. Two numbers are either equal to (*mutasábí*), or different from, each other;—if different, they are either *mutadákhal* (one an aliquot part of the other), *mutwáfak* (commensurable), or *mutabáyan* (prime to each other).*

Principle. CCCXX. They are *mutadákhal*, or one an aliquot part of the other, when the smaller being substracted twice or oftener from the greater, exhausts it completely, and the smaller does not exceed half the greater*(*h*).

(*h.*) It is optional to designate it *mutanásib*, or proportional, as three, six and nine;—four, eight, and twelve.*

Principle. CCCXXI. They are *mutwáfak* when the smaller (of them) being substracted once or oftener from the greater, the remainder is more than one (*i*).*

(*i.*) As ten and twelve, for when you subtract ten (from twelve), the remainder is two; and if you subtract two from ten several times, the latter is completely exhausted.*

Principle. CCCXXII. If after subtraction, the remainder is two, the numbers are said to agree in half; if it is three, the agreement is in a third; and so on up to ten; and if it is eleven, then the agreement is in a fraction of that number.*

---

* *Sharáya ul-Islám*, pp. 464 & 465.

CCCXXIII. Two numbers are said to be *mutabáyan*, or prime to each other, when the smaller being subtracted from the greater (of them), once or oftener, the remainder is unity.* Principle.

As thirteen and twenty; for, if thirteen is subtracted from twenty there remains seven; and if seven is subtracted from thirteen, there remains six, and if six is subtracted from seven, there remains only one.* Example.

Arrangement.

CCCXXIV. If the parts (or numbers) of a divisor agree with the shares (of the parties entitled thereto), so that the estate can be divided (among them) without a fraction, then there is no difficulty.* Principle.

As when there is a sister by the same father only, with a husband (of the deceased), then the division is by two. Or, when the deceased has left two daughters, and both parents, or both parents and a husband, then (in each of these cases) the division is by six; and the estate (in all these cases) can be divided without a fraction.* Example.

But if there is a fraction in the division, yet the same may occur, either with respect to one set of heirs (1), or with respect to several of them (2).*

In the first case.—

CCCXXV. The number of the individuals (whose shares are fractional) is multiplied by the whole of the divisor if there is *no* common measure between the number and shares of the individuals.* Principle.

As, for instance, if there are both parents and five daughters (left by the deceased), then the divisor is six, and the shares of the daughters are four (the same constituting two-thirds), and there is no common measure (between four and five), so the (whole) number of their persons, which is five, will be multiplied by six, and the product (30) will settle the case: the share of each heir, as it stood before the multiplication, will now be multiplied by five, and the product will be the amount to which each will be entitled.* Example.

---

* *Sharáya ul-Islám*, pp. 463 & 464.

Principle.

CCCXXVI. But if there is a common measure between the number of the persons and their shares, then the measure of the number of their persons, and not of the shares, must be multiplied by the divisor.*

Example.

As when there are both parents, and six daughters (of the deceased), the share of the daughters are four or four-sixths, which cannot be divided among them without a fraction; but their share agrees in half with the number of their persons (that is half is the common measure of the numbers of their share and persons), so three, which is half of the number of their persons, is multiplied by the divisor which is six, and the product gained is eighteen. Previously, the shares of the parents were two out of the original divisor, or the root of the case, now they are multiplied by three, and the product, which is six, is for them: the daughters had four out of the original divisor, the same is now multiplied by three, and the product twelve will be for them all,—two parts for each daughter.*

In the second case, that is,—

Principle.

CCCXXVII. If a fraction occurs in the shares of more than one set, then there may be a common measure between the shares and individuals of *all* those sets of heirs whose shares are fractional (1), or there may be *no* common measure between them (2), or there may be a common measure in *any* of them, and not in others (3). In the first instance, the number of the heirs or individuals of all those sets are reduced in correspondence with the common measure; in the second, all the numbers are to be dealt with as they are; and in the third, the (number of the individuals of the) set with respect to which (that is between whose number and shares) there is a common measure, is to be reduced in correspondence with the common measure, and the rest is to be dealt with as it is.*

---

* *Sharáya ul-Islám*, pp. 463 & 464.

After all this has been done, the resulting numbers will be found to be similar or equal (*mutamásal*), one an aliquot part of the other (*mutadákhal*), commensurable (*mutwáfak*), or prime (*mutabáyan*) to each other.*

CCCXXVIII. If the numbers are equal or similar (*mutamásal*), it is sufficient to take one of them, and multiply it by the original divisor.* *Principle.*

As where the deceased has left two brothers by the same father and mother, and two brothers by the same mother only, there the original divisor of their shares is three,† and three cannot be divided among them without a fraction; so one of the two numbers, that is two, is multiplied by the original divisor three, and (the product is six, out of which) two go to the brothers by the same mother only to be divided between them (equally), and four go to the brothers of the whole blood.* Illustration.

CCCXXIX. If the numbers are *mutadákhal*, or one an aliquot part of the other, then reject the least of the numbers, and multiply the greater by the divisor.* *Principle.*

As where the deceased has left three brothers by the same mother only, and six by the same father only, the divisor of their shares is three, which cannot be divided among them without a fraction; the number, however, of one of the sets (of heirs) is half of that of the other. So the numbers being *mutadákhal* (that is one an aliquot part of the other), six, the greater number, must be multiplied by the divisor (3), and the product will be eighteen, which settles the case (without a fraction).* Illustration.

CCCXXX. If the numbers are *mutawáfak*, or commensurable, you are (first) to multiply one of those numbers by the measure of the other (that is, by the quotient of the other when divided by the measure), and then to multiply the product by the root of the case or the original divisor. *Principle.*

As when the deceased has left four wives and six brothers, the (original) divisor is four, but by this the estate cannot be divided without a fraction: there is, however, a measure between four and six, which (measure) is half, or two, so you are to Illustration.

---

* *Sharáya ul-Islám*, p. 464.

† Of which two go to the brothers of the whole blood, and one goes to the brothers of the half blood.

multiply (six, which is) one of the numbers by two, which is half of the other number (*i.e.*, four), and the product will be twelve, by which you are to multiply the original divisor, which is four, and this product is divisible without a fraction.*

Principle. CCCXXXI. If the numbers are *mutabáyan*, or prime to each other, one of them is to be multiplied by the other, and then the product by the (original) divisor.*

Illustration. As when there are two brothers by the same mother only, and five by the father alone, the divisor is three, but this cannot be divided among them without a fraction, and the numbers are neither commensurable, nor one an aliquot part of the other, one of them is, therefore, to be multiplied by the other, and the product, which is ten, is to be multiplied by the original divisor, which is three, and the product of this (latter) multiplication will satisfy the case.*

Mode of Distribution.

Principle. CCCXXXII. If (the number of the units or parts contained in) the divisor falls short of the shares (to be allotted), a case that can only happen when a husband or a wife intervenes,—yet the divisor is never increased;* but the deficiency falls on the person or persons related through the father.†

Example. As when the deceased has left both parents, two or more daughters, and a husband or wife;—or both parents, a daughter, and a husband;—or one parent, two or more daughters, and a husband. In these cases, the husband or wife takes the small or reduced share appointed for him or for her,‡ each of the parents has a sixth, and the remainder goes to one daughter, or to two or more daughters,—the divisor never being increased.*

In like manner, when there are two brothers by the same mother only, and two or more sisters by the same father and mother, or by the same father only, with a husband or wife, or a brother or sister by the same mother only, with a sister and husband, then, in these cases, the husband or wife takes his or her (appointed) share,‡ and the deficiency falls especially on the sister or sisters by the same father and mother, or by the same father only.*

---

* *Sharáya ul-Islám*, p. 465.

† See *ante*, pp. 213 & 214.

‡ See *ante*, pp. 182 & 184.

CCCXXXIII. If the estate can be divided without a fraction, well and good (*a*), if not, you must multiply the shares of those whose portions out of the original divisor will not quadrate (*b*).* *Principle.*

(*a.*) As an example of the first case, suppose that the deceased has left both parents, a husband and five daughters, here the divisor is twelve,† (of which) the husband has three, the parents four, and the remaining five, which are for the daughters, are divisible among them without a fraction. **Example.**

(*b.*) As an example of the second case, suppose there are three daughters (instead of five), then the (remaining) five shares will not be divisible among them without a fraction, so three must be multiplied by the original divisor, and the product will settle the case (without a fraction).* **Example.**

CCCXXXIV. If (the units or parts contained in) the divisor exceed the shares (to be allotted), the excess or surplus is returned to the sharers, excepting the husband‡ and wife, and the mother, when there are brethren, as already stated.§ And when there is a person who has two causes of inheritance, with another who has only one cause,—the master of two causes has a preferable right to the return over the master of one.* *Principle.*

1. When a deceased has left both parents and one daughter, and there are no brethren, the return is made in fifths; but if brethren intervene, the return is in fourths, and the original divisor of the return is multiplied by the divisor of the case.‖ **Examples.**

2. In the case of there being one parent and two or more daughters, the surplus returns in fifths, so five is multiplied by the original divisor.‖

3. In the case of there being a brother or sister by the same mother only, with a sister by the same father only, the return is made to them in fourths, according to the most correct doctrine.‖

---

* *Sharáya ul-Islám*, p. 465.

† See *ante*, p. 312.

‡ *Vide*, however, *ante*, pp. 223—225.

§ See *ante*, p. 291.

‖ *Sharáya ul-Islám*, pp. 465 & 466.

4. In case of there being two brothers or sisters by the same mother only, with a sister by the same father only, the return is made in fifths, and five is multiplied by the original divisor, and the product divided without a fraction.*

On the Munásakhah, or vested inheritances.

Principle. CCCXXXV. By *munásakhah* we understand that a man has died, and before partition has been made of his estate, one of his heirs has died also,—so that two partitions are to be made of one original estate.*

Principle. CCCXXXVI. The way to dispose of the above is to arrange the first case, and to take out of it the portion of the second deceased; then if the heirs of the second deceased are (also) the heirs of the first, without any difference in the division, the partitions would be as if one only.*

ANNOTATIONS.

CCCXXXV. By *Munasákhah* is here meant that a person has died, and while yet his estate has not been divided, there died another who is an heir of the first deceased: in this case, sometimes the two inheritances are divided by the partition of one (*i.e.*, the original) estate.—Rouzat ul-Ahkám, p. 76.

Thus if the heirs and inheritances be not different, then the (two) inheritances will be assumed as one, and there will be no need of a new (process of) partition. The meaning of the heirs not being different is, that the heirs of the second deceased are, without any difference, the heirs of the first deceased—as being a child, a brother, one of the spouses, or the like. For example, a man has died leaving four brothers and two sisters, all of whom are of the whole blood, or by the same mother only; subsequently a sister and two brothers have died, leaving no heir except the two brothers and one sister: in this case, the estate is divided among them in the proportion of two shares to a male and one share to a female—if they are related by both parents, but if they are related by the same mother only, it will go to them in equal shares: those who died (before the partition) are considered as if they did not at all exist, or as if the first deceased did not leave any heir except the latter (who survived).—*Ibid.*

* *Sharáya ul-Islám*, p. 166.

As when a deceased has left three brothers and three sisters all related on the same side, and subsequently one of the brothers has died, then another; after this one of the sisters has died, and then another, and there remained only one brother and one sister surviving them: now among these the property of the first deceased is to be divided in *thirds*,* or in *equal* shares.† Example.

CCCXXXVII. But if there is a difference in the right or in the heirs, or in both, then the portion of the second deceased must be looked to: if the same is divisible (among his heirs) without a fraction, there is an end of it.† Principle.

As a person has died leaving a widow, a father, and a daughter, then the widow's portion (being an eighth), is three parts out of twenty-four. Subsequently the widow has died leaving a son and a daughter† (and her share is obviously divisible among her heirs without a fraction). Example.

But if the second deceased's share cannot be divided among his heirs without a fraction, then the case represents two aspects:—

CCCXXXVIII. *First.*—There may be a common measure between the second deceased's portion (out of the first estate), and the (number of the) parts into which the second estate is to be divided; if so, then multiply the measure of the second estate or inheritance by the (whole number of) parts of the first estate,‡ and the product will settle both the estates;§ that is, it will suffice to divide them without a fraction. Principle.

ANNOTATIONS.

cccxxxvii. If the second partition can be made out of the first without a fraction, (that is, if the portion received by the second deceased out of the original estate can be divided among his heirs without a fraction,) then both (the divisions) will be considered as one, and this happens when the second division or arrangement agrees with the second deceased's share in the first estate.—Rouzat ul-Ahkám, p. 78.

---

* *In thirds*, if the surviving brother and sister are related by both parents or by the father only, and *in equal shares*, if they are related by the mother alone.

† *Sharáya ul-Islám*, p. 466.

‡ That is the parts into which the first estate is divided.

§ *Sharáya ul-Islám*, p. 446.

CCCXXXIX. *Second.*—The portion of the second deceased (out of the first estate) and the number of the parts (into which his own portion is to be divided among his heirs) may be prime to each other, then (the whole number of the parts of) the second divisor is to be multiplied by the original divisor, and the product will suffice to make both the divisions without a fraction; and every person who had anything in the first estate, will take the same multiplied by (the number of) the second.*

Principle.

Illustration and solution of the first aspect of the above case,—

A woman dies leaving two brothers by the mother alone, and two brothers by the same father only, and also a husband: subsequently the husband dies leaving a son and two daughters.† Here the original divisor is six, which does not quadrate; the same, therefore, must be raised to twelve.‡ Now the husband's share is six (*i.e.*, half of twelve), which is not divisible (without a fraction) into four parts (as required for distribution among his heirs), the same, however, agrees in half with (the number of) the second division (that is there is a common measure of 6 and 4, which is 2), so, *two*, the measure (of the number) of the second estate, must be multiplied by the (raised) divisor = 12 of the first estate, and not by the original divisor, and the product (=24) will satisfy both: each person who had anything in the estate

---

* *Sharáya ul-Islám*, p. 466.

† This example is more fully explained in the *Rouzat ul-Ahkám*, which is as follows:—

"A woman dies leaving her husband, two brothers by the same mother only, and two paternal brothers: subsequently the husband dies leaving a son, and two daughters born of the womb of a wife other than the deceased: (in this case,) the original divisor is six, from which both half and a third can be extracted, but as the remainder, which is one, does not quadrate with the paternal brothers, the original divisor (six) must be multiplied by the number of their persons, and the product (twelve) will suffice for the division without a fraction. Out of the above (12), the portion of the husband is six, and as the divisor of the shares of his heirs is four, so there is an agreement in half between (the number of) this divisor and that (of the) portion; consequently, the measure (=2) of the former is multiplied by (the whole number of) the (raised) divisor of the first estate, which is twelve, and the product, which is twenty-four, will be divided (among all the heirs) in integral portions.—Rouzat ul-Ahkám, p. 78.

‡ See the above note.

will now have the same multiplied by two.*—Sharáya ul-Islám, p. 466.

Illustration and solution of the second aspect of the above case :—

A woman dies leaving a husband, two brothers or sisters by the same mother only, and a brother by the same father alone : subsequently the husband dies leaving two sons and a daughter. Here the original divisor is six, out of which the husband's portion is three, which cannot be divided (without a fraction) into five parts (receivable by his heirs), and there is no common measure (between three and five). Five, therefore, must be multiplied by the original divisor, and the product will satisfy both the partitions.*—*Ibid,* p. 467.

CCCXL. When there is a *mundsakhah* (or vested inheritance) in more than two estates,—that is, when more than one heir has died before partition of the first estate,—then you must see if the portion of the third (deceased) is divisible among his heirs without a fraction, if not, then you must proceed with the third in reference to the two (preceding) estates, as you have done in the second with reference to the first. And so on, if we suppose that there has been a fourth death or more.—*Ibid,* p. 467. *Principle.*

The abstract or substance of the principles or rules cccxxxvi—cccxxxix is, that, in the division of the first deceased's estate, if the divisor, determined, falls short, or cannot satisfy all the sharers in integral numbers, then it is multiplied by the number of the persons whose shares are fractional; and thus raised to a number that suffices for the purpose.

ANNOTATIONS.

cccxl. In this manner, if further deaths occur among the heirs, then the third, fourth, and other divisors (that is the divisors in the third, fourth and other deaths) will be determined, and compared with the fixed portions of the second, third and fourth (and also other) deceaseds, and the amount of the measure (in the case of agreement), or the whole number of the parts of the division (in the case of disagreement) must be multiplied by the first, or original divisor, and the product divided.—Rouzat ul-Ahkám, p. 78.

* See the following Abstract and Tables.

In the division of the second deceased's estate, if the divisor, determined, agrees in a number with what is in hand (that is, the portion left by the second deceased as his share in the estate of the first deceased), then the measure of this divisor will be multiplied by the whole of the original divisor, and accordingly the number of the shares already received by the *then living heirs* of the first deceased will be multiplied by the measure of the second divisor, in order to give them the proportionate numbers or parts of the product of the multiplication of the second divisor by the first. In like manner, the measure of the portion in hand must be multiplied by the measure of the second divisor, and the product will be divided among the heirs of the second deceased, or, in other words, their respective portions out of the second divisor will be multiplied by the measure of the portion in hand. But if, instead of agreement, there be disagreement between the second divisor and the portion in hand, then the whole of this divisor will be multiplied by the whole of the original, or the first, divisor, and also by the whole of what is in hand; and the products of the two multiplications will be divided among, and given to, the heirs of the first and second deceaseds, as done in the (above) case of common measure. All these will be more clearly, and at the same time more easily, learnt from the two following tables, which are nothing more than the above two examples simplified in tabular forms. The first, in Table I, and the second, in Table II.

TABLE I.

First deceased—*Hindah*. A case of common measure.

Heirs						Remarks
Heirs ...	Husband Zayid 6.	Maternal Sister Zaynab 2 × 2 = 4.	Maternal Sister Rabiyah 2 × 2 = 4.	Paternal Sister Mariyam 1 × 2 = 2.	Paternal Sister Rukiyah 1 × 2 = 2.	The first or original divisor 6. Raised to 12. 12 × 2 = 24, as arranged in the second division.

Second deceased—Zayid, the husband.

Heirs				Remarks
Heirs ...	Son Khálid 2 × 3 = 6.	Daughter Khudíjah 1 × 3 = 3.	Daughter Máriyah 1 × 3 = 3.	Divisor 4. In hand 6. They agree in half, *viz.*, 2 & 3. 3 × 4 = 12.

Thus the whole estate of Hindah, the first deceased, is divided into 24 parts, and given to the surviving heirs in proportion to their respective rights, *viz.*:—

Zaynab 4. Rabiyah 4. Mariyam 2. Rukiyah 2. Khálid 6. Khudíjah 3. Máriyah 3.

TABLE II.

First deceased—*Fátimah*. A case of disagreement.

Heirs					Remarks
Heirs ...	Husband Bakr 3.	Maternal Brother Khálid 1 × 5 = 5.	Maternal Brother Amar 1 × 5 = 5.	Paternal Brother Usmám 1 × 5 = 5.	The first or original divisor 6. 5 × 6 = 30, as arranged in the second division.

Second deceased—Bakr, the husband.

Heirs				Remarks
Heirs ...	Son Háshim 2 × 3 = 6.	Son Munáf 2 × 3 = 6.	Daughter Rabiyah 1 × 3 = 3.	Divisor 5. In hand 3. There is no measure, as they do not agree. So 3 × 5 = 15.

Thus the whole estate of Fátimah, the first deceased, is divided into 30 parts, and given to the surviving heirs in proportion to their respective rights, *viz.*:—

Khálid 5. Amar 5. Usmán 5. Háshim 6. Munáf 6. Rabiyab 3.

N. B.—This is the form and way in which the Muhammadan lawyers invariably write the detailed part of their *Fatwás*.

LECTURE XII.

ON PERMANENT MARRIAGE.

Principle. **CCCXLI. Marriage (contract) requires declaration (*ijáb*) and acceptance (*kabúl*) for its constitution to demonstrate intention without ambiguity.***

Principle. CCCXLII. The terms expressive of the declaration are two: "*Zawwajtu-ka*" and "*Ankahtu-ka*"† (both meaning I have married thee).*

Principle. CCCXLIII. In (regard to the term) "*Muttatu-ka*" (I have taken thee to enjoy), there is a doubt (as to its sufficiency), but the most preferred opinion is, that it is legally sufficient.*

Principle. CCCXLIV. Acceptance is (expressed) by saying—"I have accepted the *tazwíj* (union)," or—"I have accepted the *nikáh* (marriage)," or by any term of the like import; or the same may be shortened by saying—"I have accepted."*

ANNOTATIONS.

cccxli. Marriage requires declaration and acceptance which constitute (and complete) the contract.—Tahrír ul-Ahkám.

cccxlii. There are two terms to express declaration, *viz.*, "*Zawwajtu-ki*" and "*Ankahtu-ki*" (I have married thee).—*Ibid.*

cccxliii. Acceptance is effected or expressed by the words "*Kabiltu nikáha, wa at-tazwíja*" (I have accepted the marriage).—*Ibid.*

In marriage, the contracting parties, if adult, are required to express declaration and acceptance by such words as indicate the intention of (their) mind; as "*zawwajtu-ka, ankahtu-ka,* and *muttatu-ka*" (I have married thee) permanently or temporarily.—Mafátíh.

The first and second expressions are generally used in a permanent marriage, and the third, in a temporary marriage.—*Ibid.*

---

* *Sharáya ul-Islám*, pp. 261 & 262.

† More literally '*zawwajtu-ka*' signifies 'I have joined or united thee. and '*ankahtu-ka*,' 'I have connected thee in wedlock.'

CCCXLV. It is required that those two (that is, declaration and acceptance) be expressed by words of the past tense.* However,— *Principle.*

CCCXLVI. If the proposing party use the expression in the imperative mood, or in the indicative mood, but in the future tense, and the other party reply in the past tense, a valid marriage will take place. *Principle.*

Thus the *Sharáya ul-Islám*:—" If the imperative be employed, and thereby the above be intended to take place, as by the man's saying—' marry me to her,' and then if the other party answer— ' I have married thee,' it is said that the marriage is valid. In like manner, if a word in the future tense be employed, as by the man's saying—' I shall marry thee,' and the woman should answer—' I have married thee,' the marriage would be lawful. It is, however, said that after this the man should utter the words of acceptance; that is, he should say in reply—' I have accepted.' " P. 262.

So the *Mafátíh*:—" In contracting a marriage, it is allowable to use an expression in the imperative mood, or in the future tense, but not any other."

CCCXLVII. In the acceptance, it is not a condition that the same should *verbally* agree with the declaration; but the declaration would be valid by (the utterance of) one word, and the acceptance by another,* (which may not *verbally* agree with each other). *Principle.*

So if a woman should say—" *zawwajtu-ka* " (I have married thee) and he (the husband) should say—" I have accepted *nikáh* or marriage;" or (if the former should say) " *ankahtu-ka*" (I have married thee), and then (the latter should reply) "I have accepted the *tazwíj* (union)," the marriage would be valid.* **Example.**

If one should say—" hast thou married thy daughter to such a one?" then if he (the person addressed) say—" yes," and thereupon if the husband should reply " I have accepted," there would be a valid marriage, inasmuch as the expression " yes " involves a repetition of the question, though it is not repeated verbally. In this point, however, a doubt is entertained.* **Example.**

---

* *Sharáya ul-Islám*, p. 262.

Principle. **CCCXLVIII. It is not required that the declaration should precede (the acceptance).***

Example. If one should say—"*tazawwajtá*" (hast thou married), and then the guardian should say—"*zawwajtu-ka*" (I have married to thee), the contract is valid.*

Any deviation from the above two terms by translating them into a language different from the Arabic—except in the case of inability to use Arabic words,*—is unlawful. Hence,—

Principle. **CCCXLIX. If either of the contracting parties is unable (to speak *Arabic*), then each of them should employ what (language) is best known to him or to her.***

Principle. **CCCL. If both the contracting parties are, or one of them is, dumb, then the person who is speechless may indicate the contract by a sign or hint.***

Annotations.

cccxlviii. It is not a condition that declaration should invariably precede the acceptance.—Tahrír ul-Ahkám.

cccxlix. The contracting parties are to speak the words in *Arabic*, but if any of them is unable to do it, he or she may employ that language which is best known to him or her.—Mafátíh.

cccl. If any of the contracting parties is unable to speak at all, or is dumb, then it will suffice if he or she indicates the contract by a sign or hint.—*Ibid.*

The contracting parties, if able (to speak), are required to use such expression as would indicate declaration and acceptance. But if both are, or one of them is, unable to speak, then a sign on the part of the person unable to speak, such as would indicate his or her assent, would be sufficient.—Tahrírul-Ahkám.

---

* *Sharáya ul-Islám*, p. 262

CCCLI. Marriage is not contracted by (the use of) the word *bayi* (sale), *hibah* (gift), *tamlík* (owning), or *ijárah* (lease), whether the same be used with or without dower.* Principle.

CCCLII. Marriage is not contracted by writing (but by the utterance of the words as above).—Tahrír ul-Ahkám. Principle.

CCCLIII. It is not required that the parties entering into the contract be both males, since, to us, a contract entered into by a female is valid, whether it be in person or through a *wakíl*.—Mafátíh. Principle.

The articles or provisos of the contract of marriage are the following:—

CCCLIV. In marriage no regard is to be paid to the words of an infant whether in expressing the declaration, or the acceptance; nor to the words of an insane person.* Principle.

CCCLV. The marriage contracted by a person so drunk as to be incapable of discernment, is, according to the prevalent opinion, invalid, even though it be confirmed by that person when sober. Principle.

Thus the *Tahrír ul-Ahkám*:—"The expression of declaration and acceptance used by minors either for themselves or for others are not taken to account,—such also is the case with a person drunk, even though he make it (*i.e.*, the contract) binding, after he became sober."

So also the *Sharáya ul-Islám*:—"With regard to the marriage contracted by the person who is so drunk as to be incapable of

ANNOTATIONS.

cccli. The contracts (of marriage) are not effected by the word "*hibah*" or *sadakah*, not also by *bayi*, nor by *ijárah*, whether dower be mentioned in all or every one of them, or not.—Tahrír ul-Ahkám.

ccclv. The author of the *Mafátíh*, however, says that, according to a correct tradition which is followed by the Shaikh and a body of the doctors, the marriage contracted by a person drunk would be invalid, unless he or she confirmed it after becoming sober.

* *Sharáya ul-Islám*, p. 262.

discernment, a doubt is entertained: the most approved opinion, however, is that it is not valid, even though confirmed by the person when sober."*

There is, however, a tradition according to which, if a woman should contract herself in marriage while drunk, and afterwards, becoming sober, if she should declare her consent to the marriage, or, if being enjoyed while intoxicated, she should, on becoming sober, acknowledge the man (to be her husband), there would be a concluded marriage.*

Principle. CCCLVI. In the marriage of a discreet female (*rashídah*), no guardian is required. The presence of witnesses, too, is not necessary in any matter regarding marriage. And if a marriage was contracted by the spouses themselves or their guardians in private, the same would be valid, and if there were an injunction to secrecy, *that* would not invalidate it.*

Principle. CCCLVII. When a person after making a declaration has fainted away or become insane, the effect of the declaration is rendered null, and if it were accepted after this (occurrence), the acceptance is void.*

Principle. CCCLVIII. If (on the other hand) the acceptance was first expressed, and the acceptor lost his understanding, and the guardian (or the party on the other side) made a declaration subsequently to this occurrence, the same also would be void, as in a case of sale.†

Principle. CCCLIX. If an option be stipulated for with regard to dower especially, it would be valid, without vitiating the contract (of marriage).†

Principle. CCCLX. When a man has declared himself to be the husband of a woman, and she assented to the truth of the declaration, or when a woman has declared herself (to be the wife of a man), and he has acquiesced therein, they are adjudged to be ostensibly married, as having mutual rights of inheritance. But if one of them made such declaration, judgment for the effects of the contract is to be given against him or her alone, and not against the other.†

---

* *Sharáya ul-Islám*, p. 262.

† *Sharáya ul-Islám*, p. 263.

CCCLXI. It is required that the female spouse, contracted in marriage, should be distinguished from others by a sign or signs, by name, or by description.—Tahrír ul-Ahkám. *Principle.*

If a man, having several daughters, gave one of them in marriage without naming her at the time of the contract, but only fixing her in his mind, and subsequently the father and husband are disagreed with respect to the identity of the *one* contracted in marriage, in this case the contract would be void if the husband did not see those (daughters).* Illustration.

If a man should claim a woman as his wife, and her sister should (on the other hand) claim him as her husband, and both parties adduce proof (in support of their claims), then if the man had connubial intercourse with the female claimant, preference is to be given to her proof, as *that* is manifestly corroborated by the man's own act. So also, if it (the woman's proof) was prior in date (to that tendered by the man). But in the absence of both these circumstances, preference is to be given to the proof adduced by the man.*

CCCLXII. In the marriage contracted by a sickman, consummation is a necessary condition; so if he should die without consummating the marriage, the same is invalid, and the woman is entitled neither to dower nor to inheritance.—Mafátíh. *Vide* Succession of Spouses in Lecture IX. *Principle.*

On the Causes of Prohibition in Marriage.

CCCLXIII. These are six in number:—*First*, Consanguinity; *second*, Fosterage; *third*, Affinity; *fourth*, Completion of number; *fifth*, *Lián* or Imprecation; *sixth*, Infidelity.† *Principle.*

ANNOTATIONS.

ccclxi. It is required as a condition in marriage that the wife be distinguished from all others by distinctly pointing her out, or by name and description.—B. Dig., Part II, p. 5.

---

* *Sharáya ul-Islám*, p. 263.

† *Vide Sharáya ul-Islám*, pp. 266—273.

On Consanguinity.

Principle. CCCLXIV. By consanguinity seven classes of women are prohibited to a man, namely: 1. The man's mother, and also maternal and paternal grandmothers, how high soever; 2. Daughter, daughter's daughters how low soever, and son's daughters to the lowest degree in descent; 3. Sisters, whether by the same father or by the same mother only, or by both parents; 4. Daughters of sisters, and daughters of their children; 5. Paternal aunts, whether they be the man's father's sisters of the whole or of the half blood, likewise the sisters of his grandfathers how high soever; 6. Maternal aunts by the same father or by the same mother alone, or by both parents, likewise father's as well as mother's maternal aunts how remote soever in ascent; 7. Daughter of his brother of the whole or half-blood, whether the daughter be the immediate child of the brother himself, or the daughters of his daughter or son, or their daughters how low soever.*

Annotations.

ccclxiv—ccclxvi. God has mentioned in his Book fifteen women prohibited to be married to a man: some of these are related by consanguinity, and the others by affinity. Those related by consanguinity are: 1, the mother; 2, daughter; 3, sister; 4, paternal aunt; 5, maternal aunt; 6, brother's daughter; and 7, sister's daughter.—Tahrír ul-Ahkám.

The detail of the seven women related by consanguinity and prohibited in the text of the *Kurán* is as follows:—1, The mother, which comprehends also grandmothers how high soever; 2, daughter and daughter's daughters how low soever; 3, sister; 4, brother's daughter; 5, sister's daughters how low soever; 6, paternal, and 7 maternal, aunts how high soever,—that is, paternal and maternal aunts of the father and mother, grandfather and grandmother.—Mafátíh.

* *Sharáya ul-Islám*, p. 266.

The general rule (deduced from the above) is as follows:—

CCCLXV. To a man are prohibited his roots and his branches, the branches of his first root, and the first branch of every (other) root how high soever.—Tahrír ul-Ahkám. *Principle.*

CCCLXVI. The consanguinous women, besides the above, are lawful; that is,—all the consanguinous relatives are prohibited, except the children of paternal and maternal uncles and aunts how high soever.—Mafátíh. *Principle.*

CCCLXVII. The like classes of men also are prohibited to a woman.—So that her father how high soever, her son how low soever, her brother and his son, her sister's son, her paternal uncle how high soever, and her maternal uncle in like manner* (are unlawful to her). *Principle.*

Nasab, or consanguinity, is established by a valid marriage or by the semblance of it; but not by *ziná*, or illicit intercourse.* Hence,—

If a man should have such (*i.e.*, illicit) intercourse with a woman, and a child be generated of his seed, it is not legally related to him in law.*

As to the question whether such child is prohibited (to be married) to the man or woman who had the illicit intercourse between them, the most approved doctrine is, that such child is unlawful to him and to her, because it is the product of his (the man's) seed, and is accordingly 'his child' in common parlance.† Hence,—

CCCLXVIII. The mother or putative father of an illegitimate child is prohibited to marry such child. *Principle.*

---

* *Sharáya ul-Islám*, p. 266.

† *Sharáya ul-Islám*, pp. 266 & 267.

*On Fosterage (the Second Cause of Prohibition).**

Principle. **CCCLXIX. The pillars or essentials are three:—1, milk; 2, the nurse herself; and 3, her husband.—Tahrír ul-Ahkám.**

This cause requires the consideration of its conditions and effects.†

The first condition is that the milk must proceed from marriage; for it does not occasion prohibition when it has its source in *ziná*, or illicit intercourse.†

The second condition has reference to the quantity (*a*) of the milk that is required to occasion prohibition, and it must be such as to give increase to the flesh and strength to the bones.† However,—

Principle. CCCLXX. There is no doubt that when the acts of suckling amount (at least) to fifteen, or are continued for a day and night, illegality is induced.†

They are nevertheless restricted by these conditions, *viz.*: Each act must be complete in itself; and the acts must be consecutive and direct from the breast (*b*).†

It is further necessary that the milk should be in its natural state; for if another liquid is put into the child's mouth just before it is sucked, and the milk is thus so much diluted as to be no longer deserving of the name, there is no prohibition.†

(*a*.) In determining the quantity of each, regard must be had to what is customary.†

(*b*.) When it is said that the acts of suckling must be consecutive, what is meant by it is, that only one woman should be engaged in making up the number.†

The third condition is that the suckling of the infant should take place within two years (from its birth).‡ Hence,—

---

* Fosterage is placed immediately after consanguinity, because in the *Hadis*, the former is considered to be equal to the latter.

† *Sharáya ul-Islám*, p. 367.

‡ *Sharáya ul-Islám*, p. 268.

CCCLXXI. If a child is continuously suckled, full fifteen times or more within the period of two years, from the breast of a woman, then they are prohibited to marry each other, and not otherwise. *Principle.*

But if the child is suckled the full number of times except one, and then completes its two years, after which it is again suckled to make the full number, there is no prohibition. So also, there is no prohibition if the two years expire without any attempt to complete the number by adding the last. But the prohibition is incurred whenever the full number is completed within two years.*

CCCLXXII. The fourth condition is that the milk should arise from the intercourse of one male. *Principle.*

If a woman suckle a hundred children on the milk caused by *one* man, they would all be unlawful to each other. So also, if one man were to marry ten women, and each of them should give suck to one or more children, none could lawfully intermarry.* But,— *Illustration.*

If a woman suckle two children on the milk caused by different men, such children would not be unlawful to each other.*

There is a tradition on the other way upon this point, but that has been rejected.*

CCCLXXIII. There is no doubt that the woman's own children by natural descent (*nasab*) are unlawful to any who may have been nursed by her.* *Principle.*

On the Effects of Fosterage.

CCCLXXIV. When a prohibiting fosterage has taken place, the prohibition spreads from the nurse and her husband to the child whom she has suckled, and from it back to them both;—so that the nurse becomes its mother, the nurse's husband its father, *their* parents, its grandparents, *their* children, its brothers and sisters, and *their* brothers and sisters, its paternal and maternal uncles and aunts.* Hence,— *Principle.*

---

* *Sharáya ul-Islám*, pp. 268 & 269.

CCCLXXV. Neither the nurse of a child, nor any of her relatives, as above, can marry the child, nor can the child marry any of them.

Principle.

Principle. CCCLXXVI. Every one in the relation of child to the (nurse's) husband, either by natural descent or by fosterage, is prohibited to the foster child, and so, also, every one in the relation of child to the foster-mother by *natural* descent, how low soever (is prohibited to the foster-child); but those so related to the foster-mother only by fosterage, are not prohibited to it* (the child).

Principle. CCCLXXVII. The natural father of a child that has been suckled cannot intermarry with any of the children by natural descent or by fosterage of its foster-father, nor with any of the children by natural descent of his wife, the foster mother, for they have become like his children.*

Principle. CCCLXXVIII. The other children of the natural father, who have not been suckled on the milk of their brother's or sister's foster-mother, may, however, intermarry with her children, or with those of her husband.

Thus *Sharáya ul-Islám* :—"Whether his other children, who have not been suckled on the milk, can intermarry with the children of the foster-mother, or of her husband, is a question that has been answered in the negative. But it seems more agreeable to the principle of law that such a marriage would be lawful."*

Principle. CCCLXXIX. If a woman should suckle a son of one family, and a daughter of another, the brothers and sisters of one of the two children so suckled by her, may intermarry with the brothers and sisters of the other of them, as there is neither consanguinity nor fosterage between them.*

ANNOTATIONS.

ccclxxiv, ccclxxv. According to the *Nasús*, as well as the general assent of the learned, whatever is prohibited in consanguinity, the same is prohibited in fosterage.—Mafátíh.

The nurse is in the place of the (child's) mother, and her husband is in the place of its father, and so on. This is the general rule.—*Ibid.*

* *Sharáya ul-Islám*, p. 269.

CCCLXXX. A prohibiting fosterage not only forbids beforehand the intermarriage of the parties between whom it exists, but also cancels an existing marriage to which it attaches.* *Principle.*

Thus if a man should marry an infant at the breast, and it is subsequently suckled by his mother, grandmother, or sister, or by the wife of his father, or brother, when the author of her milk, the marriage is vitiated.* Illustration.

If a man has two wives, one an adult and the other an infant at the breast, and the infant is suckled by the adult wife, they are both rendered perpetually unlawful to him, if he had consummated with the adult wife; but if not, the adult wife is alone prohibited to him.* Illustration.

On Affinity (the Third Cause of Prohibition).

Affinity is established by valid or lawful coition, and seemingly also by *ziná*, or illicit intercourse, and by intercourse under a semblance of right, as also by seeing or touching.—Sharáya ul-Islám, p. 271.

CCCLXXXI. By reason of affinity are prohibited (to a man) mothers how high soever, and daughters how low soever, of a wife, whether the latter (*i.e.*, the daughters) were born before or after her marriage (to the man), also the wife's sister during the subsistence of marriage of the former, but not after (the dissolution of) it, and also the father's wife how high soever.—All these are unlawful according to the *Ijmaa*, as well as the ***Kurán*** and *Sunnat.*—Mafátíh. *Principle.*

CCCLXXXII. These are rendered unlawful even by the mere contract being entered into permanently or temporarily.—*Ibid.* *Principle.*

So the *Tahrír ul-Ahkám*:—"If a man married a woman, but did not consummate the marriage, still her mother is for ever unlawful to him according to two reports most generally received. Her daughters how low soever are also prohibited to be married to him in conjunction with herself" (*a*).—Tahrír ul-Ahkám.

---

* *Sharáya ul-Islám*, p. 269.

(*a.*) By this it is meant that if the man had divorced a wife (before consummation), he could lawfully marry her daughter or daughters (by another husband). Still, however, such marriage would be abominable, if he had seen those parts of their mother (the former wife) which it is unlawful for a stranger to see.—*Ibid.*

So also the *Sharáya ul-Islám*:—"Whether a mother is rendered unlawful to a man by the mere contract with her daughter (without coition), is a question on which there are two different opinions: according to the more authentic of which she is (thereby) rendered unlawful to him."*

Principle. CCCLXXXIII. When a man has had connubial intercourse with a woman, either by virtue of a valid contract (of marriage), or a right of property, he is rendered unlawful to the mother, how high soever, of the woman so enjoyed, and also to her daughters in any stage of descent,—whether born before or after the intercourse, and whether living under his protection or not.*

Principle. CCCLXXXIV. In like manner, the woman is rendered unlawful to the father, how high soever, of the man who has had intercourse with her, and to his sons in every stage of descent, by a perpetual prohibition.*

Principle. CCCLXXXV. The taking of a son's wife—whether under a permanent or temporary contract, or by right of property—is for ever prohibited to a man.—Tahrír ul-Ahkám.

ANNOTATIONS.

ccclxxxiii. If a man cohabited with a woman under a valid marriage, right of property, or temporary contract, her mother, how high soever, becomes unlawful to him, also her daughters, how low soever,—whether these be daughters of her daughter or of her son, whether they were born before or after the intercourse, or whether they lived under his protection or not. All these are for ever prohibited to be married to him permanently as well as temporarily, or are unlawful to be enjoyed by right of property.—Tahrír ul-Ahkám.

---

* *Sharáya ul-Islám*, p. 271.

CCCLXXXVI. In like manner, a father's wife, whether married under a permanent or temporary contract, or by right of property, and whether enjoyed by him or not, is for ever unlawful to the son.—Tahrír ul-Ahkám. *Principle.*

There is no difference between a real father and one who is constructively so.—*Ibid.*

CCCLXXXVII. If there has been only a contract of marriage without coition, (still) the wife is rendered unlawful to the father and son (of the man); but the woman's daughter is unlawful (to the man) not in *herself*, but only in conjunction with her mother,—so that if the man should separate himself from the woman, he may lawfully marry her daughter.* *Principle.*

CCCLXXXVIII. *Ziná*, or illicit intercourse, though a prohibitory cause, has no retrospective effect, that is, an illicit intercourse with the relation of a woman *after* she was taken to wife does not vitiate her marriage. *Principle.*

Thus the *Sharáya ul-Islám*:—"With regard to *ziná*, or illicit intercourse, if it be supervenient, the prohibition is not incurred thereby. Thus if a man should marry a woman, and then have illicit intercourse with her mother or daughter, or should commit fornication with the enjoyed slave of her father or son, in none of these cases would the act have a retrospective effect (in rendering the wife unlawful to her husband). But if the illicit intercourse should have occurred *before* the contract, then, according to the generally approved doctrine, the daughter of a paternal or maternal aunt would be rendered unlawful to the man, if he has had such intercourse with her mother.†—Whether the illicit intercourse with a woman or women other than those two *previous* to a contract would occasion the prohibition

---

* *Sharáya ul-Islám*, pp. 271 & 272.

† That is his cousin, whom he might otherwise have legally married, would be prohibited to him by his incestuous intercourse with his aunt.—Note by Mr. Baillie.

of affinity in the same way as a valid or legal intercourse, is a question in which there are two traditions,—according to the most correct one of which, it has that effect, but according to the other, it has not.—Pp. 271 & 272.

Among the consequences of affinity is the prohibition of a wife's sister, *not in herself*, or singly, but in conjunction with the wife; and her sister's or brother's daughter without her consent: so if she permits the union, it is valid. The paternal and maternal aunts of a wife may be taken in conjunction with her, though the junction with her be abominable. But if a man should marry his wife's niece, whether she be a daughter of her brother or sister, without the wife's permission, the contract would be void.*

Some of the doctors are of opinion that (in such cases), the paternal and maternal aunts would have an option either to allow such marriage or to cancel it, without the cancellation being a divorce. But the first opinion (according to which the contract is void) is the most correct.*

With respect to marrying two or more women related to each other, the rule is, that—

Principle. **CCCLXXXIX. It is unlawful to marry such two women as, if one of them had been a male, he could not lawfully marry the other.—Mafátíh.**

However,—

Principle. CCCXC. If a maternal or paternal aunt gave her consent, her niece could be married in conjunction with her.—Mafátíh.

Principle. CCCXCI. It is unlawful to marry a wife's sister *in conjunction* with her, whether the wife was enjoyed or not.—Tahrír ul-Ahkám. So,—

ANNOTATIONS.

cccxc. It is unlawful to marry in conjunction with a wife her brother's daughter or sister's daughter, except with the consent of the paternal and maternal aunt (that is, the former wife).—Tahrír ul-Ahkám.

cccxci. If a man should have married two sisters, the contract with the first is valid. If both (sisters) are married under one contract, it is maintained by some (of the doctors) that the marriage of both is void.

* *Sharáya ul-Islám*, pp. 271 & 272.

CCCXCII. If the husband had *irrevocably* divorced his wife, then he could lawfully marry her sister: but if he had divorced her *revocably*, he could not lawfully marry her sister *before* the completion of the *iddat*.—Tahrír ul-Ahkám. *Principle.*

CCCXCIII. If a man married two sisters by one and the same contract, their marriage is void. But if there were (two) contracts one after the other, then the second contract is void, and not the first.—*Ibid.* *Principle.*

CCCXCIV. The marrying of a slave on a free woman, (that is, *after* marrying a free woman) is unlawful, except with her consent, and such contract is void, if entered into without waiting for her consent.* *Principle.*

If, on the other hand, a man should marry a free woman on a slave, the contract is lawful, but the free woman, if ignorant of the existing connection, has an option with regard to herself.*

It is maintained by some of the doctors that the free woman has an option: she may either cancel or allow the marriage (with the slave), or cancel her own contract. But the first opinion is more agreeable according to the general principles of law.*

CCCXCV. If a free woman and slave are married by one contract, the contract as to the free woman is valid, but not as to the slave.* *Principle.*

CCCXCVI. If a man married a woman during her *iddat*, knowing her to be in that state, knowing also the unlawfulness of the act, there must be a separation between *Principle.*

ANNOTATIONS.

But there is a tradition that the man has an option, and may choose whichever of them he pleases. The first opinion, however, is more agreeable according to the general principles of the law, and the tradition is weak, or insufficiently authenticated.—Sharáya ul-Islám, p. 272.

cccxcvi, cccxcviii. If a man has married a woman during her *iddat*, with knowledge of the fact, she is for ever unlawful to him. If he were ignorant of the fact or of the unlawfulness of marriage, then, if consummation has followed, the prohibition is, in like manner, incurred. But if consummation has not taken place, the existing contract only is void, and he is not prohibited to enter into another with her, *de novo*.—Sharáya ul-Islám, pp. 272 & 273.

* *Sharáya ul-Islám*, pp. 272 & 273.

them, and never again she shall be rendered lawful to him, whether he had cohabited with her or not, and whether the *iddat* was observed for a revocable or irrevocable marriage, or for death.—Tahrír ul-Ahkám.

Principle. CCCXCVII. But if he was aware of both the *iddat* and unlawfulness, or was aware of only one of them, still, if he had cohabited with her, she shall be for ever prohibited to him, and he shall be liable to pay the dower: the woman, moreover, must observe two *iddats*,—one for the first husband, and the other on account of the second husband.—*Ibid.*

Principle. CCCXCVIII. When a man has married a woman during her *iddat*, and pregnancy has ensued, the child, of which she may be delivered, is to be affiliated to him,—if he were ignorant of its mother being in *iddat* at the time of her marriage to him, or of the unlawfulness of the marriage in such circumstances,—provided that the child is born at six months or more from the time of consummation. The (marrying) parties are nevertheless to be separated, and the husband is liable for the dower mentioned in the contract, while the woman must complete her *iddat* for the first marriage, and then enter into another on account of the second.*

Principle. CCCXCIX. When a man has had illicit intercourse with a woman, he is not thereby prohibited to marry her, even be notoriously profligate.*

Principle. CCCC. But if a man should commit adultery with a woman who has a husband, or who is in her *iddat* for a revocable divorce, she is rendered perpetually unlawful to him according to the generally received opinion.*

ANNOTATIONS.

cccxcix. If a man had illicit intercourse with a widow, or with a woman who was not observing *iddat* in a revocable divorce, he is not, without difference of opinion, prohibited to marry her, though she be notoriously profligate.—Mafátíh.

cccc. It is declared by the doctors without difference of opinion that if a man committed adultery with a woman having a husband, during her *iddat* in a revocable divorce, she is for ever unlawful to him, even though he was ignorant of the fact.—*Ibid.*

---

* *Sharáya ul-Islám*, pp. 272 & 273.

CCCCI. A woman who has a husband is not lawful to another man till after her separation from the husband, and the completion of her *iddat*, if she is liable to observe one.* *Principle.*

CCCCII. If a man has committed an unnatural act with a youth, he can not lawfully contract marriage with his mother, sister, or daughter, but none of these to whom he may have been previously contracted is thereby rendered unlawful to him.* *Principle.*

CCCCIII. When a *mahrim* (*a*) has entered into a contract of marriage with a woman, knowing that it is not lawful for him to do so, she is for ever unlawful to him. But if he were not aware of the illegality, then, though that contract is vitiated, the woman herself is not prohibited to him* (that is, he may lawfully enter into another contract with her). *Principle.*

(*a.*) A pilgrim after he has come within the sacred territory, and put on the *ihrám*, or pilgrim's dress.*

CCCCIV. When a man has had sexual intercourse with a girl under the age of nine years, and has ruptured the parts,† it is unlawful for him to have further connection with her, but she is not released from her ties, if connected with him by marriage or slavery. If no rupture has taken place, the prohibition is not incurred according to the most valid opinion.* *Principle.*

ANNOTATIONS.

cccci. According to the *Nasús*, as well as the general assent of the learned, a married woman who has her husband living is prohibited to another man, except after separation from the husband and completion of the *iddat*, whether the same be observed in a revocable or irrevocable divorce, or for death of the husband.—Mafátíh.

cccciv. It is unlawful for a man to cohabit with his wife before she is nine years old, but if he has committed the unlawful act, and ruptured* the parts, there must be a separation between them, and never again shall she be lawful to him (the husband), who will be liable to pay the fine, and her maintenance as long as she lives.—Tahrír ul-Ahkám.

---

* *Sharáya ul-Islám*, p. 273.

† Arab. '*Ifza*,' which here signifies the rupturing of the skin between the two private passages of nature.

Completion of Number.

By number is here meant,—First, the number of wives to which a man restricted, and,—Second, the number of divorces which renders a woman unlawful to her divorcer.*

Principle. **CCCCV.** A free man cannot have at a time more than four wives permanently married, but if any of these died or was separated by the dissolution of marriage, then he can, if he likes, permanently marry one or more that would not exceed, but fill up the number (four).

Thus the *Sharáya ul-Islám*:—"When a free man has filled up the number of four wives by permanent contracts, any in excess of that number is prohibited to him; and it is not lawful for him to have more than two slaves by contract out of the four. When a slave has filled up the number of four wives who are slaves, or two who are free women, or three, one of whom is free, and the others slaves, any in excess of these is prohibited to him. But each of the two parties (that is the free man, or the slave,) may marry, by temporary contracts, as many as he pleases."—P. 273.

So the *Tahrír ul-Ahkám*:—"It is not lawful for a free man to marry permanently more than four free women. It is not also lawful for him to marry permanently more than two slaves. So if a free man has permanently married four free women, the permanent marriage of any wife beyond those four is unlawful, unless any of those four was separated by death, divorce, or the like,—such as *lián*,† and so forth."‡

So also the *Mafátíh*:—"It is not lawful for a free man to marry permanently more than four wives. And if one of them is divorced, still he cannot marry another during her *iddat* in a revocable divorce."

Principle. **CCCCVI.** When a man has divorced one of his four wives, he cannot lawfully enter into another marriage contract, until she has completed her *iddat*, if the divorce were revocable. But if it were absolute or irrevocable, he may

---

* *Sharáya ul-Islám*, p. 273.

† *Vide* Lecture XVI.

‡ That is '*Khulá, Mubárát*,' &c., *vide* Lecture XVI.

immediately enter into a contract with another woman. And the rule is the same as to marriage with the sister of his wife.*—Sharáya ul-Islám, p. 274.

CCCCVII. When a man has divorced one of his four wives irrevocably, and married two others, then if one of them was married before the other, the contract with the former is to be sustained, and if the contracts were simultaneous, both are void.—*Ibid.* *Principle.*

There is one tradition, however, that he has a right of choice (between the two), but it is weak, that is insufficiently authenticated.—*Ibid.*

CCCCVIII. The free woman who has filled up the number of three divorces is unlawful to the divorcer, until she has been married to another husband, whether she was the wife of a free woman or of a slave.—*Ibid.* *Principle.*

CCCCIX. And when a bond-woman has filled up the number of two divorces, she is unlawful to her husband, even she was the wife of a free man.—*Ibid.* *Principle.*

CCCCX. When a divorced woman has filled up the number of nine divorces for the *iddat,*† being intermediately married to two other men, she is for ever prohibited to the first divorcer.—*Ibid.* *Principle.*

Lián, or Imprecation.‡

CCCCXI. Imprecation is a cause of perpetual prohibition of the imprecated woman (to be re-married to the imprecator). And such slanders of a deaf or dumb woman, as would occasion *lián* with regard to one not so afflicted, has the same effect, though *lián* does not actually take place.—*Ibid.* *Principle.*

Annotations.

ccccix. A free woman thrice divorced by a husband, is not lawful to him until another man has married her.—Mafátíh.

ccccxii. If a man has been separated from his wife by *lián*, or imprecation, she is for ever prohibited to him, according to the general con-

---

* It is, however, abominable to marry the sister of a wife notwithstanding the latter became absolutely separated.—*Sharáya ul-Islám*, p. 274.

† This will be explained in the Lecture on Divorce.

‡ *Vide* Lecture XVI, wherein it is treated of *in extenso*.

On Infidelity.

CCCCXII. Without difference of opinion, it is not lawful for a muslim to marry a woman from any class of infidels,—or one who is not a *Kitábiyah*,—whether under a permanent contract or under a temporary one, or by right of property.—Tahrír ul-Ahkám.

So also the *Sharáya ul-Islám*:—"It is not lawful for a muslim to marry a woman who is not a *Kitábiyah;* so far all are agreed.*

With regard to the unlawfulness of a *Kitábiyah,* who is a Jewess or a Christian, there are two traditions, and according to the most generally received of these,*—

CCCCXIII. A permanent marriage with either of them (*i.e.* a Jewess or a female Christian) is forbidden, but a temporary marriage, or one by right of property, is lawful. And the rule is the same with regard to a *Majúsiyah*, or fire-worshipper, according to the most approved traditions.*

CCCCXIV. If one of the two spouses should apostatize from the Muhammadan faith before connubial intercourse has taken place, their marriage is cancelled on the instant, and the right of dower becomes extinct if the apostasy is on the wife's side; but if it is on the side of the husband, she is entitled to half of the dower.* But,—

ANNOTATIONS.

sent of the learned. There is no difference of opinion as to whether she was enjoyed by the husband or not, and whether the judge has passed a decree or not, she will become unlawful (to her husband) even though no one should hear of it.—Mafátíh.

ccccxii. According to the *Nas* as well as general assent, it is not lawful for a Muslim to marry an infidel except a *Kitábiyah*.—Mafátíh.

ccccxiv. With respect to a *Kitábiyah* there are different opinions. The most prevalent of which allows a man to marry her temporarily and prohibits to marry her permanently.—*Ibid*.

* *Sharáya ul-Islám*, p. 274.

CCCCXV. If the apostasy does not take place till after connubial intercourse, the cancellation of the marriage is suspended till the expiration of the *iddat,* whether the husband or the wife be the apostate; and no part of the dower abates, because the right to it has been fully established by consummation.* *Principle.*

CCCCXVI. If the husband was born in the faith, and then apostatized, marriage is cancelled *immediately,* though the apostasy should have occurred after connubial intercourse; because (in this case) a return to the faith is not allowed.* *Principle.*

CCCCXVII. When the husband of a *Kitábiyah* woman is converted to the Musalman faith, his marriage is unaffected by the conversion, whether it takes place before or after the conversion.* But,— *Principle.*

CCCCXVIII. If the wife of a *Kitábí* should embrace the faith of *Islám* before the consummation of her marriage, it is cancelled, and she has no right to dower. If, again, her conversion takes place after consummation of the marriage, the cancellation of the marriage contract is suspended till after the expiration of the *iddat.** *Principle.*

CCCCXIX. If one of the married couple, who were not *Kitábís,* but belonged to a class of infidels, became a Musalmán, then, if the conversion took place *before* connubial intercourse, the marriage would be *immediately* dissolved, *Principle.*

ANNOTATIONS.

ccccxvii. When a husband, who was a *Kitábí,* embraced the Muhammadan faith, but the wife did not, her marriage will remain unaffected, whether the husband become a Musalmán before or after consummation of the marriage.—Tahrír ul-Ahkám.

ccccxix. As respects the persons who are not *Kitábís,* their marriage is cancelled by the conversion of either of the married couple to the faith of *Islám,—immediately,* if the conversion was *before* connubial intercourse, but not till after completion of the *iddat,* if it was *after* such intercourse.—Sharáya ul-Islám, p. 274.

---

* *Sharáya ul-Islám,* pp. 274 & 275.

but if *after* that, then the marriage will remain in suspense till the (completion of the) *iddat;* and if the other party became a Musalmán within the *iddat,* the marriage will remain in *statu quo;* otherwise the contract would be annulled.—Tahrír ul-Ahkám.

Principle. CCCCXX. A change of religion is a cancellation of marriage, not a *talák*, or divorce. If the change is on the part of the wife, and it takes place *before* consummation, she has no right to any dower; while if it is on the part of the husband, she is entitled to half the dower according to the generally received doctrine. But if the change occurs *after* consummation, the woman's right having been once established, is not affected by the supervening event.*

Principle. CCCCXXI. If the dower (mentioned in the contract) is invalid, the proper dower (*mahr-i-misl*) is due if cancellation took place *after* consummation, and also before it, when half of the proper dower becomes due if the cause of cancellation be on the part of the husband.*

Principle. CCCCXXII. If no dower has been mentioned (in the contract), a present is only incumbent on the husband when he has given cause for the cancellation, though on that point there is some difference of opinion.*

Principle. CCCCXXIII. According to the *Nasús* and *Ijmá,* as it is a condition to marry an equal, it is not lawful that marriage should be contracted between *unequals.* The most correct doctrine, however, is, that it is sufficient if both parties be *Muslims.*—Mafátíh.

---

* *Sharáya ul-Islám,* pp. 275—277.

LECTURE XIII.

ON THINGS CONNECTED WITH MARRIAGE—DOWER—GUARDIANSHIP IN MARRIAGE.

On things connected with Marriage.

THESE are seven in number:—

CCCCXXIV. *First.*—Equality is a condition in marriage, that is, equality in respect of *Islám*, or the general profession of the Muhammadan religion.* *Principle.*

Whether it is also a condition in respect of *Imám*, or true belief, is a question on which there are two traditions; but, according to the most notorious or generally received of these, equality in respect of *Islám* is all that is required.*

The author of the *Tahrír ul-Ahkám*, however, upon the authority of the *Shaikh*, adds to *Islám*, the man's ability to support the woman. He says, "as to equality, the *Shaikh* has declared it to be faith, and the man's ability to support the woman.—Tahrír ul-Ahkám.

CCCCXXV. It is lawful for a free woman to marry a slave, or for an Arabian woman to marry a Persian, or for a woman of the tribe of Háshim to marry a man of another tribe, and *vice versâ*,—the reverse is also lawful.* *Principle.*

CCCCXXVI. If the *walí*, or guardian, of a woman marry her to a person who is not her equal, she has a right to cancel (the contract), though such contract would be binding upon her when entered into by herself.—*Ibid.* *Principle.*

It is abominable for a woman to marry a profligate, and the abomination is aggravated by his being a confirmed

* *Sharáya ul-Islám*, p. 278.

wine-drinker. So also it is abominable for a woman who is a true believer, to marry a *mukhálif*, or opposer. But there is no objection to her marrying a *mustazif*, or one weak in his belief, who does not know the grounds of controversy.*

Principle. **CCCCXXVII.** *Second.* — **Where a man has married a woman, and afterwards discovers that she had been previously guilty of fornication, he has no right to cancel the marriage; nor has he a claim against her guardian to refund the dower.***

Third.—It is not lawful to court a woman during her *iddat* for a revocable repudiation, for she is still the wife (of another man); but a woman who has been repudiated three times may be lawfully courted during (the *iddat*),—either by the (repudiating) husband or by another man, though by neither should it be done in direct terms.*

With regard, again, to a woman who has been repudiated nine times with two intermediate marriages to other men,† it is not lawful for the divorcing husband again to pay his address to her, but another may lawfully do so, though not directly during her *iddat* for the first husband, or for either of the two others.*

A *mutaddah*, or woman in *iddat*, for an absolute separation (from her husband), either by *Khulá*,‡ or by cancellation, may lawfully be courted by the husband or by the other man, and in express terms by the husband, but not so by the other.*

Fourth.—When proposals of marriage have been made to a woman, and she has accepted them, it is maintained by some of the doctors that it is unlawful for another to pay his addresses to her; yet if she should marry the other, the contract would be valid.§

---

* *Sharáya ul-Islám*, p. 278.

† *Vide* Divorce in Lecture XV.

‡ *Vide Khulá* in Lecture XVI.

§ *Sharáya ul-Islám*, p. 279.

CCCCXXVIII. *Fifth.*—In every case in which it is said that the contract is valid, the woman is rendered lawful by coition to the first divorcer *after* she has been legally separated (from the second husband), and her *iddat* has expired; and in every case in which it is said that the contract is invalid, she is *not* rendered lawful (to the first divorcer), for coition with another man is not alone sufficient (for that purpose), without a valid contract.* *Principle.*

CCCCXXIX. *Sixth.*—A *Shighár* marriage is void: that is, when two women are married to two men with a condition that the marriage of each is to be the dower of the other (both marriages are void). But if each of two guardians should marry his ward to the other, and they should stipulate for each (of their wards) a known dower, the marriages would be valid.* And,— *Principle.*

CCCCXXX. If one of the guardians should marry his ward to the other, and stipulate that the other should reciprocate by marrying his ward to him, for a known dower, both contracts would be valid; but the dower would be void,* (and the women entitled to their proper dower). *Principle.*

Because with the dower there is a stipulation for marrying which is not binding (on the party), and marriage does not admit of an option. The woman is, therefore, entitled to her proper dower. Upon this point, however, there is room for some doubt or hesitation.*

CCCCXXXI. Such also would be the result (*a*) if one of the guardians should marry his ward to the other and stipulate that the husband should marry such a one to him, without any mention of dower.† *Principle.*

(*a*.) That is, the contracts would be lawful, and the woman entitled to her proper dower. Further,—

CCCCXXXII. If one person should say to another, "I have married my daughter to thee, on condition that thou shalt marry thy daughter to me, so that the marriage of my daughter shall be the dower of thy daughter," the marriage of his daughter would be valid; but that of the daughter of *Principle.*

---

* *Sharáya ul-Islám*, p. 279.

† *Sharáya ul-Islám*, p. 379.

the person spoken to would be void. But if he should say, "on condition that the marriage of thy daughter shall be the dower of my daughter," the marriage of the speaker's daughter would be valid, and that of the other's daughter void.*

Principle. CCCCXXXIII. *Seventh.*—It is abominable for a man to enter into a contract of marriage with a nurse who has brought him up, and with her daughter; or to marry his son to the daughter of his wife by another husband, whom she has borne *after* her separation from himself. But there is no objection to such a contract if the daughter were the fruit of a marriage previous to his own. It is also abominable for a man to marry a woman who was co-wife with his mother, previous to her (the mother's) marriage to his father, or a woman who has been guilty of fornication without repentance for her fault.*

"Property, or one of the parties being the slave of the other, is not expressly mentioned by the author of the *Sharáya* among the causes of prohibition in marriage; but it seems to be assumed. For it is stated (at p. 48 *post*†) that 'if a person should marry a female, the property of several owners, and should purchase the share of one of them in his wife, that would cancel the marriage;' and the author had already said, in the Book of *Tijárat* (p. 177), 'that, when one of two spouses becomes the proprietor of the other, the right of property is confirmed; but the *zowjíat*, or relation of husband and wife, is *not* confirmed.' Moreover, it is expressly stated in the *Imámiyah* Digest (p. 131), on the authority of the *Tahrír*, that 'if a husband purchase his own wife, or a wife acquire her husband in property, it is valid; but their marriage is thereby annulled.' It would seem, therefore, that there is no difference between the Shíáhs and the Hanífites on the point in question."—B. Dig., Part II, p. 38, note.

On Dower.

Although the non-mention of dower in a marriage contract, or the express stipulation therein that there shall be no dower, does not invalidate such contract,‡ yet dower

* *Sharáya ul-Islám*, p. 379.

† Ballie's Imámiyah Digest.

‡ The mention of dower is by no means a condition (of validity) in a contract of marriage. If, therefore, a man should marry a woman without any mention of dower, or with an express condition that there shall be none, the contract would (still) be valid.—*Sharáya ul-Islám*, p. 292.—B. Dig., Part II, p. 71.

The mention of dower in a marriage contract is not necessary, though proper.—*Tahrír ul-Ahkám*.

appears in almost all cases as a concomitant of marriage; that is, whether dower be not mentioned in the contract, or whether it be expressly stipulated that there shall be no dower, the law will presume it by virtue of the contract itself and award it in all cases except two or three. But,—

CCCCXXXIV. If dower has been mentioned in a contract, it must be specified in such a manner as to remove all doubt and uncertainty about the same.* *Principle.*

CCCCXXXV. Dowers are principally of three descriptions (*viz.*);—*mahr-us-sunnat*, or traditional dower; *mahr-ul-mithl* (*b*),† or proper dower; and *mahr-us-sahíh*, or valid dower.‡ *Principle.*

(*b*.) *Mahr-ul-mithl* literally signifies 'dower of the like or equals,' that is, the dower of women *equal to*, or *like*, the woman contracted in marriage.§

CCCCXXXVI. *Mahr-us-sunnat*, or the traditional dower, is that which the Prophet bestowed on each of his wives, and is said to be five hundred *dirhams*. *Principle.*

CCCCXXXVII. *Mahr-ul-mithl*, or proper dower,‡ of a woman is regulated according to her condition with respect to the nobility of her birth, beauty of her person, and the custom of her female relatives, provided it does not differ from (that is, does not exceed) the traditional dower (*mahr-us-sunnat*), which is five hundred *dirhams*. *Principle.*

Annotations.

ccccxxxvi. When a marriage was contracted upon the *Kurán*, and according to the *Sunnat* of the Prophet, the dower would be five hundred *dirhams*.—Tahrír ul-Ahkám.

ccccxxxvii. In regulating the proper dower, (*mahr-ul-mithl*,) regard is to be had to the woman's condition with respect to her beauty, nobi-

---

* *Vide* Principle ccccxlix and the illustration relative thereto.

† In India, the word "*mithl*‡" is pronounced as "*misl*." The learned Translator of the Hidáyah has rendered "*mahr ul-mithl*" by "proper dower;" and the same has been adopted by Mr. Neil Baillie.

‡ *Vide* Principle ccccxxxviii.

§ *Sharáya ul-Islám*, p. 292 *et seq.*

Principle. CCCCXXXVIII. *Mahr-us-sahíh*, or valid dower, is anything which is capable of being rightly (acquired or) owned (by a Musalmán), whether it be a substance or usufruct.*

Principle. CCCCXXXIX. Anything that can be owned as *property* (by a Musalmán), can be assigned as dower, whether the same be a property in substance, or a mere usufruct.—Tahrír ul-Ahkám. Hence,—

Principle. CCCCXL. Wine, hog, and the like are not fit subjects of dower, such things not being property to a *Musalmán*.

Principle. CCCCXLI. If both parties to a marriage contract, in which wine or a hog is the dower, be *Musalmáns*, or the husband only be a *Musalmán*, then not the contract, but the dower, is invalid, and in lieu thereof proper dower, (*mahr-ul-mithl*) is established to the wife upon the marriage being consummated.

Thus the *Sharáya ul-Islám*:—"If both parties (to a contract in which wine, or a hog, is the dower,) be *Musalmáns*, or the husband only be a *Musalmán*, some of the doctors pronounced such a contract to be null; some maintained that it is valid, and the proper dower (*mahr-ul-mithl*) is established to the wife in the event of coition; while others said that she is to receive the estimated value of the wine (or hog); but the second opinion is most generally received."*—P. 290

ANNOTATIONS.

lity of birth, and the custom of her female relatives—as mother, sister, paternal aunt and maternal aunt,—provided it does not exceed five hundred *dirhams*, but if it does exceed, it will be reduced to that amount. And as there are different customs in different towns in respect of dower, regard is to be had also to the woman's own town with reference to the women equal to her in age, knowledge, wealth, poverty, virginity, or non-virginity. In short, every description or qualification to which dower can be opposed is to be taken into consideration.—Tahrír ul-Ahkám.

* *Sharáya ul-Islám*, p. 290.

CCCCXLII. If two *Zimmís*, or infidel subjects, should enter into a marriage contract for wine or for a hog, it would be valid, because these are things which may be lawfully (acquired and) owned by them; but if either or both of them should be a *Musalmán* or *Musalmáns* before possession has been taken (of such dower), the husband must deliver its value, as the thing itself is incapable of being the property of a *Musalmán*.* *Principle.*

CCCCXLIII. Marriage may be lawfully contracted for the usufruct of a free man, that is, for service to be rendered by him.* *Principle.*

As the teaching of an art, or in a chapter of the *Kurán*, or any lawful business, even for the husband's covenanting to serve in person for a fixed period.* Example.

Some of the doctors, however, have prohibited (the latter) on the authority of a report which is but weakly authenticated, and falls short of imposing the prohibition.*

CCCCXLIV. The amount or quantity of the dower depending upon the mutual agreement of the husband and wife, there is no limit to the *maximum* or to the *minimum* thereof, so long as it is not destitute of any legal value. *Principle.*

Thus the *Sharáya ul-Islám*:—"There are no bounds to the amount or quantity of the dower, but it should be that which is mutually agreed upon by the husband and wife, so long as it is not destitute of value, though it be very little, as a grain of wheat, for example; in the same manner there is no limit to its maximum."†

So also the *Tahrír ul-Ahkám*:—"There is no limit to the minimum or maximum of dower; but the amount (or quantity) mutually agreed upon by the married couple will be the valid dower."

Annotations.

ccccxliii. If the contract was for the usufruct of a freeman—as the teaching of an art, or a portion of the *Kurán*, or for any other lawful property,—the same is valid.—Tahrír ul-Ahkám.

---

* *Sharáya ul-Islám*, p. 290.
† *Sharáya ul-Islám*, p. 291.

Some of the doctors have declared that a dower cannot legally exceed (the amount of) the *mahr-us-sunnat*, that is, the dower bestowed by the Prophet on his wives; and that any excess over that amount must be returned (to the husband); but this opinion is not to be relied on.*

Principle. CCCCXLV. Either the husband or the wife may be appointed to fix the amount or quantity of the dower: and when the husband is to do so, he may lawfully fix any amount or quantity that he pleases, he being restricted neither on the side of more, nor on the side of less; but when the wife is appointed for the purpose, she is restricted, not on the side of less, but on the side of more, and cannot lawfully exceed the dower of *sunnat*,† that is five hundred *dirhams*.‡

If the judge, or referee, should die *before* fixing the amount, and *previous* to coition, some of the doctors have said that the dower is cancelled, and the wife is entitled only to a *mutát*, or present, while others insist that she has no right to either; but the first opinion is supported by traditions.‡ Hence,—

Principle. CCCCXLVI. If the judge, or referee, should die before fixing the amount, and previous to consummation of the marriage, the dower is cancelled, and the wife is entitled only to a *mutát*, or present.

Principle. CCCCXLVII. If subsequent to their contract of marriage, the parties agree upon the settlement of a dower, it is legal and valid.‡

For the right is with them, whether the amount (agreed upon) is equivalent to the proper dower, or be more or less than the same, and whether the parties, or one of them, be acquainted with the proper dower, or be ignorant thereof, inasmuch as the settlement of dower rested with them at the first, and it is equally lawful to the end.‡

---

* *Sharáya ul-Islám*, p. 290.

† See *ante*, p. 251.

‡ *Sharáya ul-Islám*, p. 293.

Moderation in the amount of the dower is, however, commendable, and it is abominable to exceed the *mahr-us-sunnat,* that is the dower which was bestowed by the Prophet on (each of) his wives, and which amounted to five hundred *dirhams.* As it is also (abominable) for a husband to have connubial intercourse with his wife till he has first paid her dower, or some part of it, or has given her something else, though it be a present or gift.*

CCCCXLVIII. It is sufficient in the (assignment of) dower that the article (which is the subject of it) be seen, if produced, though it be of unknown quality, quantity or weight, like a heap of grain for instance, or a bit of gold.* *Principle.*

If a man should marry a woman for a servant or slave, without being seen or described, it is said that a slave of medium quality must be delivered to her; and the same rule applies to a man's marrying for a *bayit,* or house, stipulated for, in general terms, on the ground of a report by *Alí Ibnu Alí Hamzah;* as also to (his marrying for) a *dár,* or mansion, as recorded by *Bin Abú Amir* from some of the doctors, quoting the authority of *Abú Al-Hasan,* on whom be peace.*

CCCCXLIX. It is indispensable (in marriage contracts) that the dower be specified in such a manner as to remove all doubt and uncertainty (*a*).* *Principle.*

(*a*.) Thus if the dower agreed upon is instruction in a chapter of the *Kurán,* the chapter must be specified.* **Illustration.**

CCCCL. If the dower is left in general terms, it is invalid, and the woman is entitled to her proper dower (*mahr-ul-mithl*) in the event of the marriage being consummated.* *Principle.*

Annotations.

ccccl. It is necessary that the dower be fixed and specified. But if it is left undetermined, proper dower becomes due (to the woman) upon consummation, while only a present in the case of divorce *before* consummation.—Tahrír ul-Ahkám.

---

* ***Sharáya ul-Islám*, pp. 291 & 292.**

CCCCLI. If a husband should assign as the dower of his wife to teach her an art or a business which he does not know well, or a chapter of the *Kurán*, of which he is ignorant, such dower is, nevertheless, valid, for the engagement is established on the husband's responsibility; and if he is unable to perform it himself, he is bound to pay the hire of such instruction.*

Principle.

If, again, he assign to her as dower a vessel said to contain vinegar, and it afterwards appears that its contents are wine, some of the doctors have maintained that she is entitled to have the value of the wine as if it were lawful, but it is better to say that she is entitled to a similar quantity of vinegar. In like manner, should he marry by assigning (to his wife) a particular slave, and if it afterwards appear that the person is free, or the property of another, the woman is to receive a slave of like value as the person mentioned.* Hence,—

Principle. CCCCLII. If a man should assign as dower a lawful article said to be contained in a vessel, and it afterwards appears that another article, which is unlawful to a Musalmán, is contained therein, the wife is entitled to receive from her husband the quantity of the lawful article which was assigned by him, or the value thereof. In like manner, if the man should assign as dower a property which subsequently proves not a fit subject of dower, or not to belong to him, the wife would be entitled to its value.

Principle. CCCCLIII. If a man should marry a woman for one dower privately, and another openly and in public, the first is her dower.*

It is lawful to marry two or more women for one dower, which must (in that case) be divided equally among them: it is, however, maintained by some that the same is to be given them in proportion to their proper dowers. This (latter opinion) is more agreeable to the general principles of law.* So,—

Principle. CCCCLIV. Two or more women can be married for one dower, but in that case the dower is to be divided among them in proportion to their respective proper dowers.

Principle. CCCCLV. If a man had carnal connection with a woman under a semblance of right, or under an invalid con-

---

* *Sharáya ul-Islám*, pp. 291 & 292.

tract, or by violence, the woman is to have her proper dower from him.—Mafátíh.

CCCCLVI. In the case of dower being named or specified, the same becomes the woman's property upon the contract being entered into,—her ownership of the whole not being dependent upon consummation.—Tahrír ul-Ahkám. *Principle.*

CCCCLVII. According to the most general doctrine amongst *us*,* the husband is responsible for the dower. If then it should perish (before delivery), he must make good its value at the time of its loss.† *Principle.*

CCCCLVIII. If it (the dower) be found blemished, the wife may return it on account of the defect.† *Principle.*

But if it should be blemished *after* the contract, it has been said that she has an option, and take either the thing itself (blemished as it is), or its value. It were better, however, to say that she has no title to claim its value, and can only take the thing itself with a compensation† (for the blemish). Hence,—

CCCCLIX. If dower should be blemished *after* the contract, she has no title to claim its value; but she can only take the thing itself with a compensation for the blemish. *Principle.*

As respects the delivery,—

CCCCLX. Dower may be partly *muajjal* (prompt or exigible) and partly *mowajjal* (deferred), or wholly exigible or deferred according as stipulated. *Principle.*

ANNOTATIONS.

cccclviii. In the case of a blemish, or defect, the dower may be returned, though it be not much.—Tahrír ul-Ahkám.

cccclx. If they stipulate that a portion (of the dower) shall be deferred, and the remainder promptly paid, the same is valid.—Tahrír ul-Ahkám.

---

* So says the author of the *Sharáya ul-Islám.*

† *Sharáya ul-Islám*, pp. 291 & 292.

Principle. CCCCLXI. When the (payment of the) dower is left in general terms, it is exigible (*muajjal*).—Tahrír ul-Ahkám.

If they (the married couple) leave the time for payment undetermined, then the specification of the amount becomes void, and proper dower is established, which is not promptly payable.—*Ibid.*

Principle. CCCCLXII. But when a time is fixed (for payment of the dower), then the husband is obliged to pay it before the arrival of that time, whether he had coition with her or not; and the woman cannot refuse her person to him, even upon the arrival of that time.—Tahrír ul-Ahkám.

So also the *Sharáya ul-Islám*:—"If she has withheld herself (till the arrival of the stipulated period), a question may arise whether she can lawfully deny herself (till the dower is paid). To this question some of the doctors have answered in the affirmative, but others in the negative, by reason of her being bound to surrender herself before the arrival of the period agreed upon. The latter opinion is agreeable to the principles of the law.†

Principle. CCCCLXIII. If the dower is exigible (*halam* or *muajjal*), the woman can refuse to surrender her person (to the husband), so long as she does not receive it.* But if the dower is *mowajjal* or deferred, the wife cannot deny herself† (to the embraces of her husband).

A woman may refuse to surrender her person till she has received delivery of her dower, whether the husband be wealthy or in straightened circumstances.* But whether she can do so after consummation (of the marriage) is a question that has been answered in the affirmative as well as in the negative. The latter opinion, however, is more conformable to the general principles of the law, because fruition is a right that accrues as a matter of course from the contract.* Hence,—

Principle. CCCCLXIV. If connubial intercourse has once taken place, she cannot any longer refuse herself to the embraces of her husband.

---

* *Tahrír ul-Ahkám.*

† *Sharáya ul-Islám*, pp. 292—295.

CCCCLXV. If the wife is divorced *before* consummation, (and there is no dower in the contract), then she,—whether a free woman or a slave,—would be entitled to a *mutát*, or present (*b*), and not to a dower; but if (in the above case) she is divorced *after* consummation, she is entitled to her proper dower (*mahr-ul-mithl*).* *Principle.*

(*b*.) The *mutát*, or present, is regulated by the condition and circumstance of the husband. Thus a rich man is to present (his wife) with a quadruped, or a rich dress, or ten *dínárs*; a man of middle class with five dínárs, or a dress of middling value; and a poor with one *dínár*, or a ring, or the like. And no woman is entitled to a present except the woman for whom no dower has been assigned, and who has been divorced before consummation.†

CCCCLXVI. When no dower has been named in the contract, but the husband has given something to his wife, and then consummated the marriage, it has been said that the thing so given is her dower, and that the wife has no right to demand more after coition, unless it were stipulated before the coition that the dower should consist of something else.† *Principle.*

This (*i.e.*, the above) is founded on an analogical exposition of a report, and is supported by the well known opinion (of the learned).†

In the case of dower being named or mentioned in the contract,—

CCCCLXVII. The wife is entitled to only a half of it upon her being divorced *before* consummation, and to the whole thereof upon her being divorced *after* consummation, or upon the death of her husband before or after consummation. But,— *Principle.*

CCCCLXVIII. When a man has divorced his wife before consummation (of their marriage), she is entitled to half the stipulated dower (as already stated), so if the whole were paid in advance, he is entitled to a refund of it, if still exist- *Principle.*

* *Vide Sharáya ul-Islám*, pp. 292 & 293.

† *Sharáya ul-Islám*, pp. 292 & 263.

ing, or half of a similar to it, if the thing itself have perished, or half of its value, if a similar cannot be had (*c*).*

(*c*.) If there be any difference between its value at the time of contract and at the time of taking possession, the wife is bound only for the lower of the two values. If, again, the identical substance remain in her possession, but it has become injured in some of its qualities, as, for instance, if the dower were an animal which has become blind of an eye, or a slave who has forgotten the trade in which he was instructed, the husband is in this case entitled to half the value, and cannot be compelled to take the thing itself, although this decision is liable to some doubt. If, however, the diminution of value should arise merely from a change in the price, he is entitled to no more than half of the article itself, as he is also, on the other hand, entitled to the half of it if an increase in its value should take place from a rise in the market price, because no reference can be made to value so long as the actual substance remains unchanged. Where, again, an essential increase of the substance has taken place, as by natural growth in the case of a young animal, or by an addition of fat in the case of a lean one, he is entitled only to half of the original value without the increase, and the wife cannot be compelled to make over half of the thing in its improved condition, according to the best founded opinion. Further, any produce of the original dower, such as the milk or young of an animal, is the exclusive property of the wife, and the husband is entitled to no more than half of what was specified in the contract. But if he had endowed her with a pregnant animal as her dower, half of both the animal and its offspring would be his ; while, if instruction in a trade were the dower, and he had divorced her before consummation, she would be entitled to half the hire of instruction ; and if he had already instructed her previous to the divorce, he would be entitled to a refund of half the hire.*

Principle. CCCCLXIX. If a person absolutely divorces his wife, and then remarries her during the *iddat*, and again divorces her before coition, she is entitled to half the dower.*

Principle. CCCCLXX. If a marriage has been consummated before delivery of the dower, (still) the right of it is by no means cancelled by the consummation (*d*), but remains a debt against the husband (for which he is responsible,) however long or short may be the delay in its payment, and whether it be demanded or not.*

---

* *Sharáya ul-Islám*, pp. 293 & 294.

There is, however, another report, but that has been set aside or abandoned.*

(*d.*) The consummation, which is a means of establishing a right to dower, is the actual coition either naturally or against nature, and the right is by no means established by mere retirement. Some of the doctors, however, have maintained that it is so established; but the first opinion is prevalent.*

According to the most common and generally received of the two reports,—

CCCCLXXI. The dower becomes the property (of the wife) by the mere contract, and she may (therefore) deal with, or dispose of, it before taking possession of the same.† *Principle.*

CCCCLXXII. But should the husband divorce her before coition, half of it reverts to him, the other half only remaining her property; and if she should forgive him what belongs to her, the whole would be his.† *Principle.*

Such also would be the case if the person who has power to contract the woman in marriage,—that is, if her guardian, as a father, or paternal grandfather, should forgive† (the husband the portion of the dower to which the wife is entitled). So,—

CCCCLXXIII. The father and paternal grandfather may forgive (the husband) part of the dower, but neither of them can give up the whole.† *Principle.*

Some of the doctors have alleged that this power belongs to every person who has authority to contract a woman in marriage.†

ANNOTATIONS.

cccclxxi. In the case of dower being named or specified, the woman becomes the owner thereof merely upon the contract being entered into, her ownership of the whole not being dependent upon consummation.—Tahrír ul-Ahkám.

A woman is competent to dispose of her dower (even) before possession, by sale, gift, or in any other way that she pleases.—*Ibid.*

cccclxxii. If the husband divorced his wife before consummation, he is entitled to the refund of half of the dower; while before the divorce the whole is established to her.—*Ibid.*

---

* *Sharáya ul-Islám*, pp. 293 & 294.

† *Sharáya ul-Islám*, p. 295.

Principle. CCCCLXXIV. The husband's guardian, however, has no legal power to give up his ward's right (to half the dower) in the event of a divorce* (previous to consummation).

Because he is appointed to take care of the interests of his ward, who can have no possible benefit from the forgiveness* (that is the abandonment of his right).

Principle. CCCCLXXV. An adult and discreet woman is competent to excuse her husband from paying the whole or any part of her dower. And so is her *walí*, or guardian, who has power to enter into the contract. Such remission by the guardian becomes, however, valid only in the case of the female being a minor (whether a virgin or a *thayyibah*†), and the *walí* being her father or paternal grandfather.—Tahrír ul-Ahkám.

And, when either the wife has forgiven her half, or the husband has forgiven his half, in neither case does the right of property pass out of either person by the mere act of forgiveness, for that is only a right of which the transfer does not take place without possession.*

If, indeed, the dower were a debt against the husbaud, or if it should happen to perish in the hands of the wife, mere forgiveness of the responsibility would be quite sufficient, because it would be a release which does not require even acceptance according to the most correct opinion. But a tangible property (*mál*), for which a person is liable, cannot be transferred by mere forgiveness, or by anything short of actual delivery.*

Principle. CCCCLXXVI. If a woman exonerate her husband from the dower, and he then divorces her before consummation, he has a claim against her for half the dower: such also is the case, if he should enter into a *Khulá* with her before consummation (*e*). This is by general agreement.*

(*e*.) That is, if she bargain with him for release from the marriage tie, in exchange for the whole dower, and then he divorces her before consummation, he should have recourse against her for a refund for half of it.*

---

* *Sharáya ul-Islám*, pp. 295 & 296.

† A *Thayyibah* is a woman who has had connection with a man.

CCCCLXXVII. If a woman makes a gift to her husband of half of the dower diffusively, and he then divorces her before coition, he becomes thereby proprietor of the remaining (half also), but has no further claim against her, whether the dower was a debt, or something specific, because the gift comprehends all that she had any right to.* *Principle.*

CCCCLXXVIII. If a person marry a woman, assigning as her dower some property pointed out, but of unknown weight, which perishes before her taking possession, and the wife releases him from it, this is valid. As also where he has assigned her a dower, that is invalid, and the wife being in consequence entitled to her proper dower, releases him from it, or in part, such acquittal is valid, although the amount thereof is yet unascertained. If, however, a wife should exonerate her husband of the proper dower, *before* coition, such acquittal is invalid; her right to it not being yet established. *Principle.*

Because this is merely the cancelling of a right which in law is not affected by the ignorance of the amount.†

CCCCLXXIX. When anything is stipulated for in a contract of marriage which is contrary to law (*f*), the condition is void, but the contract valid together with the dower.† *Principle.*

ANNOTATIONS.

cccclxxix. If in a contract of marriage such conditions are stipulated as are repugnant to what the law provides, the same would be void. For instance, if the husband should stipulate in the contract that he shall neither marry another woman, nor shall take a female slave (for enjoyment), and that he shall neither supply her with maintenance nor make her the participator of his inheritance, the contract shall be valid (but the conditions void). While, on the other hand, if he should stipulate that he will marry another wife, or take a female slave (for enjoyment), and accompany her (the former wife) to a voyage or journey, or will give her maintenance, such condition is valid, as it is not repugnant to (law and) the contract, according to the general assent of the Learned.—Tahrír ul-Ahkám.

* *Sharáya ul-Islám*, p. 295—297.
† *Sharáya ul-Islám*, p. 294.

(*f*.) As, for example, that the husband shall not marry another woman during the lifetime of the wife with whom the contract is made, nor privately entertain a woman as his concubine.*

In like manner, if the husband should stipulate that the payment of the dower shall be made at a certaiu time, and that in the event of failing to make the payment (as stipulated), the contract shall be null, both the contract and dower are binding, and the condition is void.*

If it be stipulated in a contract of marriage that the husband shall not take away his wife from her own city or village, it has been said that such condition is binding, and there is a tradition to that effect.*

Principle. CCCCLXXX. If he (the husband) should stipulate a certain amount of dower in the event of taking her away to his own country, and somewhat less if she does not accompany him; and if after this, he attempts to take her away to an infidel city or village, she is not bound to comply, but is (nevertheless) entitled to the higher amount of dower. If, on the other hand, the removal is to a *Musalmán* city or village, the condition is binding (on her), though this is liable to some doubt.*

Principle. CCCCLXXXI. If a guardian contract her female ward for a sum smaller than her proper dower, the dower so fixed is valid.

Thus the *Sharáya ul-Islám*:—"If a guardian contract her female ward for a sum smaller than her proper dower, some doctors have alleged that the dower is null, and that she is entitled to the proper dower. Others have asserted that the appointed dower is valid, and this doctrine is the most approved."†

Principle. CCCCLXXXII. The *walís*, or guardians, of infant girls or insane females can lawfully receive their dowers, and thus their husbands may be exonerated. But neither the father, nor any other person, can receive the dower of an adult and discreet female.—Tahrír ul-Ahkám.

---

* *Sharáya ul-Islám*, p. 294.

† *Sharáya ul-Islám*, p. 296.

CCCCLXXXIII. If one should contract his infant son in marriage, and the child has property of his own, he is liable for the dower. If the child is poor, the obligation for the dower rests on the father, and in the event of his death, the same must be discharged out of the whole of his estate, whether the child should arrive at maturity and become wealthy, or die before it.* Consequently,— *Principle.*

CCCCLXXXIV. If the father should have paid the dower, and the youth should come to maturity, and then divorce his wife before coition, the son, and not the father, has a right to reclaim half (the dower);—this (payment by the father) being considered as a gift to the son.* *Principle.*

On Guardianship in Marriage.

CCCCLXXXV. No person except a father, a paternal grandfather in any stage of ascent, a mother, an executor, or a judge, has authority to contract another in marriage†. *Principle.*

The above general rule is particularized and qualified as follows :—

CCCCLXXXVI. The authority of a father and paternal grandfather over a minor girl is established even though she should have lost her virginity; and, according to the more approved of the traditions, she has no option (of cancelling the contract) after attaining majority.† *Principle.*

In like manner,—

CCCCLXXXVII. Should a father or paternal grandfather contract a boy in marriage, the contract would be binding on *Principle.*

ANNOTATIONS.

ccccLxxxv, ccccLxxxvi. In marriage, the guardianship of a father and paternal grandfather, how high soevever, is, without difference of opinion, established with respect to a minor child; whether it be male or female, an idiot, or insane from infancy.—Mafátíh.

The father or grandfather of a female, who is a minor or insane, is to act as her guardian (*walí*), whether the female is a virgin or has lost her virginity by coition or otherwise.—Tahrír ul-Ahkám.

* *Sharáya ul-Islám*, p. 296.

† *Sharáya ul-Islám*, pp. 263 & 264.

him, and he would have no option after attaining puberty and discretion, according to the most prevalent opinion.*

But whether their authority in marriage is established over a virgin who is discreet, is a question on which there are several traditions: according to the most generally approved of these, their authority over her is at an end; and it is established that she is competent to contract herself in marriage, permanent or temporary; and if either of them should enter into a contract of her marriage, the same would not be effectual without her assent.* Hence,—

Principle. CCCCLXXXVIII. Neither a father, nor a grandfather, has authority over an adult and discreet virgin, who herself is competent to enter into a marriage contract; and if they, or either of them, do contract her in marriage, the efficacy or the validity of such contract would depend upon her assent or ratification.

Principle. CCCCLXXXIX. If her (the adult and discreet virgin's) guardians should refuse to marry her to an equal, when desired by her to do so, there is no doubt that she may contract herself even against the will of both (the father and grandfather). And they (the father and grandfather) have no power over a *thayyibah* who has attained puberty and discretion; nor even over an adult and discreet male.*

Principle. CCCCXC. Their power, however, is fully established over insane persons (infant or adult), and none of them has any option after restoration to reason.*

Annotations.

ccccclxxxviii—ccccxc. Without difference of opinion, neither a father nor a grandfather, can force an adult and descreet girl† to be contracted in marriage, even though she be a virgin but discreet. But if she is under age, they can force her to marry, whether she be a *thayyibah*† or virgin, or one of unsound mind.—Tahrír ul-Ahkám.

---

* *Sharáya ul-Islám*, pp. 263 & 264.

† A *Thayyibah* (or Sayyibah, as pronounced in India) is a female who has had connection with a man.

CCCCXCI. A master may contract his female slave in marriage, whether she be a minor or major, sane or insane, and she has no option in the matter. The rule is the same also in the case of a male slave.* *Principle.*

According to the most approved tradition,—

CCCCXCII. An executor has no authority in marriage, even if it were expressly given by the testator. But an executor may contract a person in marriage, who, though arrived at majority, is deficient in understanding, when there is any necessity for contracting him or her in marriage.* *Principle.*

CCCCXCIII. In marriage, the judge has no authority over a person who is not adult, nor over an adult who has discretion. But his authority is *Principle.*

ANNOTATIONS.

ccccxcii. The most approved doctrine is, that an executor cannot act as a guardian in marriage, not even if the father had authorized him to do so,—whether the *músá-alaihi* (or the person in whose favor the will is made,) be a male or a female, or whether the (testator's) daughter be an infant or adult, or whether the father had or had not fixed a husband for his infant daughter. An executor, however, can contract in marriage one who is of unsound mind and required to be married.—Tahrír ul-Ahkám.

ccccxciii. On failure of both the father and grandfather, the Judge (*Hákim*) is the *walí*, or guardian, of an insane person: he should contract him or her in marriage, if it is considered advisable.—Tahrír ul-Ahkám.

The *Shaikh* has said that by '*Hákim*' is here meant the *Imám*, or his delegate.—*Ibid.*

The *Hákim* cannot, however, be the *walí* or guardian of an infant girl (in the matter of marriage).—*Ibid.*

An insane person cannot be contracted in marriage, except when necessary—as on his going after women,—but nevertheless his lucid interval must be waited for, when he will be given in marriage.—*Ibid.*

Such also is the case with a person who has white leprosy.—*Ibid.*

* *Sharáya ul-Islám*, pp. 263 & 264.

fully established with respect to a person who has attained majority without discretion, or one on whom a defect in understanding has supervened, and marriage is for his or her benefit.*

The person who is incompetent to perform any civil function on account of a defect in understanding, is not allowed by law to marry; if he, nevertheless, does marry, the contract is invalid. The Judge (*Hákim*), however, may permit him to marry upon a proper dower, either selecting or without selecting a bride for him.—Tahrír ul-Ahkám.

Principle. CCCCXCIV. In marriage, a mother has no power over her own child. Nevertheless, if she enters into such a contract for her son, and he consents to it, the contract is binding upon him; but if he is averse, then she is responsible for the dower.†

On the above point, however, a doubt is entertained, and the question for liability is sometimes held to depend on her having sought for the appointment of agency from her son.†

Principle. CCCCXCV. Save and except the father and paternal grandfather, none of the lineal relatives—a brother or paternal uncle, for instance,—can force a girl to marry.—Tahrír ul-Ahkám.

Principle. CCCCXCVI. When a stranger has contracted a person in marriage, (the validity of) the same depends upon the permission of the party for whom the contract is entered into.†

Some, however, have said that the contract is valid; but the first opinion is the most approved.†

ANNOTATIONS.

cccexciv. The mother has no right of guardianship in marriage.—Tahrír ul-Ahkám.

* *Sharáya ul-Islám*, pp. 263 & 964.
† *Sharáya ul-Islám*, p. 266.

CCCCXCVII. A woman adult and discreet can not only marry of her own accord and authority, but appoint an agent to contract her in marriage, and can herself act as an agent in another's marriage. *Principle.*

Thus the *Sharáya ul-Islám* :—"In a contract of marriage full regard is to be had to the words of a female who is of mature age and discreet, so that she is quite competent to contract herself, or to be the agent of another in giving expression either to the declaration, or to the acceptance."—P. 266.

So the *Tahrír ul-Ahkám* :—"An adult and discreet female can, of her own authority, contract herself in marriage."

So also the *Mafátíh* :—"It is not required that the parties entering into the contract be both males, since with us, a contract entered into by a female is valid, whether it be done in person or through an agent (*wakíl*)."

CCCCXCVIII. When an adult and discreet female has given a general appointment to an agent to contract her in marriage, he cannot marry her to himself without her (special) permission.* *Principle.*

And though she should appoint an agent expressly to marry her to himself, it has been said, on the authority of one report, that such an appointment would not be valid. The more approved doctrine, however, is in favor of its validity.*

CCCCXCIX. If a paternal grandfather should marry her to the son of another son of his than to her own father, the marriage would be lawful.* *Principle.*

D. If a woman is contracted in marriage by her guardian without her proper dower,† or for less than her proper dower, she is competent to object to the contract. *Principle.*

Thus the *Sharáya-ul-Islám* :—"Whether a woman who is contracted in marriage by her guardian without (that is for less than) her proper dower,† can object to the contract, is a question on which there is a difference of opinion; but according to the most authentic doctrine, she is competent to object."*

---

* *Sharáya ul-Islám*, p. 266.

† See Proper dower or *Mahr-i misl*, in Lecture XIII.

Principle. DI. If a girl is contracted in marriage by any person other than her father or paternal grandfather, whether the person be nearly or remotely related to her, the contract cannot be operative unless subsequently allowed, or assented to, by herself, even though the person were her brother or paternal uncle.*

Principle. DII. In the case of a virgin, the assent is inferred from her silence when the matter is propounded to her; but a woman who is not a virgin must be put to the trouble of expressing her assent by actual speech.*

Principle. DIII. If the person contracted (in marriage) be a female slave, the validity of the contract depends upon the assent of her master: if she is not a slave but under puberty, and her father or paternal grandfather allows the contract (entered into by her), the same is valid.*

Principle. DIV. An infidel, whether he be an alien enemy (*harbí*), or an alien tributary (*zimmí*), and whether he be virtuous according to his own persuasion or not, cannot be guardian of a *Muslimah.*—Tahrír ul-Ahkám.

Principle. DV. When a guardian is an infidel, he has no authority over his ward; and if the father be an infidel, the authority is established in the paternal grandfather, so also when the father is insane, or falls into a state of temporary stupor. But on the removal of the impediments, his (the father's) authority revives.*

ANNOTATIONS.

dii. An adult woman in general is required to give her assent or consent; for a *thayyibah*, in particular, it is necessary to give her assent by the utterance of words; but, as regards a virgin, her silence is sufficient (for the purpose), provided the same be not from disgust.—Tahrír ul-Ahkám.

dv. If the father be an infidel, insane, or slave, the guardianship devolves on the paternal grandfather, if he is free from such defects. But if the defect is removed from the father, his guardianship shall be restored to him.—*Ibid.*

* *Sharáya ul-Islám*, p. 265.

DVI. Profligacy of a *walí* does not extinguish his guardianship. Such also is the case with a blind person, and one following a low profession—as of a door-keeper, a sweeper, a barber, and weaver.—Tahrír ul-Ahkám. *Principle.*

DVII. A dumb person does not lose his guardianship *Principle.* if the signs made by him can be understood.—Tahrír ul-Ahkám.

It is becoming and proper for a woman, whether she be a virgin or not, to authorize her father to enter into the marriage contract (for her), and if she has neither a father nor a paternal grandfather, *then* to appoint her brother to act as guardian (in such matter), giving her confidence to the eldest when she has several brothers.*

So also the *Tahrír ul-Ahkám*:—"When a girl is adult and discreet, none at all has a right to be her guardian. Nevertheless, it becomes her to take permission of her father, and in his default to appoint her brother as a *wakíl*, or agent; and, if there are two brothers, it behoves her to entrust the matter to the eldest brother."

DVIII. If the father should select one husband, and the *Principle.* paternal grandfather another, the husband whose contract was first in date is preferred, and the contract of the other is void. But if both contracts should take place simultaneously, then that which was entered into by the grandfather is preferred, and not that entered into by the father.*

DIX. When the guardian of a female has married her *Principle.* to a person who is insane, or a eunuch, the marriage is valid; but after attaining majority she has an option (to confirm or cancel the marriage).* So, also,—

DX. When the guardian of a boy has married him to *Principle.* a female having any of the defects which are the causes for cancellation of marriage,† (he has a like option on attaining majority).*

---

* *Sharáya ul-Islám*, p. 265.

† See the Defects which are causes for cancelling marriage.

DXI. When the fathers of two young children have contracted them to each other in marriage, the contract is binding on them. And if one of them should happen to die, the other would be entitled to participate in the deceased's inheritance.*

Principle.

Principle. DXII. Should any *other* persons than the fathers of their children contract them in marriage, and one of them should happen to die before arriving at majority, the contract would be void, and both dower and the right of inheritance would fail.*

Principle. DXIII. If, again, one of them should allow the contract on attaining majority, it would be binding on *that* person; so if he or she should (subsequently) die, the share of the other in the deceased's estate must be reserved. And if such other, on attaining majority, allow the marriage, he or she must then be sworn that the marriage has not been allowed from greed of the inheritance, and inherit (the portion reserved); while if the person, who has not allowed it, should happen to die, the contract would be void, and the party would have no right to (share in) the estate of the deceased.*

Principle. DXIV. If each of an elder and younger brother of a female should select a husband (for her), she should adopt the choice of the elder brother.†

Principle. DXV. If both brothers were appointed her agents (to contract her in marriage), and they should contract her to two different men, the contract first entered into would take effect; yet if the man with whom the second contract was entered into had connubial intercourse with her, and she become pregnant in consequence, the paternity of the child is attached to him, and he is liable for her dower, though the woman must return to the man with whom the contract was previously made.† But,—

Principle. DXVI. If she had never given authority to either of them (*i.e.*, the brothers) to enter into the contract, she may approve whichever of the contracts she pleases, though it is better that she should allow that which is entered into for her by the elder brother.† If, however, before (expressly) allowing either of the contracts, she has connection with one of the husbands, the contract with him is binding on her.†

---

* *Sharáya ul-Islám*, p. 265. So also the *Tahrír ul-Ahkám*.

† *Sharáya ul-Islám*, p. 265.

LECTURE XIV.

ON TEMPORARY MARRIAGE, AND CAUSES BY WHICH PERMANENT MARRIAGE MAY BE CANCELLED.

Temporary Marriage.

DXVII. Temporary marriage (*mutá*) is contracted for a fixed time or period,—as for a day, month, or year, or for any other fixed period.—Tahrír ul-Ahkám. *Principle.*

Temporary marriages are permitted by the Muhammadan religion,* because they were permitted by the law, and there is nothing to show that the permission was ever abrogated.†

DXVIII. The pillars or essentials (of a temporary marriage-contract) are four: the form,—the subject,—the period,—and the dower.† *Principle.*

DXIX. As regards the form of the contract,—it is the expression, appropriated by law, of the declaration and acceptance by which it is constituted.† Hence,— *Principle.*

DXX. Declaration and acceptance constitute one of the essentials of temporary marriage.† *Principle.*

ANNOTATIONS.

dxx dxxi. It is necessary that there should be a declaration by saying—"*zawwajtu-ki,*" or "*ankahtu-ki,*" or "*muttatu-ki*" (I have married thee) for such a period and for such dower, and also acceptance indicating consent (of the other party).—Tahrír ul-Ahkám.

---

* That is, the religion followed by the *Shíahs*, and not that followed by the *Sunnis*, who do not admit the legality of a temporary marriage.

† *Sharáya ul-Islám*, pp. 279 & 280.

DXXI. The proper terms expressive of declaration are three—"*zawwajtu-ka,** *muttatu-ka* and *ankahtu-ka* (I have married thee);" by any of these, declaration is effected, and by none other (*a*) than any of these can the contract be made.†

Principle.

(*a.*) Such as "*tamlík* (owning), *hibah* (gift), or *ijárah* (lease)."†

Principle. DXXII. Acceptance is an expression indicative of assent to the declaration;—as "I have accepted the *nikáh* or *mutá*;" or if it is shortened by saying—"I have accepted," or "I am content," the same would be valid.†

If it be commenced with acceptance by the man saying "*tazawwajtu-ki* (I have married thee)," there would be a valid contract.†

Principle. DXXIII. It is, however, necessary that both declaration and acceptance be expressed by words in the past tense.

For, if a man were to say, "*akbalu* (I do or shall accept)," "*arzá* (I am or will be content)," there would be no contract; even if he used the words intending that they should be understood in an initiatory sense.†

It has, however, been said that, if the man were to use the expression "*atazawiju-ki* (I do or will take thee to wife)" for such a period, at such a dower, with an initiatory intention, and the woman should say "*zawwajtu-ka* (I have married thee)," there would be a valid marriage. So also if she were merely to say, "yes."†

As regards the subject of the contract,—

Principle. DXXIV. According to the more general of the two traditions, it is a necessary condition that the wife be a *Muslimah*, or a *Kitábiyah*,—that is a Jewess or a Christian, or even a *Majúsíah* (a fire-worshipper); and the husband restrain her from drinking wine and (other) unlawful practices.†

ANNOTATIONS.

dxxiv. As respects the wife, she should be a *muslimah*, or *Kitábiyah*. There is, however, a difference of opinion with respect to *Majúsíah*.—Tahrír ul-Ahkám.

---

* Literally, "I have united (myself) with thee."

† *Sharáya ul-Islám*, pp. 279 & 280.

DXXV. In the *mutá* form, a *Musalmán* woman cannot marry any but a *Musalmán;* nor is it lawful for a *muslim* to enter into a contract with an idolatress.* *Principle.*

It is not also lawful for one who is straight and strict in his own belief to contract with one of a sect notorious for enmity,—such as a *khárijí.**

A slave is not to be taken to wife in the *mutá* form by a man who is already married to a free woman, except with her consent: consequently such contract, if entered into without her consent, would be void. Such also would be the result if a man should, without his wife's consent, marry, in the *mutá* form, the daughter of her brother or sister.*

DXXVI. Those relations by affinity who are unlawful in permanent marriage are also unlawful in temporary marriage.—Tahrír ul-Ahkám. *Principle.*

It is proper, though not a necessary condition of validity, that the woman (who is the subject of the contract) should be a true believer *(muminah)* and chaste, and that due inquiries be made into her conduct, if there be any suspicion. If the woman is adulterous or addicted to fornication, it is abominable to enter into the contract with her; and, if she has committed such an act, she should be prohibited from a repetition of the same.*

It is also abominable to marry in the *mutá* form a virgin who has no father; and if one should do so, he ought to refrain from connubial intercourse with her: still that is not actually prohibited.*

As respects dower,—

DXXVII. It (*i.e.*, dower) is an essential condition of the contract in the *mutá* form; and upon failure of this, the contract itself is void.* *Principle.*

ANNOTATIONS.

dxxx. According to *Nasús*, as well as the general assent of the Learned, mention of dower is necessary in a temporary marriage, without which the contract is void.—Mafátíh.

---

* *Sharáya ul-Islám*, p. 280.

Principle.

DXXVIII. It is also a condition that dower be something owned or possessed, and known by measure, weight, inspection or description, though it be left to be determined by mutual agreement of the contracting parties, whether it be much or little* (*b*).

(*b*.) Even so little as a handful of wheat, and it becomes binding (on the husband) by virtue of the contract.*

Principle.

DXXIX. The law puts no limit to dower, but whatever may be agreed upon by, and between, the marrying parties, the same—be it little or much—is valid (dower); with this condition, however, that the quality or amount must be known by measure, weight, inspection or description, and that it must be property.†—Tahrír ul-Ahkám.

Consequently,—

Principle.

DXXX. If the contract was made for a dower which is not known and not seen, or that which could not legally be the property of the man, the contract is void.—*Ibid.*

Principle.

DXXXI. The dower is to be paid upon the contract being entered into.—*Ibid.*

Principle.

DXXXII. If the man were to make to the woman a gift of the term (that is, to waive his right to her altogether) before coition, he would be liable for half (the dower); while if coition should have taken place, the (whole) dower is confirmed to her on condition of her keeping the term (and adhering to him till its completion), but if it is not completed, the man is entitled to deduct a proportionate part of the dower.*

ANNOTATIONS.

dxxxii. If the fixed term (of the duration of marriage) is given away (to the woman) without coition, half of the dower is dropped; but, if coition has taken place, the whole of the dower becomes due.—Tahrír ul-Ahkám.

---

* *Sharáya ul-Islám*, pp. 280 & 281.

† See *ante*, p. 353.

DXXXIII. If it turn out that there was a defect in the contract, either by its appearing that the woman has (another) husband, or she is the sister or mother of the man's (already married) wife, or anything similar which is one of the causes for cancellation, then, if no coition has taken place, she has no right whatever to dower; and if she has received it, the same becomes the right of the man who can demand (of her) the refund thereof.* *Principle.*

DXXXIV. But if the defect does not transpire till after connection has taken place, the woman is entitled to retain whatever portion of the dower she may have received, if she was ignorant of the existence of the defect, otherwise she is bound to refund it. *Principle.*

Thus the *Sharáya ul-Islám*:—"But if the defect does not transpire till after connection has taken place, the woman is entitled to retain whatever she may have received, and the man is under no obligation to deliver the remainder: yet it were better to say that, in the event of her having been ignorant of the existence of the cause of cancellation, she is entitled to retain whatever portion of the dower she may have received, and that if she were cognizant of the defect in the contract, she is bound to refund."*

DXXXV. There is no maintenance for a wife married in the *mutá* form, nor is a habitation to be assigned to her.—Tahrír ul-Ahkám. *Principle.*

It is laid down by *Allamah Hillí*, that when the period of *mutá* has passed away and no coition has taken place, it is unlawful for the man to cohabit with the woman without entering into a fresh contract, whether the prevention was on the part of the wife or the husband himself; and if the wife had prevented him for the (whole) period, still the husband has no right to demand a period in lieu thereof; but if he has delivered the dower to her, he can claim the refund thereof.—*Tahrír ul-Ahkám.*

DXXXVI. Neither witness nor publicity is necessary in a *mutá* marriage.—*Ibid.* *Principle.*

DXXXVII. The (fixing of a) period or time is a necessary condition of the *mutá* or temporary *Principle.*

ANNOTATIONS.

dxxxvii. According to general assent, it is necessary that in a temporary marriage the period be mentioned, or fixed.—Mafátíh.

* *Sharáya ul-Islám*, p. 281.

contract of marriage; so that, if there is no mention of a time, the contract would become permanent.*

The (determination of the) extent of the period is left (entirely) to the parties who may prolong or shorten it to a year, a month, or a day: it is only necessary that some limit be distinctly specified, so as to guard the period from any extension or diminution. Even if the time be shortened to any part of a day, the contract would be lawful, provided that its limit is distinctly known.*

As, for example, by the declining or setting of the sun.*

If the man says "*once*," or "*twice*," and does not confine this within a fixed time, the contract would not be valid (as a *mutá*), but would become a permanent one.

Principle. DXXXVIII. If a contract were made in the above manner, it would be held to be permanent; while if the acts were brought within the compass of a particular time, the contract would be valid as a *mutá* or temporary one.*

It is also lawful to specify a month to commence immediately after the contract, or at some interval from it. If mentioned generally, the month next to the contract is to be understood.*

Principle. DXXXIX. If a man should abstain from her until a a part of the specified time has expired, that is to be deducted from the contract, but, nevertheless, she is entitled to her full remuneration, that is dower.*

ANNOTATIONS.

In this (*mutá*) contract, it is necessary to mention the known period and fix the dower. As regards the period itself, there is no limit to it, whether it should be long or short, the determination thereof depends upon the consent of the parties;—but it is necessary that the same should be fixed (by them). If the period is mentioned indeterminately, the contract is void according to the more correct of the two opinions: some, however, say the contract become permanent.—Tahrír ul-Ahkám.

dxxxviii. In respect of *mutá*, it is related in a tradition by *Ibnu Bin Tughlib*, that if a man should say (to a woman) "I take thee to wife by way of *mutá*," and then if she should answer "*yes*," she becomes his wife; or if the guardian of a woman or the woman herself should

---

* *Sharáya ul-Islám*, pp. 280 & 281.

There are eight rules of the mutá contract :—

DXL. *First.*—When the term and dower both have been mentioned, the contract is valid; but if there is a failure in respect of the dower, while the term is mentioned, the contract is void; but if there is a failure in respect of the time (while the dower is mentioned), the contract, though reckoned void as a *mutá*, is valid as a permanent marriage.* *Principle.*

DXLI. *Second.*—Every condition stipulated for in this contract must be mentioned together with the declaration and acceptance, and no effect can be given to any stipulation previous to the contract unless the same be repeated at that time ; nor to any condition hereafter made. As regards, however, the condition that has been mentioned in the contract, there is no necessity for its repetition after it.* *Principle.*

Some of the doctors, however, are of opinion that the condition should be repeated after the contract. But this is far from being correct.*

DXLII. *Third.*—According to the prevalent opinion, an adult and discreet female may contract herself in a *mutá* marriage, and her guardian has no right to object, whether she be a virgin or not.* But,— *Principle.*

ANNOTATIONS.

say "I have given to thee the enjoyment for this," and should not specify any particular time, marriage would be permanently contracted. And this is evidence that permanent marriage may be constituted by the word '*tamattua*.'—Sharáya ul-Islám, p. 262.—*Vide* B. Dig., Part II, p. 2.

dxlii. An adult and discreet female is competent to contract herself in *mutá* marriage, and it is not required that she should take the permission of her guardian, even though she be a virgin.—Tahrír ul-Ahkám.

* *Sharáya ul-Islám*, p. 281.

It is unlawful for a minor girl to marry except with the consent of her guardian.*

Principle. DXLIII. *Fourth.*—It is lawful to stipulate with a woman that she shall come by night or by day, and also to stipulate for once or twice within the specified period.†

Fifth.—The practice of *azl*‡ is lawful with a *mutá* wife, and is not dependent on her permission.§

Principle. DXLIV. If she should become pregnant (notwithstanding the *azl*),‡ the child belongs to the temporary husband, on account of (some of) the seed remaining contrary to his intention. But if he should deny the child, the denial is to be sustained apparently without any necessity for *lián*.§

Principle. DXLV. *Sixth.*—According to the prevalent doctrine, a woman so married cannot be divorced; but the parties become absolutely separated upon the expiration of the period. Nor is the woman subjcet to *I'lá* or *Lián*.‖ With regard to *zihár*‖ (in such a case), there is some hesitation; but, according to the most approved opinion, it may be exercised under this form of marriage.§

ANNOTATIONS.

dxliv. The Allámah, however, has laid down in his Tahrír ul-Ahkám that the child born in a *mutá*, or temporary marriage, is affiliated to both its parents, none of whom can legally deny its being his or her issue.—*Vide* Tahrír ul-Ahkám.

dxlv. There is no divorce in the *mutá* or temporary marriage, but separation would take place upon the term being given away to the wife, or upon the expiration thereof.—*Ibid.*

Neither *I'lá* nor *Lián* is exercised under the *mutá* marriage. There is, however, a doubt as to whether *Zihár* could be exercised, and the most approved opinion is in the affirmative.—Tahrír ul-Ahkám.

* *Tahrír ul-Ahkám.*

† *Sharáya ul-Islám*, p. 281.

‡ *Extrahere ante emissionem seminis.*

§ *Sharáya ul-Islám*, p. 282

‖ *Vide* Lecture XVI.

Seventh.—By this contract, no right of inheritance is established in favor of the marrying parties, whether there was an express condition to that effect, or whether the contract was left in general terms (without any stipulation in either way). If, however, there is a stipulation for mutual rights of inheritance, or for one of the parties to inherit (from the other), some of the doctors are of opinion that effect must be given to the same, while others maintain that the condition is not binding, because inheritance is not established except by the law, and the stipulation would be in favor of persons who are not heirs by law, and, therefore, the same as if it were made in favor of absolute strangers. The first opinion, however, is more generally approved.* Hence,—

DXLVI. If the marrying parties have stipulated in the contract that they should inherit from each other, or only one of them should inherit from the other, effect must be given to such stipulation.† *Principle.*

Allámah Hillí, has, however, said:—"In this marriage, the husband and wife do not inherit from each other, whether (their) non-inheritability is, or is not, stipulated by them in the contract. But if both or any of them stipulated for inheriting, then one of them shall inherit from the other. The Shaikh says, they would inherit according as stipulated. But in my opinion it is better to forbid."‡—Tahrír ul-Ahkám.

DXLVII. *Eighth.*—If the period of the *mutá* has expired after connubial intercourse between the parties, the woman must observe an *iddat* of two returns of her courses.* *Principle.*

ANNOTATIONS.

dxlvii, dxlviii. If no coition has taken place, no *iddat* is to be observed. But if coition has taken place, and the term has expired, or has been given away to the woman, then she must observe *iddat* for two returns of her courses, if she is menstruant; but if she does not menstruate, yet if

---

* *Sharáya ul-Islám* p. 282.—*Rouzát ul-Ahkám*, p. 38.—B. Dig., Part II, p. 44.

† See *ante*, p. 182.

‡ The opinion of the *Shaikh* is, however, received as the settled law on the point.

According to one tradition a single occurrence of them is sufficient; but this tradition is rejected.*

Principle. DXLVIII. If the woman has never had them, yet if she has not despaired, then the term (of her *iddat*) is forty-five days. On account of the death of her husband the woman must observe an *iddat* of four months and ten days, if she is not pregnant, even though connubial intercourse has not taken place; but if she is pregnant, the *iddat* must continue till the more distant of two events (that is the completion of four months and ten days, and delivery). If the woman is a slave, her *iddat*, supposing that she is not pregnant, is two months and five days.*

Principle. DXLIX. A man can lawfully marry in the *mutá* form wives above four, without limit, whether the women be free or slaves. The best opinion, however, is, not to marry more than four.—Tahrír ul-Ahkám.

Principle. DL. It is lawful for a man to marry a woman in the *mutá* form for several times,—that is, on the expiration of the term of one *mutá*, he can contract another, even though it be within the *iddat*.—Tahrír ul-Ahkám.

Principle. DLI. In like manner, after the expiration of the term, the man may marry the sister of his wife (even) before completion of the *iddat* of the latter, though he cannot marry another woman till after the completion of the *iddat*.

Principle. DLII. Having contracted with a woman for a fixed period, if the man intend to extend the period before its expiration, he can renew the contract for any term that he may wish.—*Ibid.*

ANNOTATIONS.

she is within such age as to be subject to it, she must observe *iddat* for forty-five days. And if the husband dies within the period of *mutá*, the wife must observe *iddat* for four months and ten days whether her husband had cohabited with her or not. If she is pregnant, the *iddat* must continue till the more distant of two events (that is, the completion of four months and ten days, or delivery).—Tahrír ul-Ahkám.

* *Sharáya ul-Islám*, p. 282.

On the Causes for which Marriage may be Cancelled.

Personal Blemishes in a Married Man and Woman.

DLIII. The personal blemishes in a man are three:—"Insanity," "Eunuchism," and "Impotence."* *Principle.*

The author of the *Tahrír ul-Ahkám,* after separately mentioning the two kinds of *Eunuchism,* says,—"In a man there are four blemishes: '*Insanity,*' '*Khisá,*'† '*Jabb,*'‡ and '*Impotence.*'"

DLIV. Insanity (of a husband) is a cause which empowers the wife to cancel their marriage, whether it (the insanity) be continued or occasional; so also when it is supervenient and occurs after the contract, and whether before or subsequent to connubial intercourse.* *Principle.*

DLV. Eunuchism (*a*) causes cancellation of marriage when it has occurred before the marriage contract.* *Principle.*

(*a.*) Eunuchism is the loss of both the testicles, and includes in its meaning their actual destruction by castration.*

DLVI. Impotence is a cause for the cancellation of marriage though it should occur *after* the contract, provided, however, in this case, that the man had no sexual intercourse either with his wife or with another woman.* *Principle.*

For, if he has had sexual intercourse, though only once, with his wife, or if, while impotent with regard to her, he has had connection with another woman, the wife has no option according to the most approved doctrine. So, also, if he has had connection

---

ANNOTATIONS.

dliv. It is optional with a woman to cancel marriage in the case of her husband being insane, whether he was so *before* the marriage or *after* it.—Tahrír ul Ahkám.

dlv. A woman has the option of dissolving marriage if her husband became a eunuch *before* the marriage, and *not,* if after it.—*Ibid.*

dlvi. It is optional with a woman to cancel marriage if her husband was impotent *before* the marriage, but *not* if he become so *after* consummation. So, also, if he was unable to cohabit with her, but able to cohabit with another woman.—Tahrír ul-Ahkám.

---

* *Sharáya ul-Islám,* pp. 287 & 288.

† Castrating, cutting off the testicles.

‡ Cutting off the organ of generation.

with his wife against nature,* though he was impotent in the natural way† (she has no power to cancel the marriage).

Whether *jabb*, or the removal (of the penis only) be a cause for cancellation (of marriage), is a point on which there is a difference of opinion, but,†—

According to the opinion which is more agreeable to the general principles of the law, the *jabb*, or the removal of the penis only, does not enable the wife to cancel her marriage, provided, however, that so much of the stump has *not* been left as is sufficient for coition†.

Principle. DLVII. A man cannot be rejected for any cause other than (one of) those above mentioned.†

Principle. DLVIII. The blemishes of a woman are seven:—Insanity (*b*), *jazám* (*c*) or leprosy, *bars* (*d*) or white leprosy, *karn* (*e*), *ifzáa* (*f*) or rupture, blindness, and *arj* (*g*) or limping naturally.†

(*b.*) Insanity is a total derangement of the intellect, and an option is not established by slight aberrations which easily subside, or by stupors, though of frequent occurrence; but if these are confirmed or permanent, the option is established.†

(*c.*) *Jazám* is a disorder in which there is a drying up, or withering of the members, and a falling away of the flesh.†

(*d.*) *Bars* is a whiteness which appears on the surface of the body from an excess of humours; but if there is any room for doubt as to the symptoms, that does not give the power of cancellation.†

(*e.*) *Karn* is sometimes described as a fleshy protuberance, and sometimes as a bone growing in the womb, which prevents coition: The first (description) is, however, the more approved. But if it does not prevent coition it is not a cause of cancellation.†

ANNOTATIONS.

dlviii. The blemishes of a woman are seven:—Insanity, leprosy, white leprosy, *karn*, *ifzáa*, blindness, and limping naturally.—Tahrír ul-Ahkám.

---

* There are two traditions with regard to this practice, and though according to the more generally received of these, it is not unlawful, yet it is deemed to be utterly abominable.—*Sharáya ul-Islám*, p. 260.

† *Sharáya ul-Islám*, pp. 287 & 288.

(*f.*) *Ifzáa* is the becoming of two natural passages one* (by rupture).

(*g.*) With regard to *arj*, there is some doubt; but, according to the most approved authority, it is included among the causes of cancellation, when it amounts to actual lameness.*

DLIX. *Ratak* (*h*) has been placed by some among the blemishes of a woman which give a right to cancel marriage, and it is just in the case of its totally preventing coition on account of the privation of the sexual enjoyment,—that is, when it cannot be removed, or has resisted the usual remedies.* *Principle.*

(*h.*) *Ratak* is the female organ so narrow as only to allow a passage for the urine.

DLX. A woman cannot be rejected for any other than the seven blemishes above mentioned.* *Principle.*

Rules respecting Blemishes.

DLXI. Blemishes (in a woman) that existed before the contract afford a cause for the cancellation (of marriage); but any that occurs *after* the contract or connubial intercourse does not cancel* (the marriage). *Principle.*

Annotations.

dlviii, dlx. Without difference of opinion, the husband has power to cancel or dissolve marriage if the wife was insane, blind, or leprous, or had white leprosy, or *karn*, *before* the contract, though the same was discovered after consummation. With respect to *arj*, or limpering naturally, there are different opinions, according to the third of which, it is optional with the husband, if it is obviously perceptible.—Mafátíh.

dlxi, dlxii. As regards the defects of a woman, if they occurred *after* the contract and consummation, the marriage is not thereby cancelled; and if they occurred after the contract, and previous to consummation, then also, according to the most approved opinion, the marriage shall not be cancelled. Thus marriage is cancelled only in the case of the defect occurring before the contract.—Tahrír ul-Ahkám.

---

* *Sharáya ul-Islám*, p. 288.

DLXII. With regard, again, to those that occur *after* the contract, but *before* sexual intercourse, there is room for doubt; but, according to the prevalent opinion, they are not sufficient causes for cancellation, and this is corroborated by the consideration that, at the time of the contract, it is free from objection.*

Principle.

Principle. **DLXIII. The option of cancellation must (in all cases) be exercised immediately, for, if a blemish be known to a man or woman, and he or she does not hasten to cancel the contract, it would become binding on him or her.***

The rule is the same in the case for option of *tadlís*, or deception.*

Principle. DLXIV. The cancellation on account of blemish is not a *talák*, or divorce. Hence, it does not give occasion for having the dower,† and it is not reckoned in making up the number of three (divorces).*

Principle. **DLXV. A man is competent to exercise his right of cancellation without the intervention of a judge. So also is a woman.***

True, in establishing impotence, a judge is required to fix the period allowed to the man in such cases to test his inability, yet, on the expiration of the prescribed period, the woman can cancel the marriage by herself if no connubial intercourse has taken place.*

When there is a difference (between the parties) with respect to the existence of the blemish, the word of the denier is to be received in the absence of proof.*

Annotations.

dlxiii. According to our masters, the option is to be exercised without delay, that is, as soon as practicable.—*Mafátíh.*

dlxiv. It is not necessary to have the contract cancelled, or marriage dissolved, by the Judge (*Hákim*), but either of the married couple is competent to do so of his or her own authority.—*Ibid.*

---

* *Sharáya ul-Islám*, p. 288.

DLXVI. When a husband has cancelled marriage for one of the blemishes (above described), and this is done *before* consummation, then no dower (is due); but if it is done *after* consummation, the wife is entitled to the (full) amount specified in the contract. The husband, however, has a right of recourse against the person by whom he was deceived.* *Principle.*

As respects the defect of a man,—

DLXVII. If *khisá, jabb* or impotence occurred *after* consummation, the wife has no option to cancel the marriage contract: so also if the two former occurred *after* the contract and *before* consummation. The more approved opinion, however, is, that if the husband became *majbúb after* consummation, the wife has an option to dissolve the marriage. But if the husband is insane, the wife has, at all times, an option to dissolve the marriage, even if he became so *after* consummation.—Tahrír ul-Ahkám. *Principle.*

Impotence is not established without the husband's acknowledgment (before the judge), or without proof of a previous acknowledgment by him, or his refusal to swear. If there is none of these, and the wife prefers a claim on the ground of impotence, and the husband denies, then the word of the husband is received if confirmed by his oath.*

DLXVIII. When impotence has been established, and the wife is patient (or declines to proceed in the matter), nothing further is to be said; but if she insists upon bringing it before the judge, the case is to be postponed for a year from the day of her appeal to him; and if (in the interval) the husband has had connubial intercourse with her, or with another woman, the wife has no option; but if nothing of the kind has happened, she has a right to cancel her marriage, and to half of the dower.* *Principle.*

DLXIX. If a wife should cancel her marriage *before* cosummation, she has no right to dower: while if she cancels it *after* consummation, she is entitled to the sum specified in the contract, except in the case of impotence, and also where the blemish (for which marriage is cancelled) is the eunuchism of the husband, the wife is equally entitled to her full dower if coition has not taken place.* *Principle.*

---

* *Sharáya ul-Islám*, p. 289.

On Tadlís, or Deception.

Principle. **DLXX.** When one of the married couple is deceived in respect of his or her spouse, the party deceived has a right to cancel the marriage contract, and dower becomes due if the cancellation takes place after consummation, not otherwise.

Illustrations. When a man has married a woman on condition of her being free, and she proves to be a slave, he has a right to cancel the marriage even though he had connubial intercourse* (with her).

Principle. DLXXI. If the marriage is cancelled *before* coition, the woman has no right to dower; but if the cancellation takes place *after* coition, her right to dower is established.* And the husband has right to have recourse for a refund of whatever he may be obliged to pay against the person who practised the deception upon him.*

When a woman has married a man on condition of his being free, and he proves to be a slave, she has power to cancel (the marriage) before or after connubial intercourse; but if the marriage is cancelled *before* it, she has no right to dower, while she has a right to it if the cancellation takes place *after* coition.*

If a man should marry to another his daughter who is the child of a free woman, and should send to him instead of her, a daughter of his by a slave, the husband is competent to return her to the father; but if coition has taken place, she is entitled to her proper dower (*mahr-i mithl*); for which, however, the husband has a claim against the father, who must restore to him also the daughter whom he actually married. So, also, may every man act to whom another than his own wife has been brought, whether the woman be higher or lower in degree than the person whom he has married.†

---

* *Sharáya ul-Islám*, p. 289.—*Vide Tahrír ul-Ahkám*, which is of the like import.

† *Sharáya ul-Islám*, p. 290.

DLXXII. When a man has married a woman stipulating her to be a virgin, and finds that she is a *thayyibah*,* he has no power to cancel the marriage (*a*); but he is entitled to a deduction from the dower equivalent to the difference between the dower of a virgin and one who is not so; and can claim it according to the usual custom.† *Principle.*

(*a.*) Because the marks of virginity may have been destroyed by some concealed cause other than coition.†

Some, however, maintain that the amount to be deducted is a sixth of the dower, but this is erroneous.†

DLXXIII. When a man has taken a woman in *mutá*, or temporary marriage, and it is discovered that she is a *Kitábiyah*, he has no power to cancel the marriage without giving up his right to her during the time or period (for which the marriage has been contracted); nor can he deduct any part of the dower. And even if the contract were a permanent one, the result would be the same (as above) according to one or two opinions on the subject.† *Principle.*

DLXXIV. If, indeed, there were a positive condition that the woman should be a *muslimah*, he would have the power of cancelling the marriage, should he find her to be of a different religion.† *Principle.*

DLXXV. When two men have married two different women, and the wife of each has been brought to the other, and he has had connection with her, each of the women is entitled to have her proper dower (*mahr-i-misl*), from the man who has had such connection with her, and must be restored to her own husband, who is liable to her for the dower specified (in the contract). But it is unlawful for him to have connubial intercourse with her until the expiration of her *iddat* on account of the first connection.† *Principle.*

DLXXVI. If both the women (above mentioned) should die during the *iddat*, or the husbands should die, each of the two men should inherit from his own wife, and each of the women should inherit from her own husband.† *Principle.*

---

* "*Thayyibah*" or "*Sayyibah*" is a woman who has had carnal connection with a man.

† *Sharáya ul-Islám*, p. 290.

Principle.

DLXXVII. In every place or case in which it is judged that the contract is void, the wife is entitled, upon connubial intercourse having taken place, to her proper dower (*mahr-i misl*), and not to the dower appointed for her by the contract; and in every place or case in which it is judged that the contract is valid, the wife is entitled, upon cancellation of her marriage, to the specified dower, if connubial intercourse has taken place.—Sharáya ul-Islám, page 290. So also the Tahrír ul-Ahkám.

Principle.

DLXXVIII. If no coition has taken place, she has no right to dower in the case of the marriage being void, as well as cancelled.—Tahrír ul-Ahkám.

LECTURE XV.

ON DIVORCE (TALAK).

The different kinds of Divorce.

DLXXIX. *Talák*, or divorce, is principally of two kinds—*badaí* and *sunní*.* *Principle.*

DLXXX. The *badaí* (new or heretical) form of divorce is, again, of three kinds: *First,*—the divorce of an enjoyed wife during her courses, or *nifás*,† while her husband is present with her, or absent from her, for a time short of the period conditioned or required (in such cases). *Second,*—divorce during the wife's *tuhr*,‡ or purity, in which the husband had approached her. *Third,*—three divorces without any intermediate revocation. All these (*badaí*) forms of *talák* are void with the *Imámiyah* sect, no divorce taking effect in any of these cases.§ *Principle.*

DLXXXI. Of the *Sunní*, or regular, form of divorce, there are also three different kinds: 1—The *Báïn*, or absolute; 2—The *Rajaí*, or revocable; and 3—The *talák ul-idat*, or the divorce of *iddat*.§ *Principle.*

ANNOTATIONS.

dlxxix. Divorce is of two kinds—irregular and regular (*badaí* and *sunní*). The regular divorce is either irrevocable or revocable. An irrevocable divorce is that in which the woman cannot be recalled: and a revocable divorce is that in which the wife can be recalled (by the divorcer).—Tahrír ul-Ahkám.

---

* *Vide Sharáya ul-Islám*, p. 316.

† Puerperal discharge. The extreme legal term according to the *Sunni* sect is forty days, but by the *Shiáhs* it is limited to ten days.—*Vide Sharáya ul-Islám*, p. 14.

‡ "*Tuhr*," purity: in law, it signifies the time between the occurrence of two courses of a woman.

§ *Sharáya ul-Islám*, p. 316.

DLXXXII. The *Báïn* or absolute divorce is that in which the husband has no power of revocation.*

Principle. DLXXXIII. Of the above, again, there are six different species:—the *first* is *that* in which the divorced wife was never enjoyed by the husband. The *second* is, when the divorced wife is passed child-bearing (*yáïsah*). The *third* is, when she has not yet attained puberty. The *fourth* and *fifth* are when the wife is released by *khulá*† or *mubárát*,‡ and she has not reclaimed the property for which the release was obtained. The *sixth* is the wife thrice repudiated with two intermediate revocations.*

Principle. DLXXXIV. The revocable divorce (*talák i-rajaí*) is that in which the divorcer has the power of revocation, whether he exercises it or not.*

Principle. DLXXXV. The divorce of *iddat* (*talák ul-iddat*) is *that* in which a man divorces his wife under the requisite conditions, he then recalls her and cohabits with her before the expiration or completion of the *iddat*, and then divorces her in another *tuhr* than that in which the intercourse took place, and again recalls her, has intercourse with her,

Annotations.

dlxxxii—dlxxxiv. The divorce in which the wife cannot lawfully return to, or be recalled by, the divorcer, before being married again (by him) is termed "irrevocable or absolute." This occurs in six places or cases:—The divorce of an unenjoyed woman,—of a woman passed child-bearing,—of a girl not yet arrived at the age of menstruation,—of the woman who has been separated by *khulá*,† or *mubárát*,‡ and has not reclaimed the property for which the release was obtained (by her),—the sixth is the divorce of a woman thrice divorced, even though she was (in the interim) twice recalled, or twice married, or was once recalled and once married (by the divorcer). The divorce in which the wife can be recalled during, or before completion of, the *iddat*, without entering into a contract of marriage, is termed "revocable divorce." This is besides those above mentioned.—Mafátíh.

---

* *Sharáya ul-Islám*, p. 316.

† Release obtained by a wife from the marriage tie, by giving to the husband her dower, or other property as ransom for the freedom.—*Vide* Lecture XVI.

‡ Mutual release from the marriage tie.—*Vide* Lecture XVI.

and divorces her in a subsequent *tuhr*. She then is rendered unlawful to him till she has married another husband. If she should do so, and be released from him, and her first husband should remarry her, and repeat the series of divorces as at first, she would become a second time unlawful to him until married to another husband. And if this also was done, and she was again free, and the first husband remarries her (a third time), and repeats the series of divorces, she would become after the ninth (divorce) unlawful to him *for ever*.*

The *talák ul-iddat* does not take effect unless there has been connubial intercourse after each revocation.*

If the man divorces his wife before such intercourse, the repudiation would, indeed, be valid, but it would not be a *talák* or divorce of *iddat*.

DLXXXVI. In giving a divorce, it is required that the same be done with intention. *That* divorce, therefore, which is given without intention will not take effect, even though it were pronounced *expressly*. —Tahrír ul-Ahkám. *Vide* post, pp. 394 & 395. *Principle.*

DLXXXVII. The pillars, or essentials, of divorce, according to the *Sharáya ul-Islám*, are four, namely: 1, the divorcer; 2, the divorced; 3, form; and 4, testimony;† while according to the *Tahrír ul-Ahkám*, they are three, *viz.*, the divorcer, the divorced, and the subject. *Principle.*

On the Divorcer.

DLXXXVIII. In the divorcer, four conditions are necessarily required: 1, puberty, 2, understanding, 3, choice or free-will, and 4, design or intention.† *Principle.*

ANNOTATIONS.

dlxxxviii. A divorcer is required to have majority, understanding, choice or free-will, and design or intention.—Tahrír ul-Ahkám, so also the Mafátíh.

---

* *Sharáya ul-Islám*, p. 316.

† *Vide Sharáya ul-Islám*, pp. 311, 312, 314 & 316.—B. Dig., Part II, pp. 107, 109, 113 & 117.

Consequently,—

Principle. DLXXXIX. No regard is to be paid to the words of a boy who is under age, and indiscreet.

No regard is to be had to the words of a boy who is under ten years of age. With respect to one who has arrived at the tenth (year of his age) with understanding, and has divorced (his wife) according to *sunnat*, or traditions, there is one report that the repudiation is legal, but the report is not well authenticated.* And,—

Principle. DXC. If the guardian of such a one should divorce (the wife of his ward), the act would be invalid.*

Because the right to divorce belongs exclusively to a husband; and the inhibition which the law imposes on a minor is one which in the natural course of things will soon be removed.† However,—

Principle. DXCI. If a minor should attain puberty, and be deficient in understanding, his guardian may divorce (his wife) when it becomes advisable with a due regard to his interests.†

Principle. DXCII. Divorce by an insane person is not valid, nor by one in a state of intoxication, nor by one who has lost the use of his faculties by a temporary stupor, or by drinking a narcotic, as there can be no real intention (in such cases), nor can a guardian divorce on behalf of one who is in a state of intoxication (*a*).†

(*a*.) Because the cause which prevents his own exercise of the power is likely soon to be removed, and he is for the time like one asleep.† But,—

Principle. DXCIII. A guardian may divorce for an insane person; and if he has no guardian, the *Sultán*, or any person to whom he may have delegated the superintendence of such matters, may (if necessary) divorce on behalf of the insane person.*

Annotations.

dxcii. Regard is not had to the divorce given by an insane person except in his lucid interval.—Tahrír ul-Ahkám.

The *walí*, or guardian, of an insane person can, however, divorce (his wife); and if there is no guardian, the *Sultán* or the person to whom he may have delegated the superintendence (of such matters), may divorce on behalf of the insane person, if necessary.—*Ibid.*

---

* *Vide Sharáya ul-Islám*, p. 311.

† *Sharáya ul-Islám*, p. 312.

DXCIV. Divorce given under compulsion is not valid (*b*).*

(*b.*) Three things are necessary to the establishment of compulsion: 1.—The compeller must be able to do what he threatens; 2.—There must be strong ground to apprehend that the compeller shall do what he threatens, if compliance with what he desires is refused; 3.—The threat must involve some serious injury to the compelled person himself, or to some one dear to him as his own soul—such as a father, or a child. It makes no difference whether the threat be of death, or wounding, or abuse, or beating. But in estimating the *quantum* of abuse which may be endured without amounting to compulsion, the places where the compeller and compelled are residing must be taken into consideration. A trifling injury is not sufficient to establish compulsion.* *Principle.*

DXCV. The design or intention is required for the validity (of a divorce), though an express form of words is also necessary; insomuch that divorce cannot take effect, if there is no intention on the part of the divorcer.* *Principle.*

As, for example, if the man was careless or asleep, or labouring under a mistake. And if a man forgetting that he has a wife, says—"my women are divorced," or "my wife is divorced" and should then recollect (that he is married), no separation would thereby take place. Or if, after divorcing (his wife), he should say "I did not intend it;" outwardly his assertion must be received and credited, though inwardly and in conscience he is bound by his intention, whatever it may really have been. This is the case, even though he should make some delay in explaining his intention, provided that the woman is still in her *iddat*, because it is a declaration of his intention.* So,— *Example.*

DXCVI. To effect a valid divorce, the divorcer must be adult and discreet, and he must pronounce it intentionally and of his free will. *Principle.*

ANNOTATIONS.

dxciv. Divorce given under compulsion does not take effect.—Tahrír ul-Ahkám.

dxcv. Intention is required in giving a divorce. So, when a man has pronounced the divorce by mistake, inadvertently, or when asleep, it will not take effect; so, also, when he is drunk or not in possession of his senses and faculties.—Tahrír ul-Ahkám.

---

* *Sharáya ul-Islám*. p. 312.

DXCVII. An absent person may lawfully appoint an agent to divorce his wife without any difference of opinion. So also may a husband who is present (with his wife), according to the most correct opinion.*

Principle.

Although the *Shaikh* has said that the appointment of a woman as her husband's agent to divorce herself would not be valid, yet it would seem that such an appointment is lawful.* Hence,—

Principle.

DXCVIII. A husband can lawfully appoint his own wife as his agent to divorce herself.*

If a man should say (to his wife) "Divorce thyself *thrice*," and she should do so *only once*, it has been said that the divorce would be void, while others insist that a single divorce would take effect. And so also if he should say "Divorce thyself *once*," and she should do so *three times*, it has been said that the divorce would be void; but here also others maintain that one would take effect; and this opinion is more in conformity with the general principles of the law.*

The Divorced,† or the subject of Divorce.

Principle.

DXCIX. The subject of divorce is every woman over whom a man (*i.e.*, the divorcer) has complete power under a permanent and valid contract of marriage.—Tahrír ul-Ahkám.

With respect to the (woman) divorced, there are five conditions.

Annotations.

dxcvii. It is not required that the husband should pronounce the divorce in the presence of, or directly to, his wife; for when the husband appointed an agent, and the latter pronounced the divorce in the absence of his or her client, it would be valid.—Tahrír ul-Ahkám.

dxcix, dc. For a woman (to be the subject of divorce) it is required that she be at *that* time a *wife* (of the divorcer).—Máfátíh.

If a man should say (to his wife) "I am repudiated to thee," the words would have no effect, as a man is not a fit subject of divorce.—Sharáya ul-Islám, p. 315.

* *Sharáya ul-Islám*, p. 12.

† The second pillar of divorce.—See *ante*, p. 393.

DC. The first condition is, that she must be (the divorcer's) *wife** (at the time).

Principle.

Because, if a man should divorce a woman whom he has enjoyed by virtue of a right of property, or if he should divorce a woman who was at the time a stranger to him, though he should subsequently be married to her, the divorce would have no effect ; so, also, if a man should suspend a divorce on marriage, (that is make it conditional on the occurrence of the event), the divorce would not be valid.*

DCI. The second condition is, that the woman be married by a permanent contract.* *Principle.*

For there can be no divorce of a legalized slave, or of a woman enjoyed under a *mutá,* or temporary contract, even though she be free.*

DCII. The third condition is, that she be not (*then*) in her courses, or in a *nifás*† after child-birth (*c*).* *Principle.*

(*c.*) The above condition is applicable only to a woman who has been enjoyed, and is ordinarily subject to the courses, and whose husband is present with her, or if absent, has not been away from her so long as to be assured that she has passed from the period of purity in which he had connubial intercourse with her to another such period.*

If a man should divorce his wife while they are both living in the same city, or he has been absent from her less than the time mentioned, and she is then in her courses, or in a *nifás,*† the divorce is void, whether he were aware of the fact or not.* But,—

If he has been absent from her so long as to feel assured that she must have passed from one period of purity to another, and he should then divorce her, the divorce would be quite valid, even though they both subsequently agree that she was actually in her courses at the time : so, also, if he should have departed from her during a period of purity in which he had not approached her matrimonially, her divorce would be valid.* And,—

DCIII. If a man should divorce a wife with whom he never had connubial intercourse, the divorce would be lawful, though she were actually in her courses at the time.* *Principle.*

---

* *Sharáya ul-Islám,* p. 312.

† See the foot-note at p. 391.

DCIV. The fourth condition is, that the woman be *mustabrát*,* or purified (*d*).†

Principle.

For if a man should divorce his wife during a *tuhr*, or period of purity, in which he has had connubial intercourse with her, the divorce would be ineffectual.†

(*d.*) The above condition is not required in a woman who is passed child-bearing (*yâïsah*), nor in one who has not attained puberty, or who is pregnant.†

With regard again to a *mustabarát*,* when three months have passed without any appearance of the monthly discharge, if such a one is divorced before the expiration of the three months, the divorce is without effect.†

Principle.

DCV. The fifth condition is, that the woman divorced be distinctly indicated (*e*).†

(*e.*) That is, by the man's saying "such a one is divorced," or by pointing her out in such a manner as to remove all doubt on the subject.†

Principle.

DCVI. If a man has only one wife, and should say "my wife is divorced," the divorce would be valid, as there is no room for ambiguity. But if he has two or more wives, and should say "my wife is divorced," then if he intended some one of them, the divorce is valid, and his explanation (of the one whom he intended) must be accepted.†

If, again, he had no particular one in his mind, (or he used the words without any positive intention), some of the doctors maintain that the words would be entirely nugatory for want of distinct indication, while others insist that there would be a valid divorce, and that the particular woman must be picked out by lot. This (last) opinion seems more agreeable to the general principles of the law.†

Principle.

DCVII. If a man, supposing a stranger to be his wife, should say to her "Thou art divorced," his wife would not be divorced, for the man must be assumed to have intended the person addressed.†

---

* That is purified from the menstrual flux, and has had no sexual intercourse with her husband since the purification. The object of this condition seems to be to prevent a confusion of seed and the consequent doubt of paternity. if the woman should marry again, and have a child.—Note by Mr. Neil Baillie.

† *Sharáya ul-Islám*, pp. 312 & 313.

DCVIII. It is necessary that divorce be given affecting the whole person of the wife. Consequently, should the husband say "thy hand, leg, or hair is divorced," it shall not be operative.—Tahrír ul-Ahkám. *Principle.*

*On Form.**

As a general rule, marriage being an act of chastity, favored by the law, and in its own nature not admitting of being dissolved, it is necessary in taking off or removing the tie to adhere strictly to the terms of legal permission.†

DCIX. The form of the words especially appointed for dissolution of the marriage tie is—"Thou art divorced," or "such a one, or this person is divorced," or any similar word indicative of the individual who is intended to be divorced.† *Principle.*

DCX. Divorce cannot be effected in writing, nor in any other language than the *Arabic*, when there is ability to pronounce the (Arabic) words especially appointed, nor by signs except where the party is unable to speak. So,— *Principle.*

DCXI. If the husband is dumb, divorce may be effected by any signs indicative of his purpose.† And,— *Principle.*

ANNOTATIONS.

dcix. The express divorce is given by a single term, which is by saying, "thou art divorced," or "this person, or such a one, is divorced," and the like.—Tahrír ul-Ahkám.

The approved opinion is that the utterance (of divorce) be *express* or unequivocal—as "thou art divorced," and the like.—Mafátíh.

dcx. Being unable to speak *Arabic*, should the husband expressly pronounce the divorce in another language, it would take effect, but not if he is able (to speak Arabic).—*Ibid.*

dcxi, dcxii. In like manner, divorce would not take effect without speaking, unless the divorcer was unable to speak,—as a dumb man, for instance, would give divorce by a sign; but being able to speak, if a man, whether absent or present, writes out the sentence of divorce, it will not be operative; while being unable to speak, if he writes out the sentence of divorce, it will take effect.—Tahrír ul-Ahkám.

---

* The third pillar of divorce.—See *ante*, p. 393.

† *Sheráya ul-Islám*, p. 314.

Principle. DCXII. Though divorce cannot be given in writing by one who is present and able to pronounce (the proper words), yet, being unable to speak, if he (the divorcer) writes them, thereby intending divorce, it is valid and effective.*

Some doctors are of opinion that divorce takes place by writing if the husband were absent from his wife, but this opinion is not to be relied upon.*

Principle. DCXIII. Divorce given implicatively or ambiguously does not take effect whether intended or not. Tahrír ul Ahkám.

Illustrations. If a man should say (to his wife) "Thou art vacated," or "free," or "the reins are on thy neck," or "betake yourself to thy people," or "thou art absolutely separated," or "thou art unlawful or cut off,"† nothing (*i.e.*, no divorce) would take place, whether the same be intended or not.‡

If a man should say (to his wife) "count," intending divorce thereby, it is maintained that there would be a valid divorce, and there is a tradition to that effect, recorded by *Halbí* and *Abú Abdullah* (on whom be peace); but this has been disputed by many of the doctors, whose opinion is more in accordance with the general principles of the law.‡

Principle. DCXIV. If the husband of a woman being asked "if he has divorced his wife," say "yes," there would be a valid divorce.

Thus the *Sharáya ul-Islám* :—"It is said that if a person were asked 'Hast thou divorced such a person,' and he should answer 'yes,' there would be a valid divorce. But if the question were—'Hast thou separated, or vacated, or released?' and he should answer 'yes,' then nothing would follow."‡

Principle. DCXV. Divorce, in respect of its form, must be entirely free from any condition or description.‡

"For" (says the author of the *Sharáya ul-Islám*) "I take no account of those who think differently from me (on the subject)." And,—

---

* *Sharáya ul-Islám*, p. 314.

† According to the Hanífites, however, divorce, if intended, would take place by any of these terms. *Vide* pp. 412 & 413 of Lecture XIII. delivered by me in 1873.

‡ *Sharáya ul-Islám*, p. 314.

DCXVI. Even though the husband, in pronouncing the divorce, should merely explain himself by saying "twice," or "thrice," only a single divorce would take effect.* *Principle.*

Some insist that it (*i.e.*, the above) would be void. Others, however, maintain that a single divorce would take effect by reason of the word "divorced," the rest being surplusage; and this latter opinion is supported by the more generally received of the two traditions.*

DCXVII. Should the husband say to his wife "thou art divorced according to the *Sunnat*," the divorce would be valid, if she were then in her purity (*tuhr*). *Principle.*

Thus the *Sharáya ul-Islám*:—"If he should say 'thou art divorced for the *Sunnat*,' the divorce would be valid, provided the wife were *then* in purity; and so also if he said 'for the *badát*.' It were, however, better to say that (in the latter case) divorce would not take effect; because we do not allow that kind of divorce; so the latter is without meaning. Further, if a husband should say (to his wife) 'Thou art divorced this very instant, if divorce can be effected upon thee,' the *Shaikh* has said that there would be no divorce by reason of its being made dependent on the condition; and this is right, if the divorcer were not aware (of the woman's state at the time); but if he knew that she was in a state to be legally divorced, effect should be given to his words; for though there is a condition in appearance, there is none in reality."* Hence,—

DCXVIII. If a husband should say to his wife "Thou art divorced at this instant, if divorce can be effected upon thee," she would be divorced if the husband knows that she was then in a state to be legally divorced. *Principle.*

DCXIX. If the husband should say (to his wife) "Thou art divorced the most just, or the most perfect, or the best, or the best and worst, of divorces," the divorce would be valid, as it is not impaired by the words superadded.* *Principle.*

---

* *Sharáya ul-Islám*, pp. 314 & 315.

*On Testimony.**

DCXX. It is necessary that two (just) witnesses be present and hear the divorce given, *Principle.* whether they are called upon to attest it or not.†

DCXXI. It is also necessary for the validity of a divorce, that the witnesses hear the wording of the divorce; so that if they are merely present, and do not attest, divorce does not take effect, though all other conditions may have been complied with. Hence,—

Principle. DCXXII. No divorce would take place if there be only one witness to it, though he be a just man, nor even with two witnesses if they are not just, or are reprobates; but it is necessary that there be present two witnesses of known probity.†

Some of the doctors however, think it sufficient that the witnesses are *Muslims;* but the first opinion is better founded on traditional authority.†

Principle. DCXXIII. It is necessary that the witnesses be present *together* when divorce is given.—Tahrír ul-Ahkám.

Consequently,—

Principle. DCXXIV. If one of the witnesses should testify to the constitution (of the divorce), and then the other testify to it *separately* from the first, divorce would not take effect.†

ANNOTATIONS.

dcxx. It is necessary that two witnesses of known integrity be present; and hear the divorce pronounced, or see the writing, or giving a sign in the case of (the divorcer) being dumb or unable to speak.—Mafátíh.

dcxx—dcxxvi. Divorce does not take effect unless the same be (pronounced) in the presence of two just witnesses who should hear (the utterance thereof), whether they attest it or not. The testimony of women, whether given separately or in conjunction with a man, is not accepted.—Tahrír ul-Ahkám.

* See fourth pillar of divorce. See *ante*, p. 393.

† *Sharáya ul-Islám*, p. 316.

DCXXV. But when they testify to the acknowledgment of the fact, it is not necessary that their testimony should be given *together*.* Yet if one should testify to the fact of the divorce, and the other to the acknowledgment of it, their testimony could not be received.* *Principle.*

DCXXVI. Testimony of women, whether they be alone or together with men, cannot be received in respect of divorce.* *Principle.*

DCXXVII. If a man should divorce his wife without witnesses, and then divorce her again when witnesses are present, the first divorce would go for nothing.* *Principle.*

DCXXVIII. When a divorce is given in the presence of witnesses, it takes effect provided that the appropriate words are employed.* *Principle.*

Divorce by a Sick Man.

DCXXIX. It is abominable for a sick man to divorce (his wife); yet if he should do so, the divorce is valid, and he would inherit from her (if she should happen to die) during the *iddat* for a revocable divorce. But he has no such right if the divorce were absolute (*báïn*), or her death should not occur till after the expiration of *iddat*.† *Principle.*

DCXXX. The wife (on the other hand) has a right to inherit from him if he should die at any time within a year from the divorce, whether it were revocable or absolute, provided that (in the *Principle.*

ANNOTATIONS.

dcxxix. It is abominable for a sick man to divorce (his wife); yet, if he divorce her, it is valid. They will inherit from each other if the wife returned or was recalled during her *iddat*. But they shall not inherit either before or after the *iddat*, if the divorce was irrevocable.—Tahrír ul-Ahkám.

dcxxx. The woman will inherit from the husband in the irrevocable as well as revocable divorce during one year from the date of the divorce.

* *Sharáya ul-Islám*, p. 316.

† *Vide* Lecture XVII.

meantime) the woman has not married, nor the man has recovered from the disease in which he had divorced her. But if he should recover, fall sick again, and then die, she would not inherit, unless she were *still* in her *iddat* for a revocable divorce.*

Principle. If he (the sick man) say "I divorced her three times when in good health," his word is to be received, and she is not to inherit from him, though it would seem that no credit ought to be given to his word as against her.*

Principle. DCXXXI. If a sick man should slander his wife and should go through the form of the *lián*, or imprecation, against her, then she would be absolutely divorced by the *lián*,† and would have no right of inheritance in virtue of the special effect of a divorce in sickness.*

But the question is—whether she should have such a right on account of the suspicion which attaches to his slandering her in such circumstances? This question has been answered in the affirmative. The usual effect of divorce in sickness is, however, given (to his act) without any regard to the suspicion attaching to it.*

Principle. DCXXXII. A wife loses also her right of inheritance if separated on her own solicitation, under a *khulá*, or under a *mubárát*.‡

Thus the *Sharáya ul-Islám*:—"There is also a doubt regarding her right to inherit when divorced on her own solicitation. And here it is more in accordance with the general principles of law to say that her right of inheritance is lost. So also when she has been released from the marriage tie by a *khulá*, or *mubárát*."‡

ANNOTATIONS.

Provided, in the mean time, she did not marry, or the divorcer did not recover. But if he recovered, again fell sick, and died within a year, or if the woman married another man before or after a year, she will not inherit.—Tahrír ul-Ahkám.

---

* *Sharáya ul-Islám*, pp. 317 & 318.

† According to the *Shiahs*, this is the immediate effect of *lián*, or imprecation; while according to the Hanífites, there is no separation of the parties without a divorce by the husband, or a decree by the judge.

‡ *Vide* Lecture XVI.

LECTURE XVI.

ON KHULÁ, MUBÁRÁT, ZIHÁR, ÍLÁ AND LIÁN

On Khulá.

In the event of disagreement between a husband and wife, or for any other cause, the latter, on payment of a compensation or ransom to the former, is permitted by law to obtain from him a release from the marriage tie. Such release is technically termed "*khulá*."

DCXXXIII. The pillars or essentials are: the *kháli*, or the grantor of release; the *mukhtaliah*, or the woman obtaining the release; the form; and the two exchanges.—Tahrír ul-Ahkám. *Principle.*

DCXXXIV. The conditions required in the *kháli*, or the grantor of the release, are four: puberty, sanity, freedom of choice, and intention.* Hence,— *Principle.*

DCXXXV. To effect a valid *khulá*, or release from the marriage tie, the man granting it must be adult in age, sane, free in choice, and it must be granted intentionally.*—Consequently,— *Principle.*

DCXXXVI. No *khulá* is valid if granted by a boy under puberty, or by an insane person, or by one acting under compulsion, or in a drunken state, or in a paroxysm of such anger as to take away all real intention.* *Principle.*

ANNOTATIONS.

dcxxxiv, dcxxxv. *Khulá* does not take place if the grantor of it be a minor, though he be a *muráhik*, or one approaching puberty, and grant it with the permission of his guardian or another person; not also if he is an insane. It is not also effected under compulsion, nor in a drunken state, nor in a paroxysm of anger such as to take away all intention.—Tahrír ul-Ahkám.

* *Sharáya ul-Islám*, pp. 329 & 330.

The author of the *Tahrír ul-Ahkám* says:—"The *khulá* granted by an idiot is valid, yet if the ransom is delivered into his hands, the woman is not exonerated from the liability, so she must pay it to his *walí* or guardian."

DCXXXVII. If *khulá* is considered in the light of a divorce (*talák*), it is void when entered into by a guardian for his ward; but if *khulá* is not a divorce, it is valid when given by a guardian for something in exchange.*

Principle. **DCXXXVIII. On the part of the *mukhtaliah*, or the woman receiving a *khulá*, it is required, that she remain *táhirah*, or pure, no connubial intercourse having taken place during (that) *tuhr*, or purity,—in case she be a woman whose marriage has been consummated, who is not past child-bearing, and whose husband is present with her. It is also requisite that she has some aversion to her husband.***

Principle. DCXXXIX. *Khulá* of a pregnant woman is valid, even if there should be some appearance of a discharge of blood, as divorce would be valid in such circumstances, though it might be said that the courses are upon her. So, also, of a woman whose marriage has not been consummated, though she were actually subject to them at the time.*

Principle. DCXL. A woman who is past child-bearing may be the subject of a *khulá*, though connubial intercourse would have taken place during the *tuhr* or period of purity* (in which it is effected).

ANNOTATIONS.

dcxxxviii. As regards the *mukhtaliah*, or the woman obtaining release from the marriage tie, it is required that she should obtain it, during a *tuhr* or period of purity in which the husband did not approach her, in the case of her being an enjoyed wife and not past child-bearing, not a minor, not also pregnant, and her husband being present with her, but not otherwise.—Tahrír ul-Ahkám.

dcxxxix. The *khulá* of a pregnant woman is valid even though she be menstruating, in the same manner as her divorce becomes valid.—*Ibid.*

dcxl. The *khulá* of a woman who is passed child-bearing, or is a minor, or is pregnant, is valid, though connubial intercourse has taken place with her at the time.—*Ibid.*

* *Sharáya ul-Islám*, pp. 329 & 330.

The Form of Khulá.

DCXLI. It is required that it be express and given solely by the word "*khulá*" or "*talák*" (divorce); and that it be free from any condition.—Tahrír ul-Ahkám. *Principle.*

Illustration. As if a man should say "I have released thee from the marriage tie for so much (*khulátu-ki alá kazá*)," or "such a one is released from the marriage tie for so much (*fulánatun mukhtaliatun alá kazá*)." If it be asked whether release from the marriage tie (*khulá*) is effected by this (*i.e.*, the above) alone, the tradition is in the affirmative. The *Shaikh*, however, insists that it is not effected by those words unless they are followed up by *talák*, or divorce.*

DCXLII. If a man should enter into a *khulá* and stipulate for a power to revoke it, the *khulá* would not be valid. So, also, divorce for an exchange would be invalid with a like condition.* *Principle.*

There is no doubt that it (the *khulá*) is not effected by the expression "I have liberated thee for a ransom (*fudaitu-ki*)" without the addition of the word *talák* (divorce); nor by the expression "I have cancelled thee (*fasakhtuki*)," "I have separated thee (*ábantu-ki*)," nor by "I have cut thee off (*battaktu-ki*)," nor by "*takail* (dissolution)."* So,—

Supposing that the word "*khulá*" is sufficient, another question rises whether it is cancellation of the marriage contract or a divorce. *Murtazá* says, "It is a divorce," and this opinion is supported by traditions. The *Shaikh*, however, appears to consider it as a cancellation; and i his view of it no account thereof can be taken in the number of divorces.*

DCXLIII. Divorce, when given for a ransom, takes effect absolutely, though no use has been made of the word *khulá*.* *Principle.*

DCXLIV. If a woman should ask her husband for a divorce in exchange for something, and he should grant her *khulá*, or release her from the marriage tie, without using the word divorce (*talák*), it would take effect.* *Principle.*

---

* *Sharáya ul-Islám*, pp. 329 & 330.

DCXLV. When a *khulá* has become valid, the husband has no power of revocation, the wife, however, may reclaim the ransom during the subsistence of the *iddat*; and if she should do so, he may then revoke the *khulá* if he please.* So,—

Principle.

DCXLVI. In the case of the ransom not being reclaimed before completion of the *iddat*, the *khulá* becomes *thereafter* an absolute divorce.*

Principle.

A *mukhatalah*, or woman released by *khulá*, is not affected by a divorce pronounced *after* the *khulá;* because the latter is subject to the condition of the *ransom* being reclaimed. Yes, if the woman should reclaim the ransom (within the *iddat*), the husband may lawfully revoke (the *khulá*), and *then* divorce her *de novo.** But,—

Principle.

DCXLVII. If the woman is one who should not observe *iddat*,—that is, if she is unenjoyed, past child-bearing, or an infant,—the husband cannot at all revoke the *khulá*, whether the *khulá* was given by the word *talák*, or by any other word, and whether he returned the exchange or not.—Tahrír ul-Ahkám.

Principle.

DCXLVIII. In *khulá* it is necessary that there should be two just witnesses to it, and that there be intention, as in divorce.*—Tahrír ul-Ahkám.

On the Exchange or Ransom for Khulá.

Principle.

DCXLIX. As respects the exchange or ransom, it is required that the same be known by sight, or

---

ANNOTATIONS.

dcxlv. When a man has granted *khulá*, he cannot revoke it, unless within the *iddat*, the woman should reclaim what she gave as an exchange for the *khulá*.—Tahrír ul-Ahkám.

dcxlviii. It is further required for the validity of the contract that it should be entered into before two witnesses present at the time. It is also necessary that it be free from conditions.

When the husband grants a *khulá* to his wife for a thousand, without expressing the meaning and intention, the *khulá* is invalid.—Sharáya ul-Islám, p. 329.

---

* *Sharáya ul-Islám*, p. 331.

description, so that there be no ignorance respecting its quantity, description and species; and that it be *mál* or property (with respect to a *musalmán*).—Tahrír ul-Ahkám.

DCL. Whatever may be validly given as dower,* is also valid as the ransom of *khulá;* and there is no limit (to the amount or quantity) of the same, so that it may lawfully exceed whatever was given to the woman as her dower, or on any other account.† Hence,— *Principle.*

DCLI. If the ransom is something the property in which is unlawful to a *musalmán*, as wine, for instance, it is invalid.† *Principle.*

If the *khulá* was for vinegar, and it proves to be wine, the transaction is valid, but the husband is entitled to have that quantity of vinegar.†

Where, however, the ransom is a fœtus, cf which a beast or a female slave is pregnant, the *khulá* is not valid.†

DCLII. When a ransom is not produced, its kind, quality and quantity must be mentioned; but if produced, mere inspection is sufficient. When it is money, it must be paid in the coin most prevalent in the city, unless some particular currency is mentioned, when it must be paid in that.† *Principle.*

DCLIII. The ransom may be disbursed by the woman herself, or by her agent (*walí*), or by one who has become her security for it, with her permission.† *Principle.*

ANNOTATIONS.

dcl. Anything that can validly be a dower can validly be a ransom, whether it be a thing itself or usufructuary,—as suckling, *hizánat*, maintenance, and the like.—Mafátíh.

dclvi. There is no limit of ransom; but it is necessary that the same should be known in order to be capable of delivery.—*Ibid.*

---

* See *ante*, p. 352.

† *Sharáya ul-Islám*, p. 329.

But whether it may be paid by a mere voluntary, is liable to doubt, the better opinion being against such payment.*

If the ransom (of *khulá*) be the suckling of the husband's child, it is valid, provided that the time during which the suckling is to last is distinctly specified.*

So, also, if a man should divorce his wife in exchange for the child's maintenance (the transaction would be valid), subject to the condition that the quantity of the food and clothing which may be required, and the time for which they are to be provided, are distinctly specified.*

If (in either of the last two cases) the child should die before completion of the time, the divorcer would be entitled to a compensation for so much of it as would remain unexpired, namely, the hire of a like (nurse), if the ransom were the suckling of the infant; but if it were the infant's maintenance, the value of the food and clothing that would have been required for him for such period.*

If a husband should enter into a *khulá* with his wife for a consideration sufficiently described, and which, when delivered, does not come up to the description, he may return what has been so delivered, and demand its exchange for something corresponding to the description.*

So, also, if the thing delivered be blemished, he may return it, and claim an exact similar unblemished thing, or its value; or he may retain the thing, and require a compensation for the blemish.*

Principle.

DCLIV. If a *khulá* is made with two women for one ransom, the *khulá* is valid, and the ransom is payable by them equally.*

If two women should say (to their husband), "Divorce us for a thousand," and he divorces only one of them, he is entitled to half the sum; but if he should subsequently divorce the other, the divorce would be revocable, and he would have no title to the remainder on account of his delay in responding to what required an immediate answer.*

---

* *Sharáya ul-Islám*, pp. 329 & 330.

DCLV. If a man enters into a *khulá* with his wife for a specific article which belongs to another person, the *khulá* is valid, and the husband entitled to the value of the article, or something similar to it, if it belong to the class of similars. *Principle.*

Thus the *Sharáya ul-Islám*:—"If a man should enter into a *khulá* with his wife for a specific article which proves to be the property of another, it has been said that the *khulá* is void; but it were better to say that it were valid, and the man entitled to the value of the specific article, or something similar to it, if it belong to the class of similars."*

DCLVI. It is lawful to appoint a *wakíl*, or agent, in *khulá* on behalf of the woman, to ask divorce from the husband, to fix the amount of the exchange or ransom, and to deliver and pay the same; also one on behalf of the man, to stipulate for the exchange, to take possession of the same, and to effect the divorce.*— *Principle.*

DCLVII. If the exchange is destroyed before possession thereof was taken (by the husband), the right thereto is not lost, the woman is bound to give property similar to that (destroyed), or the value thereof, if there is nothing similar thereto.* *Principle.*

So also the *Tahrír ul-Ahkám*:—"When the husband granted *khulá* for a property, and it was destroyed before being taken possession of (by him), the woman is bound to give property similar to the one destroyed, or the value thereof, if there is nothing similar."—Tahrír ul-Ahkám.

DCLVIII. When a woman has appointed an agent for her *khulá* generally, the ransom must not exceed her proper dower, to be paid in the coin of the place. And, in like manner, when the husband appoints an agent for *khulá* in general terms, and the woman's agent gives more than the proper dower, the ransom is void, and the divorce takes effect revocably without the agent being responsible. And if the husband's agent should grant the *khulá* for less than the proper dower, the *khulá* would be void. So, also, if he should divorce her for such a ransom, the divorce would not take effect, as he acted contrary to his instructions.* *Principle.*

---

* *Sharáya ul-Islám*, p. 330.

DCLIX. When a woman's father says to her husband —"Divorce her, and thou art free from her dower," and he does divorce her, the divorce is valid *revocably,* and she is neither obliged to discharge her husband from the payment of the dower, nor is her father responsible.*

Principle.

Principle. DCLX. If a stranger obtained *khulá* for a woman from her husband, it is valid, provided it was with her consent and property, because the man acted only as her *wakíl,* or agent.*

Principle. DCLXI. If a sick woman† obtains *khulá* for her proper dower (*mahr-ul-mithl*), or for less, it is valid; but if for more, the excess must not exceed one-third of the whole of her estate.—Tahrír ul-Ahkám.

So also the *Sharáya ul-Islám*:—"If a woman should enter into a *khulá* during her death-illness, the transaction would be valid, though the ransom exceed a third (of her estate). But in respect thereof it is maintained (by some of the doctors), that any excess over the proper dower (*mahr-ul-mithl*) must come out of one-third (of her estate), and this opinion is in accordance with the principles of the law."‡

Khulá, granted by a sick man for the (woman's) proper dower, or without it, is valid, since he is competent to grant a divorce without an exchange.—Tahrír ul-Ahkám.

The conditions which nullify *khulá* are those which the contract itself does not require.‡

For instance, if the husband should say "If you revoke, I revoke," this condition would not nullify the contract, as it is one which the *khulá* requires. So, also, if the wife should stipulate for a right to reclaim the consideration, (the *khulá* would still be valid). But if the husband should say "I have given you a *khulá,* if you wish it," the *khulá* would not be *valid,* though she should wish (the same); for this is not a condition which the contract requires; so, also, if he should say "If thou wilt be responsible to me for a thousand," or "If thou wilt give me," or words to the like effect; so, also, if he should say, "when," or "whenever," or "at any time," (the *khulá* would not be valid).‡

---

* *Sharáya ul-Islám,* pp. 329—331.

† Here by a "sick woman" is meant a wife in her death-illness.

‡ *Sharáya ul-Islám,* p. 331.

The Rules of Khulá.

These may be gathered from the following cases :—

DCLXII. If a man should compel his wife into (an arrangement for) a ransom, he would do what is unlawful; and if he should thereupon divorce her, the divorce would be valid without any obligation (on her part) to deliver the ransom to him. This divorce, however, would be revocable.* *Principle.*

DCLXIII. If a husband should grant a *khulá* to his wife, while their dispositions and tempers are still in harmony, the *khulá* would not be valid, and he would not become the proprietor of the ransom. And if he should divorce for an exchange in like circumstances, he would not become the proprietor of the exchange, but the divorce would be valid, though with liberty to him to revoke.* *Principle.*

If a woman has been guilty of any profligate act, her husband may lawfully annoy her to ransom herself. It has been said, however, that this is abrogated, and is no longer permitted.*

DCLXIV. When a *khulá* has become valid, the husband has no power of revocation; the wife, however, may reclaim the ransom (at any time) *during* the *iddat*, and when she does so, the husband may revoke (the *khulá*) if he please.* *Principle.*

DCLXV. If a man should grant a *khulá* to his wife with stipulation for revoking it, the *khulá* would not be valid.* *Principle.*

ANNOTATIONS.

dclxiv. When the contract for ransoming has become valid, the husband has no right to revoke; the wife, however, can reclaim the ransom *before* completion of the *iddat;* and, upon her doing so, the husband is competent to revoke (the contract) if he please.—*Mafátih.*

---

* *Sharáya ul-Islám*, p. 331.

Mubárát, in law, signifies mutual liberation, or release from the marriage tie.

Principle. DCLXVI. *Mubárát* is like *khulá*, with this exception or difference, that *mubárát* is founded upon the mutual aversion of husband and wife, while *khulá* is founded on the aversion of the wife alone; and that in *mubárát* the husband can take (in exchange for it) no more than what the wife had received from him, any excess being unlawful, while in *khulá* it is quite lawful.*

According to the general agreement,—

Principle. DCLXVII. In *mubárát* the use of the word *talák* (divorce) is necessary to effect separation.

Thus the *Sharáya ul-Islám*:—"We are all agreed that in *mubárát* the word *talák* is necessary to effect a separation between the parties, while (with regard to its being required) in *khulá*, there is a difference of opinion."*

Principle. DCLXVIII. *Mubárát* is effected by the husband's saying "*Báritu-ki alá kazá, fa anti tálikun*" (I have liberated thee for so much, so thou art liberated).*

Annotations.

dclxviii. The form (of *mubárát* as well as of *khulá*) should be express, as: "*khalátu-ki li-káza*, or *alá kazá* (I have released thee from the marriage tie for this or upon this);" "*Báritu-ki li-káza* or *alá kazá* (I have liberated thee for this or upon this);" or the like.—Mafátih.

Murábát is effected in the case of mutual aversion (between husband and wife), as by the husband's saying "*Báritu-ki, ala kazá, anti tálikun* (I have liberated thee for this, thou art divorced);" but if he should divorce her without using the word *mubárát*, an absolute divorce would take place, and the exchange must be redelivered; but if the word *mubárát* is alone used without the word *talák*, then *talák*, or divorce, shall not take place according to the *Ijmáa* or concurrence of the Learned.—Tahrír ul-Ahkám.

In *mubárát* it is not lawful for the husband to take more than what he gave her.—*Ibid.*

---

* *Sharáya ul-Islám*, p. 333.

In *khulá* and *mubárát*, the conditions or requisites are the same as in *talák*, or divorce, and each of them is a *talák* for an exchange. There are, however, additional requisites, one of them is the wife's being willing to give the exchange; another condition, which is peculiar to the *khulá*, is her aversion to the husband, as without it the *talák* will not be valid, and the husband will not be the proprietor of the exchange. There are two other conditions which are peculiar to the *mubárát*,—one of them is the mutual aversion, and the (other is the) exchange not exceeding the (woman's) dower. If there is no aversion, then, according to the generally received opinion, the *talák* is valid, but the exchange void: such also is the case when the husband compels his wife to give the exchange, and grants a divorce for it; but when he gives a *khulá* for it, the same becomes void by reason of the exchange being so.—*Mafátíh.*

Mubárát is founded upon the mutual aversion of the husband and wife; and it is a condition that this (*i.e.*, *mubárát*) be followed by the word *talák* (divorce), insomuch that if the husband should stop at the word "*mubárát*," no separation would thereby take effect* (between the spouses). And,—

DCLXIX. If, instead of "*Báritu-ki*," he should say "*Fásakhtu-ki*," or "*abantu-ki*" or any other (like) expression, the same would be equally effective, if followed by the word "*talák*," since it is the utterance (of that word) alone which is required for the separation, and nothing else.* *Principle.*

Even if the husband should shorten (the sentence) into "Thou art divorced for so much," it would be valid, and there will be a *mubárát*, or mutual release, effected, as it is an expression of divorce for an exchange with mutual repulsion between the spouses.*

DCLXX. The same conditions are required in the man and woman entering into a *mubárát*, as those entering into a *khulá*.* *Principle.*

ANNOTATIONS.

dclxx. The conditions with respect to the parties mutually released are the same as those with respect to the giver and taker of the *khulá*. Tahrír ul-ahkám.

* *Sharáya ul-Islám*, p. 333.

Principle. DCLXXI. Divorce for an exchange or ransom is absolute, so that the husband has no power to revoke it, unless the wife should reclaim the ransom, which she can do during the *iddat;* and if she should avail herself of the right, he may also revoke the divorce.*

Principle. DCLXXII. After the expiration of the *iddat,* none of them can revoke or reclaim.—Tahrír ul-Ahkám.

On Zihár.

Principle. DCLXXIII. *Zihár* is repudiating one's wife by likening her to the back of his mother, or of any other woman related to him within the prohibited degrees, not by affinity, but by consanguinity, or fosterage. By such likening separation takes place, which would be absolute, unless the sin is expiated for.*

Principle. DCLXXIV. The form must be express, as if the husband should say "Thou art on me (or to me) like the back of my mother;" so also if he should say "this person," or "my wife," or "such a person" (is on me like the back of my mother).—Tahrír ul-Ahkám.

So also the *Sharáya ul-Islám:*—"As respects the form, it is as if one should say (to his wife) 'Thou art on me like the back of my mother;' so, also, if he should say 'This person,' (or make use of any other word indicative of the particular individual), 'is on me like the back of my mother,'* (the *zihár* would be constituted)."

ANNOTATIONS.

dclxxi. In *mubárát,* an absolute divorce takes place as in the *khulá,* unless the exchange is reclaimed by the woman within the *iddat;* in which case it may be revoked during the *iddat,* provided the husband did not marry a fourth wife, or the sister of the divorced (wife).—Tahrír ul-Ahkám.

* *Sharáya ul-Islám,* p. 333.

The particular word of *connection* is of no consequence; so that if the man should say "thou art *to* me," or "*with* me," it would make no difference.*

But if the man should liken her to the *hand* of his mother, or to her *hair*, or to her *belly*, it has been said that there should be no *zihár*, though there is a weak tradition in favor of its taking effect in such a case accordingly.*

If the likening were to any other than his mother, in any part of her person, but the back, there is no doubt there would be no *zihár*.*

According to general agreement, *zihár* takes place by likening (the wife to the back of the mother).* However,—

DCLXXV. If the man should liken his wife to the back of another woman who is one of those with whom marriage is for ever prohibited, the *zihár* would take place.—Tahrír ul-Ahkám. *Principle.*

So also the *Sharáya ul-Islám*:—"If, again, the man should liken her to the back of one of the women related to him within the prohibited degrees of *consanguinity*, or *fosterage*, there are two traditions on the subject, and according to the most generally received of these, *zihár* would take effect."—p. 333. Hence,—

DCLXXVI. If the man should liken his wife to a woman prohibited to him only by *affinity*, even though the prohibition were perpetual (*b*), *zihár* would by no means take effect.* *Principle.*

(*b*.) As a wife's mother, or the daughter of an enjoyed wife, or the wife of a father or son.† Such also would be the case if he likened the wife to her sister, or to her aunt, maternal or paternal, or if he said "like the back of my brother, or my father, or my paternal uncle," nothing would result (therefrom); so, also, if the woman should say "thou art on me like the back of my father, or my mother."*

---

* *Sharáya ul-Islám*, pp. 333 & 334.

† *Tahrir ul-Ahkám.*

Principle. DCLXXVII. As respects the *muzáhir*, or the husband uttering the *zihár*, it is required that he be adult, perfectly sane, have freedom of choice, and intention.—Tahrír ul-Ahkam.

So also the *Tahrír ul-Ahkám* :—" With respect to the *muzáhir*, the requisites are the same as in divorce,—that is puberty, sanity, free choice, and intention."*

Consequently,—

Principle. DCLXXVIII. The *zihár* by an infant, by an insane person, by one acting under compulsion, or by one temporarily incapable of intention through drunkenness, stupor, or a paroxysm of passion,* is invalid.

If one should intend divorce by *zihár*, there would be neither divorce for want of the proper word *talák* (divorce), nor *zihár* for want of intention.*

Zihár by a eunuch is valid, if we say that dalliance short of connubial intercourse is prohibited by it, so, also, it is valid when pronounced by an infidel, or a slave.*

Principle. DCLXXIX. With regard to the *muzáhirah*, or the woman who is subject to the *zihár*, it is a condition that she have been married by contract.*

Accordingly *Zihár* cannot take effect with reference to one who is a stranger (to the *muzáhir* at the time), though he should suspend it, or make it dependent on his marrying her.*

Principle. DCLXXX. It is also a condition that the woman be *táhirah*, or pure, in that *tuhr*, having no connubial intercourse (during it), and her husband be present with her, and that she be of an age to be subject to the courses.*

Annotations.

dclxxx & dclxxxi. It is also a condition that the *muzáhir* be *married* to the woman ; that she be a *táhirah* having no connubial intercourse during that *tuhr* ; that the husband be present with her ; and that she be not an infant, nor *yás*, nor pregnant.—Tahrír ul-Ahkám.

---

* *Sharáya ul-Islám*, pp. 334 & 335.

If any of these conditions is wanting, the *zihár* is valid, though they were on her at the time.*

With regard to a woman married by a temporary contract (*mutá*), there are various opinions; but according to *that* which is best supported by authority, *zihár* may take effect on such woman.* *Principle.*

DCLXXXI. It is a condition that two just persons be present when *zihár* is pronounced, and hear the words of the *muzáhir*, (that is, the wording of *zihár* uttered by the husband), and that the *zihár* take effect immediately (*c*). *Principle.*

(*c*.) So that, if the effect be suspended till the expiration of the month, or entering upon a Friday, there would be no *zihár* according to the best opinions.*

On the important effects of Zihár.

DCLXXXII. When *zihár* has taken place with its conditions, it is unlawful for the husband to have connubial intercourse (with the wife) before expiation.—Tahrír ul-Ahkám. Thus,— *Principle.*

The *muzáhir* is prohibited from having connubial intercourse until he has made expiation,—whether the expiation be by emancipation, by fasting, or by feeding the poor; and if he should have connubial intercourse with her (that is, if he break the prohibition) during the fast, he must begin it anew.*

Expiation is not due merely on pronouncing the *zihár*, but is rendered incumbent by a return to the wife, by which is meant an intention to resume connubial intercourse. And the more correct view seems to be that nothing is established by the *zihár* itself, except a prohibition of such intercourse until expiation is made.*

If connubial intercourse should take place *before* expiation, two expiations would be necessary; and if repeated, the expiation must be repeated also.*

ANNOTATIONS.

dclxxxi. The *zihár* should take place in the presence of two just witnesses.—Tahrír ul-Ahkám.

* *Sharáya ul-Islám*, pp. 334 & 335.

When a *muzáhir*, or the man uttering the *zihár*, is unable to make any expiation, or offer any other substitute for it than asking pardon of God, prohibition continues, according to some, until expiation is made; but others, with more probability, maintain that to ask pardon is enough.*

Principle. DCLXXXIII. If the *mazáharah*, or the woman who is the subject of the *zihár*, chooses to have patience, no other person has a right to object. But if she brings the matter before the judge, the husband must be put to his choice, either to make expiation and return to his wife, or to repudiate her, and three months are to be allowed to him to make up his mind. If the time be allowed to expire without making his choice, he is not to be compelled by means of straitening to repudiate his wife, nor is the judge empowered to make the repudiation in his stead.—Sharáya ul-Islám, p. 335. So also the Tahrír ul-Ahkám.

The expiation of *zihár* requires the emancipation of a slave; or, in the case of inability to emancipate, fasting for two successive months; and in the case of inability to fast for that time, the feeding of sixty poor persons.*

On Ilá.

Ilá, in its primitive sense, signifies a vow. In law, it implies a husband swearing to abstain from carnal knowledge of his wife for any time above four months, if she is a free woman; and two months, if she is a slave.

Principle. DCLXXXIV. There can be no *ílá* except (by swearing) in the names of God, the purest; and the same may be effected in any language when so intended.†

Annotations.

Ilá is an oath to refrain from having carnal connection (with one's wife).—Mafátíh.

dclxxxiv. It does not take effect unless it be in the name of God Almighty; and may be uttered in any language as may be practicable; but it must be with intention, and its words must also be express—as "I swear in the name of God that I will not have carnal connection with thee."—*Ibid.*

---

* *Sharáya ul-Islám*, pp. 335 & 336.

† *Vide Sharáya ul-Islám*, p. 343.

The words by which it is constituted are either plain and express (*a*), or especially appropriate to such act (*b*), or those which do not expressly indicate the same, but are capable of being so interpreted.*

(*a.*) As,—"By God, I will not have carnal connection with thee."*

(*b.*) As, when the man should say—"I will not cohabit with thee, or I will not have carnal connection with thee."*

DCLXXXV. The above will effect *ílá* if intended; but without intention, it will not be effected.* *Principle.*

The oath should be free from any condition.—Tahrír ul-Ahkám.

Whether *ílá* can be made dependent on a condition, is a question on which there are two reports of the *Shaikh's* opinion. According to the most notorious or generally received of these, it cannot be constituted either in dependence on a condition, or to take effect from a future time, and, if attempted, the condition would be surplusage.*

DCLXXXVI. The *ílá* does not take effect unless the oath be absolute, perpetual, or for a period exceeding four months, or dependent on an act, which generally does not occur except *after* it. If the husband approach the wife within the period, it is necessary for him to make expiation for the oath taken.—Tahrír ul-Ahkám. *Principle.*

DCLXXXVII. As regards the *múlí*, or the man pronouncing the *ílá*, it is required that he be *adult* *Principle.*

ANNOTATIONS.

dclxxxiv. The oath must be taken in the name of God Almighty.—Tahrír ul-Ahkám.

dclxxxv. It is a condition that the wording of the oath be uttered intentionally, though it may be in any language.—*Ibid.*

dclxxxvii. As respects the *hálif*, or the swearer, it is required that he be adult, perfectly sane, have freedom in choice, and intention.—*Ibid.*

* *Sharáya ul-Islám*, p. 343.

and sane, and have freedom of choice, and intention.* And,—

Principle. DCLXXXVIII. As regards the *múlá*, or the woman who is the subject of the *ílá*, it is necessary that she be married by contract, and not merely by virtue of a right of property; and that the marriage be consummated.*

With regard to a woman married by temporary contract (*mutá*), there is some doubt; but according to the more approved opinion she is not a subject for *ílá*.*

It makes no difference whether the woman be free or a slave; and in either case she is competent to bring the matter before a judge to have a time fixed, and after its expiration to demand a return of conjugal intercourse.*

Principle. DCLXXXIX. *Ilá* may apply to a revocably divorced woman, within her *iddat*, and not to one absolutely divorced.—Tahrír ul-Ahkám.

The rules of *ílá* are the following:—

Principle. DCXC. *Ilá* is not constituted unless the prohibition is absolute, perpetual, or for a time exceeding four months, or to continue until the occurrence of something which certainly cannot happen, or in all probability will not happen, before the expiration of that time (*c*).†

(*c*.) As if a man, being in Irák at the time, should say—"Until I go to, and return from, a town in Turkey."†

ANNOTATIONS.

dclxxxviii. The woman who is subject to *ílá*, is required to be permanently married and enjoyed.—Tahrír ul-Ahkám.

* *Sharáya ul-Islám*, p. 343.

† *Sharáya ul-Islám*, pp. 143 & 144.

DCXCI. The time for the woman to wait is four months, whether she be free or a slave, or whether her husband be the one or the other; and this time is the husband's right; so that within this time she cannot demand his return to her. Nor when it has expired is she divorced by the mere expiration. Neither has the judge any power to divorce her. But if she should bring the matter before him, the husband then must make his choice either to divorce her, or to return to her. If he should divorce her, that would put an end to her right, though the divorce be revocable, according to the best opinions. So, also, if he should return to her, that would equally put an end to her right.* *Principle.*

But if he refuse to do either of the things required of him, he is to be imprisoned and straitened until he either divorces her, or returns to her. The judge, however, has no power to compel him to do either of these in preference to the other.*

DCXCII. If the *ílá* should be for a definite time, and he procrastinates, after the matter is brought before the judge, till the time expires, the effect of the *ílá* abates; and he is not liable for any expiation though he should have connection with his wife. And if she should deem it her right to demand a return, it would not be thereby extinguished.* *Principle.*

Lián, or Imprecation.

DCXCIII. The pillars, or essentials, of *lián* are four: *First*, the causes of *lián*; *second*, the imprecating husband (*muláïn*), who is required to be adult and sane; *third*, the imprecating wife (*muláïnah*), who is required to be adult, sane, free from deafness and dumbness, and married by a *Principle.*

ANNOTATIONS.

dcxci. If the period has expired without connubial intercourse, still the woman will not be divorced without a divorce being (formally) given; and the judge has no power to give a divorce on behalf of the husband.—Tahrír ul-Ahkám.

---

* *Sharáya ul-Islám*, pp. 143 & 144.

permanent contract; and, *fourth,* the mode or form in which it is conducted.*

Principle. DCXCIV. The causes are two in number: 1, scandal of the wife; and 2, denial of a child.†

Principle. DCXCV. *Lián,* or imprecation, is not induced by the first cause, which is scandal, except when the husband charges his chaste wife (*muhsinah*), whom he has enjoyed, with adultery, and alleges that he has had ocular demonstration of the fact, but has no other proof of it.†

Principle. DCXCVI. It follows from the ocular demonstration being required on the part of the husband, that there can be no *lián* for scandal in the case of a blind man, though there may be for the denial of a child.†

If the accuser has proof, but he declines to produce it in order to (prove) a *lián,* it is a question whether *lián* would be valid. According to the *Khiláf,* it would; but this is denied in the *mabsút,* on the ground that the want of proof is made a condition in the sacred text; and this opinion is more agreeable according to the general principles of law.†

Principle. DCXCVII. It is not lawful for a husband to accuse his wife on a mere supposition, nor even with a strong presumption (of her guilt) founded on information given to him by a person in whom he can confide, nor, though it should be notorious, that such a one has committed adultery with her.†

ANNOTATIONS.

dcxciv. The causes are two,—the charge of adultery, and denial of a child.—Tahrír ul-Ahkám.

dcxcv. With respect to the first, it is required that the wife charged with adultery be chaste (*muhsinah*), enjoyed, and free from deafness and dumbness; and that the man should have seen her in the act, but have no other proof.—*Ibid.*

dcxcvi. So no *lián* can be established to a blind man if he brings such charge (against his wife), though the denial of a child may be established in his favor.—*Ibid.*

---

* *Vide Sharáya ul-Islám,* pp. 446—449.

† *Sharáya ul-Islám,* pp. 346 & 347.

DCXCVIII. For the establishment of *lián* by denial of a child, it is necessary that delivery should take place at six months or more from the time of conjugal intercourse, and not beyond the extreme period of gestation: it is further requisite that the intercourse should have been under a permanent contract. *Principle.*

Consequently,—

"If the woman should give birth to a full grown child *within* six months from the conjugal intercourse, the child is not affiliated to her husband, and may, therefore, be denied by him without *lián*." But if they differ after consummation as to the time of pregnancy, recourse must be had to mutual *lián*.*

A child is not affiliated to the husband unless access to his wife was possible, and he was capable of having matrimonial intercourse.*

DCXCIX. If he (the husband) should die, whether before or after attaining majority, without denying the child, it must be affiliated to him, and both the wife and child are entitled to appropriate shares in his inheritance.* *Principle.*

DCC. If the husband should die before the (commencement) of the *lián*, or before its completion, both the wife and the child denied will inherit from him; on the other hand, if the wife should die before the *lián*, or before its completion, the husband will inherit from her.—Tahrír ul-Ahkám. *Principle.*

DCCI. The husband can deny the child whether it be a mere fœtus in the womb, or separated from its mother. *Principle.*

ANNOTATIONS.

dcxcviii. With respect to the second, it is required that apparently, there be a possibility of the child being his,—by its being born at or after the sixth month, or a longer period from the time of connubial intercourse; and that the wife be enjoyed under permanent contract.—Tahrir ul-Ahkám.

---

* *Sharáya ul-Islám*. pp. 346 & 347.

When he denies it after its separation from the mother's womb, he must do it without delay; but if he delays it, though he was able to do so without delay, such denial is void.*

Principle. DCCII. If he refrain from denying a child of which his wife is pregnant till her delivery, he may lawfully deny it after its birth according to both opinions.* But,—

Principle. DCCIII. A person who has (once) acknowledged a child expressly, or impliedly (*a*), cannot afterwards deny it.*

(*a.*) As if, when congratulated on its birth, he has answered in the words indicative of satisfaction. For instance, if the terms of congratulation were, "God has blessed you in your child," and he should answer "Amen," or "if it please God." But if he should say by way of answer, "God has blessed thee," or "God has done good to thee," there would be no acknowledgment.*

Principle. DCCIV. It is required that he (the imprecating husband) be adult and sane.†

Principle. DCCV. *Lián*, or imprecation, is in no case valid without speech or approved signs.†

Principle. DCCVI. The imprecation by a dumb person is valid when his meaning can be ascertained by approved signs, in the same way as divorce and acknowledgment by him are valid.†

Principle. DCCVII. It is required that the imprecating woman (*muláïnah*) be adult, sane, married by a permanent contract, and free from deafness and blindness.†

With respect to consummation there are several reports: according to one of these, there is no *lián* without it; according to another, the *lián* is lawful; while a third restricts its legality to a case of scandal excluding denial of a child.†

Lián is established between a free man and a slave wife. Here also there are two opinions, of which, one forbids it, while the other allows it only for denial of a child, to the exclusion of slander.†

---

* *Sharáya ul-Islám*, pp. 346 & 347.

† *Sharáya ul-Islám*, pp. 348 & 349.

DCCVIII. *Lián*, or imprecation, is valid with respect to a pregnant woman.*

DCCIX. A *lián*, or imprecation, is not required to reject a child born of a female slave, a simple denial being sufficient for the purpose; for, as such child, though begotten by the master of its mother, is affiliated to him only by his acknowledgment, so it is cut off from him by his mere denial.* *Principle.*

DCCX. *Lián* is not validly effected except in the presence of the judge (*hákim*), or some one appointed by him for the purpose; yet if the parties are content with a private person, and take the *lián* before him, it is lawful.* *Principle.*

Form.

DCCXI. The proper form of *lián* is, that the man should four times call God to witness that he is among the truth-speakers in respect of what he has laid to the charge against his wife, and that he should then add, "May the curse of God be upon him, if he be among the liars!" The woman should then call God to witness four times that he is among the liars in respect of what he has laid to her charge, and should then add, "May the wrath of God be upon her, if he is among the truth-speakers."* *Principle.*

ANNOTATIONS.

dccxi. When a man charges his wife with adultery, and intends to have the *lián* effected, it is required that the matter be brought before the judge (*hákim*), or the person appointed by him for the purpose; and the man should first say four times "I call God to witness that I am among the truth-speakers in respect of what she is accused of." After that he should say—"May the curse of God be upon me if I am among the liars." Then the woman should say four times—"I call God to witness that he is among the liars with respect to what he has accused me of;" and she should then say—"May the wrath of God be upon me if he be among the truth-speakers."—Tahrír ul-Ahkám.

---

* *Sharáya ul-Islám*, pp. 348 & 349.

The words of testimony are as just mentioned, and it is proper that such husband should stand when uttering them, and that the woman should also stand when so doing. The man should first begin to utter (the formula), and then the woman.*

If, instead of saying "I testify by God," the parties should say "I swear," using the word "*halaf*, or *kasam*," (which signifies an oath), or the like, the formula would not be lawful.*

Principle. DCCXII. If the man deny the child, he should add—"This child is the fruit of adultery, and not of my connection." If he should shorten his speech into one of the phrases, it would not be valid.—Tahrír ul-Ahkám.

The parties should also make use of the Arabic language if able to do so, and this is only to be excused by inability.*

The Rules of Lián.

A man by slandering his wife becomes liable to punishment (*hadd*), but his liability ceases on his taking the *lián*.†

Principle. DCCXIII. The child is cut off from the man, but not from the woman: she ceases to be (his) wife, and becomes perpetually prohibited to him.†

Principle. DCCXIV. If the man should give himself the lie (or retract) after the *lián*, the child is affiliated to him, and would inherit from him; but neither the father nor any one related through him can inherit from the child, while the mother and those related through her retain their right of inheritance from him. Her wifehood, however, does not return, nor is there any abatement of the prohibition.†

ANNOTATIONS.

dccxiii. Upon the *lián* being established with respect to them (both), the child is cut off from the husband, but *not* from the wife; separation shall ta[illegible]lace between them, and they shall perpetually be unlawful to each other.—Tahrír ul-Ahkám.

* *Sharáya ul-Islám*, p. 349.

† *Sharáya ul-Islám*, pp. 349—351.

The effect of *lián* is established upon the mere order when pronounced.*

DCCXV. If there has been a failure in any of the appropriate words of *lián*, it is not valid, and any order which the judge may have passed upon it is inoperative.* *Principle.*

DCCXVI. The separation induced by *lián* is a cancellation of the marriage, and not a divorce.* *Principle.*

---

* *Sharáya ul-Islám*, pp. 349—351.

LECTURE XVII.

ON THE REVOCATION OF A DIVORCE, OR RECALLING A DIVORCED WIFE, AND REMARRYING HER,— AND ON IDDAT.

Principle. DCCXVII. The (husband's) right of recalling is established with respect to *that* (divorced) wife who is liable to observe *iddát* (for a revocable divorce),* and who has not yet completed the term thereof.†—Tahrír ul-Ahkám.

Principle. DCCXVIII. A divorce (revocable) may be validly revoked, or the wife (so divorced) may be recalled, by words (*a*), or by deed (*b*), or even by the husband's kissing or touching her amorously. Permission by the divorced woman is not necessary, she being still his wife. And it is not necessary, though proper, to have witnesses to (such) revocation.‡

(*a*.) As by his saying "I have recalled thee."‡

(*b*.) As by connubial intercourse.‡

ANNOTATIONS.

dccxvii. The revocation or recalling is established by (the husband's) words, or act. And it is not required that the woman be cognizant of it, and there be a witness to it.—Tahrír ul-Ahkám.

According to the most approved opinion, the revocation of a divorce, or the recalling of a divorced wife, is effected by express words, or by an act, or by writing intentionally.—Mafátíh.

---

* *Vdie—"Iddat," post*, p. 435.

† The term of *iddat* is the return of three courses for a free woman whether her husband be a free man or a slave; and *two* for a female slave, whether her husband be a free man or a slave.—*Tahrír ul-Ahkám*. *Vide Iddat*.

The power of revocation lasts till the expiration of the *iddat*, after which divorce becomes absolute.

‡ *Sharáya ul-Islám*, p. 319.

DCCXIX. Even a mere denial of the divorce would be equivalent to revocation, as it implies a recalling or retention* (of the woman as his wife). *Principle.*

If a husband should say to his wife "I have recalled thee, when thou wilt, or if thou wilt," the revocation would not take effect, even though she should answer "I have willed." This, however, is open to doubt.*

DCCXX. Revocation by a dumb man may be effected by a sign or signs indicating the same.* *Principle.*

Some say that he ought to raise the veil of her face, but this opinion is rarely entertained.*

If a man should revocably divorce his wife, and recall her after she has apostatized from the faith, the revocation would not be valid, in the same manner as marriage (with an apostate) would not, *ab initio*, be valid. Upon this point, however, there is room for doubt, arising from the consideration that the woman revocably divorced is still a wife; and if after that she should return to the faith, the revocation would revive.*

When a man who has divorced his wife while he is absent from her, enters into her apartment on his return, and then claims that the divorce was effective, his claim is not to be received.* Because it is to be presumed that a *Musalmán's* acts are in accordance with the law, and his claim gives the lie to what is tantamount to proof. Accordingly, if there is a child it is affiliated to him.*

When a man has divorced a pregnant wife, and recalled her, he may lawfully have connubial intercourse with her, and then divorce her a second time for the *iddat*. This is by general consent.*

Some, however, maintain that it is unlawful to do so according to the *sunnat;* but the opinion in favour of its legality is more agreeable to the principles of law.*

ANNOTATIONS.

dccxx. In the case of the husband being dumb, it is sufficient if an intelligible sign is made by him.—Mafátíh.

---

* *Sharáyä ul-Islám*, pp. 317 & 319

On the Husband's remarrying a Wife irrevocably divorced.

Principle. DCCXXI. When a woman has been divorced three times with the requisite conditions, she is rendered unlawful (to the divorcer) until she has been married to another husband.*

In removing the prohibition, regard must be had to four conditions (which are as follows):—

1*st.*—The (new) husband must be adult;—for though there is some difference of opinion in respect of a *muráhik,*—that is, a boy approaching to puberty,—yet it is more agreeable according to the principles of law to say that he does not legalize (the woman to her first husband).*

2*nd.*—He (the new husband) must have carnal connection with the woman in the natural way, so as to require ablution* (*a*).

3*rd.*—This (*i.e.*, the above) must be under a contract of marriage, and not merely by virtue of property, or permission from her master.*

4*th.*—The contract must be permanent, and not a *mutá* or temporary one.*

Annotations.

dccxxi. Every woman who has completed the number of three divorces is unlawful (to the divorcer) unless she was married to another husband, whether she was enjoyed by her former husband (the divorcer), or not, or whether she was recalled by him or not.—Tahrír ul-Ahkám.

Every woman who has completed three divorces, is unlawful to the divorcer, until she has married another man.—Mafátíh.

Every woman on whom three divorces have been fulfilled is rendered unlawful (to the divorcer,) until she marries another husband; and it makes no difference whether he has enjoyed her or not, or whether he had recalled or abandoned her.—Sharáya ul-Islám, p. 316.

It is not (also) lawful for a man to marry the woman who has been thrice or twice divorced by him, until after she has been married by another man.—Tahrír ul-Ahkám.

To legalize a woman (to her former husband) it is required that she be married to an adult; consequently, she is not legalized if married to a *muráhik.*—Tahrír ul-Ahkám.

---

* *Sharáya ul-Islám*, pp. 317 & 318.

When all those (above) conditions have been fulfilled, the prohibition incurred by three divorces is removed.*

(*a.*) The intercourse with the new husband in the natural way, though it should take place without emission, is sufficient to legalize the divorced woman (to her former husband), because the act is the occasion of mutual pleasure to the parties.*

DCCXXII. If the legalizer, after marrying a divorced woman, should, before connubial intercourse with her, apostatize from the faith, any subsequent intercourse with her during his apostacy would not be sufficient to render her lawful to her first husband, because the contract was cancelled by his apostacy.* *Principle.*

With respect to the value of a second marriage in effacing the effect of any number of divorces less than three, there are two traditions. Of these, the one which is most generally received is in favour of the extinction.* So that,—

If a woman, who was once divorced, should be married to another, and, after the dissolution of that marriage should be remarried to her first husband, she would abide with him on a fresh footing as to three divorces, the effect (of the divorce) being cancelled* (by the intermediate marriage to another person).

If after the lapse of some time she (the thrice divorced woman) should allege that she was duly married to another husband, and after being completely separated from him, has fulfilled her *iddat*, and if all the occurrences could possibly have taken place in the interval since the third divorce, some of the doctors maintain that her word must be received, because in the whole matter, a fact, that is coition, is involved, which cannot be ascertained except from herself. There is one tradition, however, which is to the effect that it is only when she is a trustworthy person that her assertion is credited under such circumstances.*

Hence,—

DCCXXIII. If after the lapse of a probable time, a thrice-divorced woman, who is trustworthy, should affirm that she had been intermediately married to another man from whom she has been completely *Principle*

---

* *Sharáya ul-Islám*, pp. 318 & 319.

separated (by divorce or otherwise) after connubial intercourse (in the natural way), she is legalized to her former husband, who can again take her under a permanent marriage contract.

Principle. DCCXXIV. When a legalizer has entered into the woman's apartment, and she asserts that connubial intercourse took place (between them), she is rendered lawful to her former husband, provided that the legalizer assent to the assertion.*

Principle. DCCXXV. Every woman who has completed nine divorces by being intermediately married to two men, is rendered for ever unlawful (to the first husband).†—Mafátíh.

But,—

The divorces, *after completion of the iddat*, do not render a woman perpetually unlawful to the divorcer, though they should amount to nine.

A man divorces his wife, and she completes her *iddat ;* he then marries her a second time, divorces her again, and leaves her to complete her *iddat;* after which he marries her a third time, and this time he divorces her. She now becomes unlawful to him till she has been married to another husband. After which, if separated from him, and her *iddat* from him has expired, her first husband may lawfully return to her,—that is, marry her again ; and a wife so treated is not perpetually prohibited even after the ninth divorce. But the *iddat* which she has to observe does not prevent her from becoming immediately prohibited to him after the third,—that is, until she has been married to another.‡

Recapitulation. In the case of a revocable divorce, the divorcer, can, *before* completion of the *iddat*, recall and take back the divorced wife, without remarrying her, simply by words of mouth, or by an act indicative of revocation ; while in the case of an irrevocable divorce being effected, he cannot take her back without remarrying her. And after she has been divorced three times, he must wait till she is married to another man adult in age, and separated from him after

---

* *Sharáya ul-Islám*, pp. 318 & 319.

† See *Talak ul-iddat, ante*, pp. 392 & 393.

‡ *Sharáya ul-Islám*, pp. 316 & 317.

consummation, and then it is that the former husband becomes entitled to take her back by marrying her for the second time. But a man can never take back that wife whom he has divorced nine times, before completion of *iddat** at any time.

On Iddat.

Iddat is a woman's abstaining for a fixed period from uniting in marriage, or from carnal connection, with another man, in order that it might be ascertained whether or not he is pregnant by her husband from whom she has been separated by death, or divorced after consummation.

DCCXXVI. No woman whose marriage has not been consummated (*a*), whether she was divorced by her husband, or separated from him by cancellation of the marriage, is obliged to observe *iddat* except only when it is for his death.† *Principle.*

Because a widow is bound to observe an *iddat* even though her marriage was not consummated (*a*). For observing the *iddat*, the rule is the same in all kinds of dissolution, except that by death.—Tahrír ul-Ahkám.

(*a*.) Consummation is established by the insertion of the *glans penis*, without emission, even though the husband be a eunuch. Some have said that an *iddat* is also incumbent if he was a *majbúb* from the possibility of pregnancy by friction; but this is liable to doubt, as *iddat* is dependent on coition. If, however, pregnancy should ensue, an *iddat* must necessarily be observed till delivery.†

DCCXXVII. According to the most generally received opinion, *iddat* is not necessary to be observed in consequence of mere retirement (of the husband and wife) without coition.† *Principle.*

Annotations.

dccxxvi. The wife not enjoyed is not bound to observe *iddat* for divorce and cancellation of marriage, except in death.—Tahrír ul-Ahkám.

There is no *iddat* for an unenjoyed wife, though she was absolutely divorced or separated (for another cause).—Mafátíh.

*** The completion of *iddat* renders the divorce irrevocable.**

† *Sharáya ul-Islám*, p. 321.

Principle. DCCXXVIII. For women who are free and subject to the courses, whether their husband be free or not, the *iddat* is prescribed for three *kurahs*, by which is understood (according to the most generally received of the two traditions) three *tuhrs* or periods of purity.*

If a man should divorce his wife while the courses were actually upon her, the divorce would have no effect (as already mentioned). But,—

If the divorce were given in a *tuhr*, or period of purity, it would be valid, though the woman should menstruate when the man had done speaking, without an appreciable instant of time intervening, as it took effect in the *tuhr*. Still, however, that *tuhr* could not be reckoned in the *iddat*, because, it did not follow the divorce, and three new *kurahs* or *tuhrs* would be required after the menstruation.*

Principle. DCCXXIX. The woman who is not subject to the courses, though she has arrived at the proper age, must observe an *iddat* of three months after divorce, or other cancellation of her marriage, provided that it has been consummated, and she is free.*

Annotations.

dccxxviii. The *iddat* of a divorced woman, who is free, enjoyed and menstruant, is the period of three *tuhrs*, whether she was the wife of a free man or of a slave.—Tahrír ul-Ahkám.

The (period of) *iddat* to be observed by an enjoyed woman, who is free and menstruant, is three *tuhrs* for divorce or separation, or for coition under a semblance of right.—Mafátíh.

dccxxix. The *iddat* of a free woman who does not menstruate, though she is at the age of menstruating, is three months, for any of the above causes (except death).—Tahrír ul-Ahkám.

If a woman does not menstruate, though she is of that age in which women do menstruate, her *iddat* is for three months, if she is (free and) enjoyed.—Mafátíh.

---

* *Vide Sharáya ul-Islám*, pp. 321 & 322.

DCCXXX. With regard to a *yáïsah*, or a woman who is past child-bearing (*a*), as well as one who has not yet arrived at puberty, there are two traditions. According to one of these, they are both obliged to observe an *iddat* of three months; but according to the other, which is more generally received, no *iddat* of any kind is obligatory on either of them.* *Principle.*

(*a*.) The age when women are passed child-bearing is fifty years, though it is said that among the *Kuresh* and *Nabatiáns* the age is sixty years.*

If, in a particular case, the monthly discharge should have ceased while women of the same age are generally subject to it, the *iddat* is three months by general agreement.*

In such a case (as the above) the woman should have regard to courses and to months; so that if three *tuhrs* should first be completed, or if three months should first expire, the *iddat* would be at an end in either case. But if she should perceive the discharge in the third month, and the second and third appearance should be delayed, she must have patience for nine months, for the possibility of her being pregnant, and then keep an *iddat* for three months. This of all the *iddats* is the longest.†

DCCXXXI. A woman whose courses occur only once in four or five months, should keep *iddat* by months.† *Principle.*

When a woman has been divorced at the beginning of the *hilál*, or the first appearance of the new moon, the three months of the *iddat* are to be reckoned by *hiláls*. Where, again, she was divorced in the middle of a month, the *iddat* is to be measured by two *hiláls*,

ANNOTATIONS.

dccxxxi. The term of *iddat* is mentioned to be three months of a woman who menstruates once after every three months, six months or seven months, or who is always in a state of menstruating, or who has not arrived at the age of menstruating, or who sometimes menstruates and sometimes does not menstruate, or who is not expected to give birth to a child, or who has ceased to menstruate though not considered to be past child-bearing, or who, not always, but sometimes, discharges yellow fluids.—Mafátíh.

* *Sharáya ul-Islám*, p. 322.

† *Sharáya ul-Islám*, pp. 322 & 323.

and so much of the third month as to make up for what was wanting of the first. Some, however, are of opinion that here also the three months must be reckoned by three *hiláls*, and the opinion seems to be more in accordance with the general principles of the law.*

If there should be any suspicion of pregnancy before the expiration of the *iddat*, the woman should refrain from entering into another contract of marriage. And it would be proper to do so when there is any suspicion of the kind, even though the *iddat* should have expired. In this, however, it is right to observe, that the marriage would be lawful so long as there is no certainty of the woman's being pregnant. But in all the cases, if she should subsequently prove to have been pregnant, a second marriage entered into under such circumstances would be void by reason of the *iddat* being still subsisting at the time of the contract.* Hence,—

Principle. **DCCXXXII. A marriage contract entered into after completion of the *iddat* is not void unless the woman be found to have been pregnant subsequently at the time of the contract.**

Principle. **DCCXXXIII. A pregnant woman, when divorced, must observe *iddat* till she is delivered of her child.***

Principle. DCCXXXIV. If a man should divorce a pregnant wife revocably, and then die, while her *iddat* is still unexpired, she must observe anew an *iddat* on account of his death. But if he should divorce her *irrevocably*, she is only required to complete the *iddat* already commenced for the divorce.*

ANNOTATIONS.

dccxxxiii. A pregnant woman must observe *iddat* for the above three causes till her delivery, even though she was delivered immediately after any of the occurrences, whether the child so delivered was perfectly formed or imperfectly, and whether it was alive or dead.—Mafátíh.

Of a pregnant woman the term of *iddat* is till her delivery, whether she be a free woman or slave.—Tahrír ul-Ahkám.

dccxxxiv. When the husband of a free woman married under a valid contract dies, she, if not pregnant, must observe *iddat* for four months

---

* *Shara'ya ul-Islám*, pp. 322 & 323.

If a woman should declare that her *iddat* has expired, and subsequently she be delivered of a child at six months more from the date of the divorce, some are of opinion that the child is not affiliated to the divorcer; but the better opinion seems to be that it ought to be ascribed to him, so long as the time does not exceed the extreme period of gestation.*

DCCXXXV. A free woman married by a valid contract should observe *iddat* for the death (of her husband) during four months and ten days, if she is not pregnant, whatever be her age (that is, whether she be a child or full grown), and whether her husband had attained majority or not, and whether he had matrimonial intercourse with her or not; and her connection with him is cut off at the sunset of the tenth day.* But,— *Principle.*

DCCXXXVI. If she is pregnant, she must observe *iddat* for the largest of the two periods,—that is, if the delivery takes place before the expiration of four months and ten days (from her husband's death), she must wait to complete that time.* *Principle.*

ANNOTATIONS.

and ten days, whether she is a minor or major, whether her husband was adult or not, and whether she was enjoyed (by him), or not. But if she is pregnant, her *iddat* is the longer of the two periods, and if she is delivered of a child before the expiration of four months and ten days, she must continue in *iddat* until that period has expired; while, on the other hand, if this period has expired before the delivery, she must continue (in it) till she is delivered of her child.—Tahrír ul-Ahkám.

dccxxxv. If a woman is free and married under a valid contract, and not pregnant at the time, the *iddat* for her husband's death is four lunar months and ten days, whether she is adult or infant, whether her husband was adult or not, whether she was enjoyed by him or not, whether she was married under a permanent or temporary contract, and whether she is menstruant or not.—Mafátíh.

dccxxxvi. If she is pregnant, she must observe *iddat* for the longer of the two periods.—*Ibid.*

* *Sharáya ul-Islám*, pp. 322 & 323.

Remark. The observance of *iddat* for the death of a free woman's husband appears to have been ordained as part of the act of mourning which is incumbent on a widow; and whence it is that no distinction is made in this respect between women infant and adult, enjoyed and unenjoyed, as it is evident from the following passage:—

"*Hidád*, or mourning, is incumbent on a widow, by which is to be understood abstinence from everything in dress and ornaments intended to adorn and beautify the person. In those respects there is no difference between young and full grown, the *Muslimah* and the *Zimmíyah*. But there is some doubt with respect to a slave, on whom it would seem that the *hidád* is not incumbent. Neither is it incumbent on a woman who has been divorced by her husband revocably or irrevocably."*

Principle. DCCXXXVII. If a man died after having carnal connection with a woman under a semblance of contract, she should observe the *iddat* prescribed in divorce (not that prescribed for a husband's death), whether she be pregnant or not, the observance being due to the carnal intercourse, and not to the contract, as in reality she is not a wife.*

If no intelligence is received of a missing person, and no person maintains his wife, she may bring the matter before the judge (*kázi*), who thereupon should postpone the consideration of the subject for four years, and make diligent inquiry in the meantime with respect to the husband. If some certain intelligence of him be then received, she must still have patience, but it is incumbent on the *Imám* to maintain her out of the public treasury (*bayit-ul-mál*). If, on the other hand, nothing can be heard of her husband, the judge should direct her to observe the *iddat* as for his death, upon the completion of which she can marry again.* Hence,—

Principle. DCCXXXVIII. If after making diligent inquiry with respect to a missing person, and receiving no intelligence of him, the judge should direct his wife to observe *iddut*, she can observe one for death, after the completion of which she can marry another man. So,—

---

* *Sharáya ul-Islám*, p. 324.

DCCXXXIX. If the missing person should reappear *after* his wife had completed the *iddat*, and married again, he is without any remedy against her. But if he should reappear while she is still in her *iddat*, he retains his right to her.* *Principle.*

But if the *iddat* has expired, and she has not been married, there are two traditions on this point, and by the most generally received of these, he is entirely without any remedy against her.*

DCCXL. If a woman is married under a doubtful contract, and not enjoyed, separation (at once) takes place between the marrying parties, and no *iddat* is to be observed, even upon the death of the husband. But if the woman was enjoyed, then separation would take place, and *iddat* observed for *three tuhrs* from the time of separation if she is menstruant; but if she is not so, her *iddat* is for three months; while, if pregnant, her *iddat* would be till delivery. She is not to observe *iddat* for death; but if the husband died before separation, the *iddat* should be observed as abovementioned.—Tahrír ul-Ahkám. *Principle.*

DCCXLI. As regards a woman married under a temporary contract,—if she is free and her husband died *before* the expiration of the term, her *iddat* is four months and ten days, whether she was enjoyed or not; while if she was pregnant (at the time), her *iddat* is the longer of the two periods, as is the case in a permanent marriage. But if the husband died *after* the lapse of the term, then she must observe and complete the *iddat* for separation, and that is two *tuhrs*, or a month and a half, because the expiration of the term is similar to an absolute divorce.—Tahrír ul-Ahkám. *Principle.*

ANNOTATIONS.

dccxli. The woman married under a temporary contract, if enjoyed, must observe *iddat* till the return of her courses from the expiration of the term, or upon its being given in gift.—Mafátíh.

If she is one who does not menstruate, though not yet past child-bearing, her *iddat* is forty-five days, whether she be a free woman or a slave; while if she is pregnant, it is till her delivery.—*Ibid.*

The *iddat* for death is four months and ten days if she is not pregnant; but if pregnant, it is the longer of the two periods.—*Ibid.*

---

* *Sharáya ul-Islám*, p. 324.

Principle. DCCXLII. A divorced woman is to observe *iddat* from the time of divorce, whether the divorcer is present or not.—Tahrír ul-Ahkám.

Principle. DCCXLIII. If she was apprized of the divorce, but was ignorant of the (particular) time when it was given, she must observe *iddat* from the time of receiving intelligence (thereof).—Tahrír ul-Ahkám.

Principle. DCCXLIV. If the husband died in the presence of the wife, then *iddat* must be observed by her from the time of his death; while if he died when absent, she is to observe *iddat* from the time of receiving the intelligence, whether the informer be a just man or not.—*Ibid.*

But when the husband divorced his wife during his absence, and the divorce is not known (to her), till after the expiration of the *iddat*, he can lawfully marry her without observance of another *iddat de novo*.—*Ibid.*

LECTURE XVIII

ON SHUFÁ, OR PRE-EMPTION.

Shufá is the right of one of two co-sharers to his partner's share in consequence of its transfer by *sale* (1).*

The Things in which Shufá is established.

DCCXLV. *Shufá*, or right of pre-emption, is established with respect to lands,—such as dwellings, vacant tracts, orchards, and the like.—Tahrír ul-Ahkám. *Principle.*

DCCXLVI. The right of pre-emption is not established with respect to movables.* *Principle.*

Thus the *Sharáya ul-Islám*:—"As to whether it (*i.e.*, the right of pre-emption) is established with respect to movables,—such as wearing apparel, household utensils, shipping, and animals,—there are different opinions. Some doctors have answered in the affirmative to obviate the inconvenience of division, and upon the ground of a report by *Yunas* from Abú Abdullah, on whom be peace! Others, again, have answered in the negative upon the principle that the conferring of dominion over the property of a Musalmán ought to be restricted to those cases in which all are agreed, and also upon the ground of the report alluded to being weak or not well authenticated. This (latter) doctrine is the most approved."*

ANNOTATIONS.

(1.) *Shufá* is the right which one of two co-sharers has to his partner's share in the *akár* capable of division, and which has originated from its being transferred by *sale*.—Tahrír ul-Ahkám.

dccxlv. By general agreement of the Learned, *Shufá*, or the right of pre-emption, is established with respect to lands,—such as dwellings, vacant spaces, and orchards.—Sharáya ul-Islám, p. 418.

* *Sharáya ul-Islám*, p. 418.

So the *Mafátih* :—"According to *Nass*, as well as the general agreement of the Learned, the right of pre-emption is attached to *akár*."

So also the *Tahrír ul-Ahkám* :—"As to whether or not the right of pre-emption is established with respect to *moveable* property, there are two different opinions, the more approved of them is in the negative."

Principle. DCCXLVII. With respect to date and other trees and buildings, the right of pre-emption is established if they are sold as appendages of the ground on which they stand, but if sold separately, the same difference of opinion, as above stated, exists.*

Some of the doctors have allowed the right of pre-emption in respect of slaves, and not other animals.*

Principle. DCCXLVIII. The right of pre-emption would be established with respect to rivulets, ways, baths and the like, provided the *division* thereof would not occasion a loss or damage (*a*), such as to render the property useless, otherwise it would not.

Thus the *Sharáya ul-Islám* :—"With regard to the establishment of *Shufá* in respect of rivulets, ways, and baths, the division of which would occasion loss or damage (*a*), a doubt has prevailed; but the most approved opinion denies its operation as to those.*

(*a*.) By "damage," we understand such injury as would render the property useless after division, in which case, the person who would be injured cannot be compelled to make a partition.*

Principle. DCCXLIX. Where again the bath, or way, or rivulet is of such a character, that its utility would not be destroyed by division, the co-owner may be compelled to admit of a partition; and (if he should sell his share), the right of pre-emption would have effect in favour of his partner.*

Principle. DCCL. In like manner, in the case of a well, to which there is waste ground adjoining as an appendage, so as to admit of a division without loss or injury by surrender of the well to one person, of the land to another, the judgment of the law would enforce a partition of the joint property, and establish the right of pre-emption if one partner should sell his share.*

---

* *Sharáya ul-Islám*, pp. 418 & 419.

DCCLI. The right of pre-emption has no effect as to fruits, even when sold, on date and other trees, in connection with the root and the ground which they occupy.* *Principle.*

DCCLII. The right of pre-emption is established in respect to land which has been divided off, where a road or rivulet (passing through it) continues to be held in joint property, and one of the partners (in the latter) sells his share together with his portion of the divided land:* *Principle.*

For, *there* the other partner's right of pre-emption attaches not only to the share in the road or rivulet, which was held as joint property, but extends also to the portion of the land divided off as being connected in sale with the other.†

DCCLIII. If, however, the land should be sold separately, no right of pre-emption would attach to the same.* *Principle.*

DCCLIV. With respect to the road and rivulet (which continued as joint property), the right of pre-emption is established only when it is wide enough to admit of a division.* *Principle.*

DCCLV. If a person should sell a piece of land which is his exclusive property, and with it his share in another (joint tenement), by *one* bargain (*safkat*), the right of pre-emption attaches to the *share* exclusively, at the due proportion of the price.* *Principle.*

DCCLVI. It is an indispensable condition for the operation of the right of pre-emption that the share (of the property) should have been transferred by *sale*. So,— *Principle.*

DCCLVII. If the share has been assigned as a dower, or given in charity, or bestowed by way of gift, or in composi- *Principle.*

ANNOTATIONS.

dcclv. If a person sold, by *one* bargain, properties partly divided and partly undivided, the right of pre-emption is, by general agreement, established with respect to the divided property only, and not to that which is undivided.—Mafátíh.

dcclvi, dcclvii. The transfer (to which the right of pre-emption should attach) must be by *sale* (and not otherwise). So, if the transfer

* *Sharáya ul-Islám*, pp. 418 & 419.
† B. Dig., Part II, p. 177.

tion (for a claim), it is not subject to the claim of pre-emption.*

Principle. DCCLVIII. If a mansion should be partly *wakf*, or appropriated for pious and charitable purposes, and partly free, and the portion which is free be sold, the person entitled to the benefit of appropriation has no right of pre-emption, not even if he be a single individual.

Because he is not the actual owner of the property* (but is entitled only to its usufruct).—Murtazá, however, says the right of pre-emption would be established.*

On the Shafí or the person to whom the right of pre-emption belongs.

Principle. DCCLIX. The *Shafí* is every owner of a share in a joint and undivided property who is able to pay the price (of the share sold). It is, moreover, a condition that he be a *muslim*, when the purchaser is of that religion.† Consequently,—

Principle. DCCLX. An infidel's right of *Shufá* is not established against a muslim even though he should have purchased from a *Zimmí*, or infidel subject; but only against another infidel (that is a purchaser of his own persuasion); while, on the other hand, a musalmán's right of pre-emption is established against a musalmán as well as against an infidel.†

ANNOTATIONS.

be made as a dower, or as a gift, or in compromise, then, according to the prevalent doctrine, there is no right of pre-emption.—Mafátíh.

dcclix. When the purchaser is a Musalmán, the person to be the *Shafí*, or claimant by right of pre-emption, must also be a Musalmán.—*Ibid.*

dcclx. Neither an infidel subject (*zimmí*), nor an alien enemy (*harbí*), has a right of pre-emption against a muslim, though it is established, on the other hand, that a muslim has a right of pre-emption against a *zimmí*, and a *zimmí* against one like him or any other infidel; and an infidel against an infidel, or a *zimmí*.—Tahrír ul-Ahkám.

* *Sharáya ul-Islám*, pp. 418 & 419.

† *Sharáya ul-Islám*, p. 419.

DCCLXI. The right of pre-emption does not belong to a neighbour, nor does it attach to the property that has been divided, unless the road or rivulet of water (if any running through it) be still in joint tenancy.* *Principle.*

DCCLXII. It is a necessary condition that the person claiming the right of pre-emption should at *that* time be (actually) a co-sharer (of the seller).—Mafátíh. *Principle.*

DCCLXIII. The right of pre-emption is established between two co-sharers* (and no more).† *Principle.*

Thus the *Sharáya ul-Islám* :—"When there is more than one claimant by right of pre-emption, opinions are divided as to the establishment of the right. According to one of these, it is established absolutely, whatever be the number (of the claimants). According to another, it is established with a plurality of partners when the claim is for land, but not when it is for more than a single slave; and according to the third, it is not established with respect to anything when there is more than *one* (co-sharer). And *this* (last opinion) is the most prevalent."*

So the *Tahrír ul-Ahkám,* which says:—"According to most of the doctors, the right of pre-emption is extinguished in the case of there being several *Shafís,* or claimants by right of pre-emption; and this doctrine is adopted by the modern lawyers."

So also the *Mafátíh* :—"According to the prevalent doctrine, there should be only one co-sharer (of the seller), and the right of pre-emption is extinguished in the case of there being many part-proprietors."

ANNOTATIONS.

dcclxi. Without any difference of opinion, the privilege of *Shufá* does not belong to a neighbour.—Mafátíh.

* *Sharáya ul-Islám,* p. 419.

† According to the Haníftes, several persons may have the right, and exercise it.—Note by Mr. Neil Baillie, *vide* B. Dig., Part II, p. 179.

Principle. **DCCLXIV.** The right of pre-emption is not established by the *Shafi's* inability to pay the price, by his delaying to claim the privilege, or by his absconding at the time of the sale.*

Principle. **DCCLXV.** If he allege the absence of funds to pay (the price), a delay of three days is to be allowed to him, and *then* if he be unable to produce the money, his right of pre-emption is extinguished.*

Principle. **DCCLXVI.** If, again, he should say that his property (money) is in another town (*balad*), a time proportionate to enable him to obtain the same should be granted to him, and three days additional, unless the purchaser would be injured thereby.*

Principle. **DCCLXVII.** The privilege of *Shufá* is established in favour of persons who are absent, imbecile, insane, or under age;—the guardians of all of whom should avail themselves of the right, provided the same be for the advantage of their wards (*a*).*

(*a.*) So, where the assertion of the claim is of no advantage to the ward, and still the guardian has made it, the same is invalid.†

Annotations.

dcclxiv. The *Shafi* must be able to pay the price, though it be by borrowing; he must not procrastinate, or abscond: if he does so, his right is extinguished.—Mafátíh.

dcclxv. If he allege the absence of funds to pay the price, a delay of three days is to be granted to him, and then if he does not produce it, the right is extinguished.—*Ibid.*

dcclxvi. If, again, he should say that the purchase-money is in a different town or village (*balad*), a time proportionate to enable him to go (thither), take the money and come back will be granted to him in addition to three days. This decision is followed in practice.—*Ibid.*

---

* *Sharáya ul-Islám*, p. 419.

DCCLXVIII. The guardian's fault in delaying to make the demand, does not, however, extinguish the right.—Mafátíh. *Principle.*

DCCLXIX. If the guardian should abandon the claim, the minor on attainnig puberty, and the insane person on recovering his reason, may still assert it.* *Principle.*

Because (in either case) there is a sufficient legal excuse for the delay† (in prosecuting the claim).

DCCLXX. A person who was absent is entitled to prefer his claim, though the period of absence was long, in case he was, during absence, unable to prosecute it in person or through a *wakíl*.—Mafátíh. *Principle.*

DCCLXXI. A sick man unable to prefer his claim is like an absent person, and so is one imprisoned.—*Ibid.* *Principle.*

DCCLXXII. If a father or grandfather should sell the share of his ward (child or grandchild) in the property held in joint ownership with himself, he may lawfully assert the right of pre-emption in his own favor, any ground of objection being obviated by the consideration that it is no more than selling the ward's share directly to himself.* *Principle.*

DCCLXXIII. And, under the above circumstance, an executor appears to have the same power. *Principle.*

Thus the *Sharáya ul-Islám* :—"But has an executor the same power? The Shaikh says—'he has not,' on account of the suspicion (which attaches to such a transaction) : the affirmative, however, is better supported, as in the case of an agent"* (who may lawfully claim the privilege under such a circumstance).

ANNOTATIONS.

dcclxvii—dcclxix. The *walí* is, likewise, entitled to make the demand on behalf of his client during his absence, also during the minority or insanity of his ward, as well as before or after his attaining majority, or recovering from insanity, and also after his ward, who was an idiot, obtained intellect.—Mafátíh.

---

* *Sharáya ul-Islám*, p. 419.

The Mode of Claiming, &c.

Principle. DCCLXXIV. The *Shafí* is entitled to assert his claim on the conclusion of the contract without waiting for the expiration of the option stipulated to the purchaser alone.

Thus the *Sharáya ul-Islám* :*—" The *Shafí* is entitled to assert his claim on the conclusion of the contract and expiration of the option; for it is *then* that the contract becomes binding. Some doctors, however, maintain that (the right is established) by the mere contract, without waiting for the expiration of the option, on the principle that transfer is legally effected by the mere contract; and this opinion is the most generally approved. But if an option is stipulated only to the purchaser, the *Shafí's* right is established on the mere conclusion of the contract by reason of transfer to the purchaser being completed."†

Principle. DCCLXXV. A *Shafí* cannot relinquish his privilege in part (and exact it, as to the remainder of the property to which it applies); but, on the contrary, he must either take the whole, or abandon his right entirely.*

Principle. DCCLXXVI. He must take at the contract price, though the value of the share be more or less (than the same); and he is not liable for any contingent charges incurred by the purchaser,—such as brokerage, agency, or the like.*

Principle. DCCLXXVII. If the purchaser add something to the price after (completion of) the contract and expiration of the period of option, such addition is not an increase (of the price), but a gift, and the *Shafí* is not obliged to pay it.*

---

* *Sharáya ul-Islám*, p. 421.

† This is the approved doctrine of the modern authorities.—*Vide Tahrír ul-Akhám. Mafátíh*, &c.

If, however, the augmentation is made during the period of option, the *Shaikh* has declared that it constitutes a part of the original price, and is the same as stipulated in the contract; but this opinion is attended with some difficulty, as being inconsistent with what has been already said of the transfer being completed by the contract.*

DCCLXXVIII. In like manner, if the seller should make any abatement from the price, such abatement is unconnected with the contract; and the purchaser is by no means bound to surrender the share until he has received the (full) price at which the contract was entered into.* *Principle.*

DCCLXXIX. If the price be of the class of similars,—such as gold or silver,—the *Shafí* must give a similar to it,* (that is, an equal quantity of either metal). *Principle.*

DCCLXXX. But if there is no similar to the price, then the *Shafí* can take the property at its value at the time of the contract. *Principle.*

Thus the *Sharáya ul-Islám*:—"But if there is no equivalent to the price, as where it is an animal, or a price of cloth, or a jewel, some doctors have said that the right of *Shufá* must drop for want of an equivalent to the price, and also by reason of a tradition by Alí Bin Riáb from Abú Abdullah, on whom be peace! Others, however, maintain that the *Shafí* may take the property at its value at the time of the contract; and this doctrine is more generally approved."*

ANNOTATIONS.

dcclxxix, dcclxxx. According to the most correct opinion, the *Shafí* must pay an equivalent to the price if it is of the class of equivalents, if not, then the value thereof.—Mafátíh.

---

* *Sharáya ul-Islám*, pp. 421 & 422.

Principle. DCCLXXXI. A *Shafí* should prefer his claim as soon as he is informed of his right of pre-emption; but should he delay (to do so) from any cause preventing his making the claim in person, or, through an agent (on his behalf), his right of pre-emption is not extinguished.*

Principle. DCCLXXXII. If the *Shafí* did not make his claim of pre-emption upon being misinformed of the amount or kind of the price, or if he could not assert it by reason of being imprisoned and unable to appoint a *wakíl*, his right would not be extinguished.

Thus the *Sharáya ul-Islám*:—"In like manner, if he should abandon (his claim) on the supposition of the price being high, when it was really (subsequently) proved to be low or moderate; or on the supposition of its being gold, when it turned out to be silver; or an animal, when it proved to be some other article, the dereliction in such circumstances would have no effect in extinguishing his right. Such also (would be the case) if he is imprisoned for a claim which he is unable to discharge, or unable to appoint an agent (to claim on his behalf)."—p. 422.

Principle. DCCLXXXIII. It is at the same time incumbent on him to use all proper diligence in preferring his claim as soon as he becomes acquainted with his right, but yet so far as is customary.*

Annotations.

dcclxxxi. When the (transaction of) sale is known to him, the *Shafí* must hasten to assert his claim of pre-emption, according as is customary.—Mafátíh.

dcclxxxii. If he fail to do so without a good cause, his right is extinguished according to the opinion of the greater part of the Learned,—nay, it is affirmed by the Shaikh that the above opinion has received the general assent.—*Ibid.*

But if, for a good cause, a delay has occurred in preferring the claim *in propriâ personâ*, or by the appointment of a *wakíl*, the right is not extinguished.—*Ibid.*

---

* *Sharáya ul-Islám*, p. 422.

Insomuch that when travelling with that intent, he is not obliged to use greater expedition in his journey than is habitual to himself. Further, should he be engaged in the performance of any religious duty, whether indispensable or discretionary, he is not obliged to break it off, but may lawfully wait till it is completed. In like manner, if the time of prayer is at hand, he may wait till he has purified himself, and then performed his devotion without hurry or restraint.*

DCCLXXXIV. Should he receive intelligence of the occurrence of his right of pre-emption whilst on a journey, and unable to prefer his claim by personally appearing or appointing an agent, the right is not extinguished even though he should also neglect to call upon witnesses to attest his intention to demand it.* *Principle.*

DCCLXXXV. If, however, while able to use the proper exertions in person, or by appointing an agent, he should neglect to do so, his right is entirely lost.* *Principle.*

DCCLXXXVI. If the two contracting parties dissolve the contract, the right of pre-emption is not extinguished; and the *Shafí* is competent to annul the dissolution. However,— *Principle.*

ANNOTATIONS.

dcclxxxvi. The right of *Shufá* is not annulled on the dissolution of sale on the part of the seller and purchaser, because the right is established by virtue of the (original) contract, and cannot be cut off by (any subsequent act of) the contracting parties, moreover, the *dark*, or future responsibility, rests still on the purchaser.†—Sharáya ul-Islám, p. 422.

dcclxxxvi. If the two contracting parties dissolve the contract, yet the right of pre-emption is not lost; since such right has accrued in the (original) contract; consequently, they have no power to extinguish the same; on the contrary the responsibility lies with the purchaser; because the above is a cancellation, and not a sale (*de novo*).—Mafátíh.

---

* *Sharáya ul-Islám*, p. 422.

† That is, as the *Shafí* takes his title from the purchaser, the latter remains responsible to him, notwithstanding the dissolution for all future claims that may be made against his title.—Note by Mr. Baillie.

DCCLXXXVII. If the *Shafi* should acquiesce in the sale, and then the buyer and seller dissolve it, then he would not have the right of pre-emption.*

Principle.

Principle. DCCLXXXVIII. If the seller should ask the *Shafí* to dissolve the sale, and he should do so, the dissolution would not be valid; inasmuch as the dissolution could not take place unless it were on the part of the contracting parties themselves.—Mafátíh.

Principle. DCCLXXXIX. If the purchaser (of a share in a property) should sell it, the *Shafí* is entitled to annul the sale, and take (the subject of the sale) from the first purchaser: he may also take it from the second.*

Principle. DCCXC. If the purchaser dispose of the property in such a manner as not to be subject to pre-emption,—as a *wakf*, gift, mortgage, or conversion into a *masjid*,—still the *Shafi* can annul the same, and take the property for the price at which the contract was (originally) entered into.

Principle. DCCXCI. The *Shafí* takes possession of the property from the purchaser on whom the *dark*, or future responsibility, lies, and does not take it from the seller.* But,—

ANNOTATIONS.

dcclxxxvii. But if the *Shafi* acquiesces in the sale, and *then* the contract is dissolved by the contracting parties, the *Shafí* is not competent to claim his right of pre-emption in consequence of the dissolution.—Tahrír ul-Ahkám.

dccxc. In like manner, if the purchaser should make a *wakf*, or appropriation, of the property to any special purpose, or should convert it into a *masjid*, or place of worship, the *Shafí* can do away with all such acts, and take (possession of) the property under his right of pre-emption.—Sharáya ul-Islám, p. 422.

* *Vide Sharáya ul-Islám*, p. 422.

DCCXCII. If the property has still remained in the hands of the seller, the purchaser will not be put to trouble to take possession thereof, and then deliver it to the *Shafí*, as the object may be gained without such process, the possession taken by the *Shafí* being tantamount to his (the purchaser's) possession.—Mafátíh. *Principle.*

But if, when he makes his demand, and the property is in the hands of the seller, it may be said to him,—"Take it from the seller, or relinquish your right;" and the purchaser cannot be put to the trouble of taking pessession from the seller if he decline to do so, even though acquired by the *Shafí*. In such circumstances, the *Shafí's* possession comes into the place of the purchaser's, the *dark*, or responsibility for future claims, resting notwithstanding on the purchaser; and the *Shafí* has no right to cancel the sale. On the contrary, if he attempt to do so, and take possession from the seller, the act would be invalid.*

DCCXCIII. If the subject of sale should perish or become damaged, and if this happens without the act of the purchaser, or by *his* act, but before it was demanded by the *Shafí*, then it is optional with the latter to take the property at the full price, or abandon it entirely; and in the event of his taking it, he is entitled to all the ruins or fragments that remain, whether they are still on the spot, or have been removed from it.* *Principle.*

Because they are obviously opposed to part of the price.*

DCCXCIV. If, on the other hand, a defect or injury (to the property) has occurred by the act of the purchaser *after* demand (made by the *Shafí*), the purchaser is responsible.* *Principle.*

ANNOTATIONS.

dccxciii. If the subject of the sale became blemished before it was demanded by the *Shafí*, then he is at liberty either to take it at the full price, or to abandon it entirely. This is according to the prevalent doctrine.—Mafátíh.

dccxciv. Should any part of the subject perish or be destroyed, the *Shafí* is entitled to a compensation in proportion to the loss.—*Ibid.*

---

* *Sharáya ul-Islám*, p. 422.

Some doctors, however, have asserted that no responsibility attaches to him, because the *Shafi* does not become proprietor in virtue of his demand, but by taking possession. The first opinoin, however, is better supported and more generally adopted.*

Principle. DCCXCV. If the purchaser should plant trees or erect buildings upon the ground (which is the subject of pre-emption), and the *Shafi* should afterwards demand (the same by virtue of his right), the purchaser is entitled, if he think proper, to pull up and remove his trees and buildings, and it is not incumbent on him to level the ground; while, on the other hand, it is optional with the *Shafi* to take it at the full price, or to relinquish (his right) altogether.*

Principle. DCCXCVI. If, again, the purchaser should decline to remove (the trees or buildings), the *Shafi* has three things in his option: he may either remove them himself, paying the purchaser compensation for any loss he may sustain thereby, or he may take possession of the whole, paying, in addition to the price, the value of the trees or buildings which thus became his property with the consent of the purchaser, or he may abandon his claim altogether.*

Principle. DCCXCVII. If the subject of *Shufá* should increase in such a manner that the increase is connected with it (*b*), the advantage belongs to the *Shafi*; but if the increase be separated [from the original subject (*c*)], it belongs to the purchaser.*

ANNOTATIONS.

dccxcvii. Any increase to the property (the subject of pre-emption), if separate from the property itself, belongs to the (intermediate) purchaser, but if connected with it, the same belongs to the *Shafi* (the subsequent purchaser).—Mafátíh.

---

* *Sharáya ul-Islám*, pp. 422 & 423.

(*b*.) As, for example, if a young plant or shoot of a date or other tree is sold together with the ground on which it stands, and it becomes enlarged by natural growth.*

(*c*.) As residence in a mansion, or the fruit of a tree.

DCCXCVIII. If a person should sell his share in two mansions, and (the partner or) *Shafí* in both is one and the same person, he may lawfully take or abandon both, or if he takes one and foregoes his claim of pre-emption to the other, the same would be valid. But in the case of a single mansion, he cannot forego his claim to a part.* *Principle.*

DCCXCIX. If the price is a specific article, and it turns out to be the property of some person other than the purchaser, there can be no right of pre-emption by reason of the sale being null. If the price, however, was not specific, but was merely stipulated for in general terms (*d*), the right would be fully established, by reason of the purchase being good (in such circumstances). And although after delivery of the price by the *Shafí* it should turn out to be the property of another person, that would not affect his right in either of the cases supposed.* *Principle.*

(*d*.) As if it were a quantity of some commodity estimable by weight or measure.*

DCCC. If the subject of sale should appear to be defective, and the purchaser, in consequence, should receive a compensation for the defect, the *Shafí* is entitled to take the property for what remains after deduction of the compensation. And if the purchaser should determine to keep the subject of sale without seeking any compensation for the defect, the *Shafí* must either take it at the (full) price, or abandon* (his claim altogether). *Principle.*

DCCCI. The *Shafí's* right is not lost by relinquishment upon misinformation by the purchaser as to the subject, or quantity, or terms of his purchase. *Principle.*

---

* *Sharáya ul-Islám*, pp. 422 & 423.

If a person should say "I purchased the half for a hundred," upon which the *Shafí* relinquishes his claim, and it subsequently appears that he purchased a fourth for fifty, the privilege is not lost, (and he may still assert his claim). So also if it were said, "I purchased the fourth for fifty," upon which the *Shafí* relinquished his claim, but if it should subsequently appear that he purchased a half for a hundred, the privilege would not be lost; because in the one case the *Shafí* might not be able to give the larger price; and in the other he might not be inclined to avail himself to the defective or partial sale.*

Illustration.

Principle. DCCCII. Relinquishment by the *Shafí* upon misinformation in respect of the purchaser does not also extinguish his right of pre-emption.

Illustration. If the *Shafí* is informed that there are two purchasers, and thereupon he abandons his claim, after which it appears that there was only one; or if he was informed that there was only one (purchaser), and it turns out there were two; or if he was told that the purchaser bought for himself, and it afterwards appears that he bought for another; or the reverse of this is the case,—(in all these instances), the right is not lost, because (in each) he might have a different object in view* (which was frustrated by the false information).

Principle. DCCCIII. The price must first be delivered by the *Shafí*, and if he should decline to deliver it, the purchaser is not bound to make delivery (of the subject of sale) till he has received the full amount.*

Principle. DCCCIV. Where the land is a sown field, it must be suffered to remain (in that state until the crop is gathered), and it is optoinal with the *Shafí* either to take immediate

ANNOTATIONS.

dccci, dcccii. If he (the *Shafí*) had abandoned (his claim) upon supposition that the price was excessive, and it appeared subsequently that the same was moderate; or that the price was gold, and it afterwards appeared that the same was silver; or that half (of the property) was purchased, and it turned out to be a fourth, or *vice versâ;* or that there was one purchaser, and it subsequently appeared that there were many purchasers; or the contrary, and the like,—the right of preemption is not lost.—Mafátíh.

* *Sharáya ul-Islám*, pp. 423 & 424.

possession (of the ground allowing the crop to remain), or he may wait until it is reaped.*

Because in this (option) he has an interest, that is the use of his money, while he is precluded from the benefit of the land so occupied. There is, however, some doubt as to the legality of this delay without prejudicing the right of *Shufá.**

When a person has purchased for a price deferred, or on credit, it has been stated in the *Mabsút* that the *Shafí* may take possession immediately (on paying down the price), or may wait (till the stipulated time of payment arrive), and then pay the price and take possession. But it is laid down in the *Niháyah* that the *Shafí* may take immediate possession (of the subject of sale) on his own responsibility for the price, provided that he be in opulent circumstances, if not, he must give security for the amount. And this doctrine is the more approved.* Hence the settled law on the subject is, that,—

DCCCV. Where a property is sold on credit, the *Shafí* may take immediate possession thereof on his own responsibility if he is in opulent circumstances, otherwise by giving a security for the price. *Principle.*

Mufíd and *Murtazá* have pronounced the right of *Shufá* to be hereditary. But the *Shaikh* has declared that it is not so, on the authority of a report by *Talhá bin-Zayid*, who is a *battarí*:† the first doctrine, however, is more approved, as being agreeable to the general and comprehensive sense of the sacred text on the subject of inheritance.‡ Hence,—

DCCCVI. The right of pre-emption is hereditary,§ and, as such, it is inherited like (any other) property.‡ *Principle.*

ANNOTATIONS.

dcccvi. *Shufá*, or the right of pre-emption, is inherited like any other property, whether the *Shafí* had demanded it or not.—Mafátíh.

---

* *Sharáya ul-Islám*, pp. 423 & 424.

† A particular sect of Zaydians held in detestation by the followers of the twelve Imáms, as disputing the title of their seventh spiritual leader, Imám Músá Kásim, son of Imám Jaáfar Sádik, in favour of another brother. See Sale's Preliminary Discourse to the Translation of the *Kurán*. See also Lecture VI, p. 165.

‡ *Sharáya ul-Islám*, p. 424.

§ According to the Hanífites, the right abates on the death of the *Shafí*.

So that if the *Shafí* should leave a widow and a child, an eighth of it goes to the widow, and the remainder to the child.* Further,—

Principle. DCCCVII. If one heir should relinquish his share (of the right), it would not drop or be extinguished, but the other might take the whole.*

This, however, is liable to some doubt, which is not strong.*

When the *Shafí* sells his own share (of the property), after being apprized of his right of pre-emption, the *Skaikh* has declared that his right is extinguished, because such share is the (sole) ground of his claim; but that if he should sell his share before being informed of his right, it would not be extinguished, as his right existed previous to (his own) sale. It would, however, be better to say, that in neither of these cases would he have any claim to exercise his right of pre-emption.* So the approved doctrine is, that—

Principle. **DCCCVIII. When a person sells his own share of a property, he cannot claim his right of pre-emption upon the other share of the property being sold.**

Principle. DCCCIX. If a person in his death-illness should sell his share of the joint property to one of his heirs, by a contract

ANNOTATIONS.

dcccvi, dcccvii. Some of the Learned have maintained that the right of pre-emption is one of the properties which can be owned, given up in compromise, succeeded to as a heritage, and divided among one's heirs in proportion to their respective shares; and that it cannot be given up by some of them; but, on the contrary, the rest of the heirs are entitled to take the whole (if partly given up by some).—Mafátíh.

dccc If the *Shafí* has sold his own share with the knowledge of the sale made by his co-sharers, his right of pre-emption is extinguished.—Tahrír ul-Ahkám.

Sharáya ul-Islám, p. 424.

of *muhábát,** that is, for a price under its value, and if the abatement does not exceed a third part† of his estate, the contract of sale is valid, and establishes a right of pre-emption in the partner (of the deceased). But if it does exceed a third part of the deceased's estate, and the other heirs refuse to ratify the sale, it is valid only to such extent as is opposed to the price, and so much more as the third of the estate will admit of: consequently, to this extent only the privilege of *Shufá* can operate in favor of the partner.‡

DCCCX. If a *Shafí* makes a compromise giving up his right of pre-emption, it is valid, and his right is thereby extinguished.‡ *Principle.*

For it is a right to property, and compromise is effectual in respect of the same.‡

If a share of a property is sold, and the *Shafí* stands security (*Zámin-ud-dark*), either for the seller or for the purchaser, or if both the contracting parties should stipulate an option to the *Shafí*, his right of pre-emption would not be extinguished (in either case). Neither would it be so if he acted as an agent (in the sale) for either of the parties. Upon this point, however, there is room for some doubt, in consequence of his acquiescing in the sale.‡

DCCCXI. When the *Shafí* has taken possession of the property and discovered therein a defect which existed prior to the sale, then if both he and the (intermediate) purchaser were aware of the defect, neither of them has any option (in the matter); but if they were both ignorant of the defect, and the *Shafí* returns the property to the purchaser, the latter has an option either to reject the sale altogether, or to demand a compensation for the defect from the seller (*e*). If, however, the *Shafí* should elect to retain the property, the purchaser has, in that case, no right to cancel the sale, because the share has passed out of his hands.‡ *Principle.*

(*e*.) The *Shaikh* has said that the purchaser has no right to demand a compensation for the defect; but it is better to say that he has such right.‡

---

* *Vide* p. 80 of Lecture II.

† To which amount the operation of a death-bed gift is limited.

‡ *Sharáya ul-Islám*, pp. 424 & 425.

DCCCXII. Such also is the case if the *Shafí* was acquainted with the defect, and not the purchaser. But if the purchaser was apprized of it, and not the *Shafí*, the latter only would have the right of rejection.*

Principle.

There are devices for defeating the right of pre-emption, two of which are the following :—

The property may be sold for a price above its value, and then something of trifling value may be received in exchange for it, which would compel the *Shafí* to pay the full price if he choose to avail himself of his privilege.—Sharáya ul-Islám, p. 426.

In like manner, if the property is sold at an excessive price, and the seller receives part of it, giving a release for the remainder, this also obliges the *Shafí* either to submit to a considerable loss or to abandon his claim.—*Ibid.*

* *Sharáya ul-Islám*, p. 423.

LECTURE XIX.

ON WAKF OR APPROPRIATION.

DCCCXIII. *Wakf* is a contract, the fruit or effect of which is to tie up the original of a thing, and leave its usufruct free. (*Tahbís ul-asali wa itlák ul-munfiati*).* *Principle.*

Because he (the Prophet), on whom be peace, has said—"Tie up the original, and give away the fruit (*Habbis ul-asala wa sabbil us-samarata*)."*

DCCCXIV. The express term by which *wakf* can be constituted is—"*wakaftu* (I have appropriated)," and not any other.* *Principle.*

For, as respects the terms "*Harramtu* (I have consecrated)," and "*Saddaktu* (I have bestowed)," they do not constitute *wakf* without accompanying circumstances,—as by themselves they are susceptible of another interpretation besides *wakf.**

DCCCXV. If, however, they are used with the design of constituting "*wakf*," they are obligatory on the conscience of the person employing them without any circumstance to fix their meaning. And if he should actually acknowledge that he used them with that design, judgment should be given against him* (in terms of his acknowledgment). *Principle.*

ANNOTATIONS.

dcccxiii. *Wakf* is to tie up a thing itself and leave its usufruct free; as it is in the *Hadís* of the Prophet.—Mafátíh, p. 414.

---

* *Shárája ul-Islám*, p. 234.

DCCCXVI. The *wakf* is not obligatory except by giving possession. Being (so) completed, it becomes binding, and cannot be revoked if made in health.* But,—

Principle.

Principle. DCCCXVII. Made in death-illness, a *wakf* or appropriation becomes valid (to the full extent) if allowed by the heirs; otherwise, only to the extent of a third (of his property) in the same way as a gift, or *mahabát*† in sale. The same rule is to be observed when a person has made bequests.*

Some, however, have said that it should be sustained to the extent of the whole of the original estate left by the deceased; but the first (that is the above) opinion is the more approved.*

Principle. DCCCXVIII. If a person should, in death-illness, make a *wakf*, gift and *muhabát* sale, and emancipate a slave, and the acts be not allowed by his heirs, then they would be valid if they can be carried into effect out of a third of his estate; otherwise, they are to be preferred according to priority of date (*a*), and effect is to be given to each in order until the third of the estate is exhausted, after which any that may remain is void.*

(*a*.) In the case of priority not being determined, some of the doctors maintain that the third should be rateably divided among all the different objects; but it would be better if the same be determined by lot.*

ANNOTATIONS.

dcccxvi. Without difference of opinion, the delivery of possession is a necessary condition for the validity of the *wakf*. So if the *wákif*, or appropriator, die before it (that is before delivery of possession), the property (appropriated by him) shall be his inheritance. But upon delivery of possession, the *wakf* becomes binding or obligatory according to the opinion of all. And *after* that, the same cannot be lawfully revoked.—Mafátíh.

---

* *Sharáya ul-Islám*, p. 234.

† *Vide* p. 80 of Lecture II.

Conditions relating to the subject of Wakf.

DCCCXIX. The subject of the *wakf* must be a substance the property of the appropriator, capable of yielding benefit without itself being consumed, and capable of being delivered.* Hence,— *Principle.*

DCCCXX. The *wakf* of any thing not existing in substance is not valid (*b*). *Principle.*

(*b.*) As *Dayin*, or indeterminate things.*

DCCCXXI. Even the *wakf* of a thing in substance is invalid if not mentioned in particular. *Principle.*

If one should say "I have appropriated *a* house, or *a* mansion," without mentioning some one in particular, the *wakf* would be invalid.* *Example.*

DCCCXXII. The *wakf* of *akár* or lands and houses, of clothes, furniture and lawful instruments, is valid.* *Principle.*

DCCCXXIII. The rule is, that the *wakf* of any thing from the use of which benefit can be lawfully derived with the preservation of the thing itself is valid.* Thus,— *Principle.*

The *wakf* of a trained dog, and cat (is valid) from the possibility of benefit being derived from them. The *wakf* of a hog is not valid, because it cannot lawfully be the property of a *Musalmán*, nor of an absconded slave, because it cannot be delivered.* *Illustration.*

Whether *dínárs* and *dirhams*† can be validly appropriated, is a question, which some doctors have answered in the negative, and their opinion is transcendant, since no benefit can be derived from them except by expending.*

ANNOTATIONS.

dcccxix. With respect to the thing appropriated, it is a necessary condition that the same be in substance, be owned by the appropriator, and be capable of yielding benefit with the preservation of the original. So the *wakf* of a *dayin*, or of a thing indeterminate, is not valid by reason of there being no certainty or identity of the same. The *wakf* of a profit is not also valid by reason of non-stability.—Mafátíh.

---

* *Sharáya ul-Islám*, p. 234.

† *Dínár*, money, a ducat. *Dirham*, a silver coin of which from 20 to 25 have at different times passed current for a *dínár* (nearly equal to a ducat or sequin, about nine shillings).

DCCCXXIV. If one should appropriate a thing which is not his own, the *wakf* is not valid. But if the real owner consent to the appropriation, the *wakf*, or appropriation, is thereby valid according to some of the doctors,—the sanction being, in their opinion, tantamount to a new appropriation; and this is good and approved.*

Principle.

Principle. DCCCXXV. The *wakf* of a *musháa*, or undivided share in a thing, is valid, and possession of it is (to be taken) in the same way as in the case of a sale.*

Conditions relating to the wákif or appropriator.

Principle. DCCCXXVI. It is required that he (the appropriator) be of full age and sound understanding, and unrestrained in the use or disposition of his property.*

Principle. DCCCXXVII. It is lawful for an appropriator to retain the superintendence of the *wakf* to himself, or to appoint another in the office. If he has not appointed any superintendent, the duty of superintending belongs to the person in whose favor the *wakf* is made, on the ground of the right of property being vested in him.*

It is required that the *Názir*, or superintendent, appointed, be a righteous man and know how to perform his duty. It is not necessary that he should formally accept the office, and remain permanently employed.—Mafátíh.

ANNOTATIONS.

dcccxxv. The *wakf* of a *musháa*, or undivided share in a thing, is valid without difference of opinion amongst us, and its possession is (to be taken) in the same manner as in a sale.—Mafátíh.

dcccxxvii. The appropriator may lawfully make himself the superintendent of his *wakf* or another person though not forthcoming at the time, but thereafter.—*Ibid.*

* *Sharáya ul-Islám*, p. 234.

Conditions required of the object of Wakf.

DCCCXXVIII. He (in whose favour a *wakf* is made) must be in existence, capable of owning property, and distinctly indicated: he must not be one in whose favour it is unlawful to make a *wakf*.* *Principle.*

Consequently,—

DCCCXXIX. If one should make a settlement beginning with a person not in existence (*c*), the *wakf* would not be *valid*. But if it were in favour of one not in existence, in succession to a person actually in being, it would be quite good.* *Principle.*

(*c.*) As, for instance, one to be born, or a fœtus not yet separated* (from the womb of its mother). *Principle.*

DCCCXXX. A *wakf* made in favour of a slave is not valid, nor can the thing appropriated be used by his master, the same being contrary to the intention of the *wákif*, or appropriator.* *Principle.*

DCCCXXXI. A *wakf* for *masálih*, or works of general utility,—such as bridges and *masjids*, or places of worship,—is valid; as such a *wakf* is, in truth, a settlement on all *Musalmáns*, though some only participate in its advantages.* *Principle.*

ANNOTATIONS.

dcccxxviii. It is required that the person in whose favour the *wakf* is made be in existence, or held to be so, or one whose existence be usually possible; and that he be capable of a *wakf* being made in his favour. So, the *wakf* made in favour of one without existence is invalid.—Mafátíh.

dcccxxxi. A *wakf* for works of general utility (*masálih*)—as bridges, *masjids*, shrouds of the dead, and the like—is valid, the same, in truth, being for the poor.—*Ibid.*

---

* *Sharáya ul-Islám*, p. 235.

DCCCXXXII. If one should make an appropriation for a *maslahat*, or object of general utility, which has ceased to be used, it is to be applied to any good and pious purpose. And if it is for such purpose *generally*, it is to be expended on the poor and indigent, and in any other way by which an approach is made to Almighty God.*

Principle.

Principle. DCCCXXXIII. A Musalmán cannot make a *wakf* in favour of an alien enemy (*harbí*), though he be a blood-relation, but he can make it in favour of an infidel subject (*Zimmí*), even though he be a stranger, or in no way related to him.* Yet,—

Principle. DCCCXXXIV. A *wakf* made for Jewish synagogues or Christian churches is not valid.*

A *wakf* in favour of a *Zimmí*, or infidel, subject is lawful; because it is a transfer of property, and like permission to take the usufruct. Some say, however, that it is not valid, because it implies a pious intention, and is good only when made for the benefit of a parent; while others maintain that it is good when for the benefit of any relative. But the first opinion is most approved. So, also, the appropriation in favour of an apostate is valid, while there is some doubt as to one in favour of an alien enemy (*harbí*); the more approved opinion being entirely against it.*

ANNOTATIONS.

dccccxxxii. If one should make a *wakf* for a *maslahat*, or object of general utility, but that has ceased to be used, it will, according to the approved doctrine, be applied to any good or pious purpose. It will, however, be better to apply the same in reference to the true intention of the appropriator. So the *wakf* for a *Masjid* will (in case of the intended *Masjid* not being in existence) be applied to another *Masjid*, and that for a *Madrassah*, to another like *Madrassah*, and so on, regard being had to the same description of object as was intended by the appropriator.—Mafátíh.

When a *wakf* is made for a good purpose in general, it will be applied to any good purpose by which an approach is made to Almighty God.—*Ibid.*

* *Sharáya ul-Islám*, pp. 235 & 236.

DCCCXXXV. A *wakf* in favour of fornicators, highway robbers, or drinkers of wine, is not valid; nor for the copying of what are *now* called *Towrít* and *Injíl* (the books of Moses and Gospels), since they are altered and perverted variations. But if such appropriation were made by an infidel, it would be lawful.* *Principle.*

DCCCXXXVI. No *wakf* which is productive of sin is valid.—Mafátíh. *Principle.*

DCCCXXXVII. A *wakf* made in favour of Muslims is to be applied for the benefit of all those who pray towards the *Kiblah*;† but one in favour of true believers (muminín), is to be applied only for the benefit of the followers of the twelve *Imáms.** *Principle.*

DCCCXXXVIII. If the *wakf* is made in favour of the *Shíahs*, it is to be applied to the *Imámiyahs* and *Jarúdiyahs*, and not to the others of the *Zaydiah* sect.* *Principle.*

DCCCXXXIX. If a Musalmán should make a *wakf* in favour of the poor, it is to be applied for the benefit of the poor *muslims* only, to the exclusion of all others: and if an infidel made a similar appropriation, it is to be applied, in like manner, to the poor of his *own* persuasion.* *Principle.*

DCCCXL. Whenever the *moukúf alaihi* (*i.e.*, the person in whose favour a *wakf* is made) is described by a particular relationship, all those who *Principle.*

ANNOTATIONS.

dccccxxxv. *Wakf* made by an infidel is valid.—Mafátíh.

dccccxl, dccccxli. Whenever the *moukúf alaihi*,* or the person in whose favor a *wakf* is made, is particularized by a description or relationship, all those who come within the same are included; and both males and females participate though the description is given in the masculine gender;—as the term "*Háshimí*" comprehends also the females of that family.—*Ibid.*

* *Sharáya ul-Islám*, pp. 235 & 236.

† That to which people direct their faces in prayer; (especially Mecca, towards the *Káaba*, or temple, of which city the Muhammadans, in whatever quarter of the world they are, turn themselves when praying). The tomb of Muhammad at Mecca

come within it are held to be included in the benefits of the *wakf* (*d*).*

(*d.*) So that if the *wakf* is in favour of the *Imámiyahs*, it is for all the followers of the *Imáms*. In like manner, when it is for the *Zaydiyah*, all those who assert the Imámship of *Zayid*, the son of *Alí* (the second),† are included.* Likewise,—

Principle. DCCCXLI. When the connection is a relation to a particular ancestor, all those lineally descended from him by their fathers (*e*) are included.*

(*e.*) As, for instance, "*Háshimís*," who comprehend all those descended from *Háshim*, through *Abú Tálib*, *Hárith*, *Abbás* and *Abú Lahab*; or "*Tálibís*," who are the descendants of *Abú Tálib*, on whom be peace! both males and females participate if connected with him on the side of their fathers, from a regard to custom; though upon this point there is some difference of opinion.*

If one should make an appropriation for the *Baní Tamím*, it would be valid, and should be applied to any of them who can be found.—Mafátíh.

Principle. DCCCXLII. If a person should make an appropriation for (his) neighbours (*jírán*), a reference should be made to custom for determining who are to be thereby comprehended.‡

Some say, however, that any one whose house is within forty cubits is a neighbour, and this opinion is good, or well supported; while others maintain that the meaning of the term extends to all the occupants of forty houses on either side; but this opinion is now abandoned.*

ANNOTATIONS.

dcccxli. With respect to a person who belongs to a family through his mother, there are two opinions, of which the one approved is that he is not included in the description.—Mafátíh.

---

* *Sharáya ul-Islám*, pp. 235 & 236.

† *Vide*, Introductory Discourse, p. 165.

‡ According to the Hanífites, the term "*Jírán* or neighbours" signifies all who worship in the same *masjid*.

DCCCXLIII. If a man should make a *wakf* without mentioning its object, such *wakf* is void; so, also, if the object is not distinctly specified (*f*).* *Principle.*

(*f*.) As, if he should say "for one of these two," or "for one of the two *mashhids* or *fakírs*," the whole will be void.*

DCCCXLIV. If the settlement were on maternal and paternal uncles, they would share *equally* together.* *Principle.*

DCCCXLV. If a person made *wakf* for the nearest of mankind to him, his parents, and children how low soever, should (first) be taken, and so long as these exist, there shall be nothing for any of the (other) relatives. On failure of them, the grandparents, and brethren (with their children) how low soever; after them, the paternal and maternal uncles in the order of inheritance; but all of them shall participate *equally* unless some are specially mentioned in detail.* *Principle.*

If one should make a *wakf* in favour of his children and his brethren, or his kindred, so general an expression requires participation of males and females, and of the near and remote, with equality of division among them, unless some order or detail is made a condition, or some one is especially indicated.*

Conditions relating to the wakf itself.

DCCCXLVI. The *wakf*, or appropriation, must be perpetual, absolute or unconditional; possession must be given of the thing appropriated (*g*), and *Principle.*

ANNOTATIONS.

dcccxliii. If a person make a *wakf*, and do not mention the object in favour of which it is made, such *wakf* is void. So also if a *wakf* is made in favor of one not distinctly specified.—Mafátíh.

dcccxlvi. The universally approved opinion is, that the property appropriated must be transferred from the appropriator.—*Ibid.*

It is a necessary condition that *wakf* should be perpetual, so it will be void if made only for a period. This is the approved opinion.—*Ibid.*

Without difference of opinion, *wakf* should be made *at once:* it cannot be made to depend on the occurrence of an event (in future), unless the same be quite certain and positive.—*Ibid.*

* *Sharáya ul-Islám*, pp. 235 & 236.

it must be entirely taken out of the *wákif*, or appropriator.*

So if it (the appropriation) is restricted to a particular time, or made dependent on some quality of future occurrence, the same is void. Such also is the case when it is made in favor of persons who will probably fail. As, for instance, if one should make a settlement on *Zayid*, with a restriction to himself, or extend it to generations that would probably fail; or if he say generally, "for his successors," without mentioning what is to be done after they fail,—in these cases, it is maintained by some that the *wakf* would be entirely void; but others insist that due course should be given to the purposes actually named, and this is approved. Then, upon their failure, the property would revert to the heir of the *wákif*, or appropriator; but some of the doctors maintain that it reverts to the heirs of the *moukúf alaihi*, or the person in whose favour the *wakf* is made. The first opinion, however, is the most approved.*

If one should say "I have appropriated when the beginning of the month should come, or if *Zayid* will arrive," the appropriation would not be valid.*

(*g.*) Seizin is a condition of the validity of *wakf*. So that if one should make an appropriation, and die without giving possession, the subject of it would be his inheritance. The seizin that is required is that of the first of the *moukúf aliahi* or the person in whose favour the apppropriation is made; and all regard to possession ceases in the subsequent steps.*

Principle. DCCCXLVII. If, however, one should make a *wakf* in favour of his young children, then (no delivery of possession is required, but) his own possession would be possession on their behalf. So, also, is the case of a paternal grandfather.*

But with regard to an executor (*wasí*), there is room for doubt. The approved opinion, however, is that it is *valid.**

Principle. DCCCXLVIII. If a person make a *wakf* in favour of himself, it would not be valid. So, also, if

ANNOTATIONS.

dcccxlviii, dcccxl. If a person make a *wakf* in favour of himself, it is invalid without difference of opinion. But if he made a *wakf* in favour of the poor (*fakírs*), and afterwards he himself become a *fakír*, he can lawfully participate in the benefits thereof.—Mafátíh.

* *Sharáya ul-Islám*, pp. 236 & 237.

he made it first in favour of himself, and then in favour of another.*

Some, however, maintain that it would be void only with respect to himself, and valid with regard to the other. But the first opinion is the more approved.* In like manner,—

DCCCXLIX. If the *wakf* were made in favour of another with a condition for the payment of the *wákif's* (appropriator's) debts, and current expenses, it would not be valid.* But,— *Principle.*

DCCCL. If one should make a *wakf* for the poor, and should himself subsequently become poor, or for the Learned in law (*fakíh*), and should himself become a lawyer (*fakíh*), there is no objection to his participating in its benefits.* *Principle.*

DCCCLI. If one should make a *wakf* with a condition that the property (appropriated) is to revert to him in case of necessity, the condition would be valid, but the *wakf* void; and the property would remain in the state of being tied up until the necessity should arise, and will be inherited* (upon his death).

DCCCLII. If he (the appropriator) make it a condition of excluding whomsoever he may please, that would invalidate the *wakf*. But if the condition were that he may add to those in whose favour the *wakf* is made, some yet to be born, the *wakf* would be *valid*, whether it was made for his own children, or for others.* *Principle.*

DCCCLIII. If, again, the condition were that he (the appropriator) may make an entire transfer from those on whom the settlement has been made to others subsequently to come into being, that would not be lawful, and the *wakf* would be *void*.* *Principle.*

Some doctors have said that when one has made a *wakf* in favor of his young children, he may lawfully make others participate with them without reserving any power to that effect; but this opinion is not to be relied upon.*

---

* *Sharáya ul-Islám*, p. 237.

DCCCLIV. In the case of a *wakf* being made for the poor, or for the Learned in law, a superintendent (*kayyïm*) must be appointed to take possession of the *wakf*-property,—while in the case of a *wakf* being made for a *maslahat*, or useful purpose, the creation of the *wakf* is sufficient, the condition of acceptance being entirely dispensed with; and as to possession, that of the *Názir*, or superintendent, is sufficient.*

Principle.

Principle. DCCCLV. If a person should appropriate a *masjid*, or place of worship, the appropriation is valid, though only one person should pray therein.* In like manner,—

Principle. DCCCLVI. If a person appropriate a cemetery, the same becomes valid by the interment therein even of a single corpse.*

But though people should pray in a *masjid*, or bury in a cemetery without the formal words of *wakf* being pronounced, neither would pass out of the property of the owner. Such also would be the result if possession was not given of the *wakf* property, though the appropriate words were used.*

Appendages to Wakf.

Principle. DCCCLVII. The subject of *wakf*, or appropriation, is transferred so as to become the property of the *moukúf alaihi*, or the person in whose favour the *wakf* is made, for he has a right to the advantage or the benefits to be derived from it, and prohibition to sell does not negatve the same; and,

ANNOTATIONS.

dcccliv. If a *Názir*, or superintendent, is appointed, it is required that he be righteous, and know for what purposes he should make the expenditure. It is not necessary that he should formally accept the office and remain permanently employed.—Mafátíh.

dccclv, dccclvi. If the *wakf*-property be a *masjid* or cemetery, it will be sufficient if a single person said prayer, or a single corpse be buried, therein.—Mafátíh.

* *Sharáya ul-Islám*, p. 237.

indeed, the sale of *wakf* property is sometimes in a manner valid* (as will be seen hereafter).†

If a person has made a settlement on the children of his children, the children of sons and daughters, males as well as females, participate, without any superiority of one over another. But if he should say—"those among them who are (lineally) related to me," the children of daughters would not be included. And if he made the settlement "on his children," it should be applied to the children of his loins; the children of his children will not be included with them.*

Some maintain that they would all participate together; but the first opinion is the most approved; because a child's child would not be understood by the use of the word "child."* And,—

If he should say—"on my children, and children of my children," it would be confined to two generations.* And,—

If he said—"on my children, and when they fail, and the children of my children fail, then on the poor," the *wakf* should be for his children, and on their failure, some (of the doctors) maintain, that the proceeds should be expended on the children of his children, and when *they* fail, on the poor; while others are of opinion that the proceeds are not to be expended on his children's children, for they are not comprehended in the *wakf*, but their failure is only a condition of the application to the poor; and this opinion is the more approved.*

DCCCLVIII. When a person has made a *wakf*, or appropriation, "in the way of God," it is applied to whatever is productive of reward in a future state, such as religious warfare, the greater or lesser pilgrimages, the erection of *masjids*, and bridges. So also, if he (the appropriator) should say,—"in the way of God, in the way of reward, and in the way of good," the purposes are all considered as one and the same, and there is no necessity for dividing the proceeds (of the *wakf*) into three different parts.* *Principle.*

DCCCLIX. When a person has made a *wakf* of a *masjid*, and it has fallen into ruins, or the village or quarter (in which it is situated) has gone to decay, it (the *wakf*-property) does not revert to, and *Principle.*

---

* *Sharáya ul-Islám*, pp. 237 & 238.

† *Vide* Principles dccclxi & dccclxii.

become the property of, the appropriator; nor does the sale thereof cease to be *wakf*, nor is the sale of it lawful and valid.*

Principle. DCCCLX. No person is competent to consume the original, or the corpus, of a *wakf*, by sale, gift, or in any other way, as such disposition frustrates the purpose of the *wakf*, which is to tie up the original property.—Mafátíh. But,—

Principle. DCCCLXI. If dissensions arise among the persons in whose favour the *wakf* is made, and there is apprehension of the property being destroyed, while on the other hand the sale thereof is productive of benefit, then, in that case, its sale is lawful. It is thus laid down in the *Sahíh.—Ibid.*

Principle. DCCCLXII. If the mansion belonging to a *wakf* should fall into ruins, the space would not cease to be *wakf*, nor would its sale be lawful. If (however) dissensions should arise among the persons for whom it was appropriated, insomuch as to give room for apprehension that it will be destroyed, its sale would be lawful.*

And even if there should be no such differences, nor any room for such apprehensions, but the sale would be more for the advantage of the parties interested, some are of opinion that the sale would be lawful; but the approved doctrine is to forbid it.*

Principle. DCCCLXIII. When a person has made a *wakf* for the poor, it is to be applied to the poor of the (deceased's) town who are present: so also should it be done when a *wakf* is for the descendants of *Alí*. And when a *wakf* is made for the children or descendants of an ancestor who are scattered in different places, the income is to be applied to those forthcoming, and there is no necessity for following, into difficult places, those who are not present.*

ANNOTATIONS.

dccclix. It is not necessary to distribute the profits of a *wakf* among *all* the persons comprehended in the description, but among those who may be in the town (*balad*) of the *wákif*, or appropriator.—Mafátíh.

---

* *Sharáya ul-Islám*, pp.—237239.

INDEX

TO THE

FIVE LECTURES ON MUHAMMADAN LAW

ACCORDING TO THE

SUNNI SCHOOL.

INDEX

TO THE

MUHAMMADAN LAW OF THE IMÁMIYAH SCHOOL.